The 21st Century Webster's
Family Encyclopedia

D0004668

The 21st Century
Webster's
Family Encyclopedia

Volume 6
Lao - Naia

1999 Edition

IMPORTED BY/IMPORTE PAR
DS-MAX CANADA
RICHMOND HILL, ONTARIO
L4B 1H7

ENGLAND
WENTWALK LTD.
278A ABBEYDALE ROAD, WEMBLEY
MIDDLESEX, HA0 1NT

MALAYSIA
PRO ENTERPRISE SDN BHD
LOT 605, SS13/1K, OFF JLN.
KEWAJIPAN, 47500 SUBANG JAYA
SELANGOR D.E., MALAYSIA

DS-MAX
IRVINE, CA 92618
IMPORTER: #16-1241510
949-587-9207

TRIDENT PRESS INTERNATIONAL

The 21st Century Webster's Family Encyclopedia
is based on the Spectrum Database

editors:
Bart Drubbel
Tjeerd van der Velde
Saskia van Iperen

Laos

Capital:	Vientiane
Area:	91,400 sq mi
	(236,800 sq km)
Population:	5,261,000
Language:	Lao
Government:	People's republic
Independent:	1953
Head of gov.:	Prime minister
Per capita:	U.S. $350
Mon. unit:	1 Kip = 100 at

Laocoön, in Greek mythology, priest of Apollo who warned the Trojan people not to accept the gift of the wooden horse from the Greeks, with whom they had been at war for 10 years. When Laocoön was killed while worshipping, the Trojans took this as a sign of the gods' displeasure with him and brought the horse into Troy. The horse was filled with Greek soldiers, who seized the city.
See also: Mythology; Trojan War.

Laos, officially Lao People's Democratic Republic, Southeast Asian country formerly part of French Indochina. It is bordered by China to the north, Vietnam to the east, Kampuchea to the south and Thailand and Burma to the west. It is a small country (650 mi/1,046 km-long and in places barely 50 mi/81 km-wide). The administrative capital is Vientiane. The total population is over 4,000,000.
Land and climate. Laos is dominated by mountain chains and plateaus, cut by deep, narrow valleys, covered by forests interspersed with patches of grassland. The Mekong, the river that creates the important Mekong Basin, forms the border with Burma and most of Thailand. Laos has a tropical monsoon climate, with near-drought from Nov. to Apr. and a wet season from May to Oct.
People. The people of Laos include various ethnic groups, the largest being the Lao, who total over half of the population. Their language, Lao, is the official language. Most practice Hinayana (Theravada) Buddhism. The rest of the population consists of the Kha—original inhabitants of Laos—and mountain tribes, which include the Mons, Thai, Meos and Hos. The education system is poorly developed. There is one university, at Vientiane, the University of Sisavang Vong. Smaller urban areas include Luang Prabang (the royal capital), Pakse and Savannakhet.
Economy. Laos is one of the poorest countries in the world. The people of Laos are mostly primitive farmers who mainly grow rice. Some coffee, corn, hemp, cotton and opium poppies—although illegal—are grown, and the Mekong River and its many tributaries provide fish for local consumption as well as the major means of transportation. The forests provide good teak and bamboo, charcoal, benzoin (used in perfumes) and stick lac (for shellac). Rich iron ore deposits are known to exist, but only the tin ore is exploited

commercially. Industry is on a very limited scale. There are no railways and few reliable roads. There is an international airport at Vientiane.
History. Part of the Khmer empire, the territory was settled from the 10th to 13th centuries by Thai Lao. By the 17th century a powerful Lao kingdom had emerged; but in the early 1700s it split into the principalities of Luang Prabang, Vientiane, and Champasak. In 1893 France made Laos a protectorate. After World War II national insurgency of various factions (including the Communist Pathet Lao with Vietnamese support) won the country independence within the French Union in 1949; it remained in the French Union until 1954. In 1959 renewed civil war between the neutralist premier Souvanna Phouma and right- and left-wing rivals brought intervention from the great powers. A coalition government was formed in 1973. In Dec. 1975 the king abdicated, and the country became a Communist republic under the Pathet Lao, strongly influenced by Vietnam. In 1990 a small guerrilla resistance force took action against the communist government, but the effect was minimal. In 1997 Laos signed a trade agreement with the United States.

Lao Tzu, or Lao Tze (Old Master), legendary Chinese philosopher of the 6th century B.C., said to be the founder of Taoism and the author of *Tao-te-ching*. Tao, or the Way, emphasizes simplicity, naturalness, and spontaneity in life. *See also:* Taoism.

La Paz (pop. 1,049,800), largest city and administrative capital of Bolivia (the legal capital being Sucre). Founded in 1548 by the conquistadors, it is located in the La Paz river valley in western Bolivia. At some 12,000 ft (3,700 m) above sea level, it is the world's highest capital. Local products include cement, glass, textiles, and consumer goods. Lake Titicaca, South America's largest freshwater lake, is a popular tourist attraction of the region. *See also:* Bolivia.

Lapland, region in the extreme north of Europe, the homeland of the Lapps (or Finns, as they are called in Norway). Lying primarily within the Arctic Circle, it embraces northern parts of Norway, Sweden, and Finland, and the Kola Peninsula of the former USSR, with an area of 150,000 sq mi (388,000 sq km). It has tundra vegetation, with some forest vegetation in the south. Its wildlife, especially the economically important reindeer, were severely hurt by radioactive contamination from the 1986 Chernobyl nuclear disaster.

Lapps *See:* Lapland.

Lapwing, or peewit (*Vanellus vanellus*), shore bird found in Western Europe and the British Isles. The lapwing, named because of its slow, ungainly wingbeat, has an iridescent green-black back, blue-black throat, white belly, and long, wispy, black crest.

Laramie (pop. 24,410), city in southeast Wyoming, county seat of Albany County, and the third largest city in the state. Named after Jacques La Ramie, a French-Canadian trapper, it was settled in 1868 and grew with the onset of railroad, mining, and cattle-producing industries. Laramie is the home of the University of Wyoming. *See also:* Wyoming.

Larceny, in law, the unlawful removal of the property of another person without the owner's consent and with intent to steal. Grand larceny, a felony, is generally the theft of valuable property, while petty larceny, usually a misdemeanor, involves less valuable goods. Embezzlement, robbery, and fraud are generally considered larceny.
See also: Crime.

Larch, pine (genus *Larix*) that is unusual in being deciduous rather than evergreen, shedding its needles in winter, becoming completely bare. The several kinds of larch flourish in the Northern Hemisphere as far north as the Arctic Circle. The European larch is a source of turpentine, and several larches, including the tamarack (*L. laricina*), yield a timber that lasts well in water and is used for piers.

Lardner, Ring (1885-1933), U.S. sports journalist and short-story writer. Stories like "You Know Me, Al" (1916), satirize vulgarity and greed in U.S. life. Short-story volumes include *What of It?* (1925) and *Round Up* (1929). With G.S. Kaufman, he wrote the play *June Moon* (1929).

Laredo (pop. 133,239), city in southern Texas, on the Rio Grande River. Laredo, founded in 1755, is a principal port of entry, with one-half the tourists and 60% of the U.S.-Mexico import-export trade passing through its customs stations. Industries include natural gas production, oil refining, clothing manufacture, agriculture, and ranching.
See also: Texas.

Lares and penates, in Roman mythology, household guardian gods. The lares were godly ancestor figures; the penates were guardians of the store-room.
See also: Mythology.

Lark, any of a family (*Alaudidae*) of small terrestrial songbirds of Europe, Asia, North America, and Africa. The birds are streaked brown or gray, and feed on insects and seeds, walking or running at great speed along the ground. Larks are known for their beautiful songs, usually delivered on the wing.

Larkspur, any of a genus (*Delphinium*) of flowering plants of the buttercup family, growing mostly in the temperate zones of the Northern Hemisphere. The loosely clustered flowers, which grow on spikes ranging from 1 to 7 ft (30 cm to 2.1 m), have 5 sepals, one of which forms a spur. Larkspurs may be white, blue, or pink.

La Rochefoucauld, François, Duc de, François, Duc de (1613-80), French writer. He is known for his *Memoirs* (1662) of the Fronde, and his *Maxims* (1665), a collection of more than 500 moral reflections and epigrams, generally paradoxical, often pessimistic, usually acute.

La Rochelle (pop. 75,800), French city on the Atlantic coast, capital of the Charente Maritime department. The city, chartered in the 12th century, is a yachting and fishing center. During the persecution of the Huguenots (French Protestants) by the Roman Catholics in the 16th century, La Rochelle was among the 100 communities established by the Edict of Nantes as a haven

for Protestants. In 1627 the city was forced to return control to the French government.
See also: France.

LaRouche, Lyndon Hermyle, Jr. (1922-), U.S. political leader and thrice-unsuccessful candidate for the presidency of the United States. In 1948, he began his career with the progressive Socialist Worker's Party, but in the 1970s he began to ally himself with reactionary interests, founding such organizations as the National Caucus of Labor Committees and the National Democratic Policy Committee. In 1989 he was sentenced to 15 years in prison for mail fraud and conspiracy.

Larva, metamorphic stage of development in some animals in which the young are noticeably different in feature and behavior from their parents. Larvae most often occur in the metamorphoses of insects and aquatic animals. The length of the larval phase varies according to species. Examples of larvae are the tadpoles of frogs and toads and the caterpillars of butterflies and moths.

Larynx, specialized organ of the respiratory tract used in voice production. It lies above the trachea in the neck, forming the Adam's apple, and consists of several cartilage components linked by small muscles. Two folds, or vocal cords, lie above the trachea and can be pulled across the airway so as to regulate and intermittently occlude air flow. It is the movement and vibration of these that produce voice.

La Salle, Jean *See:* Jean Baptiste de la Salle, Saint.

La Salle, Robert Cavelier, Sieur de (1643-87), French explorer and fur trader in North America who claimed the Louisiana territory for France. In Canada from 1666, he commanded Fort Frontenac, sailed across Lake Michigan (1679), explored the Illinois River, and followed the Mississippi River to its mouth on the Gulf of Mexico. In 1684, sailing to plant a colony there, his fleet was wrecked by storms and Spanish raiders. He was killed by a mutinous crew.

Las Campanas Observatory *See:* Mount Wilson Observatory.

Las Casas, Bartolomé de (1474-1566), Spanish missionary in Central America. He exposed the forced labor of the Indians, persuaded Madrid to enact the New Laws for Indian Welfare (1542), and in his *History of the Indies* recorded data valuable to modern anthropology.

Laser, device that produces an intense beam of light with a precisely defined wavelength. The name is an acronym for "*l*ight *a*mplification by *s*timulated *e*mission of *r*adiation." The light produced by conventional sources travels in all directions. With lasers, the source atoms radiate in step with each other and in the same direction, producing coherent light. Laser beams spread very little as they travel and thus provide high-capacity communication links. They can be focused into small spots and have been used for cutting and welding—notably for refixing detached retinas in the human eye. Lasers also find application in distance measurement by interference methods, in spectroscopy, and in holography.

Laski, Harold Joseph (1893-1950), English political therorist and economist, active in the Fabian Society and the Labour Party. A lecturer at the London School of Economics (1920-50), his books include *Democracy in Crisis* (1933), *Liberty in the Modern State* (1948), and *The American Democracy* (1948).
See also: Fabian Society; Labour Party.

Lassen, Mount, volcano in Lassen Volcanic National Park, northeastern California. The peak rises to an altitude of 10,457 ft (3,187 m). It erupted on May 30, 1914, and again in 1921.

Lasso, Orlando di (1532-94), Flemish Renaissance singer, choirmaster, and composer of a wide range of more than 2,000 sacred and secular works. Orlando di Lasso is the Italian version of his Flemish name, Roland de Lassus.

Last Supper, the final passover meal held by Jesus and his disciples in Jerusalem before his crucifixion. In it he distributed bread and wine to them, instituting the Christian sacrament of Holy Communion. Leonardo da Vinci's well-known fresco of the Last Supper is in Milan.
See also: Jesus Christ; Passover.

Las Vegas (pop. 741,459), city in southwestern Nevada, seat of Clark County. It is renowned for "The Strip," with its casinos (state-legalized gambling), luxury hotels, bars, and nightclubs. The city is also a mining and cattle-farming center. There are artesian springs nearby. It is one of the fastest growing cities in the United States.
See also: Nevada.

Latakia, or Al-Ladhiqiyah (pop. 234,000), principal seaport city in western Syria, on the Mediterranean Sea, about 110 mi (177 km) north of Beirut. Latakia dates to antiquity, when it was the Phoenician city Ramitha. Exports include tobacco, cotton, bitumen, asphalt, and coffee.
See also: Syria.

Lateran, district of southeastern Rome, given to the church by Emperor Constantine I in 311. The Lateran palace—the papal residence until 1309—was demolished and replaced in the 16th century. The basilica of St. John Lateran is the cathedral church of the pope as bishop of Rome.

Lateran Treaty, concordat between the papacy and the government of Italy, signed 1929 in the Lateran palace and confirmed by the 1948 Italian constitution. It established Roman Catholicism as Italy's state religion and Vatican City as an independent sovereign state.

Latex, milky substance extracted from various plants and trees that serves as the source of natural rubber. Synthetic latex has been used since the 1940s to make paints and coatings. Its properties are hardness, flexibility, toughness, adhesion, color retention, and resistance to chemicals.
See also: Rubber.

Lathrop, Julia Clifford (1858-1932), U.S. social worker, founder of the first U.S. Juvenile Court (1899) and first head of the Children's Bureau of the Department of Labor (1912-21).

Latimer, Hugh (c.1490-1555), English Protestant martyr and Reformation leader. He defended Henry VIII's divorce from Catherine of Aragon, and was made bishop of Worcester in 1535. With Nicholas Ridley, he was burned at the stake as a heretic by order of the Roman Catholic Queen Mary I.

Latin, Indo-European language of the Italic group, language of ancient Rome, and ancestor of the Romance languages. Originating in Latium (about 8th century B.C.), Latin spread with Roman conquests throughout the empire, differentiating into vulgar Latin and classical (literary) Latin. It is a logical and highly inflected language that has furnished scientific and legal terminology and is still used in the Roman Catholic Church. It was the international language of scholarship and diplomacy until the 18th century. About half of all English words are Latin in origin.

Latin America, 33 independent countries and 13 other political entities in Central and South America where Romance languages are spoken: Spanish in most of Latin America; Portuguese in Brazil; and French in Haiti. Sometimes the term includes Guyana, Suriname, and French Guiana in South America, and, less often, also all the Caribbean islands.
People. The population growth of almost 2% per year is one of the highest in the world. The population lives by the Pacific or Atlantic oceans, rivers, or in highland farm areas. The people are of European, African, Indian, and mixed ancestry. After World War II, large numbers of people moved from rural to urban areas in search of employment, and most large cities suffer from overcrowding, pollution, homelessness, inadequate medical services, and high unemployment.
The literacy rate varies from less than 50% (Haiti) to more than 90% (Argentina).
Economy. Historically, Latin America economies depended on one export commodity—oil, copper, tin, coffee, bananas, livestock, fish—to earn foreign currency. In several countries there have been efforts at diversification, but economic development is hampered by poor transport, political instability, and burdensome effects of foreign aid. Although about half of the people work on the land, agriculture is mostly primitive and inefficient.
Important changes in recent decades include the emergence of Brazil as a leading industrial power, and use of oil revenues in Mexico and Venezuela to finance economic growth. Argentina, Brazil, Mexico and other nations borrowed huge sums from the International Monetary Fund and from private banks, leading to a near-crisis in the 1980s when they were unable to repay their debts.
History. Before the arrival of Columbus in 1492, several highly developed civilizations flourished in the region, most notably the Mayans, Aztecs and Incas. During the conquest the indigenous populations were decimated by war and European diseases. Spanish and Portuguese colonial rule lasted about three hundred years, and by 1825 most of the colonies, inspired by the leadership of Bolivar and San Martin, gained their independence. Power and wealth, however, remained in the hands of tiny minorities, and political life was marked by corruption and instability. In the 20th century, several countries have enjoyed long peaceful periods of constitutional rule while others have experienced military dictatorships, revolution, and violent factional strife.

Latin-American literature, literature of the Spanish-speaking countries of
the Western Hemisphere. It also includes Brazil, where the native language
is Portuguese, not Spanish. The literary period began with the explorations
in the 1400s and lasted some 300 years. The earliest literature was written
by soldiers and missionaries describing new lands and civilizations. Her-
nando Cortés, the conqueror, wrote his *Five Letters* (1519-1526) for King
Charles I of Spain, outlining his campaign in great detail. Many works deal
with the period of conquest. Bartolomé de las Casas wrote of the brutal
treatment of the Indians by the Europeans in *The Devastation of the Indians:
A Brief Account* (1552). *La Araucana* (1569-1589) by Alonso de Ercilla y
Zúñiga is considered the greatest poem of the time and heralded the bravery
of the Chilean Indians in resisting the Spanish invaders.
The ornate baroque style arose in the latter 1600s. The Mexican nun, Sor
Juana Ines de la Cruz, wrote plays, satire, philosophical works and poetry in
the baroque style.
In the early 1800s, Romanticism, stressing individualism, nationalism and
artistic freedom spread to Latin America. Nomadic cowboys called Gauchos
became a literary topic. The best example of this is the epic poem *Martin
Fierro* (1872-79) by José Hernandez of Argentina. The Romantic period
gave rise to the novel. Jorge Issacs of Columbia wrote a sentimental love
story *Maria* (1867) that remains popular today. The "noble savage" theme
was popular among the romantics who felt that the Indians were superior to
the corrupt Europeans. Realist writers, seeking to capture external reality in
an objective way, emerged in the 2nd half of the 19th century. The modern
period lasted from 1888 to 1910 and Nicaraguan poet Rubén Darió gave it
its form. His books of poems *Azul* (1888) marked the beginning of the period.
Jose Martí of Cuba was a celebrated journalist, essayist and poet of this
period.
In the 20th century women poets emerged with work dealing with love and
the role of women in society. Gabriela Mistral of Chile won the Nobel Prize
for literature (1945). Novels explored social and political problems. The
Mexican revolution (1910) inspired Mariano Azuela's novel *The Underdogs*
(1916). Poets experimented with form and technique. Vincente Huidobro
and Pablo Neruda of Chile, César Vallejo of Peru, Mario de Andrade of
Brazil and Jorge Luis Borges of Argentina created poetry with unusual
imagery. In the mid 1940s the "new novel," combining authentic subject
matter with various themes and experiments, appeared. *The President* (1946)
by Miguel Angel Asturias of Guatemala and *The Edge of the Storm* (1947)
by Augustín Yáñez of Mexico are well known examples of the new novel.
Since the 1950s Latin American novelists have enjoyed international renown. The best known authors of this period are Carlos Fuentes of Mexico;
Alejo Carpentier of Cuba, who coined the term "magical realism;" Julio
Cortázar of Argentina; Mario Vargas Llosa of Peru; and Gabrial García
Márquez of Colombia, who brought the use of realism to its greatest
expression in his novel *One Hundred Years of Solitude* (1967), considered
by many one of the most important literary works of the 20th century.
Márquez was awarded the Nobel Prize for literature in 1982.

Latin literature, all literary works of ancient Romans, written in Latin. Latin
literature, beginning as a derivation of Greek literature, and evolving over
several literary eras, came to express the nature, politics, and history of the
people, and developed into a highly distinctive standard for all written

language. Although early Latin literature (240 B.C.) contained translations of the Greek classics, poetry, and drama, much of it has been preserved in the form of comedies.

The comedies of Plautus and Terence were based on Greek themes with creative variations. Cato the Elder (f. 160 B.C.) produced the most impressive prose of the early period. He also wrote the first history of Rome in Latin. The early period ended with a new kind of poetry by Gaius Lucilius. The *Satires* of Juvenal are also of this era. The apex, or Golden Age, occurred around the 1st century B.C. Cicero was the most accomplished writer of this period. His literary works are a treasure chest of information about life in Rome. His works on education, philosophy, and oratory have endured throughout the ages as classics. In this period, Julius Caesar wrote his works on the Gallic and Civil Wars. The lyric poetry of Catullus appeared at this time. The reign of the emperor Augustus (27 B.C. to A.D. 14) saw the creation of Vergil's *Aeneid* and *Georgics*. The work of Horace and Ovid also appeared in this era.

After the death of Augustus, Roman writers demonstrated new styles. The works of Seneca, Lucan, and Petronius' *Satyricon* are of this era. The *Satyricon* is considered the first Latin novel. Other notable writers are the historian Tacitus and Pliny the Younger. The foundations of Christian Latin literature were laid during the 4th and 5th centuries by church fathers like Augustine, Jerome, and Ambrose.

Latitude, distance from the equator, measured in degrees, of any point on the surface of the earth. The equator is considered 0° latitude; the north pole is 90°N, the south pole 90°S. Lines of latitude run parallel to one another. *See also:* Equator; Longitude.

Latium, historic region of Italy, "the cradle of the Roman people," extending from the Tiber River to the Alban Hills. It is now part of the western region of Lazio, and includes the provinces of Rome, Frosinone, Latina, Rieti, and Viterbo.

Latrobe, Benjamin Henry (1764-1820), English-born U.S. architect and engineer. His work includes the southern wing of the Capitol in Washington, D.C., and the Roman Catholic cathedral in Baltimore. A pioneer of the Classical revival, he was the first major professional architect in the United States.

Latter-day Saints, The Church of Jesus Christ of *See:* Mormons.

Latvia (Republic of), independent country, bordering on the Baltic Sea (west), between Estonia (north), Russia (east), and Lithuania (south). Its capital is Riga.
Land and climate. It is a lowland country, covering some 24,938 sq mi (64,589 sq km), with a moderate continental climate.
People. Nearly a third of the people are Russians, but the majority are Latvians, an ancient Baltic people. Minorities include Byelorussians, Ukrainians, Lithuanians, and Poles. The official language is Latvian. Over 90% of the population are Christians.
Economy. While cattle and dairy farming, fishing, and lumbering are of considerable importance, highly developed industries also exist and include

Latvia

Capital:	Riga
Area:	24,938 sq mi
	(64,589 sq km)
Population:	2,385,000
Language:	Latvian
Government:	Republic
Independent:	1991
Head of gov.:	Prime minister
Per capita:	U.S. $2,270
Mon. unit:	1 Lat = 100 santims

shipbuilding, engineering, and the manufacture of steel, textiles, cement, and fertilizers. The country hardly has any natural resources.

History. Christianized by the German Livonian Knights in the 13th century, Latvia was ruled by Poles, Swedes, and, from the 18th century, Russians. From 1920 to 1940 (when it was reabsorbed into the USSR (Soviet Union)), it enjoyed a precarious independence. Beginning in the late 1980s, Latvia, together with Lithuania and Estonia, was involved in a sometimes violent struggle for economic self-determination, religious freedom, and autonomy from the central Soviet government. With the collapse of communism in the USSR in 1991 Latvia formally attained independence. After independence Latvia pursued Western political and economic policies, and its relationship with Russia deteriorated.
See also: Union of Soviet Socialist Republics.

Laudanum *See:* Opium.

Laud, William (1573-1645), archbishop of Canterbury from 1633 and a chief advisor of Charles I. He enforced High Church beliefs and ritual, and his persecution of English Puritans and Scottish Presbyterians provoked parliamentary impeachment (1640). He was executed for treason.
See also: Church of England.

Laue, Max Theodor Felix von (1879-1960), German physicist awarded the 1914 Nobel Prize for physics for his discovery of X-ray diffraction in crystals.
See also: Physics; X ray.

Laughing gas *See:* Nitrous oxide.

Laughton, Charles (1899-1962), English-born actor, a U.S. citizen from 1950. Films include the award-winning *The Private Life of Henry VIII* (1933), *The Hunchback of Notre Dame* (1939), and *Advise and Consent* (1962). He directed *Night of the Hunter* (1955).

Laureate *See:* Poet laureate.

Laurel, family (Lauraceae) of evergreen trees and shrubs that grow in the tropics and subtropics. The flowers are inconspicuous and last for only a short time before forming a berry. The classical, or bay, laurel (*Laurus nobilis*), which produces the bay leaf used popularly as a seasoning, is a native of the Mediterranean. It was sacred to Apollo, and its shiny leaves were woven into garlands by the Greeks and Romans. Other laurels include avocado, camphor, cinnamon, and sassafras.

Laurel (pop. 21,897), city in southeast Mississippi, seat of Jones County. Laurel was founded in 1822 to mill and process yellow-pine timber. Other products now include petroleum, canned vegetables, chemicals, electrical parts, and textiles. The Lauren Rogers Museum of Art and the Masonite Corp. are located in Laurel.

Laurel and Hardy, famous comedy team of Hollywood films. The English-born **Stan Laurel** (Arthur Stanley Jefferson; 1890-1965) and the U.S.-born **Oliver Hardy** (1892-1957), thin man and fat man, simpleton and pompous heavy, made over 200 films between 1927 and 1945. Their style, shaped by Laurel, ranged from slapstick to slow-paced comedy of situation and audience anticipation. In the early 1990s several original films were released on videotape.

Laurencin, Marie (1885-1956), French painter and printmaker, designer of textiles, clothing, and stage decorations for the Ballet Russe and the Comédie Française. Her personal style was characterized by simplified images, usually of women, and pastel colors. Works include *The Assembly* (1910) and *In the Park* (1924).

Laurentian Plateau *See:* Canadian Shield.

Laurier, Sir Wilfrid (1841-1919), first French-Canadian prime minister of Canada (1896-1911). Leader of the federal Liberal party (1887-1919), he encouraged provincial autonomy while seeking to unite the country. Many of his attempts to protect the rights of French-Canadians, particularly in education, met with little success.

Lausanne (pop. 117,500), city in western Switzerland, on the north shore of Lake Geneva. An ancient Celtic, then Roman, settlement, it was a bishopric from A.D.590 until 1536, when it was defeated by Bern, which established Protestantism. The Bernese retained power until 1798, and in 1803 Lausanne became the capital of the new Vaud canton. It is a cultural, industrial, and tourist center. The Flon and Louve rivers flow through the city. Historic features include the Cathedral of Notre-Dame (consecrated 1275) and the tower of the former Bishop's Palace, now a history museum.
See also: Switzerland.

Lava, molten rock rising to the earth's surface through volcanoes and other fissures, or the same after solidification. Originating as magma deep below the surface, most lavas are basaltic (subsilicic) and flow freely for considerable distances. Lavas of intermediate silica content are called andesite. Silica-rich lavas, such as rhyolite, are much stiffer.
See also: Volcano.

Laval (pop. 284,200), city in Quebec province, southeastern Canada, part of the Montreal metropolitan area. Covering the island called Ile Jésus, 27 mi (43 km) long and 7 mi (11 km) wide, it is separated from Montreal, to the south, by the Des Prairies River, and from the mainland by the Mille Isles River. An amalgam of 6 former cities and 7 towns, Laval was created in 1965.
See also: Quebec.

Laval, Pierre (1883-1945), French politician who collaborated with the Germans in World War II. A socialist and pacifist, he served as premier (1931-32, 1935-36). Believing that Nazi victory was inevitable, he allowed himself to be installed as a Nazi puppet premier (1942-44). He surrendered to the Allies (1945) and was executed for treason.

Lavender (*Lavandula vera*), shrub of the mint family, cultivated for its aromatic flowers that, along with the leaves, are used for medicinal purposes. Lavender is normally used in the form of an oil derived from the flowers and distilled with water. It is used for flatulence, migraine, headache, fainting, and dizziness. It also has some antiseptic properties and is useful against putrefactive bacteria in the intestines.

Laveran, Charles Louis Alphonse (1845-1922), French army physician. He won the Nobel Prize in medicine (1907) for his research on protozoa in the generation of tropical diseases. As a surgeon in Algeria (1880), he discovered the malarial parasite and demonstrated its spread by mosquito. He joined the Pasteur Institute in Paris in 1894.
See also: Malaria.

Laver, Rod (Rodney George Laver; 1938-   ), Australian tennis player. He was the first person to win the grand slam (consisting of the Australian Open, the French Open, Wimbledon, and the United States Open) twice (1962, 69). He also played on 4 winning Davis Cup teams and captured 4 Wimbledon titles (1961, 62, 68, 69).

Lavoisier, Antoine Laurent (1743-94), French scientist, foremost in the establishment of modern chemistry. He showed that when substances burned, they combined with a component in the air (1772). In 1779 he named this substance *oxygen* (from Greek *oxys*, "acid"), believing it was a component of all acids. He discredited the phlogiston theory of combustion, proposed a new chemical nomenclature (1787), and published the epoch-making *Elementary Treatise of Chemistry* (1789). In the years before his death on the guillotine, he also investigated the chemistry of respiration, demonstrating its analogy with combustion.
See also: Chemistry.

Law, body of rules governing the relationships between the members of a community and between the individual and the state. In England, the British Commonwealth, and the United States, the law is based upon statute law, or laws enacted by legislative bodies such as Congress, and upon common law, the body of law created by custom and adherence to rules derived from previous judgments. The other main system, civil law, derives from the laws of ancient Rome and relies not on precedent but on a code of rules established and modified only by statute. This is the dominant system in most of Europe and in many other countries of the world.

All major bodies of law break down into 2 divisions, public law and private law. Public law governs matters that concern the state. Private law governs the relationship between individuals (including corporate bodies such as companies).

The first legal system of which we have any detailed knowledge is that of the Babylonian king Hammurabi in 1700 B.C., whose complex code linked crime with punishment and regulated the conduct of everyday affairs. Like the Hebrew Mosaic Law, it treated law as a divine ordinance. The ancient Greeks were probably the first to regard law as made by man for his own benefit. Roman law was based on the Laws of the Twelve Tables, compiled 451-450 B.C.

The Romans developed a complex equity system when these principles became outdated; the Byzantine emperor Justinian I produced the last definitive code in an attempt to clear up resulting difficulties. Much medieval law was based on Church law, although an independent system arose quite early in England. This grew into the common law and spread outwards with the growth of the British Empire. Napoleon revised Roman law as the basis for his Code Napoléon, the model for most subsequent civil law codes. U.S. law grew out of the common law, but has been much modified by the federal system.

Law enforcement, method used by the various levels of government to regulate social conduct. Laws, the rules by which society recognizes obedience, are enforced by agencies given public authority to impose penalties or sanctions when they are broken. These agencies are usually a combination of a police force and the courts. In the United States most municipal police forces operate independently of state influence, and city police chiefs are traditionally appointed, while sheriffs, who enforce county laws, are elected to office. The Federal Bureau of Investigation (FBI) maintains an enforcement branch and assists local authorities in federal cases. The International Court of Justice, an agency of the UN with 15 international judges, sits at The Hague, Netherlands, and hears disputes between countries.

Lawn tennis *See:* Tennis.

Law of the land *See:* Due process.

Lawrence, D.H. (David Herbert Lawrence; 1885-1930), English author. He combined a vivid prose style with a solid background of ideas and intense human insight. From a working-class background (reflected in *Sons and Lovers*, 1913), he believed that the Industrial Revolution had resulted in dehumanization. Stressing the supremacy of instinct and emotion over reason in human relationships, he advocated absolute sexual candor; his novel *Lady Chatterley's Lover* (1928) was notorious for this to the exclusion of its other themes. His other novels include *The Rainbow* (1915) and *Women in Love* (1920).

Lawrence, Ernest Orlando (1901-58), U.S. physicist awarded the 1939 Nobel Prize for physics for his invention of the cyclotron and his studies of atomic structure and transmutation.

Lawrence, James (1781-1813), U.S. naval officer. He was captain of the frigate *Chesapeake*, sunk by the British frigate *Shannon* off Boston in 1813. His dying words, "Don't give up the ship!" have become proverbial.

Lawrence, T(homas) E(dward) (1888-1935), called Lawrence of Arabia, English scholar, writer, and soldier, legendary guerrilla fighter with the Arabs against the Turks in World War I. As a British intelligence officer he joined Prince Faisal I in a successful guerrilla campaign against Turkish rail supply lines and was with the Arab forces that captured Damascus in 1918. In *The Seven Pillars of Wisdom* (1918) he described his wartime experiences and his personal philosophy. He joined the Royal Air Force and Royal Tank Corps under assumed names (1923-25, 1925-35).

Lawrence of Arabia *See:* Lawrence, T(homas) E(dward).

Lawrencium, chemical element, symbol Lr; for physical constants see Periodic Table. Lawrencium was discovered by Albert Ghiorso and co-workers in Mar. 1961. It was incorrectly identified as Lawrencium-257, later changed to Lawrencium-258. It was prepared by bombarding a mixed-isotope californium target with boron-10 or boron-11. It has also been prepared by bombarding americium-243 with oxygen-18 ions. It is a metallic element and a member of the actinide series. Lawrencium-261 has a 40 minute half-life. That is the longest of the ten isotopes of the element now known. Lawrencium is the last member of the actinide transition series.

Lawson, Ernest (1873-1939), U.S. impressionist painter. One of the eight members of the Ashcan School, he exhibited at their controversial Armory Show. Seeking a greater degree of naturalism, he specialized in serene landscapes, rendered in glowing colors, such as *Winter* (1914) and *High Bridge* (1939).

Laxative, drug or food taken to promote bowel action and to treat constipation. Laxatives may act as irritants (cascara, senna, phenolphthalein, castor oil), softeners (mineral oil), or bulk agents (bran, methylcellulose, magnesium sulphate). Laxative abuse may cause gastrointestinal tract disorders, potassium deficiency, and lung disease.

Lazarus, in the New Testament, brother of Mary and Martha of Bethany, who was restored to life by Jesus 4 days after his death (John 11:1-44; 12:1-5); also in the New Testament, beggar at the rich man's gate in a parable (Luke 16:19-25).
See also: New Testament.

Lazarus, Emma (1849-87), U.S. poet best known for the sonnet, "The New Colossus," engraved at the base of the Statue of Liberty. Much of her work is based on Jewish culture, such as the poems *Songs of a Semite* (1882).

Leacock, Stephen Butler (1869-1944), Canadian writer, scholar, and humorist. Although he was a distinguished professor of political science and wrote numerous books on political science, economics, history, and literary criticism, he was perhaps best known for his satiric essays and short stories written in dead-pan style. These humorous works were first published in newspapers and magazines and later appeared in collections. In 1946, his unfinished autobiography, *The Boy I Left Behind Me,* was published posthumously.

Lead, chemical element, symbol Pb; for physical constants see Periodic Table. Lead was known and used by the ancients. It is sometimes found native and occurs in the minerals *anglesite, cerussite, mimetite*, and *pyromorphite*. It is obtained by roasting its most common ore, *galena*, a sulfide, to its oxide and reducing with carbon in a blast furnace. Lead is a silvery, soft, heavy, metal. It is a poor conductor of heat and electricity. The metal has long been used in the lead-chamber process for the production of sulfuric acid. In the decay of uranium, thorium and actinium, a different stable isotope of lead is the end product. Lead and its compounds are used in storage batteries, X-ray shielding, cable sheathing, insecticides, detonators, solders, shot, and type metal.

Lead monoxide *See:* Litharge.

Lead pencil *See:* Graphite.

Lead poisoning, cumulative chronic disease caused by excessive lead levels in tissues and blood. Lead may be absorbed in industrial settings, through air pollution due to lead-containing fuels, or, in children, through eating old paint. Brain disturbance, with coma or convulsions, peripheral neuritis, anemia, and abdominal colic are important effects. Chelating agents are used in treatment, but preventive measures are essential.
See also: Lead.

Leadwort *See:* Plumbago.

Leaf, green outgrowth from the stems of higher plants; the main site of photosynthesis. The form of leaves varies from species to species, but the basic features are similar. Each leaf consists of a flat blade or lamina attached to the main stem by a leaf stalk or petiole. Leaflike stipules may be found at the base of the petiole. The green coloration is produced by chlorophyll, located in the chloroplasts. Most leaves are covered by a waterproof covering or cuticle. Gaseous exchange takes place through small openings called stomata, through which water vapor also passes. The blade of the leaf is strengthened by veins that contain the vascular tissue responsible for conducting water and the substances essential for metabolism through the plant. Leaves may be adapted to catch insects or to reduce water loss. Bracts, leaves produced immediately below the flowers, may be highly colored and thus mistaken for flowers (as in the poinsettia).

Leafhopper, about 70 genera and over 700 species of slender, sucking insects of the family Cicadellidae. Leafhoppers may be brilliantly colored, green, or brown, and are 1/20-1/2 in (1.3-12.7 mm) long. They occur worldwide and on almost any type of plant, particularly fruits, grains, sugar beets, and roses. Leafhoppers carry fungus and bacterial diseases and in large numbers may cause severe crop damage.

Leaf insect, any of about 25 species of herbivorous, tropical, usually nocturnal insects of the family Phylliidae, whose green, ribbed, and veined wings and flat shape make them appear leaflike. Leaf insects are 3-4 in (8-10 cm) long and have irregularly shaped bodies.

Leaf miner, name for many species of insect, including flies, moths, wasps, caterpillars, beetles, and weevils, whose larvae infest and feed within leaves. Leaf miners burrow into leaves and other plant parts and leave blotches or tunnels.

Leaf-monkey *See:* Colobus; Langur.

League of Nations (1920-1946), the first major international association of countries, set up after World War I. The charter, or covenant, was incorporated into the Treaty of Versailles by the War's victors, among them France, Great Britain, Italy, Japan, and the United States. The United States failed to ratify the treaty and join the League. Though the League grew during the 1920s, it was never effective in settling major disputes (e.g., Italy's invasion of Corfu in 1923, Japan's invasion of Manchuria in 1931, Italy's invasion of Ethiopia in 1935). After World War II proved it a failure, the League was dissolved (1946), but its successor, the United Nations, used it as a model. *See also:* United Nations; Versailles, Treaty of.

League of Women Voters, nonpartisan organization with about 125,000 members in the United States and Puerto Rico, founded in 1920 by members of the National American Women Suffrage Association. Apart from political education for its members, the league researches and campaigns economic and social issues. It does not sponsor electoral candidates or political parties. Men gained admittance to the organization in the mid-1970s. *See also:* Woman suffrage.

Leakey, family name of English archeologists and anthropologists. **Louis Seymour Bazett Leakey** (1903-72) is best known for his findings of hominoid fossils and artifacts, especially in the region of Olduvai Gorge, Tanzania, and for his (sometimes controversial) views on their significance. His wife, **Mary Leakey** (1913-96), collaborated with him. Their son **Richard Leakey** (1944-) continues their work. *See also:* Anthropology; Archeology.

Leander *See:* Hero and Leander.

Leaning Tower of Pisa, white marble bell tower, or campanile, in Pisa, Italy. Building was started in 1174, reputedly by Bonanno Pisano, but the foundations were unsound and the 184.5-ft (56-m) tower had already begun to lean by the time of its completion in the 14th century. It now tilts more than 17 ft (5 m) from the perpendicular.

Lear, Edward (1812-1888), English artist and writer, best known for his limericks and nonsense rhymes, such as "The Owl and the Pussy-Cat" (1871). His landscapes and illustrated journals are highly regarded.

Learning, the process by which behavior is modified through experience and practice. All animals are capable of learning. Humans far surpass all these in the ability to learn, especially in the ability to acquire a language.

Psychologists do not agree about how learning takes place, but certain principles seem clear.

Classical conditioning. The simplest type of learning is the formation of *conditioned reflexes* in this process, an individual learns to associate 2 events, or stimuli, and to respond in the same way to both. During early life, much behavior is learned in this way. A wide range of behavior patterns are conditioned and always occur when the right stimuli are presented.

Instrumental conditioning. Much behavior is learned as a result of random acts that *elicit*, or draw forth, a response. Satisfying *drives*, such as hunger and thirst, are important in this kind of learning. If a particular act reduces the drive, that act will more likely be repeated next time the drive seeks satisfaction. Positive reinforcement—reduction of a drive by a satisfying reward—is usually more effective than negative reinforcement; thus a child who wins approval for performing a task well is more likely to be successful than a child whose "reward" is simply the avoidance of punishment for performing the task badly. Instrumental conditioning is particularly important in the development of acceptable social behavior during the early years of life.

Problem solving and insight learning. There are 2 ways to solve a problem: firstly, by *trial and error* and secondly, by reasoning out a solution, using *insight*. Learning by trial and error is encouraged by presenting the problem a number of times and only rewarding the correct solution. Insight learning involves thinking about the problem and grasping the solution without any trial and error.

Human learning. Many psychologists agree that the upper and lower limits of a person's ability to learn are determined by inherited factors. But related factors such as personality, social background, early childhood experiences and level of motivation make it difficult to predict how well a person will perform. A given amount of time is more effective if distributed over several short sessions. Practice is more efficient if directed toward part of a learning task at a time. Trying to learn 2 similar pieces of information at the same time often leads to confusion between the 2. Actually performing a practical task is better than watching others do it. Activities such as writing down notes will lead to faster learning than just reading about or listening to the facts. Mastering one subject will make it easier to learn a closely related subject. It is easier to remember something if there is a period of inactivity, especially sleep, between learning and attempts to remember.

An especially important aid to learning is knowledge of performances as one is actually progressing with a learning task. This is one advantage of teaching machines, which only move on to a new problem after the student has correctly solved the previous one.

Learning disabilities, conditions or factors that hinder one's comprehension or impairs one's ability to use standard educational tools and methods. An inability to perform in the school environment at the same level as one's peers can be the result of an inherited condition causing mental retardation, a developmental defect, a physical handicap such as impaired hearing or vision or muscle incoordination, an allergy causing hyperactivity, or even a reaction to medications taken to control hyperactivity. Learning problems are first identified through tests that measure reading, writing, and arithmetic performance correlated to age, experience, and family background. One common learning disability is *dyslexia*, the mental reversing of printed letters

and inability thus to comprehend the meaning of written text. Its cause can lie in the brain, the eyes, or another part of the body. Writing disabilities frequently come from a lack of coordination between the brain and the muscles. A mathematics disability seems to reflect problems of memory and can exist with or without a reading problem.
See also: Dyslexia; Hyperactive child.

Leather, animal hide or skin preserved by tanning. After the hair, fat, and flesh have been removed from the hides, they are soaked in enzymes for softening, then pickled in acid. The tanned leather is lubricated with oil and resins, and often dyed.

Leathernecks *See:* Marine Corps, U.S.

Leavenworth (pop. 33,656), city in northeastern Kansas, on the Missouri River. The oldest city in the state, it was organized in 1854 by proslavery settlers near Ft. Leavenworth on the Santa Fe Trail. In 1855 it became the first incorporated town in Kansas Territory. Leavenworth is an industrial and marketing center producing wood, meat, and dairy products, structural steel, greeting cards, and mill machinery. It is the site of Leavenworth Prison.
See also: Fort Leavenworth; Kansas.

Lebanon, small republic of about 3,8 million people in southwest Asia, on the Mediterranean, bordered by Syria on the north and east and Israel on the south. Modern Lebanon is the only Arab State with a large Christian community. The capital is the free port of Beirut. Since the Civil War and subsequent conflicts (beginning in the 1970s), the strong financial and trade industries have weakened as well as other sectors of the Lebanese economy.
Land and climate. Geographically the country can be divided into 4 regions, all more or less parallel to the sea: a flat coastal strip along the Mediterranean, the Lebanon mountain range, the narrow Bekaa (Biqa) Valley, only 10 mi wide and the Anti-Lebanon Mountains of the eastern border. The Bekaa Valley, lying between the 2 major mountain ranges, is the country's most fertile area,though the coastal strip is also entirely fertile. Lebanon is fortunate in having more rainfall and a more moderate climate than most of the neighboring countries. In the past the country was famed for the cedars of Lebanon, which probably covered large tracts of its mountain ranges. Today only a few small cedar groves remain. The capital, Beirut, is a seaport of relatively recent origin. Other important cities are Tripoli (Tarabulus), the ancient Tyre and Sidon along the coast, and Zahle in the interior.
People. The people of Lebanon are of mixed ancestry, but mostly Arab. About 40% are Christians. An Armenian community also exists. Most of the remainder are Sunni Muslims, with a smaller group of the Shi'te sect. The small Druze sect has played a significant part in Lebanese history, especially as a political and military force in the recent conflicts.
History. Lebanon is the site of ancient Phoenicia. Although engulfed by successive invaders—Greek, Roman, Arab and Turkish—it preserved some degree of autonomy. Lebanon's inaccessible mountains were an early refuge for persecuted religious groups, especially Christians. Freed from Turkish rule after World War I, the country passed into French hands, becoming effectively independent in 1943. Civil war erupted in 1975 between the conservative Christian Phalangists and leftist Muslim and Palestinian mili-

Lebanon

Capital:	Beirut
Area:	4,015 sq mi
	(10,400 sq km)
Population:	3,506,000
Language:	Arabic
Government:	Republic
Independent:	1943
Head of gov.:	Prime minister
Per capita:	U.S. $2,660
Mon. unit:	1 Lebanese pound =
	100 piastre

tias, including the Palestine Liberation Organization (PLO). In 1982 after years of skirmishes with the PLO in southern Lebanon, Israel invaded Lebanon, occupying Beirut and eventually forcing many PLO guerrillas to leave the country. A multinational peace-keeping force, including U.S. marines, arrived (1982) in Beirut, but withdrew within 1 year. The withdrawal was due, in part, to a terrorist attack on U.S. and French compounds which killed over 241 Marines (Oct. 23, 1983). By 1985 Israeli troops also withdrew from all but southern Lebanon. Since 1985 various attempts at ceasefires and political settlements have been made by Syria and other countries involved in the conflict. In 1996 the violence in South Lebanon escalated when Hezbollah fired missiles at North Israel. In return, Israel bombarded Beirut and South Lebanon. The violence caused new streams of refugees.

Le Carré, John (David John Moore Cornwell; 1931-   ), English author of novels of international espionage, including *The Spy Who Came in from the Cold* (1963), *Tinker, Tailor, Soldier, Spy* (1974), *The Little Drummer Girl* (1983), and *The Russia House* (1989).

Lecithin *See:* Soybean.

Le Corbusier (Charles-Édouard Jeanneret; 1887-1965), Swiss-born, French-trained architect, a founder of the international style. His austere, rectangular designs of the 1920s and 1930s reflect his view of a house as a "machine to live in." Later influential designs (featuring reinforced concrete) include apartments at Marseilles, a chapel at Ronchamp, and buildings in Chandigarh, India.
See also: Architecture.

Lederberg, Joshua (1925-   ), U.S. geneticist awarded (with G.W. Beadle and E.L. Tatum) the 1958 Nobel Prize in physiology or medicine for his work on bacterial genetics. He showed that sexual recombination occurs in bacteria. Later he established that genetic information could be carried by bacterial viruses.
See also: Genetics.

Lederman, Leon Max (1922-   ), U.S. physicist who was part of a team
that won the 1988 Nobel Prize. Together with colleagues Melvin Schwartz
and Jack Steinberger, he discovered a new subatomic particle (neutrino) and
developed a way of synthesizing neutrinos in the laboratory. Lederman
served on the faculty of Columbia University and was an adviser to the
Atomic Energy Commission.
See also: Neutrino.

Lee, Charles (1731-82), American major general in the Revolutionary War.
He refused orders from George Washington (1776), planned betrayal while
in British captivity (1776-78), and retreated at the Battle of Monmouth
(1778), robbing Washington of a victory. He was court-martialed and
dismissed (1780).
See also: Revolutionary War in America.

Lee, Francis Lightfoot (1734-97), American patriot and revolutionary
leader. As a member of the Virginia House of Representatives (1758-76),
Continental Congress delegate (1775-79), and a signer of the Declaration of
Independence, Lee consistently advocated rebellion against England. He
helped draft the Articles of Confederation.
See also: Committees of correspondence.

Lee, Harper (1926-   ), U.S. author whose only novel, *To Kill A Mockingbird* (1960), won the Pulitzer Prize for fiction. The novel vividly depicts the
racism and prejudice of a small southern town by focusing on the sensitive
perceptions of the story's narrator, Finch's young daughter.

Lee, Henry (1756-1818), American cavalry officer in the Revolutionary
War (known as "Light Horse Harry") and father of Confederate Civil War
general Robert E. Lee. He was governor of Virginia (1791-94) and a
representative in Congress (1799-1801).
See also: Revolutionary War in America.

Lee, Richard Henry (1732-94), American Revolutionary statesman. He
was a Virginia delegate (1774-79, 1784-87) and president (1784-85) of the
Continental Congress. On June 7, 1776, he introduced the motion that led to
the Declaration of Independence. He opposed ratification of the U.S. Constitution, fearing its limits on states' rights. As a U.S. senator from Virginia,
1789-92, he helped secure adoption of the Bill of Rights.

Lee, Robert Edward (1807-70), U.S. general and commander of the Confederate Army in the Civil War. His father, Henry "Light-Horse Harry" Lee,
was a noted cavalry leader during the Revolutionary War, and 2 other Lees
were among the signers of the Declaration of Independence.
During the Mexican War (1846-48), Lee served brilliantly on the headquarters staff. After the war he was appointed superintendent of West Point
(1852-55). In 1859 Lee was sent to arrest John Brown and restore order after
the raid on Harper's Ferry.
When in 1861 civil war appeared imminent, President Abraham Lincoln
offered Lee the post of field commander of the Union forces. Although
opposed to slavery and secession, Lee declined out of loyalty to his native
state. He accepted a post in the Confederate Army and for a year served as

military adviser to Confederate President Jefferson Davis. In May 1861 he was made a full general and in June 1862 was given command of the Army of Northern Virginia.

Lee's first great success was the defense of Richmond in the Battles of the Seven Days (June 26-July 2, 1862), in which he neutralized superior Union numbers and forced retreat. After the Confederate victory at the second Battle of Bull Run, Lee invaded Maryland but was halted at Antietam, one of the bloodiest battles of the war, and withdrew to Virginia. At Chancellorsville (May 1863) Lee overcame a 2-to-1 troop disadvantage by dividing his forces and forcing the Union army to retreat. Lee again invaded the North and met the Union forces at Gettysburg, Pa. (July 1863).

During the Wilderness campaign (May-June 1864) and the siege of Petersburg (July 1864), superior Northern numbers and resources battered the exhausted Confederate Army. On Apr. 9, 1865, Lee surrendered to Grant at Appomattox Court House, Va. Lee's mastery of maneuver, his skills in communication, and his ability to inspire devotion in his men had delayed but could not prevent the Union victory. After the war, Lee became president of Washington College (later renamed Washington and Lee University), a post he held until his death.

See also: Civil War, U.S.

Leech, annelid (segmented) worm (class Hirudinea) with a prominent attachment sucker at the posterior end and another sucker around the mouth. Leeches are hermaphroditic. Freshwater or semiterrestrial animals, they feed by sucking the blood or other body fluids of mammals, small invertebrates, worms, insect larvae, or snails.

Leechee *See:* Litchi.

Leeds (pop. 721,800), city in western Yorkshire, northern England. A weaving town in the Middle Ages, it remains a major center for textiles and clothing, particularly woolens. Other industries include electronics, machinery, chemicals, aircraft, vehicles, and food products. On the River Aire, Leeds has canal links to both coasts, and the Yorkshire coal fields lie nearby. It is the site of Leeds University as well as the 12th-century Kirstall Abbey ruins and Temple Newsom, once a mansion of the Knights Templar.

See also: England.

Leek (*Allium porrum*), relative of the onion, originating in the Middle East. This biennial plant is now cultivated throughout Europe and is the national plant of Wales.

Lee Kuan Yew (1923-   ), prime minister of Singapore 1959-90. A labor attorney, Lee helped establish the People's Action Party (1954), and during his years in office has helped the country achieve political independence and a strong economy.

See also: Singapore.

Lee Teng-hui (1923-   ), Taiwanese president (1990-), became interim president of Taiwan in 1988 as a result of the death of President Chiang Kai-shek. He had formerly served as a member of the Joint Committee on Rural Reconstruction (1957-61). He was mayor of Taipei (1978-81), gover-

nor of Taiwan province (1981-84), and vice president of Taiwan (1984-88).
See also: Taiwan.

Leeuwenhoek, Anton van (1632-1723), Dutch microscopist who made
important observations of capillaries, red blood corpuscles, and sperm. He
is best known for being the first to observe bacteria and protozoa (1674-6),
which he called "very little animalcules."
See also: Microscope.

Leeward Islands, chain of about 15 islands and many islets in the West
Indies, northernmost group of the Lesser Antilles. They include Antigua,
Anguilla, Montserrat, and the British Virgin Islands (British colonies); St.
Kitts-Nevis (a former British colony, independent since 1983); St. Eustatius,
Saba, and St. Martin (Dutch); Guadeloupe and dependencies (French); and
the U.S. Virgin Islands.

Léger, Fernand (1881-1955)a

Legion, principal unit of the Roman army, having between 3,000 and 6,000
infantry with attached cavalry. By the 1st century B.C. the cohort, composed
of 6 companies, was the tactical unit. There were 10 cohorts to a legion. The
leader of a legion was a legate or a consul. Soldiers of the Roman Empire
were recruited to a legion for a term of 20 to 25 years.

Legion, American *See:* American Legion.

Legion, Foreign *See:* Foreign Legion.

Legionnaires' disease, severe lung infection. Legionnaires' disease appeared in 1976 when 182 delegates attending an annual convention of the
American Legion in Philadelphia contracted a severe respiratory infection.
Of 147 of those hospitalized, 90% developed pneumonia and 29 died. All
had stayed in, or visited, the same hotel during the 4-day convention. Five
months later, the organism responsible, a small Gram-negative, non-acid-fast
bacillus, was isolated from the lung tissues of 4 fatal cases, and was
subsequently named *Legionella pneumophila*. It is now clear that the organism is a significant respiratory pathogen, in both the United States and
Western Europe.
After an incubation period of 2 to 10 days, the illness begins with symptoms
of malaise, headache, and muscular aches and pains, succeeded in a few hours
by high fever and shivering. A dry cough, or a cough producing small
amounts of bloodstained sputum, begins on the second or third day, with
pleurisy (inflammation of the pleura, the membrane covering the lungs) a
common occurrence. Watery diarrhea with abdominal distention, occurring
in around 50% of the sufferers, may precede the onset of fever. The antibiotic
erythromycin is the most effective treatment for the disease.

Legislature, representative assembly empowered to enact, revise, or repeal
the laws or statutes of a community. The earliest modern legislatures were
the British Parliament and the French States-General, which were forerunners of the contemporary bicameral system of upper and lower houses. In
the United States the 2 chambers are the Senate and the House of Repre-

sentatives, which together are called the Congress. In most bicameral systems both chambers must approve a bill before it becomes law. Under a parliamentary system, like Britain's or Canada's, the prime minister, who heads the government, remains in power only as long as his or her party retains a majority in the main legislative chamber. Under the U.S. system, the president's stay in office is independent of the majority party in the legislature.

Legume, any of nearly 17,000 species of plant of the pulse or pea family (Leguminosae) including peas, beans, lentils, soybeans, and peanuts, fodder plants such as clover, alfalfa, and cowpeas, and hardwoods such as ebony, locust, mahogany, and rosewood. Legumes are widely distributed and variable in growth. The species are distinguished by their flowers, usually bilaterally symmetrical blooms, and by their fruits, seed pods with 2 splitting sides.

Lehár, Franz (1870-1948), Hungarian composer of Viennese-style light opera. His works include the melodious operetta *The Merry Widow* (1905).

Le Havre (pop. 199,400), French seaport on the English Channel and the Seine River. It is a transatlantic trade center that manufactures and imports ships, automobiles, electronics, petroleum products, steel, chemicals, sugar, flour, and beer. A fishing village before 1516, when Francis I began the harbor construction, Le Havre lost 80% of its buildings in World War II. The city was subsequently rebuilt, and the harbor was renovated and expanded in the 1970s.
See also: France.

Lehmann, Lotte (1888-1976), German-born U.S. soprano. She sang with the Vienna State Opera (1914-38) and in the United States at the Metropolitan (1934-45). Famous for her portrayal of the Marschallin in *Der Rosenkavalier*, she created roles in other Richard Strauss operas and was a skilled interpreter of lieder.

Lehmbruck, Wilhelm (1881-1919), German sculptor noted for his images of pathos and heroism of spirit. Influenced by Rodin, Brancusi, and Maillol, he depicted his human subjects as ascetic, angular figures, such as *Standing Woman* (1910) and *Kneeling Woman* (1911).

Lehn, Jean-Marie (1939-   ), French chemist and university professor who was part of a team that won the 1987 Nobel Prize for chemistry. Along with Americans Donald James Cram and Charles John Pedersen, Lehn created an artificial molecule that transmits signals to the human brain.
See also: Chemistry.

Leibniz, Gottfried Wilhelm von (1646-1716), German philosopher, historian, jurist, geologist, and mathematician, codiscoverer of the calculus, and author of the theory of monads. His discovery of the calculus was independent of, though later than, that of Sir Isaac Newton; it is the Leibnizian form that predominates today. He devised a calculating machine and a symbolic mathematical logic. His concept of the universe as a "preestablished harmony," his analysis of the problem of evil, his epistemology, logic, and philosophy of nature place him in the foremost rank of philosophers and

helped mold the German Enlightenment. His writings include *New Essays on Human Understanding* (1704), *Theodicy* (1710), and *Monadology* (1714).
See also: Calculus.

Leicester (pop. 285,400), important historic and industrial city in central England known for hosiery, shoes and machinery products. It is the site of the University of Leicester, Jewry Wall (built by the Romans in the A.D. 100s), landmark churches and a castle that dates back to the 1100s.
See also: England.

Leicester, Robert Dudley, Earl of (1532-88), favorite of Elizabeth I of England. Although his political and military performances were poor and his reputation was marred by suspicions of treason, wife-murder and bigamy, he wielded great power and was made a privy councillor (1558) and army commander.

Leiden, or Leyden (pop. 115,400), city in western Netherlands, center for science and light industry, particularly printing and textiles. It is the seat of Leiden University (est. 1575), the oldest in the Netherlands and important for Protestant theology and scientific research. Leiden is noted for its museums, laboratories, and botanical gardens. It was Rembrandt's birthplace and home to some of the English Pilgrims from 1609 until they sailed for the New World in 1620.
See also: Netherlands.

Leipzig (pop. 507,800), city in eastern Germany, former capital of Leipzig district. A major cultural, commercial, and manufacturing center, it has fine medieval and renaissance architecture. Composers J.S. Bach, Felix Mendelssohn, and Robert Schumann were active in the city.
See also: Germany.

Le Mans (pop. 148,400), city in northwestern France on the Sarthe and Huisne rivers, dating from pre-Roman times. A diocese from the 3rd century, Le Mans was invaded by the English in the Hundred Years War (1337-1453) and was the site of important battles in the French Revolution (1793). It is a marketing and industrial center, and is best known for its 24-hour annual sports car competition on 8 mi (13 km) of winding road.
See also: France.

Lemming, Arctic rodent, about 3-6 in (7-15 cm) in length, closely related to the vole. Genera include *Lemmus* and *Dicrostonyx*. Like many small mammals of simple ecological systems, lemmings show periodic fluctuations in numbers. These 3- to 4-year fluctuations result in spectacular mass migrations in search of food. One species, *L. lemmus*, is particularly noted for migrations that lead many members to accidental drowning in the ocean.

Lemon (*Citrus limon*), small evergreen tree that produces sour yellow fruits that are rich in vitamin C. The fruits also contain an oil that is used in cooking and the manufacture of perfume. The United States and Italy are chief producers of lemon fruit.

Lemur, family of cat-sized primates found only on Madagascar and small islands nearby, related to primitive ancestors of the whole primate group of monkeys and apes. They are nocturnal and strictly arboreal, feeding on insects, fruit, and even small mammals. The family Lemuridae includes 2 subfamilies: the Cheirogaleinae, or mouse lemurs, and the Lemurinae, true lemurs.

Lendl, Ivan (1960-), Czechoslovakian-born U.S. tennis player. Known for his power and consistency, Lendl held the number one ranking from 1985 to 1987. His achievements include victories at the United States Open (1985, 86, 87), the French Open (1984, 86, 87) and the Australian Open (1989, 90).

Lend-lease, program by which the United States sent aid to the Allies in World War II, during and after neutrality. President Franklin D. Roosevelt initiated the program in 1941 to help countries "resisting aggression." Total aid exceeded $50 billion and not only bolstered Allied defense but developed the U.S. war industries and helped mobilize public opinion.
See also: World War II.

L'Enfant, Pierre Charles (1754-1825), French-American engineer and architect who fought in the Revolutionary War and was commissioned (1791) to plan Washington, D.C. Because of opposition his plans were shelved, but in 1901 they became the basis for the development of the capital. L'Enfant also designed Federal Hall in New York City.
See also: Architecture.

Lenin, V.I. (1870-1924), Russian revolutionary, founder of the Bolshevik (later Communist) Party, leader of the Bolshevik Revolution of 1917, and founder of the Soviet state. Born Vladimir Ilyich Ulyanov, Lenin became a revolutionary after his older brother was executed (1887) on charges of plotting to assassinate the tsar. By then a follower of the ideas of Karl Marx, Lenin was arrested and exiled to Siberia in 1895. In 1900 he and his wife, Nadezhda Krupskaya, went into exile in western Europe. In 1902 he published his famous pamphlet *What is to Be Done*? arguing that only a highly disciplined party of revolutionaries could cause the overthrow of the tsar. In 1903 the Russian Social Democratic Workers Party, meeting in London, split over this and related issues. Lenin's supporters became known as the Bolsheviks (from the Russian word for "majority"); his opponents were called Mensheviks (from "minority"). Lenin and his fellow Marxists returned briefly to Russia during the unsuccessful revolution of 1905. In 1907 he went into exile again. When the tsar was overthrown by the Feb. 1917 revolution, in the midst of World War I, Lenin returned to Russia. Reacting against the rush of Socialist parties in Europe to support their own governments in World War I, he issued a call for the formation of a new revolutionary international organization. In Oct. 1917 the Bolshevik Party, under the leadership of Lenin and Leon Trotsky, seized power in Russia at the head of a popular insurrection, and Lenin became the head of the new, Soviet state. The revolutionary organization he had called for came into being as well, as the Communist International.Lenin led the revolutionary state for its first 6 years, a period that saw the civil war and the nationalization of industry. With the end of the civil war in 1921 he turned to a more liberal economic approach, known as the New Economic Policy. This allowed some development of private enterprises, especially in the countryside. At the same time, however, his government banned all opposition parties. Considerable state resources were devoted to the Communist International and to attempts to foster other revolutions in other countries, especially in Europe. In the late months of 1923 Lenin began warning about the rising bureaucratization of the state and about the growing ambition of Stalin. In Jan. 1924, however, before any of those warnings would be acted on, he died from a series of strokes. Lenin had a greater influence on communism than anyone else except Karl Marx. In fact, after his death the theory of communism came to be called Marxist-Leninism. His major contribution to the political doctrine was his concept of the revolutionary party, and he was the first to implement that concept successfully. In that sense he was one of history's greatest revolutionaries and one of the most influential political leaders of the 20th century.

Leningrad (pop. 4,468,000), second largest city and chief port of the RF, on the Gulf of Finland, and former Russian capital (as St. Petersburg, 1712-1914, and Petrograd, 1914-24). It was founded in 1703 by Tsar Peter I (Peter the Great). Linked by its port with western Europe, it rapidly became a cultural and commercial center. Industrial expansion during the 19th century was followed by a temporary decline during World War I and the Russian Revolution. The city was renamed for V.I. Lenin in 1924. Leningrad endured great destruction and loss of life in the German siege (1941-44) during World War II. Today industries include heavy machinery manufacturing, shipbuilding, chemicals, and textiles. The city is home to the University of Leningrad, one of Russia's largest universities; the Hermitage, a world-renowned museum, and the Conservatory of Music, whose graduates include the composers Sergei Prokofiev and Peter Ilich Tchaikovsky. Leningrad has figured in the writings of Russian authors A. Pushkin and F. Dostoevsky. In 1990 the name was reverted back to St. Petersburg.
See also: Union of Soviet Socialist Republics.

Lennon, John (1940-1980), rock musician, a founding member of the Beatles. Along with Paul McCartney he wrote most of the Beatles' music, including "Help" (1965), "Strawberry fields" (1966) and "A Day in the Life" (1967). As a social critic he wrote "Give Peace a Chance" (1969) and "Imagine" (1971). Lennon married Yoko Ono in 1969 and continued to compose and sing after the Beatles disbanded (1970). He was shot to death on Dec. 8, 1980 by Mark David Chapman.
See also: Beatles.

Lenoir, Jean Joseph Étienne (1822-1900), French inventor. He built the first practical internal combustion engine for use in industrial machinery and one of the first gas-powered automobiles (1862). He also invented a railroad brake (1855) and a motorboat (1886).
See also: Internal combustion engine.

Le Nôtre, André (1613-1700), French landscape architect. Under Louis XIV, his strictly geometrical creations, including the gardens of Versailles and the Tuileries, featured splendid vistas and radiating paths.
See also: Architecture.

Lens, transparent substance, usually glass, having 2 opposite surfaces, either both curved or one curved and one straight, used for refraction, (changing the direction of light rays). Lenses are used in eyeglasses to correct errors of vision, in cameras to focus images on film, and in microscopes and telescopes to magnify images. The term is also used for the part of the eye that focuses light rays on the retina.

Lent (from Old English *lencten*, "spring"), period of 40 days dedicated by Christians to penitential prayer and fasting as a preparation for Easter. In the West it begins on Ash Wednesday.
See also: Christianity; Easter.

Lentil (*Lens culinaris*), leguminous plant grown in warm parts of the Old World. It was one of the first cultivated crops. The seeds, which are rich in proteins, are cooked as porridge or soup. The mess of potage for which Esau sold his birthright (Genesis 25-28) was made from lentils.

Lenya, Lotte (1900-81), Austrian-born U.S. singer and actress. She performed on the stage in Berlin (1920-33), notably in *The Three-Penny Opera* (1928), composed by her husband, Kurt Weill, in collaboration with Brecht. She sang and acted in several Weill works, including *Mahogonny* and *Cabaret*, in the United States after 1933.

Leo, name of 13 popes. **Saint Leo I** (c. 400-461), an Italian, r. 440-461. Called "the Great," he suppressed heresy and established his authority in both the West and East. He persuaded the barbarian leaders Attila (in 452) and Genseric (in 455) not to destroy Rome. **Saint Leo III** (d. 816), a Roman, r. 795-816. He crowned Charlemagne "Emperor of the Romans" in Rome on Christmas Day, 800, thus allying church and state. **Saint Leo IX** (Bruno of Egisheim; 1002-1054),a German, r. 1049-54. He fought against simony (the selling of church offices) and vigorously enjoined clerical celibacy. The Great Schism between the Western and Eastern churches began in his reign. **Leo X** (Giovanni de Medici; 1475-1521), a Florentine, r. 1513-21. He made Rome a center of the arts and literature and raised money for rebuilding St. Peter's by the sale of indulgences—a practice attacked by Martin Luther at the start of the Reformation. **Leo XIII** (Gioacchino Pecci; 1810-1903), an Italian, r. 1878-1903. He worked to reconcile Roman Catholicism with science and liberalism and generally applied Christian principles to the religious and social questions of his time. His *Rerum Novarum* (1891), an encyclical (letter to the Roman Catholic Church) on the condition of the working classes, strengthened Roman Catholicism's links with the working-class movement and helped counter anticlericalism at home and abroad.

León, medieval kingdom of northwestern Spain, including the provinces of León, Salamanca, and Zamora. Forged in the 10th century by the rulers of Austria, the kingdom spearheaded the Christian reconquest of Spain from the Moors. It was permanently joined to Castile in 1230.

Leonard, Sugar Ray (Ray Charles Leonard; 1956-   ), U.S. boxer. He was the Olympic gold medalist in the light welterweight class (Summer Games, 1976), and won the World Boxing Council (WBC) welterweight title (1979) and World Boxing Association (WBA) junior middleweight title (1981).

After suffering a detached retina Leonard retired (1982) but staged a come-back, capturing the WBC middleweight title (1987) and WBC super middle-weight and light heavyweight titles (1988). He retired again in 1991.

Leonardo da Vinci *See:* Da Vinci, Leonardo.

Leoncavallo, Ruggiero (1858-1919), Italian opera composer. *I Pagliacci* (The Clowns, 1892), a classic *verismo* (realistic) opera, is the only one of his works that is still widely known.
See also: Opera.

Leonidas I (d.480 B.C.), king of Sparta. Leonidas, with 300 Spartans and about 1,000 other Greeks, died heroically defending the pass of Thermopylae against the huge invading Persian army of Xerxes.
See also: Sparta; Thermopylae.

Leopard (*Panthera pardus*), big cat similar to the jaguar, with a yellow coat marked with black rosettes, or with black fur (the panther). Found in a variety of habitats across Africa and Asia, it is agile and relies when hunting on its power to spring quickly. The leopard is known for its habit of dragging its kill up into a tree out of the reach of jackals and hyenas. The kill may weigh more than the leopard itself.

Leopard cat *See:* Ocelot.

Leopardi, Giacomo (1798-1837), Italian poet and philosopher, foremost writer of his time. Acutely unhappy, he expressed himself most fully in his brilliant, supple, lyric poetry: *Songs* (1836). *Moral Essays* (1827) reveals his bleak philosophy.
See also: Philosophy.

Leopold, Aldo (1886-1948), American outdoors enthusiast, naturalist, and conservationist. His writings include *Game Management* and *A Sand County Almanac*. An employee of the U.S. Forest Service (1909-27), he later held a faculty position at the University of Wisconsin.

Léopoldville *See:* Kinshasa.

Lepidoptera *See:* Butterfly; Moth.

Leprosy, or Hansen's disease, chronic infectious disease caused by *Mycobacterium leprae* and chiefly found in tropical zones. It leads to skin nodules with loss of pigmentation, mucous membrane lesions in nose and pharynx, and neuritis with nerve thickening, loss of pain sensation, and patchy weakness, often involving face and hand muscles. The type of disease caused depends on the number of bacteria encountered and basic resistance to the disease. Treatment is with sulfones.

Lepton, one of the 4 classes of elementary particles (the others are bosons, measons, and baryons). Leptons are larger than the massless bosons, but smaller than mesons and baryons. There are a total of 12 particles in the lepton class, of which the electron is probably the most familiar. These 12

Lesotho

Capital:	Maseru
Area:	11,720 sq mi
	(30,355 sq km)
Population:	2,090,000
Language:	Sesotho, English
Government:	Constitutional
	monarchy
Independent:	1966
Head of gov.:	Prime minister
Per capita:	U.S. $770
Mon. unit:	1 Loti = 100 lisente

---

come in pairs, one of each pair being positively charged, the other being negatively charged. (The positron is the positively charged mate of the electron, which is negative.)
See also: Particle physics.

Lerner, Alan Jay (1918-86), U.S. lyricist and dramatist. Along with the composer Frederick Loewe, he created such musical comedies as *My Fair Lady*, *Brigadoon*, *Paint Your Wagon*, and *Camelot*. Lerner and Loewe won an Academy Award for the title song in *Gigi*. Lerner himself won Academy Awards for the screenplays of *Gigi* and *An American in Paris*.

Le Sage, Alain René (1668-1747), French novelist and dramatist. His pica-resque masterpiece *Gil Blas* (1715-35), a witty satirical account of French society, influenced the development of the realistic novel in France. He also wrote the comedy *Turcaret* (1709).

Lesbos, Greek island in the Aegean Sea, near Turkey. Also known as Mitilini, it spans about 630 square miles (1,630 sq km) and produces olives, wheat, wine, grapes, and tobacco. A cultured center of ancient Greece, Lesbos was the home of Sappho, Aristotle, and Epicurus.
See also: Greece.

Lesch-Nyhan syndrome, hereditary metabolic disorder, affecting the central nervous system. First described in 1964 by William Nyhan and Michael Lesch, it is caused by a defective enzyme hypoxanthine-quinine-phosphoribasyl-transferase, which is normally very active in brain cells. It is characterized by mental retardation, aggressive behavior and a tendency to inflict self injury. The syndrome is transmitted by a recessive sex-linked gene and primarily affects males. There is no cure or effective treatment.

Lesotho (formerly Basutoland), land-locked kingdom surrounded by, and economically dependent on, the Republic of South Africa.
Land and climate. Part of the great plateau of South Africa, Lesotho lies mainly between 8,000 ft (2,439 m) and 11,000 ft (3,353 m). In the east and the north is the Drakensberg mountain range. The chief rivers are the Orange

River and its tributaries. Annual rainfall averages less than 30 in (76 cm), and temperatures vary seasonally from 93°F (34°C) to 30°F (–1°C). Sparsely forested, Lesotho is mainly dry grassland.

People and economy. The Basuto, who comprise 99% of the population, are chiefly rural. Education is mainly in the hands of missionaries. The literacy rate is about 80%, and around 90% of the people are Christians. An agricultural country, Lesotho is heavily dependent on livestock and food crops such as wheat and maize. Poor farming techniques have resulted in a shortage of good land. Although Lesotho was opposed to apartheid, it depended heavily upon South Africa for trade and employment.

History. The nation was established c.1829 by Chief Moshoeshoe I, who secured British protection from Boer encroachment. As Basutoland, it was under British rule from 1884, gaining independence in 1966.

Lespedeza, any of a genus (*Lespedeza*) of shrublike plants and herbs characterized by 3-parted leaves and smooth edges. The plants are grown in clusters and have pea-shaped flowers; the fruits are single seeded with short pods.

Lesseps, Ferdinand Marie de (1805-95), French diplomat and engineer who conceived the idea for the Suez Canal. Lesseps supervised the building of it (1859-69) himself. His later plans for the Panama Canal ended in bankruptcy (1888) and a conviction for misappropriation of monies. *See also:* Suez Canal.

Lessing, Doris (1919-), British novelist, raised in Southern Rhodesia (now Zimbabwe), who has dealt perceptively with the struggles of intellectual women for political, sexual, and artistic integrity. Her major works include *The Golden Notebook* (1962), *The Four-Gated City* (1969, part of the *Children of Violence* series), and *The Sirian Experiments* (1981). *Under My Skin* (1994) is the first part of her autobiography. Part two, *Walking in the Shade*, was published in 1997.

Lessing, Gotthold Ephraim (1729-81), German playwright, critic, and philosopher. He rejected French classicism and pioneered German bourgeois tragedy with *Miss Sara Sampson* (1755). He also wrote the influential comedy *Minna von Barnhelm* (1763), the prose tragedy *Emilia Galotti* (1772), and the dramatic poem *Nathan the Wise* (1779). His treatise *Laokoön* (1766) critically contrasted the natures of poetry and painting.

Lethe (Greek, "forgetfulness"), in Greek mythology, river in Hades. When the souls of the dead drank from Lethe, they forgot their lives on earth.

Lettuce, popular garden plant (genus *Lactuca*) of the composite family. Cultivated for salad since ancient times, lettuce is harvested before its flower stem shoots up to bear its small yellow flowers. There are 3 main types: leaf lettuce has a loose crown of leaves; head lettuce has compact leaves; romaine (or Cos), with elongated leaves, is the most resistant to heat.

Leucippus (c.400 B.C.), Greek philosopher who developed the theory of atomism (from Greek *atamos*, "uncuttable"). He was the first to state that matter consists of small, constantly moving particles, or atoms. Although little is known about Leucippus's life, *The Great World System* and *On The Mind* are believed to have been written by him.

Leukemia, common name for any of various cancerous diseases of the blood or bone marrow, characterized by malignant proliferation of white blood cells. It may be divided into acute and chronic forms. In acute forms, progression is rapid, with patients suffering anemia, bruising, and infection. Chronic forms may have milder systemic symptoms, including susceptibility to infection and enlarged lymph nodes. Chemotherapy and antibiotics have greatly improved survival prospects.
See also: Cancer.

Leutze, Emanuel Gottlieb (1816-68), U.S. historical painter. His large-scale, patriotic works include *Westward the Course of Empire Takes Its Way* and *Washington Crossing the Delaware*.

Lever, simplest type of machine, consisting of a rigid beam supported at a stationary point (the fulcrum) so that a force applied to one point of the beam can shift a load at another point. There are 3 classes of lever: those with the fulcrum between the effort and the load; those with the load between the fulcrum and the effort; and those with the effort between the fulcrum and the load.

Levi-Montalcini, Rita (1909-), U.S. scientist, shared the Nobel Prize for physiology or medicine (1986) with Stanley Cohen for their discovery (1952-53) of a natural substance that stimulates the growth of nerve cells.

Levine, James (1943-), U.S. pianist and conductor. In 1964-70 he was an apprentice conductor of the Cleveland Symphony Orchestra under George Szell and then assistant conductor. In 1972 he became principal conductor at the Metropolitan Opera, where he was appointed music director in 1975 and artistic director in 1983.

Lévi-Strauss, Claude (1908-90), Belgian-born French anthropologist, best known as the founder of structuralism, an analytical method whereby different cultural patterns are compared so as to examine the way they order the elements of their environment into systems. His writings include *Structural Anthropology* (1958), *The Savage Mind* (1962), and *The View from Afar* (1985).

Levites, in ancient Israel, tribe descended from Levi, son of Jacob. As priestly auxiliaries, they were assigned responsibility for the care of the Ark and the Sanctuary; in Jerusalem they had hereditary duties at the Temple.

Leviticus, book of the Old Testament, third of the 5 books of the Pentateuch, traditionally ascribed to Moses. It is a collection of liturgical and ceremonial laws.

Lewis, C(live) S(taples) (1898-1963), British author, literary scholar, and defender of Christianity. Of more than 40 books his best-known is *The Screwtape Letters* (1942), a diabolical view of humanity. *The Allegory of*

Love (1936), his major critical work, studies love in medieval literature. He also wrote a science-fiction trilogy and the *Narnia* fantasies.

Lewis, Francis (1713-1802), New York delegate to the Continental Congress (1774-79) and a signer of the Declaration of Independence. His son, Morgan Lewis, served as governor of New York (1804-07).

Lewis, John L. (1880-1969), U.S. labor leader, president of the United Mine Workers of America, 1920-60. He was one of the founders of the Congress of Industrial Organizations (CIO) in 1935, advocating the organization of workers on an industrial, rather than a craft, basis. Initially a supporter of President Franklin D. Roosevelt, Lewis turned against Roosevelt and resigned as president of the CIO in 1940, when the CIO backed Roosevelt's bid for reelection. Lewis was a militant advocate of workers' rights, organizing several strikes of coal miners during World War II and refusing to obey a court order to end a long strike in 1948.

Lewis, Meriwether (1774-1809), American explorer and commander of the Lewis and Clark Expedition, which penetrated to the Northwest Pacific coast 1803-06. In 1808 he became governor of the Louisiana Territory.
See also: Lewis and Clark expedition.

Lewis and Clark expedition, first overland expedition to the northwest Pacific coast (1804-06), under the command of Meriwether Lewis (1774-1809) and William Clark (1770-1838), with Sacagawea, the Native American wife of an expedition member, acting as interpreter and guide. Setting out from St. Louis, the expedition explored the Louisiana Purchase and crossed the Rockies, reaching the Pacific Ocean at the mouth of the Columbia River. It caught the popular imagination and played a major part in establishing the view that it was the "Manifest Destiny" of the U.S. to expand to the Pacific Ocean.
See also: Clark, William; Lewis, Meriwether.

Lewis, Sinclair (1885-1951), U.S. novelist, best known for 5 novels presenting a devastatingly critical view of life in the Middle West. *Main Street* (1920) was his first major success. *Babbitt* (1922), a portrait of a provincial small businessman, is perhaps his best-known book. He refused a Pulitzer Prize for *Arrowsmith* (1925), a satirical look at the medical profession. *Elmer Gantry* (1927) and *Dodsworth* (1929) followed. In 1930 he became the first American to win the Nobel Prize in literature.

Lewis, Wyndham (1882-1957), controversial English painter, critic, and writer, the founder of the vorticism movement, which simplified forms into machinelike angularity. He is best known for his savage satirical novel, *The Apes of God* (1930).

Lewiston (pop. 88,141), second largest city in Maine, first settled in 1770. Lewiston and Auburn, across the Androscoggin River, constitute the leading industrial area of southwestern Maine, producing textiles and footwear and housing metallurgical plants.
See also: Maine.

Lexington (pop. 348,428), second largest city in Kentucky, in the bluegrass region in the north central part of the state. The city is known throughout the United States as the leading center for raising thoroughbred horses and as a major market for tobacco.
See also: Kentucky.

Lexington, Battle of *See:* Revolutionary War in America.

Leyden *See:* Leiden.

Leyden jar, simplest and earliest form of capacitor, a device for storing electric charge, developed at the University of Leiden, Holland, in the 18th century. It consists of a glass jar coated inside and out with metal foil, and a conducting rod that passes through the jar's insulated stopper to connect with the inner foil. The jar is usually charged from an electrostatic generator. The device is now little used outside the classroom.

Lhasa (pop. 105,900), capital and largest city of the Tibet Autonomous Region of China. Once known as the Forbidden City, Lhasa was the center of Tibetan Buddhism until the Chinese invasion of 1951. The Potala, former palace of the Dalai Lama, head of Tibetan Buddhism and now in exile, is in the city.
See also: Tibet.

Lhasa apso, small dog, 10 in (25 cm) high, that originated in Tibet as a watchdog. The Lhasa apso is covered with long hair that falls over its face, and its thick tail curls over its back.

Liana, any climbing vine with roots in the ground, most often found in tropical forests. Lianas wind around trees or other plants for support. Kudzu, grapevines, and ivy are lianas.

Libel, false and malicious statement in permanent form, such as in writing or on film, tending to injure the reputation of a living person, or blacken the memory of the dead. The truth of the statement creates a valid defense in an action for libel.

Liberalism, political philosophy that stresses individual liberty and equality of opportunity. Classical liberalism developed in Europe in the 18th century as part of a rationalist critique of traditional institutions and a distrust of state power. Since the 1930s, modern liberalism has advocated state intervention in the economy but is still concerned with social issues such as civil rights and equality of opportunity.

Liberal Party, British political party, powerful from about 1832 to 1922. Originating in the Whig party, the Liberals were backed by the industrial owners and were associated with such policies as free trade, laissez-faire economics, and religious liberty, while initially opposing most social legislation. The Liberal party enjoyed its golden age under the prime ministers Gladstone, Asquith, and Lloyd George. In the 1920s it was supplanted by the Labour party as the chief opposition to the Conservative party, and by the 1930s it became a relatively small third party attracting about 10% of the vote nationally. In 1981 the party formed an alliance with the new Social Democratic party, but its strength has not substantially increased.

Liberal Republican Party, U.S. political party formed in 1872, during the administration of President Ulysses S. Grant to oppose the policies and the corruption of the administration. The Liberal Republicans nominated Horace Greeley for president, but when he was defeated (despite Democratic support), the party effectively broke up.

Liberia, independent republic on the west coast of Africa, with a land area slightly larger than the state of Ohio. It has a coastline of over 300 mi (483 km) on the Atlantic Ocean. Liberia is the oldest republic in Africa. It originated from the efforts of American philanthropists who in 1822 organized the first settlement of freed American black slaves near the place where the capital, Monrovia, now stands. In 1847 Liberia became an independent republic modeled on the United States.

Land and climate. The terrain varies from a sandy coastal plain cut by lagoons to densely forested mountains in the north. The central part consists mainly of plateau, a rolling plain broken by many hills that are encircled by swamps. Edged in places by steep escarpments above the coastal plain, the plateau ranges in height from 600 ft (183 m) to 1,500 ft (457 m) above sea level. The Nimba Mountains in the northeast rise to 4,528 ft (1,380 m). Several rivers flow from the mountains and plateau into the Atlantic, the most important being the St. Paul, with Monrovia at its mouth.

Liberia is hot and humid, with an average temperature of 80°F (26°C). The rainy season lasts from Apr. to Oct., when the region receives about 150 in (381 cm) of rain, and inland areas about 100 in (254 cm). The *harmattan*, a hot, dry wind from the Sahara, often blows during the dry season. About half the land is covered by dense tropical rain forests. Wildlife includes chimpanzees, monkeys, zebras, antelopes, the rare pygmy hippopotamus, and birds and reptiles. Among Liberia's mineral resources are rich deposits of iron ore, some gold, and diamonds.

People. Over 90% of the people are indigenous Africans belonging to more than 26 tribal groups. The leading citizens are the descendants of freed American slaves, known as Americo-Liberians. There are some Lebanese traders, and Europeans who manage the industries. Most of the tribal peoples are subsistence farmers. The Mandingos practice Islam, but most other tribal groups are christians or animists. The Americo-Liberians, who dominate the government, education, and the professions, are mainly Christians and live in the urban coastal areas.

Although English is the official language, most of the people speak one of many African languages or dialects. The education system includes public, mission, and tribal schools, but about 60% of the population is illiterate. Liberia has one university. There are few urban areas, except along the coast. The capital, largest city, and chief port is Monrovia. Eight smaller ports include Marshall, Robertsport, Buchanan, Greenville, and Harper.

Economy. The Liberian economy is underdeveloped. Its main industries are rubber plantations, established in the 1920s, and the mining of iron ore, dating from the 1950s; both have been run and maintained by U.S. firms. Liberia also exports several crops, including coffee, sugarcane, bananas, and cocoa. Foreign exchange is earned by registering foreign ships under lax rules.

History. The first repatriated slaves arrived from the United States in 1822 under the sponsorship of the American Colonization Society. The settlement

Liberia

Capital:	Monrovia
Area:	37,743 sq mi
	(97,754 sq km)
Population:	2,772,000
Language:	English
Government:	Presidential republi
Independent:	1847
Head of gov.:	President
Per capita:	U.S. $765
Mon. unit:	1 Liberian dollar =
	100 cents

was named Monrovia in honor of U.S. President James Monroe. In 1847 the settlers declared their independence. Liberia gradually extended its territory by signing treaties with local chiefs, or by buying or claiming land. Inequities in the wealth and political power have caused antagonisms between Americo-Liberians and Indigenous Africans, and resulted in the outbreak of a civil war in 1989. The war, in which about 150,000 people were killed, ended when a peace agreement was signed in Ajuba (1996).

Libertarian Party, U.S. political party that upholds the unfettered right of private property and a laissez-faire, free-market economy, and opposes restrictions on individual rights. Libertarians regard the state as the greatest threat to liberty and oppose government inteference in private lives. Founded in 1971, the party nominated a 1980 presidential candidate, Ed Clark, who was on the ballot in every state. He polled 921,188 votes, or 1.1% of the total cast.

Liberty Bell, historic bell housed near Independence Hall, Philadelphia. It was rung on July 8, 1776, to announce the adoption of the Declaration of Independence. It was thereafter rung on each anniversary of the Declaration's adoption until 1835, when it cracked. Originally called the Old State House Bell, it was renamed Liberty Bell by abolitionists about the mid-19th century.

Liberty Island, in New York Bay, it is the home of the Statue of Liberty. Prior to 1956 the island was called Bedloe's Island.
See also: Statue of Liberty.

Liberty Party, antislavery political party founded in 1839 by James G. Birney and other abolitionists. In 1840 and 1844 Birney made unsuccessful runs for president. In 1848 the party united with other groups to form the Free Soil Party.
See also: Free Soil Party.

Li Bo, Li Po, or Li Bai (A.D. 701-762), considered one of China's foremost poets. He is admired for his descriptions of nature and for his poems on ethics and morality.

Library, collection of books, manuscripts, films, musical recordings, and other materials arranged in convenient order for use but not for sale. The earliest libraries were kept by the ancient peoples of Mesopotamia; inscribed clay tablets have been found going back to about 3500 B.C. The first public library in Greece was established in 330 B.C. The most famous library of the ancient world was begun at Alexandria, in Egypt, by Ptolemy I Soter (305-283 B.C.). The Roman Empire acquired many libraries through their conquests of Greece, Asia Minor, and Syria (1st-2nd century B.C.). During the Middle Ages the Church kept the library tradition alive in Europe. The Renaissance saw the formation of many new libraries, such as the Vatican Library (1447), the oldest public library in Europe. The growth of libraries was further stimulated by the invention of printing in the 15th century. The Bodleian Library, Oxford, England, dates from 1602. It was the 18th century that saw the formation of many of the great national libraries: the British Museum Library (1753), Italy's National Central Library at Florence (1741), and the USSR's Saltykov-Shchedrin Library in Leningrad.

The oldest library in the United States originated in 320 books bequeathed by John Harvard (1638), Harvard University's chief benefactor. The present Library of Congress developed from a purchase (1814-15) of Thomas Jefferson's personal library by Congress. One of the first tax-supported public libraries in the United States was established in New Hampshire in 1833. The American Library Association, a professional association to foster the development of the nation's libraries, was founded in 1876. An important figure in library history is Melvil Dewey, whose decimal classification system has now been adopted in many countries. In the late 19th century the industrialist Andrew Carnegie was an important benefactor of libraries. In the 20th century the public library system has been extended and consolidated and has at its disposal such technological innovations as computer data banks.

Library of Congress, U.S. national library located east of the Capitol in Washington, D.C. Originally established by Congress in 1800, it now contains more than 80 million items—including books, pamphlets, maps, photographs, and the like—making it one of the world's largest research libraries. The library's catalog, the National Union Catalog, lists books in libraries all over the United States and Canada.
See also: Library.

Libya, independent Arab republic in North Africa, consisting of 10 administrative divisions that occupy an area of 685,524 sq mi (1,775,500 sq km). Less than 10% of Libya's land is fertile, most of the remainder being part of the Sahara Desert. The exploitation of oil resources (discovered in the late 1950s) provides the wealth that is transforming Libya from a poor peasant nation into an educated and affluent one.
Land and climate. Most of Libya is covered by the shifting sands of the Sahara,though the fertile strip along the Mediterranean coast, with an average rainfall of 10 in (15 cm) and mild winters, supports some cultivation. Even on the coast the rainfall fails about 2 years in every 10. Inland extreme desert conditions exist, and many areas do not see rain for several years at a time. The range of temperature is very wide, from over 120°F (48°C) in summer, to frost level in winter. Suffocating dry desert winds, the *quibli*, bring quantities of dust that destroy much vegetation in the interior. Most of the country's inhabitants live within 75 mi (120 km) of the Mediterranean coast.

Libya

Capital:	Tripoli
Area:	685,524 sq mi (1,775,500 sq km)
Population:	5,691,000
Language:	Arabic
Government:	Islamic-socialist people's republic
Independent:	1951
Head of gov.:	President
Per capita:	U.S. $9,385
Mon. unit:	1 Libyan dinar = 1000 dirham

In this belt enough rain falls to grow citrus fruit, barley, wheat, dates, olives, and almonds. Further inland is a grazing area in which only scrub or tough esparto grasses can grow. In the central part of the Sahara region, there are massifs as high as 2,000 ft (610 m) but no real mountains exist in the country other than the low Tibesti Mountains on the southern border, with altitudes of 4,000 ft (1,220 m) or more. The highest point in Libya is Bette Peak in the south, at 7,500 ft (2,286 m).

Economy. Though the economy depends on the export of crude oil, which accounts for more than 95% of export revenue, agriculture employs 15% of the labor force. In the coastal area barley, wheat, millet, oranges, olives, almonds, and groundnuts are grown. Dates are plentiful in the desert oases, and nomads raise livestock. Libya consumes much of its own agricultural produce and is a net importer of foodstuffs. Petrochemicals have been added to the traditional textile and leather industries.

History. Because of Libya's strategic position on the Mediterranean coast, it has been occupied by many foreign powers—the ancient Greeks, Egyptians, Romans, Arabs, and Ottoman Turks controlled the country successively. In 1912 Italy annexed Libya, although it was not able to end Libyan armed opposition until 1932. In World War II Libya was an Axis military base and the scene of desert fighting between the Axis powers and the British. In 1951 the United Nations declared Libya an independent sovereign state under the rule of King Idris I. He was overthrown in 1969 by a military coup led by Colonel Muammar al-Qaddafi, who proclaimed Libya a republic; it is now in effect an Islamic military dictatorship. In 1973 Qaddafi launched a "cultural revolution," including nationalization of key industries. A prominent follower of pan-Arabism, he has attempted to unite Libya with Egypt (1973), Tunisia (1974), and Syria (1980), and has intervened militarily in Chad (1980-94). Qaddafi is a fervent opponent of Israel. The United States launched an air strike on Tripoli (1986) and shot down 2 Libyan fighter (1989) in retaliation of alleged Libyan backing of terrorist activities. In 1998, negotiations began regarding the trial in The Hague of two Libyans who were involved in the Lockerbie aircraft disaster.

Lichee *See:* Litchi.

Liechtenstein

Capital:	Vaduz
Area:	62 sq mi
	(160 sq km)
Population:	31,000
Language:	German
Government:	Parliamentary
	monarchy
Independent:	1719
Head of gov.:	Prime minister
Per capita:	U.S. $32,000
Mon. unit:	Swiss franc = 100
	rappen

Lichen, name given to plants that consist of algae living in association with fungi. The fungi gets food from the algae and absorbs the water that is used by the algae to make its own food in the process called photosynthesis. This relationship is a form of symbiosis. Lichens generally live on the bark of trees, rotting wood, rocks, or soil.

Lichtenstein, Roy (1923-97), U.S. painter prominent in the Pop Art movement of the early 1960s. He depicted comic strip frames and used commercial art techniques, such as Benday dots, in his work.

Licorice, European herb (*Glycyrrhiza glabra*) with blue flowers and lemon yellow roots that contain a juice used as a flavoring. Licorice has long been used to treat sore throats and is often added to medicines to mask disagreeable tastes. It is also widely used to flavor candy.

Lidice (pop. 500), village in the northwestern Czech Republic. In 1942 the Nazis completely demolished the village, killing the men and deporting the women and children, in retaliation for the assassination of Reinhard Heydrich, Nazi governor of Bohemia, by the Czech Resistance. A new village has been built near the site, which is now a national monument.
See also: World War II; Czechoslovakia.

Lidocaine, drug used as a local or block anesthetic, which bars pain in specific areas of the body. It can be administered by injection or used topically, directly on the skin.

Lie, Trygve (1896-1968), Norwegian political leader, first secretary-general of the United Nations, 1946-53. He incurred Soviet hostility because of his support of UN action in Korea. After leaving office, he returned to Norway, serving in ministerial posts.

Liechtenstein, European principality in the Alps, between Switzerland and Austria. Vaduz is the capital. With a total area of 62 sq mi (160 sq km), Liechtenstein is one of the world's smallest countries. Because of low taxes and bank secrecy, it is the nominal headquarters of thousands of international corporations, and Vaduz is a thriving tourist center. Roman Catholicism is the state religion; German is the official language. Liechtenstein was a principality of the Holy Roman Empire from 1719. It was incorporated into the German Confederation in 1815 and became independent in 1866. Until 1919 it was closely associated with Austria, but since then its interests abroad have been represented by Switzerland, and much of its economy is owned by the Swiss.

Liège (pop. 195,400), city and cultural center on the Meuse River in eastern, French-speaking Belgium. Liège is an industrial city noted for its production of glassware and armaments

Life, despite the lack of any generally accepted definition of life, physiologists regard as living any system capable of eating, metabolizing, excreting, breathing, moving, growing, and reproducing, and able to respond to external stimuli. Metabolically, life is a property of any object surrounded by a definite boundary and capable of exchanging materials with its surroundings. Biochemically, life subsists in cellular systems containing both nucleic acids and proteins. For the geneticist, life belongs to systems able to perform complex transformations of organic molecules and to construct from raw materials copies of themselves capable of evolution by natural selection. As to the origin of life, many believe it was created by God. Scientists believe in the formation of organic substances in the atmosphere over 2 billion years ago; they joined water to form a "nutrient broth" that evolved into life.

Life expectancy, number of years a person in a particular population group is expected to live, based on actuarial calculations. A statistical quantity, it is not meant to be a prediction applied to individuals.

Ligament, band of strong fibrous tissue connecting bones at a joint or serving to hold body organs in place.
See also: Human body.

Light, the portion of electromagnetic radiation that the human eye can see. To be seen, light must have a wavelength between 400 and 750 nanometers, a range known as the visible spectrum. The eye recognizes light of different wavelengths as being of different colors, the shorter wavelengths forming the blue end of the visible spectrum, the longer the red. The term *light* is also applied to radiations of wavelengths just outside the visible spectrum: those of energies greater than that of visible light are called ultraviolet light, and those of lower energies are called infrared. For many years the nature of light aroused controversy among physicists. Although Christiaan Huygens had demonstrated that reflection and refraction could be explained in terms of waves (1690), Isaac Newton preferred to think of light as composed of material corpuscles, or particles (1704). Thomas Young's interference experiments reestablished the wave hypothesis (1801) and A. J. Fresnel gave it a rigorous mathematical basis (1814-15). At the beginning of the 20th century, the nature of light was again debated as Max Planck and Albert Einstein proposed explanations of blackbody radiation (1900) and the photoelectric effect (1905) respectively, both of which assumed that light comes in discrete quanta (bundles) of energy.

Light, invisible *See:* Infrared rays; Ultraviolet rays.

Light bulb *See:* Edison, Thomas Alva; Electric light.

Lighthouse, tower with a light at its head, erected on or near a coast or on a rock in the sea, as a warning to ships. One of the earliest lighthouses was on the Pharos peninsula in 3rd-century B.C. Alexandria, considered one of the 7 wonders of the world. In modern lighthouses, the lantern usually consists of a massive electric light with an elaborate optical system producing intense beams.

Light meter, device that measures the intensity of light. Some light meters contain photo cells made up of the chemicals cadmium sulfide or gallium arsenide, while others utilize cells of selenium. Both are used in specialized professions such as astronomy and photography.

Lightning, discharge of atmospheric electricity resulting in a flash of light in the sky. Flashes range from a few miles to about 100 mi (170 km) in length and typically have an energy of about 300 kWh and an electromotive force of 100 MV. Lightning results from a buildup of opposed electric charges, usually in clouds. The electrical nature of lightning was proved in 1752 by Benjamin Franklin.

Lightning bug *See:* Firefly.

Lignum vitae, either of 2 species (Guaiacum officinale and G. sanctum) of flowering evergreen tree of the West Indies, Mexico, and Florida. Its extremely heavy wood is used for ship construction, furniture, and mallets. The wood also contains a resin used in some drugs.

Ligurian Sea, portion of the Mediterranean Sea enclosed by the Italian regions of Liguria and Tuscany in the north and east and the French island of Corsica in the south.
See also: Mediterranean Sea.

Lilac, shrub or small tree (genus *Syringa*) whose pyramids of small, sweet-scented flowers cap heart-shaped leaves. Lilacs originated in Asia and eastern Europe and are now widely grown as ornamentals.

Liliuokalani, Lydia Kamekeha (1838-1917), last queen of Hawaii, who reigned 1891-93. She succeeded her brother, King Kalakaua. When she tried to assert her royal powers, American sugar planters living in Hawaii fomented a revolt in which she lost her throne. She wrote the well-known farewell song "Aloha Oe."

Lille (pop. 178,300), city in northern France. Best-known for its textile industry, Lille also produces automobiles, electronic equipment, and petrochemicals. Lille was founded c. 1030 by the Flemish, who gave the city to France in 1312.
See also: France.

Lillie, Beatrice (1894-1989), Canadian-born English comedienne internationally famous for her sophisticated wit, displayed in such performances as her monologue "Double Damask Dinner Napkins."

Lilongwe (pop. 234,000), capital, since 1975, of Malawi in southeast Africa. Located on the Lilongwe River, the city is the center of a rich agricultural region. Lilongwe, settled in 1902, became a city in 1966.
See also: Malawi.

Lily, common name for plants of the family Liliaceae, which have prominent flowers and grasslike leaves. True lilies have 3 showy sepals and petals and 6 stamens, and generally grow from bulbs. The best known varieties are the Madonna lily (*Lilium candidum*) and white-trumpet lily (*L. Longiflorum*), which flower in the spring and are seen at Easter. Many wild lilies flower only once in several years.

Lily of the valley, any of several species of woodland plants (genus *Convallaria*) widely grown in gardens and indoor pots. It produces white, bell-shaped flowers that hang from a long stalk and show up against a backdrop of 2 broad, overlapping leaves. The flowers are sweet-scented and are used in perfume. They produce large red berries.

Lima (pop. 5,330,000), capital and largest city of Peru, about 8 mi (13 km) inland from the Pacific port of Callao. Founded in 1535, Lima was the chief residence of the Spanish viceroys. Earthquakes in 1687 and 1746 destroyed much of the city, but many old buildings remain. The University of San Marcos dates from 1551. Rapidly expanding, Lima now has many industries, including textiles, chemicals, oil refining, and food processing.
See also: Peru.

Lima bean, any of several highly nutritious beans of the pea family, rich in protein. Native to tropical America, lima beans are now grown in warm climates throughout the world. The beans grow in 2- to 3-in (5- to 7.6-cm)-long pods on a bush, or on a vine that can be trained to grow on trellises or poles.

Limbourg, Pol de (d.1416), Flemish manuscript illuminator, one of three brothers who after 1404 worked for the Burgundian duke of Berry. Their renowned devotional book of hours, the *Très Riches Heures* (c.1415) shows courtly life and landscape in brilliant detail and dazzling color; it profoundly influenced Flemish painting.

Lime, shrublike citrus tree (*Citrus aurantifolia*) that grows a green fruit smaller and more acidic than the lemon. Limes are grown around the Mediterranean, in the West Indies, Central America, and India. Rich in vitamin C, they were once important in preventing scurvy among sailors on long sea voyages.

Lime, quicklime, or calcium oxide, a caustic industrial chemical (CaO). It is most often made by heating limestone until carbon dioxide is released. Lime's uses include purifying sugar, neutralizing acidic soil and sewage, and making porcelain and glass.

Limerick, humorous verse form consisting of 5 lines, named for the Irish city of Limerick but of unknown origin. Limericks were popularized by the English poet Edward Lear (1812-88). An example:

There was a young lady named Bright
Whose speed was far faster than light
She went out one day
in a relative way
And returned on the previous night.

Limestone, sedimentary rock consisting mainly of calcium carbonate. Some limestones, such as chalk, are soft, but others are hard enough to be used in building. Limestone may be formed inorganically by the evaporation of seawater or freshwater containing calcium carbonate, or organically from the compressed shells of mollusks or skeletons of coral on sea beds.

Lime tree *See:* Linden.

Limon, José (1908-72), Mexican-U.S. dancer and choreographer. In the 1930s he danced with the Humphrey-Weidman company. He formed his own company in 1946, choreographing *Moor's Pavane* (1949), *The Visitation* (1952), and *A Choreographic Offering* (1963).

Limonite, or brown hematite, mineral formed by the decomposition of other minerals that contain iron, found in France, Cuba, and Canada. It is used as an iron ore and as a source of ocher, a yellow iron ore used as a pigment.

Limpet, mollusk, related to the pond snail, with a conical instead of a spiral shell and a muscular foot that can cling to rocks. Limpets can trap water under their shells to survive even when exposed by the ebbing tide. They can grow as long as 4 in (10 cm), but are usually smaller.

Limpopo River, or Crocodile River, river dividing South Africa from Botswana and Zimbabwe. The Limpopo, which empties into the Indian Ocean, is about 1,000 mi (1,600 km) long.

Lincoln (pop. 213,641), capital and second-largest city of Nebraska, 56 mi (90 km) southwest of Omaha. A trade center for livestock and grain, transportation hub, and industrial and educational center, Lincoln also produces motor scooters, freight cars, rubber tires, and electrical appliances. *See also:* Nebraska.

Lincoln, Abraham (1809-65), 16th president of the United States. Lincoln led the North during the Civil War, the nation's greatest crisis. He was determined to restore the Union at any cost—and prevailed. Besides his preservation of the Union and the Emancipation Proclamation, Lincoln is remembered for his eloquent oratory, particularly his Gettysburg Address and inaugural speeches.
Early life. Lincoln was born in a log cabin on the frontier in Kentucky, to a poor carpenter and his wife. Lincoln had less than a year of formal schooling, but taught himself to read. At 22, he left home, working as a storekeeper, rail splitter, farmhand, village postmaster, and surveyor while teaching himself law. In 1837, he was admitted to the bar and moved to Springfield, Ill., to practice law. Soon after moving there, he met Mary Todd, whom he married in 1842. They had 4 children.

Abraham Lincoln

16th U.S. President

Born	Hardin Co. (now Larue Co.), Ky.; Feb. 12, 1809
Term	Mar. 1861-Apr. 1865
Vice presidents	Hannibal Hamlin; Andrew Johnson
Political party	Republican
Spouse	Mary Todd Lincoln
Children	4
Died	Washington, D.C.; Apr. 15, 1865

Political career. Lincoln, a successful lawyer, was more interested in politics. He lost his first election in 1832, but in 1834 won a seat in the state legislature, where he served 4 2-year terms. He rose quickly within the Whig party, becoming Whig floor leader in the Illinois house by age 28. In 1847, he was elected to the U.S. House of Representatives, where he served only 1 term, because his opposition to the Mexican War made him unpopular with his constituents. He returned to his Springfield law practice in 1849. A national debate over slavery brought Lincoln back into politics—he gave speeches attacking slavery as a "great moral wrong." He lost the 1854 and 1858 elections for the U.S. Senate, but his public debates with his opponent, Stephen A. Douglas, made him a national figure. In 1860, the Republicans nominated him for the presidency. The Democratic Party was split between a Northern candidate and a Southern one, helping Lincoln and his running mate, Hannibal Hamlin, to win the election.

President. Before Lincoln even took office, 7 Southern states had seceded. The great question was no longer slavery or freedom in the territories, but the preservation of the Union itself. Lincoln was inaugurated on Mar. 4, 1861; on Apr. 12, 1861, the Civil War broke out when the South attacked Fort Sumter in Charleston, S.C. Affairs began badly for Lincoln: 5 more states seceded and the North lost the war's earliest battles. The 1862 midterm elections brought sizable Republican losses, and slavery again became a major political issue. Hoping to settle at least that issue, Lincoln issued the Emancipation Proclamation on Sept. 22, 1862. It freed all slaves in states or parts of states in rebellion against the Union as of Jan. 1, 1863.

The tide of the war slowly turned in 1863, with important Northern victories. Lincoln was gloomy about his prospects of reelection in Nov. 1864, but he and running mate Andrew Johnson did win. Soon after Lincoln's second inauguration, the war ended with Gen. Robert E. Lee's surrender on Apr. 9, 1865.

Assassination. Five days later, Lincoln and his wife went to Ford's Theatre for a performance of *Our American Cousin.* During the third act, John Wilkes Booth crept into the presidential box and shot Lincoln. Lincoln died the next morning. Booth, who had fled, was eventually found and shot while trying to escape.

See also: Civil War, U.S.; Emancipation Proclamation

Lincoln, Mary Todd (1818-1882), wife of U.S. president Abraham Lincoln from 1842 until his death. Her snobbish manner made her an unpopular first lady. In addition, because she was from the South and had relatives serving in the Confederate Army, she was regarded with suspicion during the Civil War.

Lincoln, Robert Todd (1843-1926), only son of Abraham Lincoln to reach adulthood. After serving on General Grant's staff in the Civil War, he became a corporation lawyer and was later U.S. secretary of war (1881-85) and minister to Great Britain (1889-93).

Lincoln Center for the Performing Arts, in New York City, complex of buildings (constructed 1959-72) designed by leading modern architects including Eero Saarinen and Philip Johnson, to accommodate a number of vital performing arts institutions, which today include the Metropolitan Opera, New York Philharmonic Orchestra, the New York City Opera, and the Chamber Music Society of Lincoln Center. Also at Lincoln Center is a branch of the New York Public Library devoted to the performing arts; a prominent school of music, dance, and theater, the Juilliard School; and other institutions devoted to film and jazz.

Lincoln Memorial, marble monument to Abraham Lincoln in Washington, D.C., dedicated in 1922. Its 36 Doric columns represent the states of the Union when Lincoln was president. The great hall contains a huge statue of Lincoln by Daniel Chester French and 2 murals by Jules Guerin.

Lind, Jenny (1820-87), Swedish soprano who had brilliant success in opera, concert singing, and oratorio. In 1850-52 she toured the United States under the management of the promoter P.T. Barnum.

Lindbergh, Charles Augustus (1902-74), U.S. aviator who made the first solo, nonstop flight across the Atlantic, in 33 1/2 hours, on May 21, 1927, in *The Spirit of St. Louis*. The flight made him a popular hero. The kidnapping and murder of his son in 1932 led to a federal law on kidnapping, popularly known as the Lindbergh Act. Lindbergh and his wife, the writer Anne Spencer Morrow Lindbergh, moved to England in 1936. Criticized for his pro-German, isolationist stance in 1938-41, Lindbergh resigned his commission in the air reserves, but he later flew 50 combat missions in the Pacific during World War II. He won a Pulitzer Prize for his autobiography, *The Spirit of Saint Louis* (1953).

Linden, any of a family (Tiliaceae) of shade trees native to temperate regions. Lindens are also known as lime trees, bee trees, and basswoods. There are 35 species. The most common North American species is the American linden (*Tilia americana*), which can reach 120 ft (37 m).

Lindsay, Vachel (1879-1931), U.S. poet of rhythmic, ballad-like verse designed to be read out loud. Among the best known are "The Congo" (1914) and "Abraham Lincoln Walks at Midnight" (1914). *Collected Poems* was published in 1938.

Linear accelerator, device that produces beams of electrons, protons, and other charged particles and directs them against various atomic targets in order to study the structure of atomic nuclei. Linear accelerators vary in the way in which they speed up particles to produce the beams, which move in

straight paths. (Other particle accelerators produce circular paths of particles.) Usually the acceleration is accomplished by means of electromagnetic waves.
See also: Particle accelerator.

Linear electric motor, automatic device used to move vehicles without wheels. The motor consists of a row of electromagnets that are turned off and on in succession, producing a wave of magnetism that propels the vehicle. In the linear induction motor the electromagnets are located in the vehicle and face a strip of nonmagnetic metal called a reaction rail. The magnetism induces an electric current in the reaction rail, which in turn produces a second magnetic field that pushes against the first, thereby moving the vehicle. In the *linear synchronous motor* an electromagnet is mounted beneath the vehicle's track. It reacts with magnets on the vehicle itself to propel the vehicle.

Line Islands, string of 11 coral islands in the west and southwest Pacific Ocean. Also known as the Equatorial Islands, they total 222 sq mi (576 sq km) in area and are politically divided. Some of the Northern Line Islands are part of the British crown colony, while others are under U.S. jurisdiction. The Central and Southern Line Islands are part of Gilbert and Ellice Islands, a British crown colony.

Line of Demarcation, line decreed by Pope Alexander VI in 1494 to divide Spanish and Portuguese colonial possessions on a world scale. Running from north to south about 350 mi (563 km) west of the Azores and Cape Verde islands, the Line of Demarcation granted Spanish rights to all land west of the line and Portuguese rights to all land east of it. The line was moved farther west under the 1592 Treaty of Saragossa, thus allowing Portugal to claim what is now eastern Brazil and Spain to claim the Philippine Islands.

Lingonberry, small fruit of an evergreen shrub (*Vaccinium vitisidaea*), related to the cranberry. A member of the heather family, the lingonberry grows wild in northern North America. The berry is shiny and bright red. As the raw berry is bitter, it is usually cooked into jellies and sauces.

Linguistics, scientific study of language in all its aspects. This includes, first, the physical and biological factors that are involved in speech. Secondly, it embraces the study of the structure of language, which includes its range of sounds (phonology), its grammatical structure (morphology and syntax), and the relation of words to what they mean (semantics). In comparative linguistics, the aim is to study the relationship between various languages, especially in terms of comparative grammar. At its most general, comparative linguistics leads to a search for those features common to all languages, which is really the philosophical problem of finding a universal grammar. Finally, linguistics considers how language is related to human activity in general, what its function is in the active life of a society, and its importance as a medium for handing down a cultural tradition.
See also: Language.

Linn *See:* Linden.

Linnaeus, Carolus (Karl von Linné; 1707-78), Swedish botanist and physician, founder of taxonomy, the scientific classification of plants and animals. He presented his system of classification in 2 major works, *Systema Naturae* (1735) and *Genera plantarum* (1737). Although many of his particular classifications have been modified, the overall system is still in use. *See also:* Botany.

Linnet, small, seed-eating bird (*Carduelis cannabina*) of the finch family, characterized by light tan and brown feathers with darker patches on the back and shoulders. The crown and breast of the male linnet change to crimson in the spring and summer. In the fall and winter linnets flock together in open country regions, some migrating to warmer areas.

Linotype, mechanical typesetting machine that revolutionized printing and made possible the publication of low-priced books and newspapers. Invented by Ottmar Merganthaler in 1884, the machine, operated by a typewriter keyboard, assembles brass matrices of type into a line and casts the line as a single metal slug. Various photographic and lithographic printing techniques have virtually replaced the linotype machine. *See also:* Printing; Mergenthaler, Ottmar.

Lin Piao (1908-71), Chinese communist general and politician. A leader in the Long March (1934-35), he was crucial in the final defeat of Chiang Kai-shek by his capture of Manchuria in 1948. Minister of defense from 1959, he was a leader of the Cultural Revolution (1965-69). In 1969 he was designated the successsor of Mao Zedong. He died mysteriously in an air crash. *See also:* China.

Linton, Ralph (1893-1953), U.S. anthropologist best known for his studies in cultural anthropology in Africa, the Americas, and the South Pacific. His works include *The Study of Man* (1936) and *The Tree of Culture* (1955).

Lion, largest member of the cat family (*Panthera leo*), now found only in Africa, Asia, and zoos. Lions once lived in Europe, India, and the Middle East, but the expanding human population has eliminated lions from these regions. Lions live in family groups called prides. There may be as many as 30 lions in one pride, and they usually spend their time playing, resting, sleeping (a lion can sleep almost 20 hr a day), eating, and hunting. The pride tends to live together like a family for many years, but males are forced to leave at two or three years of age. A hungry lion may travel as much as 20 miles in one day in search of food. The male lion may reach 9 ft (2.7 m) and weigh as much as 400 lb (180 kg). The female can weigh up to 300 lb (140 kg) and can achieve a length of 8 ft (2.4 m). Because lions do not have exceptional speed, they must rely on the element of surprise for the hunt. They are fond of hunting at night. Most hunting is done by the lioness, and the prey is usually a large animal like a zebra, wildebeest, antelope, or buffalo.

Lipchitz, Jacques (1891-1973), Lithuanian-born French sculptor whose early works consisted of spaces and volumes in a cubist style. Beginning in 1925 he produced a series called "transparents," which, as in the *Harpist*

(1928), emphasized contour. His later work was more romantic and meta-phorical.

Li Peng (1928-   ), Chinese premier (1988-98). Li Peng has been a member of the Chinese Politburo, the policymaking arm of the government, since 1985. When citizens demonstrated for democracy in 1989, Li Peng advocated force to crush the demonstrations. In 1998, Li Peng was succeeded by Zhu Rongji.

Lipid, any of a group of organic compounds found in plants, animals, and micro-organisms that are insoluble in water but dissolve in fat solvents such as ether, chloroform, and alcohol. Lipids are classified into fatty-acids, phospholipids, waxes, steroids, terpenes, and other types, according to their products on hydrolysis.

Li Po *See:* Li Bo.

Lippi, name of 2 Italian Renaissance painters in Florence. **Fra Filippo Lippi** (c.1406-69) was influenced by Masaccio, Donatello, and by Flemish paint-ing. His frescoes in the Cathedral of Prato are his most important works. **Filippino Lippi** (c.1457-1504), his son, influenced by Botticelli, painted the brilliantly detailed *Adoration of the Magi* (1496).

Lippmann, Walter (1889-1974), influential U.S. political columnist and foreign affairs analyst. His column, "Today and Tomorrow," first appeared in the *New York Herald Tribune* (1931-62), then the *Washington Post* (1962-67); it won two Pulitzer prizes (1958, 1962). Books include *Public Opinion* (1922) and *The Good Society* (1937).

Lisbon (pop. 827,800), capital and largest city of Portugal, on the Tagus River estuary near the Atlantic Ocean. Its harbor handles the bulk of the country's foreign trade. A Roman settlement from c.200 B.C., Lisbon was conquered by the Moors in 716. It was reconquered in 1147 and became the capital c.1260. In the 16th century it was the center of Portugal's colonial empire. Much of the city was rebuilt after a disastrous earthquake in 1755. Current industries include steel, petroleum refining, textiles, chemicals, paper, and metal products.
See also: Portugal.

Lister, Sir Joseph (1827-1912), English surgeon who pioneered antiseptic surgery. Pasteur had shown that microscopic organisms (bacteria) are re-sponsible for infection, but his sterilization techniques were unsuitable for surgical use. Through experimentation Lister succeeded in using carbolic acid as a sterilization agent. This greatly reduced post-operative fatalities caused by infection.

Liszt, Franz (1811-86), Hungarian composer and virtuoso pianist who revo-lutionized keyboard technique. Director of music in Weimar, Germany, 1843-61, he later moved to Rome and took minor holy orders in 1865. His music includes 13 symphonic poems (a form he invented), symphonies such as *Faust* (1854), the Sonata in B Minor for piano (1853), *Transcendental Studies* for piano (1852); and 20 Hungarian rhapsodies. His daughter, Cosima, married Richard Wagner.

Litchfield (pop. 7,605), village in western Connecticut declared a National Historic Landmark in 1978. During the American Revolution it served as a supply point and rest stop for Revolutionary soldiers. Birthplace of the Revolutionary leader Ethan Allen and the author Harriet Beecher Stowe, Litchfield is also noted as the site of the first U.S. law school, Litchfield School of Law, which later became Tapping Reeve Law School.
See also: Connecticut.

Litchi, or lichee, evergreen Chinese tree (*Litchi chinensis*) grown in warm climates, a member of the soapberry family. Prized for its juicy fruit, the litchi has been cultivated in southern China for over 2,000 years. The round fruit ranges from 1/2 to 1 1/2 in (1.3 to 3.8 cm) in diameter and has a rough, brittle skin and white flesh with a single large brown seed inside. Rich in vitamin C, the fruit is eaten fresh or canned in a syrup. When dried, it is called litchi nut.

Literature for children, a special branch of creative writing that is geared to young readers, ranging from the preschool age to the teenage years. The literature consists of almost every genre used in adult literature: novels, plays, biographies, poetry, collections of folk tales, and informative works on the arts, science, and social affairs. These works for children are written expressly at their level, and they are designed and illustrated to capture the imagination of young readers. Some books that were written for adults have taken on the status of children's literature because of their popularity with young people. Among these are the collection of folk tales assembled by the brothers Grimm (*Grimm's Fairy Tales*), Mark Twain's *Tom Sawyer* (and to a lesser extent *Huckleberry Finn*), Daniel Defoe's *Robinson Crusoe*, and Jonathan Swift's *Gulliver's Travels*. Also, many adult works have been adapted for children in different versions, for example, the ever-popuar story of King Arthur and his knights, from Thomas Malory's *Morte D'Arthur*. Adults, of course, have told stories to children from time immemorial. It must be remembered that before the invention of printing in Europe (around the mid-1500s), there was little literacy in the general population. The ability to read was confined largely to the clergy and the nobility. Moreover, books were copied out laboriously by hand and were much prized by the few who could afford them or use them. Children's literature, under those circumstances, was, like the literature of the general public, based on an oral tradition, which consisted for the most part of myths, fables, ballads, and poems. Some early books for children were produced, but they were primarily instructional in nature. Saint Aldhelm, Bishop of Sherborne, is thought to have written the first such text for children in English sometime during the A.D. 600s. It was written in catechism style, that is question and answer, and that format for children's instructional and devotional texts remained popular for the next 1,000 years. The first recognized classic of children's literature appeared in France in 1697, a book of eight tales collected by Charles Perrault entitled *Stories and Tales of Times Past with Morals; or, Tales of Mother Goose*. In England, in 1744, John Newbury published *A Little Pretty Pocket-Book*, one of the first children's books designed primarily to amuse rather than to educate. Newbury was also one of the first important publishers of children's books.
During the 1800s, publishing and writing for children became a distinct branch of literature. Also at that time, illustration developed as a major

feature of books for children, as exemplified by John Tenniel's illustrations for *Alice in Wonderland* and *Through the Looking Glass*. It was the 20th century that saw an explosive growth in children's books. The picture book, a book where illustrations carry the story and interest as much as the text, developed in the 20th century. Beatrix Potter's *The Tale of Peter Rabbit* (1901) is the first of this genre. Books are now available for almost every stage of childhood, covering almost every possible subject. Fantasy and adventure are always popular, but children's books today deal with social problems (race, drugs, sex) as well as with history and biography. Children's books are now available in all formats and price ranges, and they are very much a part of growing up in the modern world.

Litharge, poisonous compound (PbO) of lead and oxygen, also called lead monoxide. Litharge is a yellow or reddish-yellow solid produced by heating lead or lead compounds in air. It is used in storage batteries and in making lead glass, rubber, and pottery glazes.

Lithium, chemical element, symbol Li; for physical constants see Periodic Table. Lithium was discovered by Johann August Arfvedson in 1817. It is found in nearly all igneous rocks. *Spodumene* (lithium aluminum silicate) is an important mineral of lithium. Lithium is recovered commercially from brines. The metal is produced by the electrolysis of its fused chloride. Lithium is a silvery-white, reactive metal, the first of the alkali metal group. It is the lightest of all metals and has the highest specific heat of any solid element. Lithium and its compounds are used in lithium-hardened bearing metals, batteries, heat transfer applications, special glasses and ceramics, and in medicine for manic-depressive illness.

Lithography, form of printing used in both fine art and in commercial printing, invented by Aloys Senefelder in Germany c.1798. The technique consists of making a drawing in reverse on the surface of a stone, usually limestone, with an ink containing grease. When the grease has penetrated the stone, the drawing is washed off with water. The grease resists the water, but will accept ink, which is spread over the moist stone. The stone is then used to print the drawing. In the United States, lithographic artists include A.B. Davies, George Bellows, and Currier & Ives.
See also: Printing; Senefelder, Alois.

Lithuania (Republic of), independent country bordering on the Baltic Sea, surrounded by Poland (south), Russia (exclave Kaliningrad), Byelorussia (east), and Latvia (north).
Land and climate. The country exists of a low-lying plain, with numerous rivers and lakes. The east has a continental climate, the west has a more moderate climate.
People. Roman Catholicism is the traditional religion. Lithuanian, a member of the Baltic branch of the Indo-European family, is the main language. About 80% of the population is Lithuanian; Russians and Poles are the largest minorities.
Economy. Although timber and agricultural products remain important, Lithuania is now mostly urban. As such, shipbuilding, and the manufacture of machinery and building materials have taken over as the most important

---

Lithuania

Capital:	Vilnius
Area:	25,212 sq mi
	(65,300 sq km)
Population:	3,600,000
Language:	Lithuanian
Government:	Republic
Independent:	1991
Head of gov.:	Prime minister
Per capita:	U.S. $1,900
Mon. unit:	1 Litas = 100 centas

---

industries. The chief cities and industrial centers are Vilnius (the capital), Kaunas, and Klaipeda, the main port.

History. Fourteenth-century Lithuania, which included Byelorussia and parts of the Ukraine and Russia, was central Europe's most powerful state. In 1386 Lithuania and Poland were united under Grand Duke Jagiello. In 1795 the partition of Poland brought Lithuania under Russian rule. In 1918 independence was declared, and Lithuania, like the other Baltic republics, became a separate state, although Poland occupied Vilnius from 1920 to 1939. In 1940 the Soviet Union invaded Lithuania and the other Baltic republics, and after World War II all 3 were incorporated in the Soviet Union. Nationalist sentiment grew in the late 1980s, and in 1990 the Lithuanian republican government declared independence from the USSR, a declaration not recognized by the Moscow government until 1991. After the independence, Lithuania sought affiliation with western countries and organisations.

See also: Union of Soviet Socialist Republics.

Little Bighorn, Battle of, battle in southeastern Montana, near the Little Bighorn River, June 25-26, 1876, in which Colonel George A. Custer was killed and his troops annihilated by Sioux and Cheyennes led by chiefs Sitting Bull and Crazy Horse.

Little Dipper *See:* Big and Little Dippers.

Little Rock (pop. 158,500), state capital and principal commercial center of Arkansas, on the Arkansas River. Little Rock, originally a river crossing, became the capital of the Arkansas territory in 1821. During the Civil War it was a Confederate stronghold but was captured by the Union forces in 1863. Today it produces metal products, cottonseed, cotton fabrics, furniture, hardwood products, electronic equipment, and processed meats. In 1957 Little Rock became a center of the civil rights struggle when federal troops were mobilized to enforce the desegregation of Central High School.

See also: Arkansas.

Liu Bang (248?-195 B.C.), Chinese emperor who founded the western Han dynasty, which ruled from 202 B.C. to A.D. 220 Liu Bang (r.202-195 B.C.) is

known for furthering unification by establishing regional kingdoms presided over by a central government. Although he defeated Mongolian tribes that invaded China and eliminated certain harsh laws, Liu Bang is historically considered a cruel emperor. He began his career as one of the generals who led revolutionary forces against the Ch'in dynasty in 207-206 B.C.
See also: Han dynasty.

Liu Pang *See:* Liu Bang.

Liu Shao-Ch'i (1893-1969), Chinese communist leader who succeeded Mao Tse-Tung as chair of the Chinese People's Republic (1959-68). In 1968 he was publicly denounced for embracing capitalism and dismissed. In 1980 he was posthumously exonerated by Deng Xiaoping.
See also: China.

Live oak, any of several species of North American evergreen trees (genus *Quercus*) of the beech family. The American oak, *Q. virginiana*, flourishes along the southeastern coast of the United States and is also found in Cuba. It can reach a height of about 50 ft (15 m), and many of its limbs fan out horizontally to form a dense web. Its leaves are dark green and shiny above, whitish and furry below. The live oak is both a timber tree and a popular ornamental tree.

Liver, in anatomy, the largest glandular organ in the human body, lying on the right of the abdomen beneath the diaphragm. It consists of 4 lobes made up of between 50,000 and 100,000 lobules. The metabolic cells of the lobules perform the work of the liver, which includes several functions. The liver aids in digestion by converting nutrients in the blood into a form suitable for storage called glycogen and by producing bile, which breaks down fats. The liver also purifies the blood by converting harmful substances into products that may be excreted in urine or bile. Diseases of the liver include cirrhosis and hepatitis.
See also: Human body.

Liverleaf *See:* Hepatica.

Liverpool (pop. 479,000), industrial city in northwestern England, one of its major ports, on the Mersey River, 3 mi (5 km) from the Irish Sea. The borough was chartered in 1207. In the 18th century it was a major slave-trading port. Food processing and chemicals are now important local industries.
See also: England.

Liverwort, primitive plant that lives in moist places. With the mosses, liverworts bridge the gap between the water-dwelling algae and the land-dwelling ferns and flowering plants.

Livestock, general term for animals raised to be sources of meat, milk, wool, leather, or labor. Cattle, hogs, poultry, sheep, and horses are all considered livestock. In some parts of the world donkeys, goats, mules, and rabbits are also livestock.

Livingston, Philip (1716-78), U.S. political leader, signer of the Declaration of Independence. A delegate to both the Stamp Act Congress (1765) and the Continental Congress (1774-78), Livingston was also an early promoter of King's College, which later became Columbia University in New York City.

Livingston, Robert R. (1746-1813), U.S. politician. A delegate to the Continental Congress, he helped draft the Declaration of Independence and, a year later, the New York state constitution. As chancellor of New York state (1777-1801) he administered the presidential oath of office to George Washington. In 1801 he began the negotiations that led to the Louisiana Purchase.

Livingstone, David *See:* Stanley and Livingstone.

Livy (Titus Livius; c.59 B.C.-A.D. 17), Roman historian. Of his 142-volume *History of Rome*, 35 books survive, with fragments and an outline of the rest. It traces the city from its founding in 753 B.C. to the end of the reign of Nero Drusus in 9 B.C. Although Livy is not always accurate, he is admired for his style and for his effort to view the development of the empire historically.

Li Yuan (A.D. 566-636), first emperor (618-627) and founder of the Tang dynasty (618-907), one of the greatest periods in China's history. His son, Li Shimin, forced him from power.
See also: Tang dynasty.

Lizard, any of many reptiles of the order Squamata, which also includes snakes. Lizards usually possess well-developed limbs, though these are reduced or absent in some species. Lizards typically eat insects, though some will take eggs or small mammals. Unlike snakes, lizards have ear openings and movable eyelids. The smallest are less than 3 in (7.6 cm); the largest is the Komodo dragon of Indonesia, which can be 10 ft (3 m) long.

Llama, domesticated South American hoofed mammal (*Lama glama*) of the camel family. Resembling a large, long-necked sheep, it has thick fleece that may be used for wool and is the principal beast of burden of Native Americans from Peru to Chile, thriving at altitudes of 7,500-13,000 ft (2,280-4,000 m).

Lloyd, Harold Clayton (1894-1971), U.S. comedian of the silent screen, famous as the disaster-prone naive young man in glasses and straw hat. Among his best-known films are *Safety Last* (1923), *The Kid Brother* (1927), and *Feet First* (1930).

Lloyd, Henry Demarest (1847-1903), U.S. reforming journalist. He distinguished himself as a muckraker, exposing the misconduct of big business monopolies, notably in his contributions to the *Chicago Tribune* (1872-85) and his book *Wealth Against Commonwealth* (1894), a history of the Standard Oil Company. He became an active supporter of the Socialists, and ran for Congress on the National People's Party ticket (1894).

Lloyd George, David (1863-1945), Welsh political leader, British prime minister 1916-22. Elected a Liberal Member of Parliament in 1890, he served the same Welsh constituency until his death. As chancellor of the exchequer (1908-15) under Prime Minister Herbert Asquith he led in initiating British welfare legislation. In World War I Lloyd George became, successively, minister of munitions, minister of war, and finally prime minister of a coalition government. He was one of the architects of the Treaty of Versailles, which ended the war. His coalition fell in 1922, when the Conservatives withdrew from it. In the 1930s he led the remains of the Liberal Party and opposed policies of appeasement toward Nazi Germany.

Lloyd Webber, Andrew (1948-), popular British composer whose first success was the musical *Jesus Christ Superstar* (1971). His other musicals include *Evita* (1978), a fictional account of the life of Eva Peron; *Cats* (1981), based on the poems of T.S. Eliot; and *The Phantom of the Opera* (1986), based on Gaston Leroux's novel.

Loadstone, hard black mineral (Fe_3O_4) with magnetic properties, also called lodestone and magnetite. It is found in the form of rocks, crystals, and sand in Siberia, South Africa, and parts of Italy and the United States. Loadstone was used as a precursor to the compass, when ancient Europeans discovered that if an oblong piece of it was suspended from a string, it would point north and south.
See also: Magnetism.

Lobbying, attempting to influence legislators' votes by an agent of a particular political pressure group. The word derives from the practice of agents talking with legislators in the lobby of the legislature. The system is controlled by the Federal Regulation of Lobbying Act of 1946.

Lobelia, any of several species of annual or biannual plants (genus *Lobelia*) found in pastures, meadows, and cultivated fields. Its clusters of flowers are used for medicinal purposes because of its antispasmodic, diuretic, emetic, and expectorant properties.

Lobster, large marine crustacean with 5 pairs of jointed legs, the first bearing enormous claws. True lobsters (genus *Homarus*) live in shallow water and feed on carrion, small crabs, and worms. The 2 large claws differ in structure and function, one being adapted for crushing, the other for fine picking or scraping. The dark blue pigment of the living lobster is a complex compound that turns red when exposed to intense heat.

Lobworm, also called lugworm or lugbait, seaworm (class Polychaeta) much used as bait for deep-sea fishing. Lobworms live along the Atlantic coasts of North America and Europe and near the Mediterranean Sea.

Local government, in the United States embraces a wide variety of governmental units, such as cities, counties, townships, and school districts. The average citizen comes into contact with local government quite often because it provides a variety of functions and services important in his daily life. These include garbage collection, police protection, education, firefighting, traffic regulation, street and road lighting, water supply and sewage control, public health and medical services, the recording of births, deaths, and marriages, and many others.

Municipal government includes the established authorities of cities, towns, and villages. The most common form is the *mayor-council*, of which the chief executive officer is a mayor elected on a partisan ballot. He generally has wide powers of administration and appointment, and may veto acts of the city council. The latter, also elected on a partisan ballot, raises funds for the municipality, and passes laws and by-laws. Many smaller cities have a *council-manager* system, in which an elected city council sets the broad outlines of policy and appoints a nonpartisan professional city manager to carry out the day-to-day administrative work. This system removes many government functions from the arena of politics.

County governments administer rural areas. They are usually headed by an elected board and include a number of other elected officials for specific functions such as sheriff, coroner, assessor, and clerk. Normally there is no one principal executive officer such as a mayor.

Locarno Treaties, pacts drawn up in Locarno, Switzerland, in 1925 providing for the demilitarization of the Rhineland and specifying the borders of Belgium, France, Germany, Poland, and Czechoslovakia. The participants included those 5 countries plus Britain and Italy. The "spirit of Locarno," supposedly heralding peace, died in 1936 when Hitler denounced the pacts and moved troops into the Rhineland.

Loch Lomond, largest lake in Scotland, located in the highlands about 20 mi (32 km) north of the city of Glasgow. It is 23 mi (37 km) long and 5 mi (8 km) wide at its widest point. Loch Lomond is the subject of a familiar Scottish folk song, and Scottish clans in ancient times used its shores as a gathering place.

Lock, device that fastens shut and prevents the opening of doors, windows, lids, and other objects. Types of lock include key, combination, chain, and electronic. Most common door locks have a bolt that fits into a metal plate in the door frame. The first key-operated lock, invented in Egypt c.2000 B.C., was a large wooden bolt fastened to the outside of a gate and stabilized by pegs inserted through it; a key raised the pins to free the bolt.

Locke, John (1632-1704), English philosopher, founder of empiricism, whose writings helped initiate the European Enlightenment. His *Essay Concerning Human Understanding* (1690) opposed the view that there were innate ideas; he held instead that the human mind was like a blank slate on which knowledge is inscribed by experience. His *Second Treatise of Civil Government* (1690) established him as Britain's leading philosopher of politics. In it he argued that all people had the right to "life, health, liberty, and possessions." He proposed a "social contract" to guarantee these rights. Locke also held that revolution was justified and even necessary in some circumstances, and he upheld both religious toleration and government by checks and balances, as later adopted in the U.S. Constitution. A believer in progress and the scientific method, Locke was one of the most influential thinkers of the modern era.

Lockjaw *See:* Tetanus.

Lockwood, Belva Ann Bennett (1830-1917), attorney, suffragette, and Equal Rights Party nominee for president of the United States in 1884 and

1888. The first woman authorized to argue before the U.S. Supreme Court, Lockwood won equal pay for women working in government. She is also known for her successful defense of the threatened land rights of the North Carolina Cherokee.
See also: Women's movements.

Locomotive, power unit used to haul railroad trains. The earliest railroad locomotives, invented in England in the early 19th century, used steam engines, which remained popular until the mid-20th century. Although electric locomotives have been in service in the United States since 1895, the high capital cost of converting tracks to electric transmission has prevented their widespread adoption. Since the 1950s, most U.S. locomotives have been built with diesel engines. Elsewhere in the world, particularly in Europe, much greater use is made of electric traction, the locomotives usually collecting power from overhead cables via a pantograph. Although some gas-turbine locomotives are in service in the United States, this and other novel power sources have not made much headway.

Locomotor ataxia *See:* Ataxia.

Locoweed, any of several leguminous plants of the genera *Astragalus* and *Oxytropis* native to dry regions of the west and southwestern United States. The plants are poisonous, causing livestock to become stuporous and to stagger, a disease commonly known as locoism.

Locust, in zoology, name for about 50 species of tropical grasshoppers that have a swarming stage in their life cycle. Locusts breed in huge numbers where conditions are suitable, then fly in swarms when they reach maturity. The swarms may contain as many as 100 billion insects and can cause agricultural disaster when they land and devour crops.

Locust, in botany, deciduous tree or shrub (genus *Robinia*) with large thorns. Locusts have flowers like those of sweet peas and compound leaves made up of double rows of leaflets. They grow rapidly, and their roots send up suckers, making them effective for holding shifting ground. The timber does not shrink or swell and is used to make wooden pins and railroad ties.

Lodestone *See:* Loadstone.

Lodge, name of 2 U.S. statesmen from Massachusetts. **Henry Cabot Lodge** (1850-1924), U.S. senator, 1893-1924, was a conservative Republican known for his support of the Spanish-American War and opposition to U.S. membership in the League of Nations. He was also a prominent historian. His grandson, the diplomat **Henry Cabot Lodge, Jr.** (1902-85), was a Republican U.S. senator, 1937-44 and 1947-52. He lost his seat to John F. Kennedy. He served as U.S. ambassador to the UN (1953-60), ambassador to South Vietnam (1963-64 and 1965-67), and ambassador to West Germany (1968-69). He was also chief U.S. negotiator at the Vietnam peace talks in Paris (1969).

Lódz (pop. 838,400), city in central Poland, the country's second largest. Chartered in 1423, the city was taken over by Prussia in 1793 and by Russia

in 1815. Only in 1919 did it revert to Poland. German troops occupied and severely damaged Lódz during World War II; it has since been rebuilt. Today it is Poland's leading textile manufacturing city, as well as the center of its motion picture industry.
See also: Poland.

Loeb, Jacques (1859-1924), German-born U.S. biologist best known for his work on parthenogenesis, especially his induction of artificial parthenogenesis in the eggs of sea urchins and frogs. Parthenogenesis is the process by which an unfertilized egg develops into an embryo.

Loesser, Frank (1910-1969), U.S. composer of music and lyrics. He won the Academy Award for his song "Baby It's Cold Outside"(1949) and shared the Pulitzer Prize with Abe Burrows for the musical comedy *How to Succeed in Business Without Even Trying* (1962).

Löffler, Friedrich (1852-1915), German bacteriologist who co-discovered the diphtheria bacillus in 1884. Loffler found a way to cultivate the bacillus and perfected a staining method by which it could be carefully observed under a microscope. His demonstration that some animals are immune to diphtheria influenced Emil von Behring in the development of a diphtheria antitoxin. Loffler is also credited, along with Paul Frosch, for discovering that foot-and-mouth disease is viral and for developing a serum against it.

Lofting, Hugh (1886-1947), English-born U.S. author and illustrator of the famous *Dr. Dolittle* stories, begun in letters to his children during World War I. *The Voyages of Dr. Dolittle*, the second in the series, won him the Newbery medal in 1923.

Log, in nautical measurement, device used to measure a ship's speed. It consists of a piece of board in the form of a quadrant of a circle, balanced so as to float upright. When thrown from the ship, it drags on the line to which it is attached, causing it to unwind at a rate corresponding to the ship's velocity.

Logan (1725?-80?), a leader of the Cayugas during the American colonial period. At first Logan established peaceful relations with white settlers in Pennsylvania and in the Ohio territory, but he led raids on white settlements after members of his family were killed by colonists in 1774. His explanation of his refusal to participate in peace talks was praised by Thomas Jefferson for its eloquence. During the Revolutionary War, Logan aligned himself with the Mohawk auxiliaries of the British forces.

Logan Act, U.S. law enacted in 1799 prohibiting private citizens from entering into negotiations with a foreign government involved in a dispute with the United States. The law was a reaction to the activities of George Logan, who in 1798, attempted to negotiate a settlement to a Naval dispute with France.

Logan, John Alexander (1826-86), Union general during the Civil War. Logan fought in the Western campaigns under Ulysses S. Grant and served with General William T. Sherman on his march through Georgia. After the

capture of Vicksburg, Miss., Logan was made a general in command of volunteers. In a later political career, Logan represented Illinois in the U.S. House of Representatives (1859-62, 1867-71) and in the senate (1871-77, 1879-86). He is also known as the originator of Memorial Day.
See also: Memorial Day; Civil War, U.S.

Logan, Joshua (1908-1988), U.S. director and dramatist. He shared a Pulitzer Prize with Oscar Hammerstein II and Richard Rogers for *South Pacific* (1950). He coauthored and directed *Mr. Roberts* (1948) and directed the musicals *Knickerbocker Holiday* (1938), *Annie Get Your Gun* (1946), *Fanny* (1954) and the play *Picnic* (1953).

Loganberry, hybrid bramble produced from the dewberry and the raspberry. It is named for Judge Logan, who developed it in 1881.

Logarithm, power to which a fixed number, called the base, must be raised to produce a given number. The base is usually 10 or *e*. For example: $2^3 = 8$; 3 is the logarithm of 8 to the base 2.
See also: Napier, John.

Logic, the science of dealing with formal principles of reasoning and thought. Aristotelian, or classical, logic is characterized by a concern for the structure and elements of argument based on the belief that thought, language, and reality are interrelated. Classical logic's influence on Western Civilization has been enormous and enduring. In the 19th and 20th centuries symbolic logic has achieved preeminence. It is rooted in mathematical theory (Set Theory) and has been instrumental in the evolution of modern mathematics.

Loire River, longest river in France, rising in the Cévennes Mountains of central France and flowing north and west through the Massif Central about 650 mi (1,050 km) to the Atlantic. The Loire Valley is famous for its opulent chateaux.

Loki, in Norse mythology, the god who personified trouble and deceit. Although some myths show Loki to be helpful to the gods, he is generally portrayed as evil. He is most infamous for his role in the killing of Balder, the son of the chief god Odin.

Lollards, name given to the 14th-century followers of the English religious reformer John Wycliffe (c.1328-84). Wandering preachers, the Lollards taught that ministers should be poor and that Christians should interpret the Bible themselves. They held that the Bible, and not an organized church, should be the supreme authority. Although repressed during the early 15th century, Lollard beliefs were linked with radical social unrest and remained as underground influences on later movements.

Lombardi, Vince (1913-70), U.S. football coach of the Green Bay Packers of the National Football League (NFL). Under Lombardi's leadership (1959-68) the Packers won 5 NFL titles and two Super Bowls (1967, 68). Known for his intense, uncompromising style of coaching, Lombardi is given credit for coining the phrase "winning isn't everything, its the only thing." He was inducted into the Pro Football Hall of Fame in 1971.

Lombards, Germanic people who moved from northwestern Germany toward Italy in the fourth century. In 568 they crossed the Alps and conquered most of northern Italy, dividing it into dukedoms until 584, when they united into a kingdom against the threat of Frankish invasion. The kingdom reached its height under Liutprand in the 8th century, but was soon overrun by the Franks under Charlemagne in the 770s.

Lombardy, region of northern Italy, once part of the kingdom of the Lombards, for whom it is named. Italy's main industrial and commercial region, it also has efficient and prosperous agriculture. Its capital, Milan, is a major transport and commercial center.

London (pop. 381,500), manufacturing and commercial city on the Thames River in southeast Ontario, Canada. Settled by British colonists on Iroquois land in 1826, London was destroyed by fire in 1845, but soon rebuilt. Today it is the home of more than 300 manufacturing plants, producing goods such as beverages, foods, diesel vehicles, chemical and electrical products, and telephone equipment.
See also: Ontario.

London (pop. 6,904,000), capital of Great Britain. Divided into 33 boroughs, Greater London covers over 650 sq mi (1,684 sq km) along both banks of the Thames River in southeast England. The national center of government, trade, commerce, shipping, finance, and industry, it is also one of the cultural centers of the world.
The Port of London handles over 33% of British trade. London is also an important industrial region in its own right, with various manufacturing industries. Many of the most important financial and business institutions, such as the Bank of England, the Stock Exchange, and Lloyd's of London, as well as many banking and shipping concerns, are concentrated in the single square mile (2.6 km) known as the City. The ancient nucleus of London, the City has its own Lord Mayor. To the west of the City are the Law Courts, the Inns of Court, and the governmental area in Westminster centered on the House of Commons and House of Lords.London is a historic city with many beautiful buildings; the Tower of London, Westminster Abbey, and Buckingham Palace are major tourist attractions. Home of universities, colleges, and some of the world's greatest museums and libraries, it also has a flourishing night life. London's art galleries, concert halls, theaters, and opera houses are world-famous. Distant areas of London are linked by the complex and highly efficient subway system known as the Underground.
See also: United Kingdom.

London, Jack (John Griffith London; 1876-1916), U.S. author of novels and short stories, many set during the Yukon Gold Rush and treating the struggles of men and animals to survive. His works include *The Call of the Wild* (1903), *The Sea Wolf* (1904), *White Fang* (1906), and *Burning Daylight* (1910). He also wrote an autobiographical novel *Martin Eden* (1909), and a political novel, *The Iron Heel* (1907), dramatizing his socialist beliefs and predicting the rise of fascism. Alcoholism and financial problems led him to commit suicide at the age of 40.

London Bridge, historical succession of bridges over the Thames River in London, England. The first bridge, dating from the 10th century, was wooden. In 1176-1209 it was replaced by a stone bridge with many buildings along it, including a chapel and defensive towers. Rebuilt many times, it was demolished and replaced in 1831 by a granite bridge, called New London Bridge. That structure was dismantled in 1968 and moved to Lake Havasu City, Ariz., as a tourist attraction. A new concrete bridge over the Thames replaced it.

Londonderry (pop. 98,500), seaport in northwest Northern Ireland, on the Foyle River. It was known as Derry until 1613 and is still called that by Irish nationalists. It has a traditional shirtmaking industry and some light manufacturing industries. Since 1968 it has been a center of violent conflict between Protestants and Roman Catholics.
See also: Ireland.

Lone Star State *See:* Texas.

Long, powerful political family in Louisiana history. **Huey Pierce Long** (1893-1935), known as "Kingfish," was elected both governor (1928-31) and U.S. senator (from 1930). A radical advocate of social reforms who gained national renown for his "Share-the-Wealth" programs and his corrupt and demagogic methods, he was assassinated by a political enemy, Dr. Carl A. Weiss, in Sept. 1935. **Russell Billie Long** (1918-   ), a son of Huey, served in the U.S. Senate from 1948 to 1987. **Earl Kemp Long** (1895-1960), younger brother of Huey, was governor of Louisiana three times. **George Shannon Long** (1883-1958), older brother of Huey, served in the U.S. House of Representatives from 1953.

Long, Crawford Williamson (1815-78), U.S. physician who first used diethyl ether as an anesthetic during surgery (1842). His discovery followed his observation that students under the influence of ether at a party felt no pain when bruising or otherwise injuring themselves.

Long, Stephen Harriman (1748-1864), U.S. explorer, army engineer, and surveyor. He explored the upper Mississippi River (1817), the Rocky Mts., where Longs Peak is named for him (1819-20), and the Minnesota River (1823). His survey for the Baltimore and Ohio railroad resulted in a railroad manual.

Long Beach (pop. 438,700), seaport, industrial center, and tourist area in southern California, on San Pedro Bay, about 20 mi (32 km) southeast of Los Angeles. After 1921, when oil was tapped in Signal Hill, there was a population boom in the town. Aircraft and electronic manufacturing and oil production are among its leading industries.

Longbow *See:* Archery.

Longfellow, Henry Wadsworth (1807-82), U.S. poet, one of the most popular poets of his generation. A contemporary of Hawthorne at Bowdoin College, he became a professor of modern languages there (1829-35) and at Harvard (1836-54). His principal works were the narrative poems *Evan-*

geline (1847), *The Song of Hiawatha* (1855), and *The Courtship of Miles Standish* (1858), and *Paul Revere's Ride* (1861). Famous individual poems include "The Wreck of the Hesperus" and "Excelsior."

Longinus (fl. 1st cent. ?A.D.), Greek writer to whom the ancient Greek essay on literary criticism *On the Sublime* has been attributed. The treatise discusses "loftiness of style" in literature. It quotes the Greek orator Demosthenes and the Roman orator Cicero to make comparative points about literary style, and it is the source of the text of Sappho's second ode.

Long Island, island off the southeastern coast of New York, extending east for about 118 mi (190 km) from the mouth of the Hudson River. Its width ranges between 12 mi (19 km) and 20 mi (32 km). The New York City boroughs of Brooklyn and Queens are at the western end. Nassau and Suffolk counties, which take up the bulk of the island, were predominantly agricultural until World War II but now have much residential and light industrial development. The beaches and bays of its southern shore, on the Atlantic Ocean, make Long Island a popular summer resort.

Long Island Sound, arm of the Atlantic Ocean separating the state of Connecticut from Long Island. About 110 mi (177 km) long and 20 mi (32 km) wide at most points, Long Island Sound is part of the Atlantic Intracoastal Waterway.

Longitude, measure of the distance, in angular degrees, of any point on the earth's surface east or west of the prime meridian, which is 0° longitude. The prime meridian is the imaginary great circle line, running from pole to pole, that runs through the city of Greenwich, England. Meridians of longitude and parallels of latitude form a grid that can be used to locate the position of any point on the earth's surface.
See also: Latitude; Prime meridian.

Long March, the 6,000-mi (9,656-km) march (1934-35) of the Chinese communists, from Jiangxi in the Southeast to Shaanxi in the extreme Northwest, which saved the movement from extermination by the Nationalist (Kuomintang) forces of Chiang Kai-shek. Led by Mao Zedong, the Red Army of some 100,000 trekked over 18 mountain ranges and 24 rivers under constant air and land attack by Kuomintang troops and local warlords. The march, which lasted for one year, took the lives of almost one-half of its participants.
See also: China; Mao Zedong.

Long Parliament, English legislative assembly that met between 1640 and 1660. Convened by Charles I, it tried to check his power. The conflict between the crown and Parliament culminated in the Civil War (1642-45), during which Parliament remained in session. In 1648 it was "purged" of accused supporters of the king, and in 1649 those who were left, known as the Rump Parliament, had Charles beheaded for treason. In 1653 Parliament was suspended under the Protectorate led by Oliver Cromwell. It was briefly reconvened in 1660 prior to the Restoration.
See also: Parliament.

Longstreet, James (1821-1904), Confederate general in the U.S. Civil War, who fought at Fredericksburg and Antietam. His delay in the attack at Gettysburg (1863), where he was second in command, is generally thought to have been decisive in losing the battle. He also fought in the last defense of Richmond, Va.
See also: Civil War, U.S.

Lon Nol (1913-85), Cambodian general and head of state (1970-75). In 1970 he led a coup to depose Prince Norodom Sihanouk. Although Lon Nol declared Cambodia as a republic he ruled as a dictator, cooperating with the U.S. invasion in the spring of 1970. Overthrown by Khmer Rouge guerillas in 1975 after a bloody civil war, Lon Nol fled to Hawaii, where he settled.
See also: Kampuchea.

Loon, waterbird (family *Gaviidae*) of northern countries, known in England as the diver. These birds have webbed feet set well back on their bodies and are very ungainly on land. They are best known for their eerie, wailing calls. They make their nests on the edges of ponds, and the chicks sometimes ride on their parents' backs. They catch fish by diving, sometimes below 200 ft (61 m).

Loosestrife, popular name of any of several species of primulaceous plants (genus *Lysimachia*) with leafy stems and yellow-white flowers.

López de Santa Anna, Antonio *See:* Santa Anna, Antonio López de.

López Portillo, José (1920-), president of Mexico (1976-82), during a period of rapid economic growth, especially in the energy field. He was notably assertive in his relationship with the United States.
See also: Mexico.

Loquat, subtropical evergreen tree (*Eriobotrya japonica*) of the rose family that bears an egg-shaped orange or yellow fruit. Loquats grow from 18 to 25 ft (5.5 to 7.6 m) tall and have fleshy, tough-skinned, many-seeded fruits borne in loose clusters. Most widely found in Japan, the loquat was introduced to the United States in 1784. Its fruit has a pleasant tart flavor and can be eaten raw, cooked, or in the form of jelly.

Lorca, Federico García *See:* García Lorca, Federico.

Lord's Prayer, or Our Father, chief Christian prayer, taught by Christ to his disciples (Mat. 6.9-13; Luke 11.2-4) and prominent in all Christian worship. Addressed to God the Father, it contains seven petitions, the first three for God's glory, the last four from bodily and spiritual needs. The closing doxology, used by most Protestants ("For thine is the kingdom" etc.), was added to the Roman Catholic version after the Second Vatican Council (1962-65).
See also: Christianity.

Lorentz, Hendrik Antoon (1853-1928), Dutch physicist awarded with Pieter Zeeman the 1902 Nobel Prize for physics for his prediction of the Zeeman effect (the effects of magnetism on light). Lorentz also introduced

the idea of "local time," that is, that the rate of time's passage differed from place to place. Incorporating this idea with George Francis Fitzgerald's proposal that a moving body decreases in direction of motion (the Fitzgerald contraction), he derived the Lorentz transformation, a mathematical statement that describes the changes in length, time, and mass of a moving body. His work, with Fitzgerald's, laid the foundations for Albert Einstein's theory of relativity.
See also: Zeeman effect.

Lorenz, Konrad Zacharias (1903-89), Austrian zoologist, founder of ethology, the study of animal behavior. He is best known for his studies of bird behavior and of human and animal aggression. His books include *King Solomon's Ring* (1952) and *On Aggression* (1966). He shared the 1973 Nobel Prize for physiology or medicine with Karl von Frisch and Nikolaas Tinbergen.
See also: Ethology.

Lorenzini, Carlo *See:* Collodi, Carlo.

Lorenzo the Magnificent *See:* Medici.

Loris, any of several species of primates related to the lemurs. They have large eyes, no tail, spindly legs, and hands adapted for grasping twigs. Native to the forests of southern Asia, they move slowly but deliberately along the lower branches of trees and bushes at night in search of fruit, leaves, and small animals such as insects and nesting birds.

Lorrain, Claude *See:* Claude Lorrain.

Lorraine *See:* Alsace-Lorraine.

Los Alamos, town in New Mexico, 25 mi (40 km) northwest of Santa Fe. It was selected as the site for a scientific laboratory where the world's first atomic and hydrogen bombs were developed (1942). Government research continued at this location until 1962. The Univ. of California currently operates The Los Alamos Scientific Laboratory. The laboratory has been designated as a national landmark.
See also: Manhattan Project; New Mexico.

Los Angeles (pop. 3,489,700), city in southern California, second-largest in the United States, a sprawling city of some 464 sq mi (1,201 sq km), the center of a metropolitan area with a population of over 8 million. Los Angeles is the third-largest industrial center in the United States, producing among other things aircraft, electrical equipment, canned fish, and refined oils. It is also a major center of the motion-picture and television industries, and a distribution and commercial center for the nearby mining regions, oilfields, and rich farm areas. Its port, San Pedro, handles more tonnage than any other U.S. Pacific port, and accommodates a large fishing fleet. The city has several museums and 4 universities. The geographical setting and the large concentration of automobiles and industry have created a serious problem of smog and air pollution, the worst in the United States. Founded by the Spanish in 1781, Los Angeles was taken from Mexico in 1846. It was linked with the

transcontinental railroad system in the 1870s and 1880s. Oil was discovered in the region in the 1890s, leading to rapid population growth.
See also: California.

Lost Colony, English settlement on Roanoke Island off the coast of North Carolina that disappeared without trace. It was founded in 1587 by 117 settlers led by John White, sponsored by Sir Walter Raleigh. Supplies ran out and White visited England for help. When he returned in 1591, the colony was gone, possibly having been wiped out by hostile Native Americans.

Lot, in the Old Testament, son of Abraham's brother Haran. He lived in the city of Sodom. Warned that both Sodom and Gomorrah were to be destroyed because of their wickedness, he fled with his wife and 2 daughters. Told not to look back, his wife disobeyed and was turned into a pillar of salt (Gen. 11-14:19).

Lotus, any of several kinds of water lilies. The sacred lotus of India figures in paintings of Buddha. It grows in marshes from Egypt to China, its leaves and pink flowers growing on stalks that rise about 3 ft (1 m) from the water. Related to the Indian lotus is the American lotus or duck acorn. Both are edible. The Egyptian lotus is a water lily with floating leaves 2 ft (.6 m) across and large white flowers. In ancient times it was cultivated for its fruit.

Lotus-eaters, legendary inhabitants of the north coast of Africa mentioned in Homer's *Odyssey*. They lived on the fruit and flowers of the lotus tree, which drugged them into happy forgetfulness. Tennyson wrote a poem titled after them.

Louganis, Gregory Efhimios (1960-   ), U.S. diver. He won gold medals in the Olympic Games (1984, 1988) for springboard and platform diving.

Lou Gehrig's disease *See:* Amyotrophic lateral sclerosis.

Lough Neagh, lake in Antrim, Northern Ireland. At about 18 mi (29 km) long and 11 mi (18 km) wide, Lough Neagh is the largest lake in the British Isles. Among the wild fowl found on or near the lake is the rare whooper swan. Plentiful in eel, salmon, and trout, the lake is a popular fishing site.

Louis, name of 18 kings of France. **Louis I** (778-840), Holy Roman Emperor 814-40, known as the Pious. The third son of Charlemagne, he divided the empire among his sons, thereby contributing to its fragmentation but laying the foundations of the state of France. **Louis II** (846-79), reigned 877-79. **Louis III** (c.863-82), reigned 879-82. As king of northern France he defeated Norman invaders. **Louis IV** (c.921-54), reigned 936-54. He was called Transmarinus because of his childhood exile in England. **Louis V** (c.966-87), reigned 986-87. The last Carolingian ruler of France, he was known as the Sluggard. **Louis VI** (1081-1137), reigned 1108-37. He subdued the robber barons around Paris, granted privileges to the towns, and aided the Church. He engaged in war against Henry I of England (1104-13 and 1116-20). **Louis VII** (1120-80), reigned 1137-80. He joined the Second Crusade (1147-49) in defiance of a papal interdict. From 1157 onward, Louis was at war with Henry II of England, who had married Louis' former wife, Eleanor of

Aquitaine. **Louis VIII** (1187-1226), reigned 1223-26. Nicknamed the Lion, he was a great soldier and was at first successful in his attempts to aid the barons rebelling against King John of England. **Louis IX, Saint** (1214-70), reigned 1226-70. He repelled an invasion by Henry III of England (1242) and led the Seventh Crusade (1248), but was defeated and captured in Egypt and had to be ransomed.
In 1270 he led another crusade, but died of plague after reaching North Africa. A just ruler, he was regarded as an ideal Christian king. **Louis X** (1289-1316), reigned 1314-16, a period in which the nobility reasserted their strength. **Louis XI** (1423-83), reigned 1461-83. A cruel and unscrupulous king, he plotted against his father for the throne but unified most of France. **Louis XII** (1462-1515), reigned 1498-1515. Nicknamed Father of the People, he was a popular ruler who inaugurated reforms in finance and justice and was ambitious for territorial gains. **Louis XIII** (1601-43), reigned 1610-43. A weak king, he was greatly influenced by the chief minister, Cardinal Richelieu. **Louis XIV** (1638-1715), reigned 1643-1715, known as Louis the Great and the Sun King. The archetypal absolute monarch, he built the great palace at Versailles. "The state is myself," he is said to have declared. His able ministers, Mazarin and Colbert, strengthened France with their financial reforms. But Louis squandered money in such escapades as the War of Devolution (1667-68) and the War of the Spanish Succession (1701-14), which broke the military power of France. **Louis XV** (1710-74), reigned 1715-74), nicknamed the "Well-Beloved." He was influenced by Cardinal Fleury until the cardinal's death in 1743. A weak king dependent on mistresses (especially Madame de Pompadour), his involvement in foreign wars created enormous debts. **Louis XVI** (1754-93), reigned 1774-92. Although he accepted the advice of his ministers on the need for social and political reform, Louis was not strong enough to overcome the opposition of his court and his queen, Marie Antoinette. This led to the outbreak of the French Revolution in 1789, with the formation of the National Assembly and the storming of the Bastille. In 1791 Louis attempted to escape but was brought back to Paris and guillotined. **Louis XVII** (1785-95), son of Louis XVI, king in name only. He was imprisoned in 1793 and was reported dead in 1795. **Louis XVIII** (1755-1824), brother of Louis XVI. He escaped from France in 1791 For more than 20 years he remained in exile, but after the final defeat of Napoleon in the Battle of Waterloo (1815), he became firmly established, proclaiming a liberal constitution. On his death the reactionary Ultraroyalists gained control under Charles X.

Louis, Joe (Joseph Louis Barrow; 1914-81), U.S. boxer. Louis won the heavyweight title in 1937, held it longer than anyone in boxing history (1937-49), and fought 25 successful title defenses. He retired in 1949 having lost only once, to Max Schmeling (1936), a defeat he later avenged, knocking Schmeling out in a rematch (1938). In 1950 he tried to return to the ring, but quit after losing to Ezzard Charles and Rocky Marciano.

Louisbourg (pop. 1,400), town in northeastern Nova Scotia, Canada, on the Atlantic. A French fortress founded in 1713, it was captured by American colonials in 1745, restored to France in 1748, and taken by the English in 1758. The remains of the fortress are now part of a National Historic Park, and Louisbourg is a port for coal-shipping and fishing.

Louisiana

Capital	Baton Rouge
Statehood	Apr. 30, 1812 (18th state)
Familiar name	Pelican State
Area	47,752 sq mi (123,677 sq km); ranks 31st
Population	4,352,000 (1997); ranks 21st
Elevation	Highest—535 ft (163 m), Driskill Mountain; Lowest—5 ft (1.5 m) below sea level, at New Orleans
Motto	Union, Justice, and Confidence
Flower	Magnolia
Bird	Brown pelican
Tree	Bald cypress
Song	"Give Me Louisiana"

Louisiana, state in the south-central United States; bordered by Arkansas to the north, Mississippi to the east, the Gulf of Mexico to the south, and Texas to the west.

Land and climate. Part of the lowland that lies along the entire Gulf coast of the U.S., Louisiana is divided into 3 natural regions: the East and West Gulf Coastal Plains and, between them, the Mississippi Alluvial Plain (often called "the Delta" by Louisianans, although it extends well north of the actual river delta). The Alluvial Plain averages about 40 mi (64 km) in width, but broadens toward the south to form the fertile but low and swampy delta. The Mississippi and other rivers are flanked by a system of levees (earthen walls), both natural and artificial, that prevent high water from flooding the lower backlands away from the river. The East and West Gulf Coastal Plains are composed of low, rolling hills; prairie lands; and steep bluffs toward the north, but along the Gulf are sandy beaches and inland marshes. The Mississippi is Louisiana's most important river. Its rich delta covers about one-third of the state's land area. Other major rivers include the Red, Sabine, Pearl, Ouachita, Atchafalaya, and Calcasieu rivers. The largest of the state's numerous lakes  is Lake Pontchartrain, which lies north of New Orleans. Louisiana's climate is semitropical, with long, hot, humid summers and brief, cool winters. Principal cities are New Orleans, Baton Rouge, and Shreveport.

Economy. Service industries account for about two-thirds of the total value of all the goods and services Louisiana produces in a year. A leading producer of petroleum and natural gas, Louisiana is second (after Texas) in mineral production. Soybeans are the leading farm product. Other major crops include rice, sweet potatoes, cotton, sugarcane, and corn. Livestock produced are beef and dairy cattle, chickens, eggs, and hogs.

Government. Louisiana's present constitution was adopted in 1974. The governor serves a 4-year term. The state's Legislature consists of 39 senators and 105 representatives; all serve 4-year terms. In the U.S. Congress, Louisiana is represented by 2 senators and 8 representatives. Louisiana is the only state whose legal system is derived from civil law, based on France's *Code Napoléon*, instead of on English common law and precedent. Louisiana's local government is based on parishes rather than counties.

History. Spanish explorers were the first Europeans in the area—already home to about 12,000 Indians—in the 1500s. The region was claimed by France in 1682; parts were later transferred from France to Spain and back again. The U.S. acquired it in the Louisiana Purchase (1803). Louisiana became the 18th state in 1812. The final engagement of the War of 1812, the Battle of New Orleans, was fought here in 1815. In 1861, Louisiana joined the Confederacy; it was readmitted to the Union in 1868. The discovery of large deposits of oil (1901) and natural gas (1916) attracted many new industries to Louisiana, but farmers suffered hard times in the 1920s and 1930s. World War II revived the state's industries. Rapid growth continued until the mid-1980s, when a drop in oil prices launched an economic decline and Louisiana's unemployment rate became the nation's highest.

Louisiana Purchase, territory purchased by the United States from France in Apr. 1803. It stretched from the Mississippi River on the east into the Rockies on the west, north almost to the Canadian border and south to the Gulf of Mexico, some 828,000 sq mi (2,144,520 sq km) in all. Its acquisition more than doubled the area of what was then the United States. The price was $15 million. In 1800 Napoleon persuaded the Spanish to return what had been the French province of Louisiana. President Thomas Jefferson instructed Robert R. Livingston and James Monroe to purchase New Orleans and other strategic parts of Louisiana from France. To the surprise of the U.S. delegation, Napoleon, who was expecting war with England, offered to sell the entire territory to the United States, and the envoys quickly accepted the offer.
See also: Livingston, Robert R.

Louis Napoleon *See:* Napoleon III.

Louis Philippe (1773-1850), king of France, 1830-48. Exiled from France in 1793, he traveled in Europe and the United States until 1815. He was accepted as a compromise candidate for the crown in 1830. As king he refused to extend the voting franchise, and the revolution of Feb. 1848 led to his abdication. The monarchy was abolished and Louis Philippe fled to England, where he died.

Louisville (pop. 300,000), largest city in Kentucky, on the Ohio River, whose falls provide hydroelectric power for the city. A major river port, transportation hub, and commercial, manufacturing, and cultural center, Louisville produces tobacco products, whiskey, and gin, as well as plumbing equipment, motor vehicles, and baseball bats. Among the several institutions of higher learning is the University of Louisville (1798). Incorporated in 1828, Louisville was named for King Louis XVI of France in recognition of his help during the American Revolutionary War.
See also: Kentucky.

Lourdes (pop. 17,300), town in southwestern France and site of Roman Catholic pilgrimage. The Virgin Mary is said to have appeared to St. Bernadette, then a 14-year-old peasant girl, in Lourdes in 1858. Lourdes is visited by some 3 million pilgrims annually.

Louse, any of several wingless parasitic insects of 2 orders, Mallophaga (bird lice or biting lice) and Anoplura (mammalian or sucking lice). With flattened bodies and broad, clearly segmented abdomens, lice are well adapted to moving between hair or feathers, and are usually host-specific. Bird lice feed by chewing on feather fragments or dead skin, occasionally biting through the skin for blood. Mammalian lice feed purely on blood obtained with needlelike sucking mouthparts. The human lice spread several diseases.

Louvre, historic palace in Paris, mostly built during the reign of Louis XIV, now one of the world's largest and most famous art museums. Its treasures include paintings by Rembrandt, Rubens, Titian, and Leonardo da Vinci, whose *Mona Lisa* is there. Other masterpieces in its collection are the painting *Arrangement in Gray and Black*, known as "Whistler's Mother," and the Greek statues, the *Venus of Milo* and *Victory of Samothrace* ("Winged Victory").

Lovebird, any of various small gray or green parrots known for their close pair-bond and the frequency with which they preen their mate, particularly genus *Agapornis* of Africa.

Lovelace, Richard (1618-57?), English Royalist soldier and Cavalier poet. His poems, in 2 volumes, were published in 1649 and 1660.

Lovell, James Arthur, Jr. (1928-   ), U.S. astronaut who commanded Apollo 13, the spacecraft scheduled to land on the moon in Apr. of 1970. The safety of Lovell and fellow astronauts Fred W. Haise, Jr. and John L. Swigert, Jr. was endangered when an oxygen tank aboard Apollo 13 exploded. The others were forced to cancel the mission and pilot the spacecraft to a premature landing in the Pacific Ocean. Lovell's first space flight, with Frank Borman, was the 14-day earth orbit of Gemini 7 in 1965. Gemini 7 joined in space with Gemini 6 to achieve the first successful space rendezvous. Lovell was also on the crew of Gemini 12 and Apollo 8, which was the first manned craft to orbit the moon.

Lovell, Sir Bernard (1913-), British radio astronomer. As director of the Jodrell Bank (now Nuffield Radio Astronomy Laboratories) he was instrumental in constructing one of the world's largest steerable radio telescopes (1957).
See also: Astronomy; Jodrell Bank Observatory.

Low, Juliette Gordon (1860-1927), founder of the U.S. Girl Scouts. She organized the first troop in her home town, Savannah, Ga. (1912).
See also: Girl Scouts and Girl Guides.

Lowell, industrial city in northeastern Massachusetts, on the Merrimack and Concord rivers northwest of Boston. Originally settled in 1653, it developed with the building of cotton mills (from 1822) advocated by the pioneer textile

manufacturer Francis Cabot Lowell (1775-1817), for whom it was named. Today Lowell makes electronic equipment as well as textiles and other products.
See also: Massachusetts.

Lowell, Amy (1874-1925), U.S. critic and poet of the imagist school. Her collections of verse include *Sword Blades and Poppy Seed* (1914), *Men, Women and Ghosts* (1916), and the Pulitzer Prize-winning *What's o'Clock?* (1925).

Lowell, James Russell (1819-91), U.S. poet, editor, essayist, and diplomat. His poetry includes the didactic *Vision of Sir Launfal* (1848) and the satirical *The Bigelow Papers* (1848 and 1867). He was professor of modern languages at Harvard (1855-76) and U.S. minister to England (1877-85); his speeches were published in *Democracy and Other Addresses* (1887).

Lowell, Percival (1855-1916), U.S. astronomer. He predicted the existence of Pluto (confirmed 1930). He also believed that the "canals" of Mars were an irrigation system built by an intelligent race.
See also: Astronomy; Pluto.

Lowell, Robert (1917-77), U.S. poet and playwright. His collections include the autobiographical *Life Studies* (1959), and the Pulitzer Prize-winning *Lord Weary's Castle* (1946) and *The Dolphin* (1973). His free adaptations of Greek tragedy and European poets brought him acclaim as a translator.

Lowry, Malcolm (1909-57), English novelist. His greatest work, *Under the Volcano* (1947), was concerned in part with alcoholism, which eventually proved fatal to the author. A reworking of his first novel, *Ultramarine* (1933), and two volumes of short stories were published posthumously.

Loyola, Saint Ignatius (1491-1556), Spanish founder of the Society of Jesus (Jesuits), a Roman Catholic order. A Basque nobleman and soldier, Loyola converted to religious life in 1521. His major work, *Spiritual Exercises*, was begun 1522-23. He later went to Paris with St. Francis Xavier to form the new order (1534). Loyola was its first general (1541-56). His feast day is July 31.
See also: Jesuits.

LPG *See:* Butane and propane.

LSD, or lysergic acid diethylamide, hallucinogenic drug that induces a state of excitation of the central nervous system and overactivity of the autonomic nervous system, manifested as changes in mood (usually euphoric, sometimes depressive) and perception. LSD was invented in 1938 by 2 Swiss chemists, Arthur Stoll and Albert Hofmann. No evidence of physical dependence can be detected when the drug is abruptly withdrawn. A high degree of tolerance develops and disappears rapidly. The chief danger to the individual is the psychological effect and impairment of judgment, which can lead to dangerous decisionmaking or accidents.
Responses to LSD depend on several factors, including the individual's expectations, the setting, and his or her ability to cope with perceptual

distortions. Untoward reactions to LSD apparently have become rare, but adverse reactions appear as anxiety attacks, extreme apprehensiveness, or panic states. Most often these reactions quickly subside with appropriate management in a secure setting. However, some individuals remain disturbed and may even show a persistent psychotic state. It is unclear whether the drug use has precipitated or uncovered a pre-existing psychotic potential or whether this can occur in previously stable individuals.

Some persons, especially those who are chronic or repeated users, may experience drug effects after they have discontinued use of the drug. Referred to as "flashbacks," these episodes most commonly consist of visual distortions, but can include distorted perceptions of time, space, or selfimage. Such episodes may be precipitated by the use of marijuana, alcohol, or barbiturates or by stress or fatigue, or they may occur without apparent reason. The mechanisms that produce flashbacks are not known, but they tend to subside over a period of 6 months to 1 year.

See also: Drug; Drug abuse.

Luanda (pop. 1,400,000), capital and largest city of Angola. Located on the west coast of Africa, Luanda is a manufacturing center and port. Its industries include saw and textile mills, cement, printing, and food processing plants. Luanda was founded in 1576 by Portuguese settlers who built fortresses, churches, and public buildings patterned after European styles of architecture. After Angola gained independence from Portugal in 1975, most of the Portuguese left.

Luba, African ethnic group comprised of Bantu-speaking tribes. Living predominantly in the grasslands of central and southeastern Zaire, the Luba are composed of tribes linked by similar cultures and related languages. The 3 major Luba subdivisions—the Luba-Shankaji of Shaba, the Luba-Bambo of Kasai, and the Luba-Hemba of northern Shaba and southern Kivu—are connected by history, language, and culture to other peoples of the Congo basin. Traditionally, they live in thatched-roof huts along single-street villages. During the twentieth century many Luba-Kasai moved to urban areas.

Lubbock (pop. 222,636), city in northwest Texas known for its production of cottonseed products. Lubbock developed as a cattle-ranching center in the 1880s. It was named after Confederate Lieutenant Colonel Thomas S. Lubbock.

See also: Texas.

Lübeck (pop. 215,200), city in Schleswig-Holstein, northern Germany, on the Trave River near its mouth at the Baltic Sea. Lübeck has been an important trading center since its founding in 1143. Today it is also a center of ship-building and machine manufacturing. It is also known for its candy products, especially the almond and sugar candy known as marzipan.

See also: Germany.

Lubitsch, Ernst (1892-1947), German film director, noted for the sophisticated comedies he made after his emigration to Hollywood in 1923. Among his films are *Forbidden Paradise* (1924), *Ninotchka* (1939), and *Heaven Can Wait* (1943).

Lucan (Marcus Annaeus Lucanus; A.D. 39-65), Roman poet, nephew of Seneca, best known for his *Bellum civile*, an epic literary work on the clash between Julius Caesar and Pompey. A protégé of Nero, he eventually aroused the latter's jealousy. Lucan joined the Pisonian conspiracy against Nero and when this failed, committed suicide.

Luce, Clare Booth (1903-87), U.S. playwright, editor, and politician. Her most successful play, later made into a movie, was *The Women* (1936), which satirized wealthy and idle U.S. women. Luce worked in editorial positions at *Vogue* and *Vanity Fair*. In 1935 she married Henry Luce, the founder of *Time* and *Life* magazines. She served in the U.S. House of Representatives as a Republican from Connecticut (1943-47). She was U.S. ambassador to Italy (1953-56) under the Eisenhower administration.

Luce, Henry Robinson (1898-1967), U.S. editor and publisher. He and Briton Hadden founded the weekly news magazine *Time* in 1923. He also produced *Fortune* (1930), *Life* (1936), and *Sports Illustrated* (1954). He was married to Clare Booth Luce.

Lucerne (pop. 59,100), city in central Switzerland, on the banks of the Reuss River and western shore of Lake Lucerne, capital of Lucerne canton. The city is considered one of the most picturesque in Switzerland, the old town on the bank of the Reuss containing many historic structures, including houses dating back to medieval times. Lucerne is a major European tourist center, with casinos, beaches, horse-racing and jumping competitions, and a traditional pre-Lenten carnival.
See also: Switzerland.

Lucian (A.D. 125-190), Syrian-Greek satirist. Among his best-known works are *Dialogues of the Gods*, a parody of mythology; *Dialogues of the Dead*, a biting satire on human vanities; and *True History*, a lampoon of fantastic travelers' tales, which influenced Rabelais and Jonathan Swift.

Lucifer, the devil. In the Bible, the reference to Lucifer is applied to the King of Babylon, but was misunderstood to mean the fallen angel. Lucifer thus came to be another name for Satan.

Lucknow (pop. 1,619,100), capital of the state of Uttar Pradesh in north-central India. Founded as a Muslim fort in the 13th century, Lucknow was incorporated into the British empire in 1856. Indian soldiers seized the city during the Sepoy Rebellion in 1857, but it was reclaimed by Britain the following year. Today Lucknow combines modern offices and industries with an old commercial district of silversmith and handicraft shops.
See also: India.

Lucretius (c.99-c.55 B.C.), Roman poet and philosopher. He was the author of *De rerum natura* ("On the nature of things") and the last classical exponent of atomism, a belief that everything is made up of atoms controlled by the laws of nature. Considered antireligious in his time, many of his theories were later validated.
See also: Philosophy.

Ludendorff, Erich (1865-1937), German general who with von Hindenburg did much to defeat the invading Russian armies in World War I. He was responsible for German military strategy 1917-18 and for the request of an armistice in 1918. After the war he took part in Hitler's abortive coup in Munich in 1923.
See also: World War I.

Ludington, Sybil (1761-83), American Revolutionary War hero. The daughter of Colonel Henry Ludington, Sybil Ludington is known for her heroism in rallying her father's soldiers in Putnam County, N.Y., for a fight against the British. Responding to a messenger's warning that the British were attacking Danbury, she rode nearly 40 mi (64 km) to successfully alert her father's regiment.
See also: Revolutionary War in America.

Luftwaffe, title of the German air force. Formed in 1935 under Hitler, it was commanded by Herman Goering during World War II.

Luge, winter sport competition where one or two persons ride a sled feet first down an ice covered track. The sled is about 4 ft (1.2 m) long, 18 in (46 cm) wide and 8 in (20 cm) high and is steered by shifting weight, pulling straps attached to the runners and using the feet.

Luisetti, Hank (1916-), U.S. basketball player. His revolutionary one-handed push shot increased the scoring and tempo of the game. As a Stanford University student, Luisetti broke the national college four-year scoring record, with 1,596 points. In 1938 he became the first player to score 50 points in a single game, against Duquesne University.

Luke, Saint (fl. 1st century A.D.), traditional author of the third Gospel and the Acts of the Apostles. A Gentile and a physician, he was influenced by his friend, St. Paul, whom he accompanied on missionary journeys. His feast day is Oct. 18.
See also: Bible.

Luks, George Benjamin (1867-1933), U.S. realist painter, one of the Eight and the Ashcan School. His bold and vigorous style in such works as *The Wrestlers* (1905) may have owed to his work as a cartoonist.
See also: Ashcan School.

Lully, Jean-Baptiste (1632-87), Italian-born French composer. A favorite with Louis XIV, he conducted the court orchestra and wrote numerous court ballets. He wrote stage music for Molière, and his operas, particularly *Alceste* (1674), *Amadis* (1684), and *Armide* (1686), founded a French operatic tradition.

Lumbee, largest Native American tribe east of the Mississippi River. A popular academic theory holds that the Lumbee are descended from the Hatteras tribe and the English colonists who settled on Roanoke Island in 1587. Other theories cite the Cherokee, Sioux, or Tuscarora as possible ancestors. Today, more than 40,000 Lumbee live in and around Robeson County in southeastern North Carolina. Many are farmers.

Lumber, cut wood, especially when prepared for use. There are two kinds of lumber: hardwood and softwood. Softwood comes from trees called conifers, or evergreens, such as pines and firs. Hardwood comes from deciduous trees such as oak, maple, birch, aspen, and cottonwood. Lumbering, the extraction of timber from the forest, is a major industry in the United States. In world timber production, the former USSR is first, then the United States, Japan, and Canada.

Lumen *See:* Candela.

Lumière brothers, **Auguste** (1862-1954) and **Louis Jean** (1864-1948), French inventors noted for their "Cinématographe," a motion-picture camera/projector. The Lumiere brothers are credited with producing the first movie, whose title in English is *Lunch Break at the Lumiere Factory*. Although the Cinématographe was patented in 1895, the brothers did not regard it as important as some of their improvements in color photography.

Luminescence, nonthermal (heatless) emission (particularly light) caused by electron movement from more energetic states to less energetic states. Including fluorescence and phosphorescence, types of luminescence are named for the mode of excitation. In chemiluminescence the energy source is a chemical reaction, while bioluminescence occurs in biochemical reactions.
See also: Bioluminescence; Fluorescence; Phosphorescence.

Lumpfish, common name for various fishes of the Cyclopteridae family, that inhabit cold, northern ocean waters. They have short, thick-set bodies with scaleless skin. Lumpfish have strong sucking discs on their underside, which they use to hold themselves to the sea bottom.

Luna, in Roman mythology, goddess of the moon, who drives across the night sky in a chariot. According to the myth, when Luna leaves the sky to visit her lover, the mortal shepherd Endymion, the night is moonless.
See also: Mythology.

Lunar eclipse *See:* Eclipse.

Lunda, indigenous people of Zaire, Angola, and Zambia. The Lunda people, who speak a Bantu language, had a powerful kingdom in the early 1600s, encompassing large parts of present-day Zaire, Angola, and Zambia. Although most Lunda still live in small country villages where they farm and fish for a living, many have migrated to urban areas since the 1960s.

Lundy, Benjamin (1789-1839), U.S. abolitionist. An activist whose efforts paved the way for the national antislavery movement, Lundy organized the Abolitionist Union Humane Society in Ohio in 1815. As an editor, he published *The Genius of Universal Emancipation* and the *National Enquirer*. Lundy traveled widely in search of places where free blacks could settle. In his effort to prevent slavery from expanding, Lundy worked closely with John Quincy Adams, when Adams was a congressman.
See also: Abolitionism.

Lung, major organs in the respiratory system of mammals, birds, reptiles, and most adult amphibians. These elastic organs pick up oxygen from the air and release carbon dioxide back out. The body requires oxygen to burn food for energy; carbon dioxide is a waste product. In humans, air passes through the *pharynx* and *larynx* to the *airways*, the tubes leading to the lungs. One of these tubes, the *bronchi*, branches off within the lungs, leading to the many *alveolar sacs* that make up the *respiratory units*. The exchange of gases takes place within the *pulmonary capillaries* of this part of the lungs. Lungs help clean the blood of impurities. By exhaling air that makes vocal chords vibrate, they help to effect the sound of speech.
See also: Human body; Respiration.

Lungfish, name for various fishes of Africa, Australia, and South America that can breathe through lungs. The African (family Protopteridae) and South American (family Lepidosirenidae) lungfishes are eellike, with slender fins. They can survive dry conditions by burrowing into mud and forming a cocoon. The Australian lungfish (family Ceratodontidae) has a broad body covered with large scales and cannot survive drying out. In 1997 DNA research indicated that the lungfish is the predecessor of the amphibian.

Lungwort (*Pulmonaria officinalis*), perennial plant that grows in shady areas. Its flowering herb is used medicinally for lung disorders.

Lunt, Alfred (1892-1977), U.S. stage actor generally regarded as one of the outstanding performers of his generation. Married in 1922 to the British actress Lynn Fontanne, Lunt performed in a partnership with her for most of his career. They starred together in 22 productions. Among the most famous were *Design for Living* (1933), *The Taming of the Shrew* (1935), *The Seagull* (1938), and *The Visit* (1958).

Lupercalia, ancient Roman religious festival celebrated on Feb. 15, to enhance fertility for people, animals, and land. The most noted of the activities of the celebration involved naked young men called *luperci* circling the walls of the Palentine Hill in Rome and thrashing women with whips made from the skins of sacrificed animals. It was believed that the women struck by the whips would be rendered fertile.

Lupine, plant (genus *Lupus*) found wild in North America and around the Mediterranean. Lupines range from 2 in (5 cm) to 10 ft (3 m) in height. The flowers are pealike and cluster around a tall stem.

Lupus, disease in which the immune system produces antibodies that attack healthy tissue. In Systemic lupus erythematosus (SLE) patients develop antibodies to their own cell structures, ultimately causing the failure of many organs, especially the heart and the kidneys.

Lusaka (pop. 870,000), capital and largest city of Zambia, in the south-central part of the country. Founded as a European trading post (1905), it was the capital of British-ruled Northern Rhodesia from 1935 until Zambian independence (1964). Intersecting road and railway lines make Lusaka a transportation center, with highways leding to Tanzania, Malawi, and Zim-

babwe. The city is also a commercial and government center as well as home to the University of Zambia.
See also: Zambia.

Lusitania, British passenger ship torpedoed and sunk by a German submarine during World War I, on May 7, 1915. A total of 1,198 people were killed, 128 of them U.S. citizens. The Germans claimed that ammunition was being transported on the ship. The incident aroused popular sentiment in the United States for joining the Allied side in the war.
See also: World War I.

Lute, plucked string instrument with a pear-shaped body and a fretted neck, related to the guitar. It was most popular in Europe between 1400 and 1700. Instruments of the lute type date at least from 2000 B.C. in Mesopotamia. The direct ancestor of the European lute of the Renaissance was an Arabian instrument, from which it gets its name (Arabic: *al-oud*, the wood); the Middle Eastern lute is still called an oud.

Lutetium, chemical element, symbol Lu; for physical constants see Periodic Table. Lutetium (formerly spelled "lutecium") was discovered by Georges Urbain in 1907, by separating the ytterbia then known into neoytterbia and lutetia, rare-earth oxides. It occurs in all minerals contaning yttrium, and in *monazite*, which is the source. Lutetium is prepared by reducing the anhydrous chloride or fluoride with an alkali or alkaline earth metal. Lutetium is a silvery-white, soft, reactive metal. It is the second rarest of the rare earth metals. Ion-exchange and solvent extraction techniques have led to much easier isolation of the so-called "rare-earth" elements. Lutetium and its compounds are as catalysts in organic chemistry reactions.

Luther, Martin (1483-1546), German Reformation leader and founder of Lutheranism. Following a religious experience he became an Augustinian friar, was ordained in 1507, and visited Rome (1510), where he was shocked by the worldliness of the papal court. While professor of Scripture at the Univ. of Wittenberg (from 1512), he wrestled with the problem of personal salvation, concluding that it comes from the unmerited grace of God, available through faith alone. When Johann Tetzel toured Saxony (1517) selling papal indulgences, Luther denounced the practice in his historic 95 theses, for which he was fiercely attacked. In 1520 he published *To the Christian Nobility of the German Nation*. It denied the pope's final authority to determine the interpretation of Scripture, declaring instead the priesthood of all believers, and it rejected papal claims to political authority, arguing for national churches governed by secular rulers. Luther denied the special spiritual authority of priests and advocated clerical marriage. In Dec. 1520 he publicly burned a papal bull of condemnation and a copy of the canon law; he was excommunicated in 1521. Summoned by Emperor Charles V to renounce his heresies at the Diet of Worms (1521), he refused. He was outlawed but, protected by Frederick III of Saxony, he retired to the Wartburg castle. There he translated the New Testament into German in 6 months and began work on the Old. His hymns have been translated into many languages, and he wrote 2 catechisms (1529), the basis of Lutheranism.
See also: Protestantism; Reformation.

Lutheran Church in America *See:* Evangelical Lutheran Church in America.

Lutherans, supporters of the Protestant church founded by Martin Luther (1483-1546), German leader of the Reformation. Luther, a scholar and priest, believed that faith rather than Catholic ritual would save people from sin and enable them to receive the grace of God. The largest Protestant sect in the world today, Lutheranism is the state church in the Scandinavian countries and is strong in Germany. In the 18th century German immigrants founded Lutheran churches in the mid-Atlantic American colonies, and the Evangelical Lutheran Church is now the fourth largest Christian sect in the United States.
See also: Christianity; Luther, Martin.

Luthuli, Albert John (1898-1967), Zulu chief and political leader in South Africa. As head of the African National Congress (ANC), he won the 1960 Nobel Peace Prize for his efforts to end apartheid in South Africa through non-violent passive resistance. In that same year, the ANC was banned and Luthuli's activities were severely restricted by the South African government.

Luxembourg, small independent duchy in Europe, bordered by Germany, France, and Belgium, and without access to the sea. Under their hereditary ruler, the Grand Duke, the bilingual Luxembourgers (just over one-third of a million) show a strong sense of national pride. The majority live in compact village communities. Luxembourg is one of the Low Countries and a member of the European Community. The capital is also named Luxembourg.
Land. Only 55 mi (89 km) long and 35 mi (56 km) wide, Luxembourg is divided into several topographical areas. The Oesling, or E'sleck, in the north is part of the rugged highland of the Ardennes, with large forests but poor soil. The Bon Pays, or Gutland (Good Country), in the south is a low, hilly, fertile area of intensive farming; it is also the site of the capital. The southwest region is rich in iron ore. The largest industrial center here is Esch-sur-Alzette. The area to the southeast, where the Moselle River marks the German border, is fertile and widely cultivated.
People. The native dialect, a low German with French and Dutch components, is referred to as Letzeburgesch. French and German are also widely spoken. The prevailing religion is Roman Catholic, and there are small numbers of Protestants and Jews. Education is compulsory between the ages of 6 and 15. There are several technical and professional colleges. The capital is the site of the International University of Comparative Science, founded in 1958.
Economy. The iron and steel industry, centered in the southwest, provides a large proportion of Luxembourg's gross income. Banking is also an important cornerstone of the economy. There is no coal, but fuel for the steel works is imported, and they in turn provide electricity for much of the country. Slate and limestone are the only other mineral resources. Agriculture provides 3% of the national income and employs 3% of the labor force. The fertile Gutland provides potatoes, rye, barley, oats, and wheat. Frisian cattle are kept. Near the German border the equally fertile Moselle region produces fruits and white wine.
History. Founded by Count Siegfried of Ardennes in 963, Luxembourg grew in size during the reigns of his successors. It was converted from a county

Luxembourg

Capital:	Luxembourg
Area:	999 sq mi
	(2,586 sq km)
Population:	425,000
Language:	Letzebuergic,
	French, German
Government:	Parliamentary
	monarchy
Independent:	1867
Head of gov.:	Prime minister
Per capita:	U.S. $41,210

into a duchy by Emperor Charles IV in 1354. After a long period of foreign rule, Luxembourg was granted independence at the London Conference of 1867. The Treaty of London also declared Luxembourg's neutrality and it was demilitarized. In 1945 Luxembourg became a charter member of the United Nations. Three years later it entered into a customs union with Belgium and the Netherlands, referred to as Benelux. Luxembourg was a charter member of the European Community.

Luxembourg (pop. 77,000), capital and largest city of the country of Luxembourg, located on a plateau above the Alzette and Petrusse rivers. It is an international financial center. Luxembourg grew up around a castle built by Siegfried, count of Ardennes, in A.D. 963. A picturesque city, its points of interest include the Grand Ducal Palace (16th century) and the Cathedral of Notre Dame (early 17th century).
See also: Luxembourg.

Luxemburg, Rosa (1871-1919), Polish-born German Marxist revolutionary. She was cofounder with Karl Liebknecht of the Spartacus Party, Germany's first Communist party, and editor of their journal, *Red Flag*. She was killed by soldiers during an uprising in Berlin.
See also: Marxism.

Luzern *See:* Lucerne.

Lvov (pop. 753,000), city in Ukraine, near the Polish border. A major center for industry, culture, and transportation, Lvov was founded c.1256 and became a commercial center on the trade route between Vienna and Kiev, the Ukrainian capital. The region around the city was ruled by Poland, Turkey, and Sweden between the 13th and the 18th century. In 1772 Austria took control of the city and changed its name to Lemberg, making it the capital of the region called Galicia. Poland again ruled the city from the end of World War I until 1939. Lvov is known for its university, founded in 1611.
See also: Ukraine.

Lyceum, gymnasium in ancient Athens where male youth received physical and intellectual training. In 335 B.C. Aristotle established his famous Lyceum outside the walls of the city. The school was named in honor of the god Apollo Lykeios. In the U.S. during the 19th century there was a lyceum movement which attempted to improve education.
See also: Greece, Ancient.

Lychee *See:* Litchi.

Lycopodium *See:* Club moss.

Lycurgus, ancient Greek political leader, possibly legendary, credited as founder of the legal institutions of the city-state of Sparta. Tradition says that during the 7th century B.C. Lycurgus instituted a new system of military discipline and training. Ancient historians cite him as a member of one of Sparta's royal families.
See also: Sparta.

Lydia, ancient kingdom of western Asia Minor, of legendary wealth. The Lydians invented metal coins in the 7th century B.C. Sardis was the capital and cultural center of this growing empire until the defeat of Croesus (546 B.C.) by Cyrus of Persia.

Lye, strong alkali used in soap-making and cleaning. Originally the name was given to potassium carbonate (K_2CO_3), which was obtained by soaking wood ash in water. It now most often refers to sodium hydroxide (NaOH) solution.

Lyell, Sir Charles (1797-1875), British geologist. He promoted James Hutton's theory of uniformitarianism and Charles Darwin's theory of evolution in his *Principles of Geology* (1830-33).
See also: Geology.

Lyly, John (c.1554-1606), English author best known for his *Euphues* (*The Anatomy of Wit*, 1578; *Euphues and His England*, 1580), a two-part prose romance in a highly artificial and suggestive style. Lyly also wrote elegant comedies on classical themes, influencing other Elizabethan playwrights.

Lyme disease, infection caused by the bacterium *Borrelia burgdorferi* and transmitted by ticks. It is accompanied by fever and a red, ring-shaped skin rash surrounding the tick bite. The disease is treated with antibiotics. Left untreated, it can lead to nervous disorders and arthritis. The disease derives its name from the town of Lyme, Conn. where a high incidence of the disease occurred in the 1970s.

Lymphatic system, network of vessels and nodes that carry tissue fluid, or lymph, from the tissues to the veins of the circulatory system. Lymph is a transparent fluid that carries oxygen and nutrients to cells and carries away waste products. Ingested fats are digested and absorbed into the bloodstream with the help of lymphatic vessels. The body fights infections through lymphocyte and macrophage cells found in lymph nodes in the armpits, groin, neck, and other parts of the body. Most lymph passes directly into capillaries, but some is carried back to the blood by the lymphatic system; whose main ducts feed into the circulatory system near the collarbone.

Lynch, Thomas, Jr. (1749-79), colonial politician from South Carolina. He signed the Declaration of Independence and served in the first general assembly of South Carolina and in the Second Continental Congress.

Lynx, any of various ferocious cats with a short tail, long legs, and tufted ears, found in northern regions of North America, Europe, and Asia. They are hunted for their fur and because they kill domestic animals. Species include the North American, or Canadian, lynx (*Lynx canadensis*), and the common lynx of Europe and Asia (*L. lynx*).

Lyon (pop. 422,400), city in southeastern France. Capital of the Rhône department in the Rhône-Alpes region, it is the third largest city in France. During Roman times, Christianity was introduced to the Gauls from Lyons. Since the 16th century, Lyons has been known for its textiles, and today it is a leading producer of silks and rayons. It is also known for being the center of the French Resistance during the Nazi occupation (1940-44).
See also: France.

Lyon, Mary (1797-1849), U.S. educator. A pioneer in education for women, she founded (1837) the oldest U.S. institution for women's higher education, Mount Holyoke Seminary of Massachusetts, now known as Mount Holyoke College.

Lyre, musical stringed instrument. In ancient Greece the lyre, with 3 to 12 strings, was a symbol for the God Apollo. The English term *lyric* comes from the Greek use of the lyre to accompany songs and poems. The strings were plucked either with the fingers or with a pick. They were strung vertically from a sound box to a crossbar held in place by 2 outer vertical arms.

Lyrebird, either of 2 species of Australian birds (genus *Menura*) of the family menuridae. The male has very long tail feathers he displays, shaped like a lyre, during courtship. Similar in appearance to chickens, lyrebirds nest on the ground and do not fly.

Lysander (?-395 B.C.), naval commander of Sparta. During the Peloponnesian War he led the Spartan forces to victory against Athens in the decisive battle of Aegospotami (405 B.C.). He died in battle during the Corinthian war.
See also: Sparta.

Lysergic acid diethylamide *See:* LSD.

Lysias (459?-380 B.C.), ancient Greek orator and speech writer. Although as many as 35 speeches attributed to Lysias have survived, he is best known for a simple though passionate attack on a ruling tyrant of Athens entitled "Against Eratosthenes." A citizen of Athens, he escaped after his arrest by the Thirty Tyrants, Spartan rulers installed at the end of the Peloponnesian War. When democracy was restored in Athens, Lysias returned and again wrote speeches on a professional basis.
See also: Greece, Ancient.

Lysippus (380s?-306 B.C.), sculptor of ancient Greece. Although he is said to have created some 1,500 works, no authenticated originals remain. Influenced by the earlier Greek sculptor Polykleitos, Lysippus developed more slender, active looking figures. He is known mostly for his sculptures of male athletes, cast and often copied in his preferred medium, metal.
See also: Greece, Ancient.

Lysippus (380s?-306 B.C.), sculptor of ancient Greece. Although he is said to have created some 1,500 works, no authenticated originals remain. Influenced by the earlier Greek sculptor Polykleitos, Lysippus developed more slender, active looking figures. He is known mostly for his sculptures of male athletes, cast and often copied in his preferred medium, metal.
See also: Greece, Ancient.

M

M, 13th letter of the English alphabet, corresponds with the 13th Semitic letter *mem*, represented by a zigzag, wavelike form that scholars relate to the Hebrew *mayim* (water). M is *mu* in the Greek alphabet and the 12th letter of the Roman alphabet. Its present form comes directly from classical Latin. In Roman numerals M represents 1,000. In the French language M. is the abbreviation for *monsieur* (Mr.).

Maazel, Lorin (1930-), U.S. conductor. A musical child prodigy born in France, he first conducted an orchestra in the United States at the World's Fair in New York (1939). He has gone on to become musical director of famous orchestras worldwide, including the Pittsburgh Symphony since 1986, the Cleveland Orchestra (1972-82), and the Vienna State Opera (1982-88).

Macadam, road-building system devised by the Scots engineer John Loudon McAdam (1756-1836). The soil beneath the road, rather than foundations, bears the weight, the road being waterproof and well-drained to keep this soil dry. For modern highways a first layer of larger rocks is laid, then smaller rocks and gravel; the whole is bound with (usually) asphalt or tar.
See also: McAdam, John Loudon.

Macadamia nut, edible seed from the macadamia tree (*Macadamia terrifolia*), a member of the *protea* family. Native to Australia, the nut of this tropical evergreen is an important Hawaiian crop today. Roasted, the round white nuts—also known as bush nuts, among other names—may be eaten by themselves or incorporated into baked or cooked foods.

Macao, or Macau, Portuguese overseas province in southeastern China, on the western side of the Pearl River Estuary, at the head of which is Canton. Lying just within the tropics, Macao is 6.5 sq mi (17 sq km) in area. The territory came into Portuguese possession in 1557 and was granted broad autonomy in 1976. It will revert to China in 1999. The territory comprises a narrow peninsula projecting from the mainland province of Kwangtung, as well as the adjacent islands of Taipa and Colôane. Macao is a popular gambling center and important commercial port. Fishing and some textile manufacturing are significant economic activities.

Macaque, several species (genus *Macaca*) of the Old World monkey family. They are found in North Africa, Japan, India, and Malaysia. A reddish face and rump are features seen in all macaques. The Barbary ape is tailless, while the bonnet macaque and toque monkey of southern India and Ceylon have tails longer than their bodies. The Japanese macaque has brown fur but a short tail. The rhesus monkey of India is used in medical research.

MacArthur, Douglas (1880-1964), U.S. general and hero of World War II. He commanded the 42nd (Rainbow) Division in World War I and was superintendent of West Point (1919-22). In 1930 he became chief of staff of the U.S. Army, the youngest man ever to hold the post, and was promoted to general. He retired from the army in 1937, but was recalled in 1941 as commander of U.S. Army forces in the Far East. In 1942 he became Allied commander of the Southwest Pacific Allied forces, and in 1944 general of the army. MacArthur received the Medal of Honor for his defense of the Philippines. Signatory of the Japanese surrender, he led the reconstruction of Japan, as Allied supreme commander from 1945. When the Korean War broke out (1950) he was selected commander of the UN forces sent to aid South Korea. His unwillingness to obey President Harry S. Truman's orders to restrict the war to Korea rather than extend it to China led to his dismissal the following year. Some Republicans tried unsuccessfully to nominate MacArthur for the presidency in 1944, 1948, and 1952. His memoirs, *Reminiscences*, were published in 1964.
See also: Korean War; World War II.

Macau *See:* Macao.

Macaulay, Thomas Babington (1800-59), historian and essayist. Babington was elected to Parliament in 1830, became a brilliant speaker, and served on the Supreme Council governing India before undertaking his *History of England from the Accession of James II* (5 vol, 1849-61). The clarity and readability of this work made it a success. Like the *History*, his *Essays* display great range and brilliance, together with supreme confidence of judgment. While continuing as a leading orator in Parliament and holding several government jobs, Babington also wrote *Lays of Ancient Rome* (1842), a popular collection of poems.

Macaw, any of several colorful, long-tailed parrots of the genus *Ara*. Macaws have powerful beaks, which they use for cracking open nuts, and their faces are bare of feathers. The largest parrots, macaws measure 12-39 in (30-100 cm) long and eat nuts, seeds and fruit. Easily tamed, they live in screeching flocks in forested areas of tropical America and Mexico.

Macbeth (d. 1057), king of Scotland, formerly chief of the province of Moray. Macbeth seized the throne of Scotland after killing King Duncan I in battle (1040). He upheld his wife's royal descent as his basis for claiming the crown. In 1057 Malcolm III, son of Duncan I, killed Macbeth at

Lumphanan. Shakespeare's tragedy *Macbeth* is partially based on Holinshed's *Chronicles* of these events.
See also: Scotland; Shakespeare, William.

Maccabee, Judah *See:* Judah Maccabee.

Maccabees, Books of, 2 books of the Old Testament Apocrypha that tell the story of the Maccabees, or Hasmoneans, Jewish rulers of the 2nd and 1st centuries B.C. who fought for the independence of Judea from Syria. First Maccabees, a prime historical source, was written c.100? B.C. Second Maccabees is a devotional work of low historical value, written before A.D. 70. Two other books, Third and Fourth Maccabees, are among the Pseudepigrapha.
See also: Old Testament.

MacDiarmid, Hugh (Christopher Murray Grieve; 1892-1978), Scottish poet. Founder of the Scottish Nationalist Party, he gave fresh impetus to Scottish literature. He is best known for the long rhapsodic poem *A Drunk Man Looks at the Thistle* (1926).

MacDonald, James Ramsay (1866-1937), English statesman who led Britain's first Labour Party government. He was prime minister of the first and second labour governments (1924 and 1929-35). He headed a national coalition government of Labour, Conservative and Liberal Party members (1931-35) that attempted unsuccessfully to deal with England's depressed economic conditions. He was replaced as prime minister in 1935.
See also: Labour Party.

MacDonald, J.E.H. (1873-1932), English-born Canadian landscape painter. As a member of a Canadian school of painters known as the Group of Seven, he often depicted the Ontario wilderness, combining influences from Scandinavian painters and designers from the *art nouveau* movement.

Macdonald, John Sandfield (1812-72), Canadian politician. An opponent of confederation, he served as prime minister of Canada (1862-6). When, in 1867, Canada was confederated, he served as the first prime minister for his home province, Ontario (1867-71). Educated and trained in law, he served at various posts in both Liberal and Conservative governments (1840-71).
See also: Canada.

Macdonald, Sir John Alexander (1815-91), Canadian statesman, first prime minister of the Dominion of Canada. Elected to the Ontario legislature in 1844, he became prime minister in 1857 as head of a Conservative coalition that was joined (1864) by George Brown and others. He led subsequent negotiations that resulted (1867) in the confederation of Canada, for which he was knighted by Queen Victoria. The Pacific Scandal (1873), involving corruption charges in completing the Canadian Pacific Railway, caused his government's resignation. However, Macdonald served as prime minister again from 1878 until his death.
See also: Canada.

Macedonia

Capital:	Skopje
Area:	9,928 sq mi
	(25,713 sq km)
Population:	2,009,000
Language:	Macedonian, Serbo-Croatian
Government:	Republic
Independent:	1991
Head of gov.:	Prime minister
Per capita:	U.S. $860
Mon. unit:	1 Denar = 100 deni

Macdonough, Thomas (1783-1825), U.S. naval officer who defeated the British at the decisive Battle of Plattsburgh (1814) on Lake Champlain, N.Y., during the War of 1812. His victory saved New York and Vermont from invasion.
See also: War of 1812.

MacDowell, Edward Alexander (1861-1908), U.S. composer and pianist. He is remembered for his lyrical piano works, such as the collection *Woodland Sketches* (1896). He headed the newly formed music department at Columbia University in New York City (1896-1904). His widow founded the MacDowell Colony in Peterborough, N.H., a retreat for creative artists.

Macedonia, Former Yugoslav Republic of Macedonia, until 1991 a federal republic of the Yugoslav Federation, in the South-east of Europe. In the north it borders on Servia (Yugoslavia), in the east on Bulgaria, in the south on Greece, and in the west on Albania. The capital is Skopje.
Land and climate. Macedonia is very mountainous. It is struck by earthquakes on a regular basis. The climate is largely continental. Approximately 30% of the country is covered with forests.
People. Apart from Macedonians (67%), Albanians are the largest minority (23%). The orthodox Church has the most followers. Official languages are Macedonian and Serbo-Croatian.
Economy. Macedonia is, when it comes to agriculture, just about selfsufficient. The machinery is out of date. Next to the metallurgic industry, the chemical industry and the textile industry are important. The country has several natural resources, such as coal, chrome, and nickel.
History. Macedonia as a region is mountainous, extending from the northwestern Aegean coast into the central Balkan peninsula. Divided among Greece, Yugoslavia, and Bulgaria, it covers 25,636 sq mi (66,397 sq km). Ethnically mixed, Macedonia is inhabited mainly by Slavs in the north and Greeks in the south. The region is primarily agricultural, with tobacco, grains and cotton the chief crops. One of the great powers of the ancient world under Alexander the Great, Macedonia was later ruled by Romans, Byzantines, Bulgars, and Serbs. From 1389 to 1912 it was part of the Ottoman

Empire. With the collapse of Yugoslavia in 1991 Yugoslavian Macedonia became an independent country, named Former Yugoslav Republic of Macedonia (F.Y.R. Macedonia).
See also: Alexander the Great; Greece, Ancient; Yugoslavia.

MacGregor, Robert *See:* Rob Roy.

Mach, Ernst (1838-1916), Austrian physicist and philosopher. His name is commemorated in the Mach number, used as a measure of the speed of bodies in terms of the speed of sound. His greatest influence was in philosophy; he rejected from science all concepts that could not be validated by experience. This approach helped inform the logical positivism of the Vienna Circle—a prominent group of intellectuals in Vienna at that time.
See also: Philosophy; Physics.

Machaut, Guillaume de (1300-77), French poet and composer. He was a leading figure in the 14th-century Ars Nova ("new art") school of music, which developed many new forms. His *Mass for Four Voices* was the first complete polyphonic setting by a single composer.

Machiavelli, Niccolò (1469-1527), Florentine politician and political theorist. He served the Republic of Florence, and was its emissary on several occasions. When the Medici family returned to power in 1512, Machiavelli was imprisoned and tortured on suspicion of plotting against Medici rule; on his release less than a year later he devoted himself principally to writing. Despite his belief in political morality and his undoubted love of liberty, as revealed in his *Discourses* (1531), his master-work *The Prince* (1532; written 1513) describes the amoral and unscrupulous political calculation by which an "ideal" prince maintains his power. Machiavelli also wrote *History of Florence* (1532). The expression "Machiavellian" denotes devious political manipulations.

Machine Age *See:* Industrial Revolution.

Machine gun, military small arm capable of rapid fire. After the invention of the percussion cap by Joshua Shaw, the reliability of firing was greatly increased. In 1862, Richard Jordan Gatling invented a single-barreled machine gun with a rotary chamber, it was used in the Civil War. Gatling's multibarreled gun was capable of firing up to 3,000 rounds a minute.
The first fully automatic machine gun was a single-barreled water-cooled weapon patented by Hiram Steven Maxim in 1885. In World War I, the machine gun was responsible for over 80% of all casualties. In 1957, the U.S. Air Force introduced the Vulcan gun, capable of firing up to 7,000 rounds per minute.

Machine tool, nonportable, power-driven tool used industrially for working metal components to tolerances far finer than those obtainable manually. The fundamental processes used are cutting and grinding, individual machines being designed for boring, broaching, drilling, milling, planing, and sawing. Essentially a machine tool consists of a jig to hold both the cutting tool and the workpiece and a mechanism to allow these to be moved relative to each other in a controlled fashion. A typical example is the lathe. Auxiliary functions facilitate the cooling and lubrication of the tool and workpiece while work is in progress using a cutting fluid. The rate at which any piece can be worked depends on the material being worked and the composition of the cutting point. High-speed steel, tungsten carbide, and corundum are favored materials for cutting edges. Modern industry would be inconceivable without machine tools. It was only when these began to be developed in the late 18th century that it became possible to manufacture interchangeable parts and thus initiate mass production.

Mach number *See:* Mach, Ernst.

Machu Picchu, ancient (16th-century) Inca fortress city in Peru, about 50 mi (80 km) northwest of Cusco. An impressive ruin dramatically situated on a high ridge of the Andes, the pre-Columbian city is 5 sq mi (13 sq km) of terraced stonework connected by 3,000 steps. Probably the last Inca stronghold after the Spanish Conquest (begun 1532), it was discovered almost intact in 1911 by the U.S. explorer Bingham.
See also: Peru.

Macintosh, Charles (1766-1843), British chemist and inventor. Trained as a chemist, he developed a method (1823) by which fabrics were treated with chemicals to create a waterproof garment. One raincoat, popularly referred to as a macintosh, is named after him.
See also: Chemistry.

Mack, Connie (Cornelius McGillicuddy; 1862-1956), U.S. baseball manager and owner. Known for his work and dedication to baseball, Mack helped establish the American League. As owner and manager of the Philadelphia Athletics (1901-50), he led his team to victory in 5 World Series. He was inducted into the National Baseball Hall of Fame in 1937.

Mackay, last name of father John William (1831-1902) and son Clarence Hungerford (1874-1938), both U.S. businesspeople. With wealth gained from his interests in the Comstock lode, one of the largest gold and silver mines in Nevada, John William developed the Postal Telegraph Cable Company (1886), breaking Western Union's monopoly. Clarence Hungerford, business partner with his father and subsequent director of Postal Telegraph, developed transoceanic cable communications between the United States and the Far East (1904), Cuba (1907), and both Southern and Northern Europe. The Mackay telegraph and cable companies were combined with Western Union Telegraph Company in 1943.

Mackenzie, Alexander (1822-92), Canadian politician. Born in Scotland, he emigrated to Canada in 1842. He entered the legislative assembly in 1861, having worked his way up to the editorship of a Liberal paper. From 1873 to 1878 he was Canada's first Liberal prime minister. Serving during a worldwide depression, Mackenzie confronted many national economic difficulties. He promoted democratic government and greater independence from Great Britain.

Mackenzie, Roderick (1760?-1844), Canadian politician and pioneer Commander of Fort Chipewyan (1789-93), he built it with his cousin, Sir

Alexander Mackenzie, after they had trailblazed their way west to this northeastern point in Alberta. Later, in eastern Canada, he served as a member of the Legislative Council of Lower Canada.

Mackenzie, Sir Alexander (1764-1820), Canadian fur trader and explorer. Mackenzie was the first non-native to cross the northern part of North America to the Pacific. Born in Scotland, he emigrated to Canada; in 1789 he made an expedition down the Mackenzie River (named after him) to the Arctic Ocean. In 1793 Mackenzie crossed the Rocky Mountains to the Pacific coast, becoming convinced that searching for a Northwest Passage to the Orient would be futile.

Mackenzie, William Lyon (1795-1861), Canadian journalist and politician. Publisher of the *Colonial Advocate* (1824-34) and denouncer of the governing clique, the Family Compact, Mackenzie led the Reform Party as the first mayor of Toronto (1834). After subsequent defeat he led them in an unsuccessful revolution (1837). He fled to the United States, but he was imprisoned for violating neutrality laws. He returned to Canada in 1849 after receiving amnesty, and served in Parliament.
See also: Canada.

Mackenzie River, in northwestern Canada, flowing from Great Slave Lake to the Arctic Ocean. The Mackenzie, which drains the northern portion of the Great Plains, is about 1,120 mi (1,800 km) long and is the main channel of the Finlay-Peace-Mackenzie river system (2,600 mi/4,180 km). It is navigable from June to Oct. only.
See also: Mackenzie, Sir Alexander.

Mackerel, commercially important food fish of the family Scombridae. Mackerel have small scales, deeply forked tails, and rows of finlets on the rear part of their streamlined bodies. Known as fast swimmers, the species includes the tuna (the largest, up to .75 ton/680 kg), albacore, and bonito.

Mackinac, Straits of, channel separating the Upper and Lower Peninsulas of northern Michigan. It connects Lakes Huron and Michigan and is spanned by the Mackinac Straits Bridge from Mackinac City to St. Ignace.

Mackinac Island, Northern Michigan island in the Straits of Mackinac. First settled by Native Americans, then French missionaries, this island became an outpost for the British (1780) before its present-day development as a summer resort. Today no automobiles are allowed on the island, and ferry service transports people and goods from the mainland to either Mackinac City or St. Ignace. This island contains an ancient Native American burial ground called *Michilimackinac* ("great turtle").

MacLeish, Archibald (1892-1982), U.S. poet and playwright. His works include *Conquistador* (1932), a long narrative on the conquest of Mexico; the lyrical verse of *Collected Poems 1917-1952* and *J.B.* (1958), a verse drama based on the story of Job, all of which won Pulitzer prizes. Cultural adviser to Franklin D. Roosevelt, he was librarian of Congress (1939-44) and undersecretary of state (1944-45).

Macmillan, Donald Baxter (1874-1970), U.S. arctic explorer. His 1st north-polar expedition with Commander Robert Peary in 1908 was followed by 30 others, including those he led to Labrador, Greenland, and Baffin Island (1913-37). His writings on the region include *Four Years in the White North* (1918), *Etah and Beyond* (1927), and *How Peary Reached the Pole* (1932).

Macmillan, Harold (1894-1986), British politician. Entering Parliament as a Conservative in 1924, he served in ministerial posts throughout World War II and the 1950s. As prime minister (1957-63), he restored Anglo-U.S. ties after the Suez Canal intervention, tried to improve East-West relations, and tried to gain Britain's entry into the Common Market. He served as chairman of Macmillan publishing house (1963-74) and was made an earl in 1984.

Macon (pop. 281,103), city in central Georgia, on the Ocmulgee River; seat of Bibb County. The commercial and shipping center for a cotton, truck-farming, and livestock area, its industries include textiles, chemicals, and lumber. Macon (incorporated 1823) was named for Nathaniel Macon. Near the city are the prehistoric Indian mounds and towns of the Ocmulgee National Monument.
See also: Georgia.

Macramé, art form based on knotting techniques. This art, originally an activity of 13th century Arab sailors before its popularity in Europe, was revived in the 1960s. Garment accessories, wall hangings, and other practical or decorative items are created through arrangements of knots in various patterns.
See also: Knots, hitches, and splices.

Madagascar, formerly Malagasy Republic, since 1975 the Republic of Madagascar, republic in the Indian Ocean comprising the large island of Madagascar and several small islands.
Land and climate. Separated from the southeast African mainland by the Mozambique Channel, Madagascar is the world's fourth largest island. It has rugged central highlands and fertile low-lying coastal plains. The highlands have several extinct volcanoes and mountain groups which rise to over 9,000 ft/2,743 m. In the highlands the climate is pleasantly cool, but it occasionally becomes cold. The coastal plains tend to be hot and humid, with luxuriant vegetation.
People. The people of Madagascar can be broadly divided into two groups. The Merinas, of Indonesian and Polynesian descent, live mainly in the highlands. The majority of people living in the coastal regions are of black African descent. The principal languages are French and Malagasy, an Indonesian language. Over 70% of the people live in rural areas. About 40% of the population is Christian, 5% is Muslim, and the remainder observe various traditional beliefs. The capital is Antananarivo (Tananarive).
Economy. The island is predominantly farming and stock-raising country. Coffee, cloves, and vanilla are principal foreign exchange earners. Meat and prawns are also exported. Chromite, graphite, mica, and phosphates are important minerals. Oil and gas deposits have been discovered. Growing industries include food processing, oil refining, vehicle assembly, and textile manufacture.

Madagascar

Capital:	Antananarivo
Area:	226,658 sq mi (587,041 sq km)
Population:	14,463,000
Language:	Malagasy and French
Government:	Republic
Independent:	1960
Head of gov.:	Prime minister
Per capita:	U.S. $230
Mon. unit:	1 Franc (FMG) = 100 centimes

History. The first peoples to settle Madagascar were black Africans and Indonesians some 2,000 years ago. Western Europeans did not reach the island until the 16th century. A native kingdom, the Merina kingdom, gained hegemony over the island in alliance with Europeans. At the same time, the Portuguese, English, and French strove with one another for dominance. Finally, the French invaded and annexed the island in 1885, but had to fight until 1905 to overcome a determined Merina kingdom. In 1947, a revolt against French rule was crushed, but in 1958 the island gained self government as the Malagasy Republic and became fully independent in 1960. 1972 marked the beginning of a period of political and economic unrest and in 1975 a Marxist military took power. In 1977, national elections were held to create a legislature. Didier Ratsiraka, who had ruled as Madagascar's military leader since 1975, won the first presidential election (1982); under his leadership, the government has loosened its restrictions on the economy and introduced democratic reforms in the 1990s. In 1997 he again won the presidential elections.

Madder, tropical and subtropical trees, shrubs, and herbs of the family Rubiaceae, native to northern South America. The family yields economically important crops, e.g., coffee and quinine, and ornamentals, e.g., the gardenia, madder, and bedstraw (used for mattress filling because of its pleasing odor). Also called turkey red, the true madder (*rubia tinctorum*) of southern Europe was used to create brilliant red dye pigments, now produced artificially.

Madeira Islands, archipelago, 308 sq mi (789 sq km), owned by Portugal, in the Atlantic Ocean about 350 mi (560 km) west of Morocco. Madeira, the largest island and site of the capital, Funchal, is a year-round resort; Porto Santo is also inhabited. The Desertas and Selvagens are uninhabited islands. Known to the Romans and rediscovered under Henry the Navigator in the 15th century, the islands produce sugarcane and Madeira wine.

Madeira River, largest tributary of the Amazon River. Flowing northeastward, this important South American waterway runs along the Brazil-Bolivia border and continues for approximately 2,000 miles (3,200 km)—some of which are still uncharted or explored. The river is navigable by boat for the first 700 miles (1,126 km), then a railroad follows the riverbank for more than 200 miles (320 km) of rapids. The river opens into the Amazon east of the city of Manaus, Brazil.

Madero, Francisco Indalecio (1873-1913), president of Mexico (1911-13). A democratic idealist, he opposed Porfirio Díaz in the 1910 election and was imprisoned. He escaped to Tex. and there declared a revolution; joined by Pancho Villa and Emiliano Zapata, he deposed Díaz in 1911 and was elected president (1911-13). His administration was marred by his ineptitude and division and corruption among his followers. In the face of widespread revolt he was deposed and murdered by Gen. Victoriano Huerta.
See also: Mexico.

Madison (pop. 176,000), state capital of Wisconsin, seat of Dane County, in south-central Wisconsin. The city is home to the main campus of the Univ. of Wisconsin, state government buildings, and facilities for manufacturing, trade, finance, and research. Popular for recreation, 3 lakes are found within the city borders: Mendota, Monona, and Wingra.
See also: Wisconsin.

Madison, Dolley Payne (1768-1849), wife of President James Madison. Known as an accomplished hostess during her husband's administration, she helped the widowed President Jefferson entertain during his presidency (1809-17). During the War of 1812, she fled the capital while it was under attack, rescuing a portrait of George Washington and important government documents.

Madison, James (1751-1836), 4th president of the United States. Madison, called "the father of the Constitution," was a penetrating political thinker who guided the deliberations of the Constitutional Convention. He was not a successful war president, but his last years in office inaugurated an "era of good feelings" and unprecedented economic growth.
Early life. Madison, born into a prominent plantation family of Virginia, graduated from the College of New Jersey (now Princeton University) in 1771. He planned to enter the ministry, but soon became involved in politics. In 1776, he helped draft Virginia's first constitution and its declaration of rights. He was a delegate to the Continental Congress (1780-83).
Political career. Under the Articles of Confederation, the new U.S. government was weak. Madison pushed for a stronger central authority, leaving to

---

James Madison

4th U.S. President

Born	Port Conway, Va.; Mar. 16, 1751
Term	Mar. 1809-Mar. 1817
Vice Presidents	George Clinton; Elbridge Gerry
Political party	Democratic-Republican
Spouse	Dorothea (Dolley) Payne Todd Madison
Children	None
Died	Orange County, Va.; June 18, 1836

states only matters that concerned them individually. He drafted the Virginia Plan (also called the Randolph Plan), which was developed into the Constitution. Madison wrote many of the pro-Constitution papers known as *The Federalist*. During the Constitution's ratification process, many state conventions called for it to be amended to protect individual rights. Madison, elected to the House of Representatives in 1789, helped draft what became the Bill of Rights, the first 10 amendments to the Constitution.

Madison helped to form the new Democratic-Republican Party, largely to oppose the fiscal policies of the Federalist Party's Alexander Hamilton, first secretary of the U.S. treasury. Until Madison left Congress in 1797, he led the new party in the House. His opposition of the Federalists' Alien and Sedition Acts helped unify his party.

As President Jefferson's secretary of state (1801-09), Madison helped the U.S. gain the Louisiana Purchase. His wife, Dolley (whom he had married in 1794), served as White House hostess for Jefferson. In the 1808 presidential election, Madison defeated Charles C. Pinckney, the Federalist candidate.

President. As president, Madison faced the same foreign-relations problem he had as secretary of state: the continuing war between France and Britain. Impressment of U.S. sailors, seizure of goods, and blockades had serious damaged U.S. shipping. Tensions arose until Congress declared war on Britain in June 1812.

The War of 1812 went badly for the U.S. Madison's popularity fell; New England Federalists opposed "Mr. Madison's War" and demanded his resignation. However, he won reelection five months after the war began. In August 1814, Madison—and the nation—suffered humiliation when British troops stormed Washington and burned the White House and the Capitol. The Treaty of Ghent, signed Dec. 24, 1814, ended the war in a stalemate.

With peace, however, Madison regained his popularity. His new domestic program appeased the Federalists somewhat and helped launch a "new nationalism."

Retirement. After leaving the presidency in 1817, Madison retired to Montpelier, his Virginia plantation. In 1826, he became rector (president) of the University of Virginia. He died at Montpelier in 1836.

Madonna (Madonna Louise Ciccone; 1958-   ), U.S. rock and roll performer. Madonna's early training was as a dancer studying ballet, modern, and jazz dancing. In the 1970s she performed with the Pearl Lange and Alvin Ailey dance companies. After joining a series of club bands as an instrumentalist, she set out to become a singer. The success of her singing career began when her songs became dance club favorites. She rose to superstar status with her songs and trend-setting fashions. Some of her well-known hits are "Like a Virgin," "Material Girl," and "Crazy For You."

Madonna and Child, among the most important art subjects of Christian religion. The Virgin Mary and child Jesus were first accepted as symbols of Christian faith following the Council of Ephesus in A.D. 431. The earliest Madonna and Child paintings were found in early Christian catacombs; styles developed and transformed through the Byzantine and Renaissance periods. There are 5 general styles of treatment of Madonna paintings: portrait, the Madonna enthroned, in glory (hovering in the sky with halo and attendants), in pastoral scenes, and in a home environment. Raphael's *Sistine Madonna* (1515) hangs in the Dresden Gallery in Germany. Other painters

who depicted the Madonna and Child include Luca Della Robbia, Giovanni Bellini, Leonardo da Vinci, Michelangelo, Fra Filippo Lippi, Andrea del Sarto, and Titian.
See also: Christianity.

Madras (pop. 3,841,000), large coastal city in southeastern India. Capital city of the state of Tamil on the Bay of Bengal, Madras once served as a British outpost (17th century) and center for trade. Today it serves as one of India's important ports and commercial centers. Hindu and Christian landmarks as well as the Univ. of Madras and the British Fort St. George may be found alongside modern industry and transportation.
See also: India.

Madrid (pop. 3,000,000), city, capital of Spain and of Madrid province, on the Manzanares River in New Castile. A 10th-century Moorish fortress captured by Castile in 1083, it was made the capital by Philip II (1561) and expanded by the Bourbons in the 16th century. Now Spain's administrative,financial, and transportation center, it has a wide range of industries. A cultural center, its landmarks include the Prado art museum, the royal palace, and the university city.
See also: Spain.

Madrid Hurtado, Miguel de la *See:* De la Madrid Hurtado, Miguel.

Madrigal, poetic part song for 2 or more voices singing separate melodies. Originating in 14th-century Italy, it reached the height of its popularity in the 16th century, through the works of Monteverdi and Gesualdo. *The Triumphes of Oriana* (1601) is a famous collection of English madrigals by 21 composers.

Madroña, shrub or tree (*Arbutus menziesii*) in the heath family. Commonly found on the west coast of the United States and Canada, this species also called laurelwood, grows to about 75 ft (23 m), has cinnamon-colored peeling bark, thick evergreen leaves, tall white flowers, and red berrylike fruit. The tree is used for decorative purposes.

Maecenas, Gaius (70?-8 B.C.), Roman statesman famous as the patron of Horace, Vergil, and Propertius. Friend, adviser, and agent of the emperor Augustus, he was criticized by Seneca for his extravagance. His name came to symbolize patronage.
See also: Rome, Ancient.

Maenads, in Greek and Roman mythology, female devotees of Dionysus or Bacchus. Also called *bacchantes*, they were known for their ecstatic frenzies.
See also: Mythology.

Maeterlinck, Maurice (1862-1949), prolific Belgian poet and playwright influenced by French symbolists. His works include the tragedy *Pelléas et Mélisande* (1892), set as an opera by his friend Debussy, *Manna Vanna* (1902), and the dramatic fable *The Blue Bird* (1909). He was awarded the Nobel Prize for literature in 1911.

Maffei, Paolo *See:* Maffei galaxies.

Maffei galaxies, 2 galaxies near the Milky Way, discovered behind cosmic dust clouds through the use of a special infrared-sensitive telescope and photographic system by Italian astronomer Paolo Maffei (1968). Maffei I is an elliptical galaxy of about 100 billion stars, located approximately 3,000,000 light-years away. Maffei II is a spiral galaxy of about 10 billion stars, located approximately 9,000,000 light-years away.
See also: Galaxy.

Mafia, name given in the 19th century to Sicilian secret criminal societies who sought justice outside of the established legal system and dominated the peasantry through terrorism (e.g., the vendetta). Despite repression by successive governments, including Mussolini, in the late 19th and early 20th centuries, the Mafia survived. *Mafiosi* emigrated to the United States organized in "families," and prospered in bootlegging, gambling, narcotics, labor unions, and some legitimate business.

Magdalene *See:* Mary Magdalene.

Magellan, Ferdinand (c.1480-1521), Portuguese navigator who commanded the first expedition to sail around the world. Magellan received Spanish backing (from Charles I) for his proposed voyage in search of a western route to the Spice Islands (East Indies), then believed to be only a few hundred miles beyond America. He set sail with 5 ships in 1519, explored the Río de la Plata, sailed south to Patagonia, discovered the straits now named for him, then sailed northwest across the Pacific. Near starvation, the expedition reached Guam and the Philippines in 1521; Magellan was killed 10 days later in a skirmish with natives. Only one ship, the *Victoria*, returned to Spain.

Magellan, Strait of, north of Cape Horn, separating mainland South America from Tierra del Fuego; about 330 mi (530 km) long and 2.5-15 mi (4-24 km) wide. An important route before the Panama Canal, the straits were discovered by Ferdinand Magellan in 1520.
See also: Cape Horn.

Magellanic Clouds, 2 irregular galaxies nearest the Milky Way, visible in the far southern sky. The Large Magellanic Cloud (Nubecula Major), about 15,000 light-years in diameter, is located mostly in the constellation Dorado; the Small Magellanic Cloud (Nubecula Minor) is about 10,000 light-years across and is almost entirely in the constellation Tucana. Both are about 200,000 light-years from the earth.
See also: Galaxy.

Maggot, the soft-bodied larva of a winged insect, e.g., a fly. It has no legs and lies in its food, which may be plants, meat, or decaying matter.

Magi, hereditary members of the priestly class of the ancient Persian Empire. Revered for their wisdom and their ability to interpret dreams and omens, the Magi were also the acknowledged priests of the ancient Persian religion Zoroastrianism, which advocated worship of a single supreme deity. Accord-

ing to one tradition, the Magi kept watch for a great star that was to signal the arrival of a savior. This helps to explain the connection between the Magi and the three wise men who, according to the New Testament, were led by a star to Bethlehem, where they honored the infant Jesus with gifts.
See also: Persia, Ancient; Zoroastrianism.

Magic, prescientific belief that an individual, by use of a ritual or spoken formula, may achieve superhuman powers. Should the magic fail to work, it is assumed to be due to deviations from the correct formula. In his classic work *The Golden Bow* (1890) Sir James George Frazer classified magic under 2 main heads: imitative and contagious. In *imitative magic* the magician acts upon or produces a likeness of the desired object: Rainmakers may light fires, the smoke of which resembles rain clouds; voodoo practitioners stick pins in wax models of their intended victims. In *contagious magic* it is assumed that 2 objects once close together remain related even after separation: the magician may act upon hair clippings in an attempt to injure the person from whose body they came. Magic is crucial to many primitive societies, most tribes having at least an equivalent to a medicine man, who is believed to be able to provide them with extra defense against hostile tribes or evil spirits.

Maginot Line, massive French fortifications system, built 1930-34 between the Swiss and Belgian borders. Named for war minister (1929-32) André Maginot, it linked underground fortresses and was considered impregnable. However, it was easily flanked by the German mobile advance in World War II.

Magma, molten material formed in the upper mantle, or crust, of the earth, composed of a mixture of various complex silicates in which are dissolved various gaseous materials, including water. On cooling, magma forms igneous rocks, though any gaseous constituents are usually lost during the solidification. Magma extruded to the surface forms lava. The term is loosely applied to other fluid substances in the earth's crust.

Magna Carta, or *Magna Charta* (Latin, "great charter"), major British constitutional charter forced on King John I by a baronial alliance at Runnymede (1215). A reaction to John's heavy taxation and his exclusion of the barons from government, the charter was designed to prevent royal restriction of baronial privilege and feudal rights and to safeguard church and municipal customs. Altered forms of the decree were issued on John's death in 1216 and again in 1217 and 1225. Now generally recognized as a reactionary measure to guarantee feudal rights, it has, in the past, been interpreted to suggest and defend such civil rights as habeas corpus and jury trial. It paved the way for constitutional monarchy by implicitly recognizing that a king may be bound by laws enforceable by his subjects.

Magnesia, chemical compound (MgO), also called magnesium oxide. Used in the manufacture of refined metals, crucibles, and materials for insulation, it also has medicinal purposes. Made from magnesia chloride, magnesia is a white, powdery substance that has no taste.

Magnesium, chemical element, symbol Mg; for physical constants see Periodic Table. Compounds of magnesium have been known and used for hundreds of years. It was discovered by Humphry Davy in 1808. The eighth most abundant element in the earth's crust, it is extracted commercially by the electrolysis of fused magnesium chloride taken from sea water or other brines. Magnesium is a light, silvery-white, hard, reactive, metal. It plays an essential role in both plant and animal life. Magnesium and its compounds are used in light metal alloys, incendiary devices, flash bulbs, flares, and in medicine.

Magnetic compass *See:* Compass.

Magnetic equator, also called the *aclinic line,* imaginary line around the earth where the magnetic pull of the 2 poles is equal. In theory, the earth is a magnet with poles that are magnetized in the north (Bathurst Island, Canada) and south (Wilkes Land, Antarctica). A metal object placed on the magnetic equator, near the geographic equator, will not be inclined north or south.

Magnetic pole *See:* North Pole; South Pole.

Magnetic resonance imaging (MRI), technique which produces images of tissues inside the body and allows physicians to identify abnormal tissue without surgery. MRI enables physicians to see through bones and organs using a powerful magnet, radio waves, and a computer, and has been used to detect tumors, diseases of the circulatory system, birth defects, and certain injuries. The examination is supervised by a radiologist though no radiation is involved.

Magnetic storm, temporary, violent agitation in the earth's magnetic field caused by the *solar wind*—a stream of positively charged atoms and negatively charged electrons that flow from the sun. Solar winds are caused by the energy created during bursts of solar activity.
See also: Magnetism; Solar wind.

Magnetism, name for a force that occurs naturally in certain substances and can be transferred to or induced in others. The basic properties of magnetism are its complementary forces of attraction and repulsion and its capacity to align itself on a roughly north-south axis. These properties occur naturally in magnetite and, in the form of the lodestone, were observed and exploited to some degree in ancient times. The force of magnetism is dipolar, on a north-south axis, corresponding approximately to the north and south magnetic poles of the earth. In a magnet, unlike poles attract; like poles repel. And if it is divided, the parts of a magnet will also be dipolar. It was early discovered that magnetism not only attracts iron, but can be transferred to iron. Metals which can be readily magnetized are called ferromagnetic and, besides iron and steel, include nickel and cobalt. A magnet, then, is anything that has the properties of magnetism.
Magnetism also exhibits a field. The shape of a magnetic field and its lines of force can be seen by sprinkling iron filings over a sheet of paper placed on top of a magnet. In the 19th century, scientists made discoveries about the relationship between magnetism and electricity. It was found that the forces between magnetic dipoles are identical to those between electrical dipoles and that electric currents generate a magnetic field. Further research

revealed that it is possible to generate an electric current in a conductor by changing the magnetic fields around it, a phenomenon known as electromagnetism. This interrelation between electrical charge and magnetic force is present in matter on the atomic level as well. And the earth itself has a magnetic field which scientists hypothesize is generated and maintained by large electric currents caused by movement in the planet's liquid core.

Magneto, small electric generator that produces pulses of electricity. Magnetos are used as an ignition source in airplane piston engines and motorcycle engines, among other things. In mining, magnetos are used to fire explosives. The magneto works on the principle of electromagnetic induction. It consists of a permanent magnet and a soft iron core wound with wire. The core is rotated between the poles of the magnet, generating a low-voltage alternating current in the coil windings. This low voltage may be transformed to a higher voltage by induction in a second set of coil windings.
See also: Electric generator.

Magnetohydrodynamics (MHD), method of generating electricity by passing a high-velocity stream of plasma (gas at very high temperature) across a magnetic field. As the stream moves through the magnetic field, it has an electric current generated in it. The principle is the same as that of the electric generator, except that in magnetohydrodynamics the plasma stream rather than a coil of wire acts as the conductor. If electrodes are inserted into the plasma, a current will flow in an external circuit between them. In this way heat can be almost directly converted into electrical energy. But magnetohydrodynamics is still in the development stage, and a full-scale MHD plant has yet to be built. In practice the plasma would be heated by burning fuel or by a nuclear reactor to a temperature of 2,000°C-3,000°C (3,632°F-5,432°C). At these temperatures the gas is ionized (has electrons stripped from its atoms) and becomes conducting. Strong magnetic fields are required, and these may be provided by superconducting magnets. So far a few kilowatts of power have been generated by MHD for only a few seconds, and improvements in high-temperature technology will be needed before substantial progress can be made. MHD plants could in theory be smaller than conventional power stations and achieve a much greater efficiency because of the elimination of moving parts.
See also: Electric generator; Magnetism.

Magnetometer, instrument that surveys the strength of a magnetic field and registers its results through electronic voltage. Magnetometers are used by biomedical technicians to measure the magnetic field of certain body organs, such as the brain. They are used in industry, especially by those working with superconductors, and by prospectors attempting to detect ore or petroleum beneath the ground.
See also: Magnetism.

Magnitude, measure of a celestial object's brightness. The foundations of the system were laid by Hipparchus (120 B.C.), who divided stars into 6 categories of relative brightness, as seen from the earth (apparent magnitude). On a logarithmic scale, the difference of 1 magnitude of brightness between objects is determined by a factor of 2,512 (the 5th root of 100). The sun's magnitude is 26.8; bright stars, about +1. *Absolute magnitude* (measure of

intrinsic brightness) is defined as the apparent magnitude if located at a distance of 10 parsecs.
See also: Astronomy; Hipparchus.

Magnolia, any of the evergreen or deciduous trees or shrubs (genus *Magnolia*) from the family Magnoliaceae, often with showy flowers, found chiefly in temperate zones. Principally an Asiatic genus, native American magnolia species include the southern magnolia, or the bull bay (*M. grandiflora*), the cucumber tree (*M. acuminata*), the umbrella tree (*M.tripetala*), and the tulip tree, or yellow poplar (*Liriodendron tulipfera*), whose soft, yellowish wood is valued for furniture and cabi-network.

Magnolia State *See:* Mississippi.

Magpie, long-tailed bird of the crow and jay family (especially genus *Pica*). The North American *black-billed magpie* (*Pica pica*) has black feathers and white wings and abdomen. These scavengers, collectors of bright objects, often learn to imitate words in captivity.

Magritte, René (1898-1967), Belgian surrealist painter. His style, influenced by Chirico, often combined realism with irony, as in fantasy painting such as *The False Mirror* (1928), *The Red Model* (1935), and *The Empire of Lights* (1950).
See also: Surrealism.

Maguey, plant in the agave family. The Mexican plant, which grows up to 9 ft (3 m) long and 1 ft (30 cm) wide, has long green stalks with green flowers. The pulque agave (*Agave atrovirens*) is used to make beverages, both pulque and tequila. In Indonesia and the Philippines, the maguey is referred to commonly as cantala, and fibers from the plant, which may grow to 30-60 ft (75-150 cm) long, are used to produce twine.

Magyars, dominant people of Hungary and their language (from the Finno-Ugric language group). A nomadic warrior people, originally from the Urals, they were forced into present-day Romania by the Turkish Pechenegs and then into Hungary in the 9th century. They went on to conquer Moravia, advancing into Germany until stopped by Otto I in 955. They adopted Christianity in the 11th century.

Mahabharata, Sanskrit epic poem ascribed to the sage Vyasa, comprising some 110,000 32-syllable couplets, probably written before 500 B.C. though with many later passages in 18 books. It concerns the lengthy feud between 2 related tribes, the Pandavas and the Kauravas, and has as its central episode the Bhagavad-Gita, the religious classic of Hinduism.
See also: Hinduism.

Mahan, Alfred Thayer (1840-1914), U.S. naval officer and historian. His works on the historical significance of sea power, classics in their field, stimulated worldwide naval expansion. They include *The Influence of Sea Power upon History, 1660-1783* (1890) and *The Influence of Sea Power upon the French Revolution and Empire, 1793-1812* (1892).

Mahathir bin Mohammad, Datuk Seri(1925-), prime minister of Malaysia since 1981. Trained in medicine, he has made his career in politics. Mahathir served as deputy prime minister (1976-81) before succeeding Prime Minister Hussein bin Onn. A Malay nationalist, he was elected president of his party, the United Malays National Organization, in 1981. At the 1995 parliamentary elections his party won 80% of the votes.
See also: Malaysia.

Mahatma *See:* Gandhi, Mohandas Karamchand.

Mahdi (Arabic, "the guided one"), the prophet or savior who Muslims believe will bring peace and justice to the world. A notable claimant was Ubaydullah (r. 909-34), founder of the Egyptian Fatimid dynasty. Another was Muhammad Ahmad (1843?-85), who raised a revolt against Egyptian rule in the Sudan and fought the British (1883-85).
See also: Muslims.

Mahfouz, Naguib, or Mahfuz, Nagib (1911-   ), Egyptian novelist, playwright, and screenwriter. Among his works, which focus on urban life, are *Midaq Alley* (tr. 1975), *Miramar* (tr. 1978), and the short story collection *God's World* (tr. 1973). He won the 1988 Nobel Prize for literature. His books have been banned in many Arab countries for his expression of support of the 1979 Egypt-Israel peace treaty and other controversial views.

Mahican, Native American group of tribes of the Eastern Woodlands. These Native Americans lived along the Hudson River in longhouses and spoke an Algonquian language. They were active in the 17th-century fur trade along with their rivals, the Mohawks. Today surviving Mahicans live on Stockbridge Reservation in Wisconsin, named after the western Massachusetts town to which they were driven in the 17th century. Both Mahicans and Mohegans, a tribe of the Mahican group, are often referred to as Mohicans, after the fictional tribe in James Fenimore Cooper's *The Last of the Mohicans*.
See also: Mohegan.

Mah-jongg, game of Chinese origin played with a set of 136 standard domino-like tiles and several additional tiles, usually by 4 players. It is a collecting game where tiles are drawn and discarded until 1 player has a winning hand.

Mahler, Gustav (1860-1911), Austrian composer and conductor. He completed 9 symphonies and a number of song cycles, most notably *Songs of a Wayfarer* (1883-85) and *Kindertotenlieder* (*Songs on the Death of Children*; 1901-04). The symphonies are a culmination of 19th-century romanticism, but their startling harmonic and orchestral effects link them with early 20th-century works. Mahler was director of the Imperial Opera in Vienna (1897-1907).

Mahogany, chiefly tropical trees and shrubs, family Meliaceae, whose scented, termite-resistant hardwood is used extensively for furniture. The American genus *Swietenia* and the African genus *Khaya* are the principal sources of mahogany.

Mahomet *See:* Muhammad.

Mahratta, or Maratha, central Indian Hindu warrior people. Their empire was founded by Sivaji in 1674; it dominated India for about 150 years, following the Mogul empire, but the British broke its power in 1818.

Maidenhair tree *See:* Ginkgo.

Maidu, Native Americans who lived mainly in the Sacramento Valley and the Sierra Nevada, Calif. Maidus are part of the Penutian linguistic family. Today they number fewer than 200.

Mail *See:* Postal Service, U.S.

Mailer, Norman (1923-   ), U.S. novelist and journalist. After the great success of his first novel, *The Naked and the Dead* (1948), he became a critic of the American way of life. He combines journalism, fiction, and autobiography, as in his collection *Advertisements for Myself* (1959). He has been awarded 2 Pulitzer Prizes, one for *the Armies of the Night* (1968), an account of the 1967 Washington peace march, and the other for *The Executioner's Song* (1979). Other works include *Though Guys don't Dance* (1984), and *Oswald's Tale: an American Mystery* (1995).

Maillol, Aristide (1861-1944), French sculptor. His chief subject was the female nude, which he sculpted in monumental, static forms that represent a revival of classical ideals.

Maimonides, Moses (Solomon ben Maimon; 1135-1204), medieval rabbi, physician, and Jewish philosopher. Born in Muslim Spain, his family was driven to Egypt under persecution, where Maimonides became renowned as court physician to Saladin. Two of his major works were the *Mishneh Torah* (*Strong Hand*; 1180), a codification of Jewish doctrine, and *Guide to the Perplexed* (1190), in which he attempted to interpret Jewish tradition in Aristotelian terms. His work influenced many Jewish and Christian thinkers. *See also:* Philosophy.

Maine, largest New England state in the northeasternmost United States; bordered by Canada to the northwest, north, and east, by the Atlantic Ocean to the south, and by New Hampshire to the southwest.
Land and climate. During the Ice Age, Maine was covered by glaciers that pushed down the coastline, creating offshore islands. The moving ice rounded the mountains and left hundreds of lakes and ponds. Today, forests cover nearly 90% of the state. Maine has 3 distinct land regions. (1) The Coastal Lowlands extend inward from the Atlantic 10-40 mi (16-64 km). The land is gently rolling; along the coast are many rocky bays, inlets, and rugged peninsulas, and more than 1,300 islands. (2) The Eastern New England Upland runs northeast to southwest down the middle of the state. This rolling, heavily forested land contains hundreds of rivers and lakes. The Aroostook Plateau in the northeast is the state's most fertile area. (3) The White Mountains Region covers northwestern Maine and extends into New Hampshire and Vermont. This region includes most of Maine's higher peaks, including Mt. Katahdin. Moosehead Lake is Maine's largest lake. The state

Maine

Capital:	Augusta
Statehood:	Mar. 15, 1820 (23rd state)
Familiar name:	Pine Tree State
Area:	33,215 sq mi (86,026 km); ranks 39th
Population:	1,242,000 (1997); ranks 39th
Elevation:	Highest—5,268 ft (1,606 m), Mt. Katahdin
	Lowest—sea level
Motto:	*Dirigio* (I Direct)
State flower:	White pine cone and tassel
State bird:	Chickadee
State tree:	White pine
State song:	"State of Maine Song."

has more than 5,000 rivers and streams; major rivers include the Kennebec, Penobscot, St. John, Androscoggin, and Saco. Maine's climate is moist, cooler than most of the United States. Arctic air and coastal winds make Maine colder than many other places in the same latitude. Principal cities are Portland, Lewiston, and Bangor.

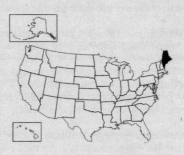

Economy. Service industries account for approximately 70% of the total value of all goods and services Maine produces in a year, but manufacturing is the main economic activity. Maine's abundant forests provide the raw materials for its paper industry and for such manufactured products as cardboard boxes, paper bags, lumber, and toothpicks. Other leading manufactured products include electrical equipment, processed foods, leather products, and textiles. Tourism, based on the striking Atlantic scenery and plentiful recreation facilities, is another major source of income for the state. Maine produces the nation's third-largest potato crop (after Idaho and Washington). Milk, eggs, and broilers (chickens) are the top livestock products. Mineral products include construction sand and gravel, cement, and crushed stone.

Government. Maine's constitution was adopted in 1819. The governor serves a 4-year term. The state legislature consists of 35 senators and 151 representatives; all serve 2-year terms. In the U.S. Congress, Maine is represented by 2 senators and 2 representatives.

History. Vikings may have been the first Europeans to explore Maine, C.A.D. 1000. Italian sea captain John Cabot probably explored the coast in 1498. The area was home to thousands of Native Americans when the first European-American settlers arrived in the early 1600s. Becoming part of the Massachusetts Bay Colony in the mid-1600s, Maine was a battleground during the French and Indian Wars; Maine soldiers played an active part in the American Revolution. In 1819, the people voted to separate from

Massachusetts, and Maine became a state in 1820. During the Civil War, it was a strong antislavery state. After the war, industrial development extended until the 1930s Great Depression and rose again after World War II, when tourism also boomed. Since the early 1970s, however, the state's economic development has been uneven. In the 1940s, Maine's Margaret Chase Smith became the first woman elected to both houses of the U.S. Congress.

Maine, U.S. battleship, sent to protect U.S. citizens and property in Cuba. It blew up in Havana harbor on Feb. 15, 1898, with a loss of 260 men. "Remember the Maine" became the war's rally cry. The incident, never satisfactorily explained though 2 inquiries were conducted, helped spark the Spanish-American War.
See also: Spanish-American War.

Mainstreaming *See:* Special education.

Maintenon, Marquise de (1635-1719), second wife of Louis XIV of France. After the death of her first husband (1660), she became governess to the sons of Louis and his mistress, Mme de Montespan. She replaced the latter in Louis' affections and, on the death of the queen, was married to him though she did not share his title and estate.

Mainz (pop. 189,400), city in west-central Germany. As the capital of the state of Rhineland-Palatinate state, it is located on a junction of two German rivers, the Rhine and the Main. Originally a Roman camp (1st century B.C.), it became an important religious and printing center in medieval times and a fortress for the German Empire (1873-1918). The city is known as home to historic buildings, a center for German Rhine wines, and manufacturing (e.g., motor vehicles and chemicals).

Maitland, Frederic William (1850-1906), English jurist and legal historian. He was particularly concerned with early English law and founded the Selden Society (1887). Notable among his works is *The History of English Law before the Time of Edward I* (1895), written with Sir Frederick Pollock.

Maize *See:* Corn.

Major *See:* Rank, military.

Major, John (1943-), former British Prime Minister from the Conservative Party who succeeded Margaret Thatcher in 1990. Prior to becoming Prime Minister, Major was a member of Parliament, Foreign Secretary, and Chancellor of the Exchequer. Major left school at the age of 16 and never attended college. He entered the banking industry at the age of 22 before entering politics. He was the youngest British prime minister in the 20th century. Following the defeat of the Conservative Party at the 1997 elections, Major resigned as party leader.
See also: United Kingdom.

Majorca, or *Mallorca*, largest of the Balearic Islands of Spain, in the west Mediterranean. Majorca is a major tourist center with many resorts, including its capital, Palma.

Major leagues *See:* Baseball.

Makarios III (Michael Christodoulos Mouskos; 1913-77), archbishop of the Cypriot Orthodox Church from 1950, and president of independent Cyprus (1960-77). During British rule he led the movement for *enosis* (union with Greece). As president after independence, he worked to reduce conflict between the island's Greek and Turkish population. He survived 4 assassination attempts and fled temporarily during the political disturbances of 1974.

Mako shark *See:* Shark.

Malabo (pop. 33,000), capital city of Equatorial Guinea. Founded by the British (1827) as Clarencetown, it was later named Santa Isabel by the Spanish (1844) until the independence of Equatorial Guinea (1973). Located on the island of Bioko in the Gulf of Guinea, the city is important in import-export trade.

Malacca, Strait of, important sea passage that links the South China Sea and Indian Ocean. Singapore is the chief port located on this 500 mi (800 km) strait, which flows between Sumatra and the Malay Peninsula. The width of the channel varies from 30 to 200 mi (50 to 320 km).

Malachi, Book of, Old Testament book, 39th and last in Authorized Version, 12th of the Minor Prophets. Written anonymously c.5th century B.C., it prophesies judgment for insincerity and negligence at the coming of the Messiah.
See also: Old Testament.

Malachite, $CU_2CO_3(OH)_2$, green, translucent mineral containing crystals of hydrated copper carbonate. It is widely distributed, usually occurring near copper deposits, in the United States, the former USSR, Chile, Zaïre, Zimbabwe and Australia. It is used as a source of copper, an ornamental stone, and, when ground, as a pigment.

Malagasy Republic *See:* Madagascar.

Malamud, Bernard (1914-86). U.S. novelist and short story writer. He won a National Book Award for his stories in *The Magic Barrel* (1958) and the Pulitzer Prize for his novel *The Fixer* (1966). Malamud's work deals mainly with Jewish life and traditions in the United States. The heroes of his books are often humble, solitary individuals, though *Dubin's Lives* (1979) marked a departure in subject matter.

Malamute *See:* Alaskan malamute.

Malaria, infectious parasitic disease causing fever, violent chills, enlargement of the spleen, and occasionally jaundice and anemia. Bouts often reoccur and can be acute or chronic. Widespread in tropical and subtropical areas, malaria is due to infection with the *Plasmodium* parasite carried by the *Anopheles* mosquitoes from the blood of infected persons. Derivatives of quinine are used both in prevention and treatment of the disease.

Malawi

Capital:	Lilongwe
Area:	45,747 sq mi
	(118,484 sq km)
Population:	9,840,000
Language:	English, Chichewa
Government:	Presidential republic
Independent:	1964
Head of gov.:	President
Per capita:	U.S. $170
Mon. unit:	1 Kwacha = 100
	tambala

Malawi, republic of east Africa lying west and south of Lake Malawi, and bordered by Tanzania to the north, Mozambique to the east and south, and Zambia to the west.

Land and climate. Malawi has a area of about 45,747 sq mi (118,484 sq km), controls much of lakes Malawi and Chiuta, and includes Malambe, Chilwa, and several other large lakes. The lakes are part of the great Rift Valley, which crosses the region from north to south and includes the Shire River valley. Bordering highlands and plateaus average 3,500 ft (1,067 m) in height, and the Shire highlands in the south and southeast rise to 9,843 ft (3,000 m) at Mlanje Peak. The valleys are hot; the highland climate is moderate.

People. The people of Malawi are almost entirely Bantu-speaking black Africans. About 75% of the people are Christians with the balance professing Islam or practicing native religions. English and Chichewa are the country's official languages, though other African languages are spoken. The largest city is Blantyre, the capital is Lilongwe.

Economy. Malawi's economy is agricultural. Tea and tobacco are grown in the highlands; cotton in the lowlands. Other crops include peanuts, corn, rice, and sugar. There is some light industry at Blantyre and Lilongwe. The Shire River is harnessed for hydroelectricity at Nkula Falls. The country's mineral resources remain mostly undeveloped.

History. Seat of a powerful black African kingdom between the 15th and 18th centuries, Malawi was later prey to the slave trade. In 1859 the British missionary Dr. David Livingstone visited Malawi. An attempt by the Portuguese to seize the south was defeated leading to the establishment of a British protectorate in 1890. Shortly thereafter the area became known as Nyasaland. In 1953 the country entered the Federation of Rhodesia and Nyasaland, but the association with white dominated Rhodesia was an uneasy one and lasted only until 1963. In 1964, Nyasaland became the independent state of Malawi. On July 6, 1966 it was proclaimed a republic under the presidency of Dr. Hastings K. Banda. Under Dr. Banda Malawi has pursued a controversial foreign policy of openly maintaining relations with South Africa. After years of one party rule, Banda introduced a multi party system and was succeeded by Bakili Muluzi in 1994.

Malaysia

Capital:	Kuala Lumpur
Area:	127,584 sq mi
	(330,442 sq km)
Population:	20,933,000
Language:	Malay (Bahasa
	Malaysia)
Government:	Federal constitutional
	monarchy
Independent:	1963
Head of gov.:	Prime minister
Per capita:	U.S. $3,890
Mon. unit:	1 Ringgit = 100 sen

Malay Archipelago (East Indies), the world's largest group of islands, off the coast of southeastern Asia, between the Indian and Pacific Oceans. It includes the 3,000 islands of Indonesia, the 7,000 islands of the Philippines, and New Guinea.

Malayo-Polynesian languages, or Austroenesian languages, family of some 500 languages found throughout the Central and South Pacific, especially in Malaysia and the Indonesian islands. There are 2 main groups: Oceanic to the east and Indonesian to the west.

Malay Peninsula, southernmost peninsula in Asia, comprising western Malaysia and southern Thailand. It is one of the world's richest producers of rubber and tin.

Malaysia, Federation of Malaysia, independent federation in Southeast Asia, comprising West Malaysia on the Malay Peninsula and East Malaysia, formed by Sabah and Sarawak on the island of Borneo.
Land and climate. East Malaysia is separated from the Malay Peninsula for a distance of about 400 mi (644 km) by the South China Sea. West Malaysia is bordered by Thailand to the north, Singapore to the south, the South China Sea to the east, and the Strait of Malacca and the Andaman Sea to the west. East Malaysia is bordered on the south and west by Indonesia, on the north by the South China and Sulu Seas and by Brunei, and on the east by the Celebes Sea. West Malaysia is mainly mountainous with narrow coastal plains and lush equatorial forests. Sarawak and Sabah also have mountainous interiors and large areas of rain forest.
People. The majority of Malaysians live on the peninsula and most are Malays or Chinese with sizable minorities of Indians and Pakistanis. Malay is the official language, but many Malaysians also speak other languages including Chinese, English, and Tamil. Islam is the official religion. The capital is Kuala Lumpur.
Economy. Malaysia is rich in natural resources, but the economy is still largely agricultural. Rice is the chief food crop, but bananas, yams, cocoa, pepper, tea, and tobacco are also grown. In addition, the forests yield valuable timber, palm oil, and coconuts. The relatively small industrial sector produ-

---

Maldives

Capital:	Male
Area:	115 sq mi
	(298 sq km)
Population:	290,000
Language:	Divehi
Government:	Presidential republic
Independent:	1965
Head of gov.:	President
Per capita:	U.S. $990
Mon. unit:	1 Rufiyaa = 100 laari

---

ces petroleum, iron ore, bauxite, coal, and gold. The country's principal exports are petroleum, rubber, tin, palm oil, and timber.

History. In the 9th century Malaysia was the seat of the Buddhist Srivajava Empire. Beginning in the 14th century the population was converted to Islam. The Portuguese took Malacca in 1511, but were ousted by the Dutch in 1641. The British formed a trading base of the East India Company in Penang in 1786, and in 1826 united Penang, Singapore, and Malacca into the Straits Settlement. Between 1888 and 1909 the British established many protectorates in Malaya and Borneo. After the Japanese occupation in World War II (1941-45), Malaya was reorganized as the Federation of Malaya (1948), gaining independence within the British Commonwealth in 1957. In 1963 the union of Malaya with Singapore, Sarawak, and Sabah formed the Federation of Malaysia. Indonesia waged guerilla warfare against the Federation from 1963 to 1965. In 1965, Singapore seceded and became an independent republic. Parliament was suspended for 22 months beginning in 1969 after race riots broke out between Malays and Chinese in West Malaysia. Racial and religious strife again broke out among Malays, Chinese, and Hindus in the late 1970s and early 80s. Ethnic and religious differences still lie behind the major divisions in national politics. In the 1980s and 90s the exportoriented economy florished. At the end of the 1990s the country suffered from terrible forest fires. 1998 saw an economic recession.

Malcolm X (Malcolm Little; 1925-65), U.S. black militant leader. He was also known as El-Hajj Malik El-Shabazz. While in prison for burglary (1946-52), he was converted to the Black Muslim faith and upon release became a Muslim minister and leader of the black separatist movement. In 1964 he split with another leader, Elijah Muhammad, to form the Organization of Afro-American Unity, speaking for black nationalism but allowing racial brotherhood. He was assassinated at an OAAU meeting in New York City in 1965, purportedly by Black Muslims. The *Autobiography of Malcolm X* (1964) is a classic concerning the black power movement of the 1960s.
See also: Black Power.

Maldives, officially Republic of Maldives, formerly Maldive Islands, republic, a series of coral atolls (115 sq mi/298 sq km) in the northern Indian Ocean, about 420 mi (675 km) southwest of Sri Lanka. They comprise some 2,000 islands, of which about 200 are inhabited. The official religion is Islam and the language, Dhivehi. Malé, the capital, is the largest island. The chief industries are fishing, coconut products, shipping, and tourism. Grains are grown on a limited scale, but most food staples are imported. Originally settled by southern Asians, the introduction of Islam in the 12th century and the arrival of the Portuguese in the 16th century strongly influenced the history of the islands. They became a British protectorate (1887-1965) with internal self-government before finally achieving independence as a sultanate in 1965. When the ad-Din dynasty, which had ruled since the 14th century, ended in 1968, a republic was declared. Britain closed its air force base on Gan in 1976. In 1988 a group of 80 Tamil Tigers attempted a coup but were unsuccessful. In 1997 the country adopted a new constitution.

Male *See:* Reproduction.

Malé (pop. 55,100), port and capital city of the Republic of Maldives, or Maldive Islands, in the Indian Ocean. Located on the island of the same name in this South Pacific atoll, Malé's main products are fish and tropical fruits and vegetables. Islam is the religion of its people, and Muslim mosques make Malé an important tourist site.

Malemute *See:* Alaskan malamute.

Malenkov, Georgi Maximilianovich (1902-88), Soviet premier 1953-55, after Stalin's death. Beginning as an aide to Stalin, followed by entrance to the politburo and deputy premiership (1946), Malenkov as prime minister curbed the power of the secret police and promoted reconciliation in his foreign policy. He was replaced by Bulganin in 1955, expelled from the Presidium in 1957, and from the party in 1961.

Malevich, Kasimir (1878-1935), Russian painter, a pioneer of abstract art. In 1913 he began painting works based on geometric shapes and published a manifesto to propagate suprematism. Among his works is *White on White* (1918).

Malherbe, François de (1555-1628), French poet; court poet to Henry IV and Louis XIII. A critic of the classical style of the Pléiade poets, he emphasized the importance of French classic language and of precision in expression. His best-known poem is *Cosolation à Monsieur du Périer* (c.1590).

Mali, officially Republic of Mali, West Africa's largest country (478,764 sq mi/1,240,000 sq km), Mali is bordered by Senegal, Guinea, and Mauritania (west), Niger (east and southeast), Algeria (north), and Burkina Faso and Ivory Coast (south).
Land and economy. The land in the south, fed by the Niger and Senegal rivers, supports the chief cash crops of peanuts and cotton and subsistence crops of rice, millet, maize, and sorghum. Exports include fish from the Niger and livestock. Extensive mineral resources are largely untapped, though some salt, gold, and phosphates are mined. Industries include textiles, food processing, and cotton ginning. Land in the north, is primarily arid, supporting minimum grazing (cattle, goats, sheep).

Mali	
Capital:	Bamako
Area:	478,841 sq mi (1,240,192 sq km)
Population:	10,109,000
Language:	French
Government:	Presidential republic
Independent:	1960
Head of gov.:	Prime minister
Per capita:	U.S. $250
Mon. unit:	1 CFA franc = 100 centimes

People. The population basically comprises 6 tribal groups, who speak the official language, French, and several indigenous tongues. About 80% are Muslims; the rest are animists.

History. The early 14th century saw the zenith of the powerful medieval empire of Mali, one of the world's chief gold suppliers. Its cities of Timbuktu and Djenné were major cultural and trade centers. The Songhai empire of Gao was prominent in the late 15th century before a Moroccan army destroyed its power (1590) and the region divided into small states. French conquest of Mali was complete by 1898, though they had faced a resurgence of Islam and were opposed by Muslim emperors. Mali became French Sudan and then part of French West Africa. After World War I, the Sudanese Union, a militant political force of the new nationalist movement, led by Modibo Keita, gained momentum, resulting in the autonomous Sudanese Republic in 1958. The republic joined with Senegal in 1959 to become the Mali Federation, a union that ended in 1960 as the Republic of Mali became fully independent and broke with the French Community. The one-party, socialist state, led by President Keita, left the French bloc (1962) but returned in 1967, due to financial difficulties. Keita was overthrown by the military (1968), displaced by Lt. Moussa Traoré as head of the military regime. In the 1970s a severe drought damaged Mali's agrarian economy and contributed to the deaths of nearly 100,000 people. A new constitution calling for civilian rule was implemented in 1979, reelecting Traoré as president. Traore's rule lasted 25 years and ended with a coup in 1991. The new leaders announced a transitional period as a stepping stone to democracy. In 1997 Swiss banks reimbursed money which had been embezzled by Traoré.

Mali Empire, one of the great Sudanese empires of West Africa. Founded in the 13th century, it reached its height under Mansa Musa, who reigned 1312-37. He and his successors were devout Muslims, and the towns of Mali and Timbuktu became centers both of the caravan trade and of Islamic culture. The empire declined in the 15th century, mainly because of expansion of the Songhai empire of Gao.
See also: Mansa Musa.

Malinke *See:* Mandingo.

Malinowski, Bronislaw (1884-1942), Polish-born English anthropologist, founder of social anthropology. In his theory of "functionalism," all the mores, customs, and beliefs of a society perform a vital function that must be taken into account in the study of that culture. His research included the cultures of Trobriand Island, Africa, and the Americas. Writings include *Crime and Custom in Savage Society* (1926), *Sex and Repression in Savage Society* (1926), and *Magic, Science and Religion* (1948).
See also: Anthropology.

Mallard, wild duck of the family Anatidae. The dull brown feathers of the female are in sharp contrast to the iridescent green head and purple chest feathers of the courting male. These ducks, which grow to 28 in (71 cm), migrate from northern marshes in summer to warmer southern wetlands in winter. They are abundant in North America, Europe, and Asia.

Mallarmé, Stéphane (1842-98), French poet, forefather of the symbolists. He held that poetry should suggest or evoke the transcendental, not describe in literal terms. Although the language of his poems is obscure and nontraditional, he had considerable influence on French poetry. His works include *Herodias* (1869), *The Afternoon of a Faun* (1876), which inspired Debussy, and *A Throw of the Dice Will Never Eliminate Chance* (1897).

Mallorca *See:* Majorca.

Mallory, Stephen Russell (1813?-73), both U.S. and Confederate politician. After his resignation as U.S. senator (1850-61) from Florida, Russell was appointed by Jefferson Davis, president of the confederacy, as secretary of the Confederate Navy. Under his leadership, the South developed a powerful force of ironclad ships that overpowered the North's naval forces until near the end of the war. After a year of imprisonment following the war, Russell, along with other Confederates, was pardoned (1867) by President Andrew Johnson.
See also: Confederate States of America; Civil War, U.S.

Mallow, shrub and herb of the family Malvaceae, usually with showy flowers and disk-shaped fruits. True mallows (genus *Malva*) of the Old World, false mallows (genus *Malvastrum*), and rose, or swamp, mallows (genus *Hibiscus*) of North America comprise the family. The perennial hollyhock (*Althea rosea*), from China, is the most popular ornamental; the pods of the mallow okra, or gumbo, are used as a vegetable; and the most economically important member is cotton. The marsh mallow of Europe is used medicinally and was once used to make marshmallow.

Malnutrition, shortage of vital nutrients. Malnutrition may be partial or total and may be the result of poor eating habits, as often occurs among the aged, or due to the unavailability or lack of food caused by disasters such as famine, drought, or war. Malnutrition may also be symptomatic of a gastrointestinal disorder, a malfunctioning of one of the body's major organs, or it may even be associated with diarrhea. Malnutrition affecting all parts of the diet is called marasmus. In marasmus, the body breaks down its own tissues to meet the needs of metabolism. The result is extreme wasting and, in children, extreme growth retardation. A shortage of the body's essential proteins is a variety of malnutrition known as kwashiorkor and shortages of essential vitamins manifest themselves as pellagra, beriberi, or scurvy.

Malnutrition is especially dangerous in pregnant women and in children. In children it can lead to growth disorders, both physical and mental, and reduce their resistance to disease. Though malnutrition is most readily associated with poor and underdeveloped countries in which its manifestations can be severe and are often fatal, it also occurs in rich and developed countries as the result of poverty or diets lacking in essential nutrients.

Malocclusion *See:* Orthodontics.

Malory, Sir Thomas (?-1471), English author who wrote *La Morte d'Arthur*. With romances (adventure stories) a favorite genre of his time, Sir Thomas Malory was the first to write, in English, the popular and legendary tales of King Arthur and his Knights of the Round Table. Believed to be completed in 1470, a first edition was printed by the first English printer, William Caxton (1485).

Malpighi, Marcello (1628-94), Italian physician and botanist who made significant advances in the understanding of human anatomy. His mastery of the microscope enabled him to perform important research on animal tissues. He discovered that lungs are made up of small air sacs, called alveoli and that the veins connect to the arteries. He was the first person to describe red blood cells. Other significant contributions were made in the study of insect and plant anatomy. Malpighi was also a professor of medicine at the University of Bologna and served as the personal physician to Pope Innocent XII.
See also: Botany; Anatomy.

Malraux, André (1901-76), French author and political activist. His social novels, such as *Man's Fate* (1933) and *Man's Hope* (1937), describe political struggles both factually and poetically. In real life, Malraux became involved in many political struggles, including the Chinese civil war, the Spanish civil war, and the French resistance against the Nazis in World War II. He was France's first secretary of cultural affairs (1958-68), under Charles De Gaulle.

Malt, product made from any cereal grain by steeping it in water, allowing it to germinate, and then drying it. This activates dormant enzymes, such as diastase, that convert the kernel starch to maltose (malt sugar). Malt is used as a source of enzymes and flavoring.

Malta, officially Republic of Malta, republic in the Mediterranean Sea south of Sicily, made up of the islands of Malta, Gozo, Comino, and some uninhabited islets, for a total area of 122 sq mi (316 sq km). The capital and chief port is Valletta.
Land. The islands are chiefly layers of limestone, with a thin topsoil, and reach their greatest height (827 ft/252 m) near Dingli, on Malta. Their fertile slopes and valleys are intensively cultivated, usually under irrigation.
People. The state religion is Roman Catholicism, and the official languages are English and Maltese, a Semitic language; Italian is widely spoken.
Economy. Malta has almost no mineral wealth or valuable natural resources and must import most of what it needs. Agriculture, tourism, shipbuilding,

Malta

Capital:	Valletta
Area:	122 sq mi
	(316 sq km)
Population:	380,000
Language:	Maltese, English
Government:	Republic
Independent:	1964
Head of gov.:	Prime minister
Per capita:	U.S. $9,385
Mon. unit:	1 Maltese lira (pound)
	= 100 cents = 1000 mils

and light industry, as well as traditional handicrafts (lave and ceramic), support the economy.

History. Malta is rich in prehistoric remains, but the first known inhabitants were the Phoenicians, who were succeeded by the Greeks, Carthaginians, Romans, and Saracens. Saint Paul was shipwrecked on Malta about A.D. 60. In 1530, after occupation by the Arabs, Normans, and Spaniards, Malta was granted to the Knights Hospitalers (later Knights of Malta), who defeated the Turks in the Great Siege (1565) and built Valletta. They were ousted by Napoleon I (1798), and 2 years later Malta passed to the British. Malta's courage under siege and intensive Axis bombardment during World War II was recognized by the award of the George Cross to the entire population. The country became independent within the Commonwealth in 1964. In 1990 Malta submitted a formal request for entry into the EC.

Malta fever *See:* Brucellosis.

Maltese, breed of toy dog. This breed probably descends from lap dogs popular 2,000 years ago with women of Greek and Roman nobility. Standing no taller than about 5 in (12.7 cm) and weighing no more than about 7 lb (1.4 kg), the long white hairs of this dog part down the middle and, sometimes, grow to floor length.

Malthus, Thomas Robert (1766-1834), English economist, sociologist, and pioneer in the study of the population problem. In *An Essay on the Principal of Population* (1798; rev. ed. 1803), he asserted that any attempt to improve the human social condition was doomed to failure since food production would never grow as rapidly as population, a condition checked only by famine, disease, war, and moral restraint. His doctrine, adapted by neo-Malthusians, has influenced such economists as David Ricardo.
See also: Population.

Maltose, malt sugar; a disaccharide sugar produced by the action of diastase on starch and yielding glucose with the enzyme maltase.

Mamba, any of 4 or 5 species of snakes in the cobra family. Found in sub-Saharan Africa, these aggressive, thin, whip-like snakes can inflict a fatal, poisonous bite to man. Hoodless, unlike the familiar image of a cobra, the green mamba grows to about 9 ft (2.7 m) and the black mamba grows to about 14 ft (4.3 m).

Mamelukes, group of ruling warriors in Egypt. First brought to Egypt as slaves (10th century), many members of this warrior caste eventually rose to power (1250-1517). After 1517, when Ottoman rule of Egypt was established, the Mamelukes became influential whenever the ruling Turks' power waned. The Mamelukes headed an unsuccessful attack against Napoleon I in Egypt (1798), and were massacred by the Turks shortly afterwards.

Mamet, David (1947-), U.S. playwright. Among his successful works, which compare the American dream with the corruption of modern society, are *American Buffalo* (1977, New York Drama Critics Circle Award), *Glengarry Glen Ross* (1984, Pulitzer Prize and New York Drama Critics Circle Award), and *Speed-the-Plow* (1988). He also wrote screenplays for such movies as *The Verdict* (1982), *The Postman Always Rings Twice* (1984), and *The Untouchables* (1987). He wrote and directed *Homicide* (1991). Other works include *The Cabin* (1992; autobiography) and *The Village* (1994; novel).

Mammal, warm-blooded animal best distinguished by the possession of milk glands for feeding its young. Hair is a feature of mammals, although some, like the whales, have little or none. All mammals, except monotremes like the platypus, bear their young alive. Other shared characteristics are a lower jaw formed from 1 bone, 3 small bones in the middle ear, a neck of 7 vertebrae (even in giraffes), a diaphragm that forms a partition under the ribs, and a 4-chambered heart.
Mammals evolved from reptiles, but due to gaps in the fossil record, various stages in their development from reptiles are as yet undetermined. It is probable that the different groups of mammals arose independently from several kinds of intermediate mammal-like reptiles, so that there was no single ancestral mammal. The first mammals are believed to have been small and lived at the same time as the giant dinosaurs.
Mammals have evolved into many forms, and constitute some 3,200 species alive today. Mammals are divided into 3 main groups. The monotremes are the most primitive mammals and include the platypus of Australia. They lay eggs and feed their babies milk secreted from pores in the skin and not from milk glands with nipples. Marsupials are the pouched animals, including the kangaroo, opossum, wallaby, and Tasmanian devil. The young are born in an undeveloped state and complete their development in a pouch. Marsupials are found only in Australia and parts of America. Placental mammals, including humans, are the largest and most successful group. The young are born in varying states of development, from the relatively helpless human offspring to those like horses that are able to run within a few hours after their birth or, in the case of whales and dolphins, are able to swim as soon as they are born.

Mammary glands, special glands present in mammals, situated ventrally in pairs, modified in females to produce and secrete milk to nourish offspring.

The milk, secreted by cells lining the small compartments, or lobules, that make up each gland, then travels from the lobules along ducts to the nipple, where it is emptied. Mammary glands, which develop in female humans at the onset of adolescence, remain undeveloped in male mammals.

Mammoth, any of several extinct, prehistoric elephants (genus *Mammuthus*) found in North America and Eurasia. Distinguishable from today's elephants by their shaggy coats, long, upward-curving tusks, and complex molar teeth, the species included the imperial mammoth of North America, 13.5 ft (4.1 m) high at the shoulder.

Mammoth Cave, limestone cavern about 85 mi (137 km) southwest of Louisville, Ky., containing a series of vast subterranean chambers. It includes lakes, rivers, stalactites, stalagmites, and formations of gypsum crystals. The mummified body of a pre-Columbian man has been found there. It is part of Mammoth Cave National Park.

Man *See:* Human being.

Management and Budget, Office of (OMB), U.S. government office that helps the president prepare the federal budget and formulate fiscal programs. The OMB was known as The Bureau of the Budget before 1970. At first part of the Treasury Department, it became part of the Executive Office of the President in 1939.

Managua (pop. 682,000), capital city of Nicaragua, located on the southern shore of Lake Managua. Made capital in 1855 to end a feud between León and Granada, it has been rebuilt on numerous occasions after destruction by earthquakes (1931, 1972) and fires (1931, 1936).
See also: Nicaragua.

Man, Isle of, island, 227 sq mi (588 sq km) in the Irish Sea off the northwestern coast of Great Britain; the capital is Douglas. It became the base for Irish missionaries after St. Patrick, and at one time was a Norwegian dependency sold to Scotland (1266). A dependency of the British Crown since 1765, it has its own legislature (Court of Tynwald) and representative assembly (House of Keys). Tourism is the main industry. The Manx language is now virtually extinct.

Manakin, bird in the family Pipridae. Found in Central and South America, these small birds are known for the male courtship rituals. In specially selected dancing grounds called leks, the males create unusual sounds and movements in competitions as the females look on. Both sexes are greenish in color, although the males have splashes of color. These birds grow to no more than 5 in (13 cm) and are believed to live approximately 20 years.

Manama (pop. 137,000), also known as al-Manamah, capital city of Bahrain. Located in the Persian Gulf, this major port for the island nation of Bahrain lies on an important trade and shipping route. Since the discovery of oil (1932), Manama has become a center for finance and commerce, with a new harbor fully equipped to dock and repair large oceangoing vessels.
See also: Bahrain.

Manassas, Battles of *See:* Bull Run, Battles of.

Manatee, large, aquatic, herbivorous mammal of tropical and subtropical Atlantic coasts and large rivers. They and the dugongs are the only living sea cows (order Sirenia). They have powerful, flat, rounded tails that provide propulsion. The forelimbs are small and hindlimbs completely absent. Manatees may be 12 ft (3.6 m) long and weigh 600 lb (270 kg).

Manchester (pop. 434,600), city in northwest England, on the Irwell, Irk, and Medlock rivers. Located about 35 mi (56 km) off England's western coast, it is connected to the Irish Sea by the Mersey River and a canal and serves as a major inland port. The city is also a center for trade and finance and is an important industrial area, the products of which include computers, chemicals, clothing, and industrial machinery. The city began as a village established around A.D. 700 on the site of what had been a Roman fort. By the 19th century, it had become an important industrial center and one of the world's major producers of cotton textiles.
See also: England.

Manchester (pop. 90,936), city in southern New Hampshire, on the Merrimack River, settled in 1722. Development of its major 19th-century textile industry was aided by water power from the Amoskeag Falls; today's manufactures include shoes, machinery, electronics, and auto parts.
See also: New Hampshire.

Manchester School, group of English businessmen and members of Parliament (1820-60), mostly from Manchester, who advocated worldwide free trade. They were led by John Bright and Richard Cobden, who formed the Anti-Corn-Law League in 1838 and brought about the repeal of the corn laws in 1846.

Manchester terrier, popular breed of dog. They were bred into existence in the 1800s in Manchester, England, when black and tan terriers were mated with swift whippets to compete in rat-killing matches. They are black with tan markings on their faces and chests and weigh 12-22 lb (5.4-10 kg). A toy variety weighs 5-12 lb (2.3-5.4 kg).

Manchineel, or poison guava tree (*Hippomane mancinella*), native to tropical regions of the United States. A member of the spurge family, manchineels grow from 10 to 50 ft (3 to 15 m) high and produce yellowish green fruit that look like crab apples. The fruit and sap are extremely poisonous and were used by ancient Carib tribes as poison for their arrows.

Manchuria, region of northeastern China comprising Heilongjiang, Jilin, and Liaoning provinces and part of the Inner Mongolian Autonomous Region; c.600,000 sq mi (1,554,000 sq km). Manchuria is bordered by the Russia, North Korea, and Mongolia. It is an important agricultural and industrial area. Historically, Manchuria was the home of the Manchus. Chinese settlement in the area increased steadily after 1900. It was a barren steppe until Western exploitation of its vast mineral resources began in the 19th century. In the 1890s Russia had declared an interest in the province; but Russia's defeat in the Russo-Japanese War (1904-05) brought Japanese domination, first of Southern Manchuria, then, in 1932, of the whole country. The puppet state of Manchukuo was created and rapidly industrialized. In 1945 Russian forces occupied the area, dismantling the industries upon their withdrawal. Bitterly contested in the Chinese civil war, Manchuria was captured in 1948 by the communists, who redrew the provincial boundaries.

Manchus, a Manchurian people descended from the Jurchen tribe of the Tungus. Originally a nomadic, pastoral people, they came to China in the 12th century, only to be driven out by the Mongols. They eventually settled in the Sungari Valley and went on to conquer China in 1644, forming the Ch'ing dynasty and reigning until 1912. The Manchus have now been racially and culturally absorbed with the Chinese, and their language is virtually extinct.

Mandalay (pop. 533,000), city in central Myanmar (Burma), on the Irrawaddy River. It is the center of Burmese Buddhism, with numerous monuments, including the Arakan pagoda, and is the country's transportation center. Mandalay was founded in the mid-19th century and served (1860-85) as the last capital of the kingdom of Burma before annexation by the British.

Mandan, Native American Plains tribe of the upper Missouri valley. Of Siouan linguistic stock, they came from the east in the 18th century to inhabit what is now North Dakota. An agricultural people, the tribe was almost wiped out by disease and war in the early 19th century. The surviving Mandans, together with other tribes, live today on reservations in North Dakota.

Mandarin, important civil servant or military official in imperial China. Mandarin Chinese, formerly an upper-class language, is the official language of China.

Mandela, Nelson (1918-), South African political leader and a major figure in the black protest movement against the racial segregation policies (known as apartheid) of the white-dominated South African government. Son of a tribal chief of the Transkei territory, he became a lawyer in 1942 and joined the African National Congress (ANC) in 1944. He gained prominence as a leader of the black protest movement in the 1950s. In 1960 he was arrested and charged with treason but was acquitted. Arrested again in 1962, he was later convicted of sabotage and conspiracy and sentenced to life imprisonment. In jail he became an international symbol of black defiance of the apartheid system. In February 1990 Mandela was released from prison and assumed leadership of the ANC, pledging to work for a peaceful end to the hated apartheid regime. In early 1991, President F.W. de Klerk of South Africa called for the end of the racial segregation laws that were the underpinning of apartheid, and Mandela's goal of a race-free state seemed possible. Despite the opposition of conservative white South Africans, apartheid was abolished and the transition to a democratic government started. Notwithstanding the growing tensions between the ANC and the Inkatha Freedom Party of Zulu chief Buthelezi, the ANC won the majority in parliament in the first democratic elections held in 1994, and Mandela became South Africa's first black president. In 1998 he married Graça Machel, widow of the former president of Mozambique.
See also: Apartheid; South Africa.

Mandela, Winnie (Winifred Nomzamo Madikileza; 1936?-   ), anti-apartheid activist in the Republic of South Africa, wife of Nelson Mandela. During her husband's imprisonment (1962-90) she frequently spoke on his behalf. Her popularity has declined since 1988 as a result of her supposed involvement in various crimes, particularly her link with the so-called Mandela United Football Club, blamed for the kidnapping and assault of African youths. In 1991, after a 14-week trial, Mandela was found guilty of kidnapping 4 black youths from a church in 1988, as part of an alleged conspiracy to discredit a white minister. The conviction is being appealed.
See also: Apartheid; Mandela, Nelson.

Mandelstam, Osip Emilievich (1891-1938?), Russian poet. At first a member of the neoclassicist Acmeist school, he was arrested in 1934 and exiled until 1937. Rearrested in 1938, he reportedly died soon afterwards in a Siberian prison. His works include *Stone* (1913) and *Tristia* (1922). After his death his widow, **Nadezhda Mandelstam** (1899-1981), spent many years collecting his verse and smuggling it to the West. Her memoirs, *Hope Against Hope* (1970) and *Hope Abandoned* (1972), were powerful indictments of Stalinism.

Mandeville, Bernard (c.1670-1733), Dutch-born English philosopher and satirist. Best known as the author of a work in verse, *The Fable of the Bees* (1714), he attempted to establish that every virtue is based on self-interest.

Mandingo, West African ethnic group, descendants of the founders of the Mali Empire, (fl.1240-1500). Most Mandingos belong to the Malinke group and practice tribal religions and customs in small rural villages. They are chiefly farmers and cattle ranchers and about one-fifth of them have converted to Islam. Their language, which has many different dialects, belongs to the Mande language group.

Mandolin, instrument of the lute family. It has a pear-shaped body, fretted neck, and 4 or 5 pairs of strings that are plucked with a plectrum. Composers who have used the mandolin in their works include Mozart and Beethoven, but it is best known as a popular Neapolitan instrument.

Mandrake, herbaceous perennial plant (*Mandragora officinarum*) of the nightshade family, with purplish or white flowers, a thin stalk, and a forked root resembling the human form. A native of the Himalayas and the Mediterranean, its poisonous root has been used to produce vomiting and bowel movements and as a pain-killer. In North America, the mayapple is called mandrake.

Mandrill, colorful monkey (*Mandrillus sphinx*) of central West Africa. Mandrills are jungle dwellers that move about on the ground and through trees and they feed on fruits and insects. They resemble baboons and may weigh up to 90 lb (40 kg). The males are brightly colored with blue, purple, yellow, and red faces and rumps and can protect groups of up to 150 against predators.

Manet, Edouard (1832-83), French painter. Influenced by Goya and Velázquez, his work, in broad, flat areas of color, introduced a new pictorial language, and was often severely criticized by the art establishment, who considered his subject matter and technique heresy. His paintings *Olympia*, a nude courtesan, and *Luncheon on the Grass*, a nude woman and a partially dressed woman lunching in the woods with 2 clothed men (both 1863 Louvre), were thought scandalously bold. He strongly influenced the impressionists, though he did not employ their techniques and refused to exhibit with them. Another major work is *The Fife Player* (1866).

Manganese, chemical element, symbol Mn; for physical constants see Periodic Table. Manganese was discovered by J.G. Gahn in 1774. It is a steel-gray, hard, brittle, reactive, metal. The element forms many important alloys with steel, as well as with aluminum, ferromagnetic alloys, antimony, and copper. It is an essential trace element in humans and animals. Manganese and its compounds are used in dry cell batteries, paint dryers, as an oxidizing agent, and in medicine.

Mange, disease of the skin that affects domestic and farm animals. Small parasites (mites) burrow into the skin and cause inflammation. The skin is usually covered with sores, and the animal's hair falls out. There are a number of different mites that can cause mange, and the exact symptoms and severity of the disease depend on the species of mite involved. Inadequate nutrition is also an important factor. Mange is treated by pesticides and by ensuring that the animal receives a nutritious diet.

Mango, tropical evergreen tree (*Mangifera indica*) of the sumac family, and its fruit, originally from eastern Asia. The trees, which can grow to 90 ft (27 m), produce a rich yellowish-red juicy fruit with a hard pit, a staple in the tropics.

Mangosteen (*Garcinia mangostana*), tropical tree of the garcinia family, native to Southeast Asia; also, the fruit of that tree. The tree grows about 30 ft (9 m) tall, bearing large, stiff leaves and large white or pink flowers. The fruit, about 2 in (6 cm) in diameter, has a thick red-brown rind and white flesh tasting something like pineapple, peach, and tangerine.

Mangrove, evergreen tree (genus *Rhizophora*) native to tropical and subtropical coasts, estuaries, and swamps. The trunk of the mangrove produces aerial roots, which support the tree and form a mass of tangled vegetation. Its fruit, a cone-shaped berry, contains a single seed that germinates within the fruit and produces a long root that imbeds the seedling within the mud when the fruit falls. The mangrove's bark is rich in tannin.

Manhattan, one of the 5 boroughs of New York City, consisting mainly of Manhattan Island, bounded by the East River, the Harlem River, the Hudson River, and New York Bay. Peter Minuit originally bought the island from a Native American tribe, the Manhattan, for $24 worth of beads and cloth in 1626 and called it New Amsterdam. The commercial and financial center of New York City, Manhattan is linked to the other boroughs by numerous bridges, tunnels, and ferries. Its many land marks and tourist attractions include the Empire State Building, World Trade Center, Central Park, Lincoln Center, the United Nations headquarters, and Rockefeller Center. Wall Street, the financial capital of the world for much of the 20th century, is located in downtown Manhattan. In addition, Manhattan is a center of the arts. Museums such as the Metropolitan Museum of Art, the Museum of Natural History, the Museum of Modern Art, and the Guggenheim Museum house some of the world's most prized and renowned exhibits. A variety of clubs, especially in the Greenwich Village area, offer many forms of music, and the Broadway area, located in the heart of Manhattan, is considered one of the premier theater districts in the world.

Manhattan Project, wartime project begun in 1942 to develop nuclear weapons. A team headed by Enrico Fermi initiated the 1st self-sustaining nuclear chain reaction. In order to obtain the necessary amounts of the required isotopes, uranium-235 and plutonium-239, centers were established in Tennessee and Washington. Actual design and construction of the atomic bombs was carried out at Los Alamos, N.M., by a group headed by J. Robert Oppenheimer. On July 16, 1945, the first atomic bomb was detonated near Alamogordo, N.M. The following month a uranium bomb was dropped on Hiroshima (Aug. 6) and a plutonium bomb on Nagasaki (Aug. 9).

Mani *See:* Manichaeism.

Mania *See:* Mental illness.

Manic-depressive disorder, or bipolar disorder, mental illness characterized either as mania (excitement, irrational judgment, increase in activity) or depression (lethargy, feelings of worthlessness, guilt), and, in some cases, alternating between mania and depression. Treatment involves the drug lithium, to control mood swings, and anti-depressants.

Manichaeism, or Manichaeanism, religion founded by Mani (c.A.D. 216-76), a Persian sage who claimed to be the Paraclete (intercessor) promised by Christ. Mani borrowed ideas from religions such as Buddhism, Christianity, Gnosticism, and Zoroastrianism; he preached dualism (between good and evil), the continuing life of the soul, and the hope of salvation. The Magians, who opposed him and his teachings, brought about his crucifixion. St. Augustine was a Manichee in his youth. The religion survived until the 6th century in the West and until the 13th century in the East.
See also: Religion.

Manifest Destiny, phrase coined in 1845 that implied divine sanction for the United States "to overspread the continent allotted by Providence for the free development of our multiplying millions." The concept was used to justify most U.S. territorial gains, especially during the Spanish-American War.
See also: Westward movement.

Manila (pop. 1,600,000), city (founded 1571) on Manila Bay, capital of the Philippines (before 1948 and after 1976). It is the commercial, industrial, and cultural center, developed by Spanish missionaries and then taken by the United States (1898) in the Spanish-American War, and chief port of the islands. Manila was occupied by the Japanese (1942-45), nearly destroyed in the Allied attack, and almost completely rebuilt after the war. Buildings of interest include the Church of San Agustin (1606) and the Philippine Cultural Center complex. Industries include textiles, chemicals, and automobiles.

Manila hemp *See:* Abacá.

Manioc *See:* Cassava.

Manitoba, sixth largest province in Canada and easternmost of the Prairie Provinces. Manitoba is bordered by Ontario and Hudson Bay on the east, Saskatchewan on the west, Minnesota and North Dakota to the south, and the Northwest Territories to the north.

Land and climate. The province has an area of 251,000 sq mi/650,090 sq km including 39,225 sq mi/101,593 sq km of inland waterways. There are some 100,000 lakes in the province, most notably Lake Winnipeg, thirteenth largest lake in the world, as well as numerous rivers draining into Hudson Bay. Most of the province is divided by an escarpment into 2 plains regions, one of which, the Saskatchewan Plain, is Manitoba's richest farm region. About 60% of Manitoba is forested. Spruces are the most common tree, but the forests also contain balsam, fir, birches, cedars, poplars, and tamaracks. Wildlife is abundant. Manitoba has pleasant summers, but its winters are long and cold with January temperatures averaging 0ÉF/–18ÉC in the south and –20ÉF/–29ÉC in the north. About 50 in/127 cm of snow falls every year.

People. The people of Manitoba are mostly descendants of Europeans who settled in provinces, principally Scots, English, and French, but more recently also Russians, Germans, Poles, and Scandinavians. The major religious denominations are Roman Catholic and the United Church of Canada. The capital of the province is Winnipeg and more then half the population is concentrated in the city and its metropolitan area.

Economy. Manufacturing is Manitoba's largest industry, including processed foods and beverages, metal products, clothing, furniture, chemicals, and oil refining. Nickel, zinc, copper, and tantalite are mined and Manitoba's oil wells produce about 4 million barrels of oil a year. Agriculture, formerly the mainstay of the province's economy, is still one of its chief industries. Wheat is the most important crop, followed by oats, barley, flax, and rye. Wheat is also a major export. Beef cattle, dairy farming, and the fur and lumber industries also contribute to the province's economy.

History. The first European settlers to arrive in Manitoba were fur traders of the Hudson's Bay Company in 1670. French and English fur traders competed in the area until their rivalry was settled in the French and Indian War of 1763. As a result, France ceded its Canadian lands to Britain. The first farming settlement was founded by Thomas Douglas, 5th Earl of Selkirk, along the Red River in 1812. Resultant tensions between farmers and fur trappers were not resolved until 1821. The Dominion of Canada acquired the rights to land in Manitoba from the Hudson's Bay Company in 1869 and Manitoba became a province in 1870, but not before a rebellion of fur trappers and their descendants led by Louis Riel was settled. The export of wheat began in 1876. The first railroad reached Winnipeg in 1878 and rapid settlement followed. During the first half of the 20th century, agricultural expansion increased at a tremendous rate and the province's economic growth was further stimulated by the discovery of valuable mineral deposits leading, in turn, to the growth of industry and manufacturing.

Manitoba, Lake *See:* Lake Manitoba.

Manitoba, University of, major educational institution of Manitoba, in western Canada. Located in Fort Garry, a Winnipeg suburb, it was founded in 1877 and is coeducational and government-supported. The university offers undergraduate and graduate programs and degrees and consists of 4 separate colleges. There is also a branch in Winnipeg specializing in the health sciences.

Manitoulin Islands, chain of islands situated northwest of Georgian Bay and separated from the northern shore of Lake Huron by the North Channel. Manitoulin is the largest of the islands as well as being the world's largest inland island, with an area of 1,067 sq mi/2,754 sq km. Popular fishing resorts, the islands are all part of the province of Ontario except for Drummond Island, which belongs to Michigan. Manitoulin contains many lakes and is connected to Ontario by a causeway and ferry service. The Manitoulin derives from Manitou, the great god of the Chippewa.

Mann, Horace (1796-1859), U.S. educator, lawyer, and politician. As secretary of the Massachusetts Board of Education (1837-48), he revolutionized public school organization and teaching, promoting public education for all children, and established the first normal school in the United States. A member of the U.S. House of Representatives (1848-53), he became the first president of Antioch College (1852-59), and was elected to the American Hall of Fame (1900).

Mann, Thomas (1875-1955), German writer, winner of the 1929 Nobel Prize for literature. He left Germany (1933), settled in the United States (1938), and became a U.S. citizen (1944). His works include *Buddenbrooks* (1901), his first novel, which brought him fame; *Death in Venice* (1912), addressing Mann's recurring themes of the relationship between art and neurosis and the challenge to the values of an artist in a bourgeois society; and *The Magic Mountain* (1924), his major work. He denounced fascism in *The Order of the Day* (1942), a political writing. His later works include *Doctor Faustus* (1947) and *Confessions of Felix Krull* (1954).

Manned Spacecraft Center *See:* Johnson Space Center.

Mannerheim, Carl Gustaf Emil von (1867-1951), Finnish soldier and president (1944-46). He successfully led the Finnish nationalists against the Russo-Finnish communists in 1918. He also led the Finish forces in the Russo-Finnish War (1939-40), holding the *Mannerheim Line* of defense, which he planned, on the Karelian Isthmus until 1940, when the Soviets broke through.
See also: Finland.

Mannerism, artistic and architectural style (c.1520-1600) developed in Bologna, Florence, and Rome as a reaction to the classical principles of the Renaissance. Exaggeration of form, and strained and unbalanced proportions, such as those in the Uffizi Palace and Laurentian Library in Florence (planned by Vasari and Michelangelo respectively) were the trademarks of the Mannerists. Other Mannerist artists were Parmigiano, Pontormo, Tintoretto, and El Greco; sculptors were Cellini, Bologna, and Goujon of France. They confused scale and spatial relationships, used harsh lighting, and depicted bizarre forms. The end of the 16th century the Baroque replaced Mannerism.

Manners and customs *See:* Custom; Etiquette.

Mannheim (pop. 312,000), city in southwestern Germany, one of Europe's major inland ports. Founded in the early 1600s, it is situated near the junction of the Rhine and Neckar rivers in the heart of a major industrial region. It has also been a center for art, music, and drama since the 1700s and is the site of a major university containing striking examples of Baroque architecture. Heavily damaged in World War II, Mannheim was extensively rebuilt. Cultural sights include the National Theatre and several art museums.
See also: Germany.

Man-of-war bird *See:* Frigatebird.

Manometer, instrument for measuring the pressure of gases and vapors, especially those too low to be measured by a pressure gauge. A sphygmomanometer is used by doctors to measure blood pressure in the arteries.
See also: Barometer.

Manorialism, socio-economic system of Europe in the early Middle Ages. It was a decentralized form of government that replaced the central authority of the Roman Empire and continued until the revival of commerce in the towns and cities in the later Middle Ages. Centering around a powerful lord who owned a large estate (manor), manorialism depended on peasants to work the land for the lord and themselves in exchange for protection and their homes.
See also: Middle Ages.

Man o' War, U.S. racehorse. Known as "Big Red," he won 20 of 21 races, including the Belmont and Preakness stakes, in 1920 (he was not entered in the Kentucky Derby). His prize money amounted to a then-record $249,465.

Man Ray *See:* Ray, Man.

Mansa Musa (?-1337?), ruler of the Mali Empire (1312-37?). During his reign, Mali was the most powerful empire of West Africa, and the cities of Gao and Timbuktu became centers of learning, justice, trade, and culture. As a Muslim, Mansa Musa made a flamboyant pilgrimage to Mecca in 1324, bringing back scholars to help educate his people and architects to design the mosques of his cities.
See also: Mali Empire.

Mansfield, Katherine (Kathleen Beauchamp; 1888-1923), New Zealand-born English writer. Known foremost as a master of the short story, collections include *Bliss* (1920), *The Garden Party* (1922), and *Something Childish* (1924).

Manship, Paul (1885-1966), U.S. sculptor best known for his interpretations of classical mythological subjects, among which is his statue *Prometheus* (1934) at Rockefeller Center, New York City.

Manslaughter, in U.S. criminal law, unlawful but unpremeditated killing of another human being. In many states 2 kinds of manslaughter are defined: *voluntary*, where injury is intended, as in a killing arising out of a quarrel; and *involuntary*, where there is no such intent, such as death caused by reckless driving. The penalty for manslaughter in the United States ranges from 1 to 14 years in prison.
See also: Crime.

Manta ray *See:* Ray.

Mantegna, Andrea (1431-1506), Italian painter and engraver. He was a member of the Paduan school, acclaimed for his mastery of anatomy and illusionistic perspective, and was attracted to the antique, as evidenced in his collection of Greek and Roman works. Among his most famous works are the altarpiece at St. Luke's (Milan), the bridal chamber of the Gonzaga palace (Mantua), where the illusion of sky on the ceiling was widely copied during the Baroque period; and the cartoons of the *Triumph of Caesar* (1495). Also known for his copper-plate engravings and drawings, Mantegna was influential in the development of printing. His initial letters for *Geography*, by Strabo, recaptured the Roman art of inscription.

Mantid, or praying mantis, large predatory insect of the Mantidae family (or order Mantodea). Most species are native to tropical and subtropical climates, although some, including varieties that have been introduced in North America, are found in temperate zones. The nickname "praying mantis" is suggested by the posture of its front legs and by its gentle swaying movement. Mantids measure 2-5 in (5-13 cm) and tend to resemble the green or brown twigs on which they perch, camouflaging them from both predators and insect or other prey. Females are known for their practice of eating males during or after mating. Mantids are harmless to humans and are sometimes useful in consuming insect pests.

Mantle, Mickey (1931-   ), U.S. baseball player. Primarily an outfielder, he played for the New York Yankees (1951-68), hitting 536 home runs, 18 of them during World Series play. A switch-hitter (both right- and left-handed), he led the American League in 1956 with an average of .353 and 52 home runs and was voted the league's most valuable player 3 times (1956, 57, 62). Mantle was inducted into the National Hall of Fame in 1974.

Mantra, in Hinduism and Buddhism, sacred utterance believed to possess supernatural power. The constant repetition of a mantra is used to concentrate the mind on an object of meditation, e.g., the syllable *om*, said to evoke the entire Veda.

Manu, in Hindu mythology, the lawgiver. Compiled into the *Manu Smriti* (*Code of Manu*) between 200 B.C. and A.D. 200 , these laws delineated the classes (castes) in Hindu society and formed the basis for the life plan of all

Hindus in 4 stages. It also set forth the goals they are expected to attain during those 4 stages.

Manuelito (1818?-1893), Navajo tribal leader. In the 1860s he led the Navajos in their fight against white settlers encroaching on their territory in what is now northern Arizona. Manuelito's forces were defeated by the United States Army (led by Kit Carson), which was sent in to help the settlers, and Manuelito surrendered in 1866. Two years later the Navajo Reservation was set aside in parts of Arizona, Utah, and New Mexico, and Manuelito led the tribal police force founded in 1872.

Manuscript, document or work written by hand as distinguished from those typewritten or printed (although the typescript of a book is often called the author's manuscript).

The oldest manuscripts are on papyrus, made from the papyrus plant, the writing material of ancient Egypt and also used in ancient Greece and Rome until superseded by parchment. The earliest surviving papyrus manuscript dates from about 3500 B.C. The Egyptians first wrote with brushes, using ink made from lampblack and water; later they used reed pens. They pasted their papyrus sheets together to make long rolls. Those of the *Book of the Dead*, the earliest known illustrated manuscript, are more than 100 ft (30.5 m) long. Wax tablets were also extensively used for manuscript writing in the ancient world.

Parchment, or vellum—made from the skins of sheep and other animals and more durable than papyrus—was first used in Pergamum in the 2nd century B.C., but did not come into general use in Europe until about A.D. 300. Some types (palimpsests) could be washed or scraped and used again or even a third time (double palimpsests). The illumination (ornamentation and illustration) of manuscripts was developed by the medieval monastic schools of Europe.

In the Far East paper (invented by the Chinese about A.D. 100), silk, bamboo, and palm leaves were used as writing materials. Paper did not reach Europe until the 11th century and did not begin to supplant parchment until the 1400s. Even after the development of printing, parchment was used for legal and other special documents.

Manzanita, ornamental shrub (*Arctostaphylos tomentosa*), of the heath family. Native to the Pacific Coast of the United States and Canada, manzanita is an evergreen that reaches heights of 20 ft (6 m). It produces pink or white bell-shaped flowers and bright red berries and is cultivated for its decorative value.

Manzoni, Alessandro (1785-1873), Italian novelist and poet. He was a leading figure in the romantic movement, and his novel *The Betrothed* (1825-26) influenced Italian prose writers. Among his poems is the well-received *Fifth of May* (1821), on Napoleon's death. His own death inspired Verdi's *Requiem* (1874).

Maori, original inhabitants of New Zealand. Of Polynesian origin, they settled New Zealand between 800 and 1350 and were hunters and farmers. They lived in small villages of communal homes and each village shared a common ancestry. In the 1860s they fought the English colonists and lost most of their lands. Today many still practice the old customs and speak the Maori tongue, a language related to Tahitian and Hawaiian.

Mao Tse-tung *See:* Mao Zedong.

Mao Zedong (1893-1976), founder of the People's Republic of China. Born to an educated peasant in Hunan province, he joined the newly founded Shanghai Communist Party in 1921, and in 1927 led the Autumn Harvest uprising, which was crushed by the local Kuomintang militia, Mao fled to the mountains, where he built up the Red Army and established rural soviets. Surrounded by Kuomintang forces in 1934, the army was forced to embark on the famous Long March from Jiangxi to Yan'an in Shoanxi province. The appalling rigors of the march united the communists behind Mao, and he was elected chairman. In 1937 an uneasy alliance was made with the Kuomintang under Chiang Kai-Shek against the Japanese; after World War II Mao's forces expelled the Kuomintang to Taiwan. Mao then became chairman of the new People's Republic. In 1958 he turned his attentions to industrial growth, with his program the Great Leap Forward. Its failure spurred his replacement as chairman of the party, but he retained party leadership. He later (1966-69) attacked the chairman, Liu Shao-Sh'i, by organizing the Cultural Revolution, which created widespread agitation and led to a consolidation of Mao's power in the 1970s. Mao steered China ideologically away from the USSR and his teachings came to have great influence in the Third World. He appeared to favor a decree of deténte with the West, especially Europe, and in 1972 met with President Nixon, signaling closer relations with the United States.

Map, representation on a flat surface of part or all of the earth's surface, or of another spherical body, showing each point and feature on a predetermined reduced scale and in accordance with a definite projection. Globes provide the most accurate representation of the earth, with regard to area, scale, shape, and direction. Any flat map will create some distortion. The making and study of maps is called cartography. Of the many different kinds of maps, those for general reference include physical maps (relief and natural features) and political maps (national borders, administrative divisions, cities, and towns). Thematic maps include economic maps, (industrial centers, transportation routes and so on); demographic maps (distribution of the population); geological maps (classifying and dating the surface rocks); meteorological maps (information about climatic zones, rainfall, air pressures, and temperatures); historical maps and the road maps for tourists. There are also celestial and stellar maps showing the planets, stars, and constellations. Maps used for sea and aerial navigation are called charts.

Maple, common name for the deciduous trees and shrubs of the genus *Acer*, found throughout the Northern Hemisphere. Maples, which are characterized by their winged seeds, are noted for the breathtaking colors they produce in the fall. The North American sugar maple (*A. saccharum*) and the black maple (*A. nigrum*) are 2 of the species that provide the close-grained hardwood used for furniture making; they are also tapped to produce maple syrup. Two other members of the genus are the swamp, or red, maple (*A. rubrum*) and the box elder (*A. negundo*) tapped to produce maple syrup.

Maputo (pop. 544,700), capital (1907) and largest city of Mozambique. Founded around 1780 by Portuguese colonists, it was called Lourenço Marques until 1976, the year after Mozambique gained independence. Maputo is located on the Indian Ocean and is a popular beach resort. It also serves as a rail terminal for several of southern Africa's landlocked nations who ship their goods through Maputo's harbor.

Marabou, large stork (*Leptoptilos crumeni-ferous*) with a heavy bill, naked head and neck, and a pink, fleshy pouch dangling from its neck. Marabous, found in many parts of Africa, are scavengers and feed on refuse and carrion.

Maracaibo (pop. 1,152,000), city in northwestern Venezuela. Located on the shore of Lake Maracaibo, it is the capital of the state of Zulia and the hub of the nation's petroleum industry. Maracaibo was founded by the Spanish in 1571 and experienced a population boom after the discovery of oil in the lake in 1912. It is also a major coffee and seafood exporting port.

Marajó, Brazilian island in the mouth of the Amazon River. With an area of 15,500 sq mi (40,000 sq km), Marajó lies between the Amazon to the north, the Rio Pará to the south, and the Atlantic Ocean to the east. The island is flooded by river overflow 6 months of the year, and cattle and water buffalo graze the grasslands left by the flooding during the dry season.

Marat, Jean Paul (1743-93), French Revolutionary politician. A doctor and journalist, he founded the journal *L'Ami du peuple* at the onset of the Revolution. His vociferous attacks on those in power led to outlaw status and flight to England (1790, 1791). He continued to publish in secret and was elected to the National Convention in 1792, a leader of the radical faction. Chief instigator of the September Massacre (1792) in which over 1,200 died, he was an active supporter of the Jacobins and their Reign of Terror. Marat was murdered in his bath by Charlotte Corday.
See also: French Revolution.

Marathon, village and plain northeast of Athens, Greece, site of an Athenian victory (490 B.C.) over the Persians. The runner Pheidippides carried a report of the victory to Athens, after which he collapsed and died. The modern Olympic Games (1896) standardized the marathon race at 26 mi, 385 yd (42.2 km) in 1908. Boston and New York City each hold annual marathons, attracting thousands of runners.
See also: Greece.

Marble, rock form of limestone consisting of crystals of calcite or dolomite. Marble is formed when limestone is *metamorphosed* (changed by great heat and pressure) so that the rock is recrystallized and hardened. Pure marble, which is snow-white in color, has been prized by sculptors and architects since ancient times. Some of the finest marble comes from the Carrara quarries in Italy, and in the United States, from Vermont. Marble often contains impurities, which affect is color. Exposed to acid fumes and water, marble will corrode.

Marble bones *See:* Osteosclerosis.

Marbury v. Madison, U.S. Supreme Court case decided in 1803. William Marbury sued James Madison, then secretary of state, for failure to deliver a federal appointment promised by the previous administration. Chief Justice Marshall held that the act upon which this case relied was unconstitutional. This was the first decision to invalidate an act of Congress and established the judicial right to review, greatly expanding the power of the judiciary.

Marc, Franz (1880-1916), German expressionist painter, with Wassily Kandinsky a cofounder of the Blaue Reiter group. His work is characterized by vigorous lines and a vivid, symbolic use of color.

Marceau, Marcel (1923-), French mime. Marceau studied drama in Paris and rose to fame with a brief mime role in the film *Les Enfants du Paradis* (1944). His best-known characterization is the white-faced clown Bip. He became world famous with stage appearances in the 1950s.

Marcel, Gabriel (1889-1973), 20th-century French philosopher. A Christian existentialist, Marcel stressed the value of understanding life through human experience. His best-known books include *Metaphysical Journals* (1927), *Being and Having* (1935), *Homo Viator* (1945), *Man Against Society* (1951), and *Presence and Immortality* (1959).
See also: Existentialism.

March, Peyton Conway (1864-1955), U.S. Army general and chief of staff during World War I. Often credited with modernizing and streamlining the army and Department of War, March was responsible for landing 1.2 million U.S. troops in France. A West Point graduate (1888), he fought in the Spanish-American War and was in charge of United States artillery forces in France prior to being named chief of staff.
See also: World War I.

Marciano, Rocky (Rocco Marchegiano; 1923-69), U.S. boxer, considered to be one of the most powerful punchers of all time. Marciano won the heavyweight championship by knocking out Jersey Joe Walcott in the 13th round (1952), and successfully defended his title until his retirement in 1956. He is the only major prizefighter to have remained undefeated throughout his professional career, fighting 49 bouts in 9 years, winning 43 by knockout. He was killed in a plane crash.

Marcion (d. A.D. 160), founder of a heretical Christian sect. He joined the church in Rome c.140 but was excommunicated in 144. Influenced by gnosticism, he taught that there were 2 rival Gods: one, the tyrannical creator and lawgiver of the Old Testament; the other, the unknown God of love and mercy who sent Jesus to purchase salvation from the creator God. Marcion rejected almost the complete bible. This forced the orthodox church to fix its canon of Scripture. Marcionism spread widely but by the end of the 3rd century had mostly been absorbed by Manichaeism.
See also: Christianity.

Marconi, Guglielmo (1874-1937), Italian physicist, awarded (with K.F. Braun) the 1909 Nobel Prize in physics for his work in devising a wireless telegraph. By 1895 he could transmit and receive signals at distances of about

1.2 mi (2 km). On Dec. 12, 1901, in St. John's, Newfoundland, he successfully received the first transatlantic radio communication.
See also: Telegraph.

Marco Polo *See:* Polo, Marco.

Marcos, Ferdinand Edralin (1917-89), president of the Philippines (1965-
86). In 1972 Marcos declared martial law in the country and in 1973, under
a new constitution, he assumed near-dictatorial authority. Although he lifted
martial law in 1981, he retained certain broad martial-law powers. Anti-Mar-
cos forces attracted worldwide attention in Aug. 1983 when returning
opposition leader Benigno Aquino was murdered at the Manila airport while
in government custody.
In Feb. 1986 Marcos was reelected president in an election marked by
demonstrations and charges of fraud. His main opponent, Corazon Aquino,
the widow of Benigno, refused to recognize the results of the election. After
continued popular demonstrations against the government, Marcos and his
wife, Imelda, left the country on Feb. 25th to settle in Hawaii. Corazon
Aquino replaced him as president. Both Marcos and his wife were indicted
by the U.S. government on charges that they embezzled from the Philippine
treasury to purchase assets for themselves in the United States. Marcos
proved too ill to stand trial and charges against him were dropped; he died
in Hawaii. Court actions against Imelda continued into 1991 and ultimately
resulted in her acquittal.
See also: Philippines.

Marcus Aurelius (Marcus Aelius Aurelius Antoninus; 121-180), Roman
emperor and philosopher. Adopted at 17 by his uncle Antoninus Pius, he
succeeded him as emperor in 161, after a distinguished career in public
service. During this time he wrote *Meditations*, his spiritual philosophy and
a classic work of stoicism. His reign was marred by plague, rebellion,
barbarian attacks along the Rhine and Danube, and his own persecution of
Christians, considered at that time to be the chief enemies of the empire. His
government was otherwise noted for social reform, justice, and generosity.
See also: Rome, Ancient.

Marcuse, Herbert (1898-1979), German-born U.S. political philosopher
who combined Freudianism and Marxism in his social criticism. According
to Marcuse, modern society is automatically repressive and requires violent
revolution as the first step toward a Utopian society. He became a cult figure
of the New Left in the United States in the 1960s. His works include *Eros
and Civilization* (1954) and *One Dimensional Man* (1964).
See also: Philosophy; Utopia.

Mardi Gras (French, "fat Tuesday"), festivities prior to and on Shrove
Tuesday, the last day of carnival before the start of Lent. Celebrated as a
holiday in various Catholic countries, it was introduced into the United States
by French settlers and is most notably observed in New Orleans.
See also: Shrove Tuesday.

Marduk, highest god of ancient Babylon. Called "lord of the gods of heaven
and earth," Marduk rose to power by conquering Tiamat, the monster of

chaos. Some of Babylon's most elaborate temples were built to worship Marduk, and, as the conquering armies of the empire overran most of the Middle East, worship of Marduk spread to those lands.
See also: Babylon.

Mariana Islands, group of islands (184 sq mi/476.6 sq km) in the West Pacific, east of the Philippines. Discovered by Magellan in 1521 and owned by Spain until surrendered to the United States, in 1898, they were named the Ladrones (Thieves) Islands until renamed in 1668 by Jesuit missionaries. They were briefly under Japanese occupation (1941-44) and became part of the United Nations Trust Territory of the Pacific Islands in 1947. In 1978 the northern islands became the Northern Mariana Islands and a commonwealth of the United States. The majority of the population lives on the largest and southernmost island, Guam, an outlying U.S. territory. The group's economy rests on subsistence agriculture, copra export, and government and military installations.

Mariana Trench, world's deepest discovered submarine trench 210 mi (338 km) southwest of Guam. More than 1,500 mi (2,414 km) long, it averages over 40 mi (64 km) in width and has a maximum known depth of 36,201 ft (1,034 m).

Maria Theresa (1717-80), archduchess of Austria, queen of Hungary and Bohemia (1740-80), and wife of Holy Roman Emperor Francis I. As a result of the Pragmatic Sanction of 1713, she acquired the Habsburg lands upon the death of her father, Emperor Charles VI (1740); the War of the Austrian Succession, in which she lost Silesia to Prussia but gained the election of her husband, Francis of Lorraine, as emperor, was immediately launched against her. She later allied with France in the Seven Years War against Prussia but was defeated. A capable ruler, she introduced administrative, agrarian, and fiscal reforms and maintained a strong army. After 1765 she shared her powers with son Joseph II, one of 16 children, including Marie Antoinette of France and Emperor Leopold II.

Marie Antoinette (1755-93), queen of France from 1774. Daughter of Maria Theresa and the Emperor Francis I, she married the Dauphin in 1770 to strengthen ties between Austria and France and became queen on his accession as Louis XVI. The unpopular, unconsummated (for 7 yrs) marriage and youthful extravagances made her many enemies, as did her involvement in several scandals. When the French Revolution broke out she advised the attempted escape of the royal family, which ended with its capture at Varennes. She began her own negotiations, independent of her husband, first with comte de Mirabeau, later with Antoine Barnave, and even asked for Austrian intervention in France, to no avail. Imprisoned with Louis, her son, Louis XVIII, taken from her, she was guillotined 9 months after the king, in Oct. 1793.
See also: French Revolution; Louis.

Marie Louise (1791-1847), empress of France (1810-15). Eldest daughter of Francis II of Austria, she married Napoleon after he divorced Josephine (1810) and was the mother of Napoleon II. After Napoleon's exile she became duchess of Parma.

Marigold, annual plant (genus *Tagetes*) with fragrant orange or yellow flowers, native to Central and South America. Two common species, native to Guatemala and Mexico, are the African marigold (*T. erecta*) and the French marigold (*T. patula*).

Marihuana *See:* Marijuana.

Marijuana, or marihuana, nonaddictive drug derived from the hemp plant (*Cannabis sativa*). It is usually smoked, but can also be sniffed or taken as food. It is mainly used for the mild euphoria it produces; other symptoms include loss of muscular coordination, increased heart beat, drowsiness, and hallucination. The most potent form of the drug is hashish. Marijuana's use, the subject of much medical and social debate, is widespread throughout the world. In the United States, use of the drug has been prohibited by federal law since 1937.

Marin, John (1870-1953), U.S. painter and print maker best known for his expressionistic watercolors of Manhattan and the Maine coast. Among his works are *Singer Building* (1921) and *Maine Islands* (1922).

Marine biology, study of the flora and fauna of the sea, from the smallest plankton to massive whales. It includes the study of the complex interrelationship between different marine organisms and between the organisms and their environment. Through experiments with marine organisms, marine biologists can increase our knowledge of human reproduction and development and the nervous system. Scientists have also discovered substances in certain marine animals, such as sponges and seaweeds, that may be used in treating cancer, infections, and pneumonia. These substances might possibly be used as commercial drugs in the future.

Marine Corps, U.S., armed service within the Department of the Navy providing troops trained for land, sea, and air operations. The Corps was founded by the Continental Congress in 1775 and established by act of Congress on July 11, 1798. It served in the Revolutionary War, the naval war with France (1798-1801), and the war with Tripoli (1801-05). Nearly 79,000 Marines served in World War I, and over 475,000 fought in World War II. They played a major role in the Pacific theater in World War II, first with their heroic stands at Wake Island, Guam, Bataan, Corregidor, and Midway and later with the assault at Guadalcanal and the Pacific campaign. Subsequently the Corps fought in Korea (1950-53), preserved order in Lebanon in 1958 and the 1980s, ended fighting in the Dominican Republic in 1965, and served in the Vietnam War (1965-73) and the Persian Gulf War (1991). Between 1943 and 1945, the Marine Corps Women's Reserve numbered over 23,000. With the passing of the Women's Armed Services Integration Act in 1948, the women reservists became full-fledged members of the regular Marine Corps.

Marion, Francis (c.1732-95), guerilla leader in the American Revolutionary War. Commander of the South Carolina troops, he fought at Charleston in 1776. In 1780 he and his men were forced to take refuge in the swamps, from which they waged ceaseless guerilla warfare on Loyalist farms and on British troops, who nicknamed Marion "the Swamp Fox." He served in the state senate (1782-90).
See also: Revolutionary War in America.

Marionette *See:* Puppet.

Mariposa lily, or sego lily (genus *Calochortus*), tuliplike member of the lily family. Taking its name from the Spanish word for butterfly, mariposa lilies bloom in spring in the sandy soil of Western United States. They are perennials, growing from bulbs, and range in color from white or purple to yellow or orange. There are about 60 species, 40 of which are native to the U.S.

Maris, Roger (1934-85), U.S. baseball player. In 1961, Maris made sports history by hitting 61 home runs, breaking Babe Ruth's single season home run mark of 60 set in 1927. Because Maris hit his home runs during a 162-game schedule and Ruth his during a 154-game schedule, both totals are considered records. Maris was also named the American league's most valuable player twice (1960, 61). He played outfield for the Cleveland Indians (1957-58), Kansas City Athletics (1958-59), New York Yankees (1960-66), and St. Louis Cardinals (1967-68).

Marisol (Marisol Escobar; 1930-), Venezuelan-born U.S. sculptor who satirizes and caricatures human society by creating Pop Art-type figures, usually from wood and clay. Reminiscent of South American folk art, her sculptures are stark representations, with many of the details drawn on them.

Maritain, Jacques (1882-1973), leading French neo-Thomist philosopher. He turned to the study of Thomism, the system of philosophy developed by St. Thomas, after his conversion to Catholicism in 1906. He was professor of modern philosophy at the Catholic Institute, Paris (1914-39) and French ambassador to the Vatican (1945-48).
See also: Philosophy.

Maritime law, body of law, based on custom, court decisions, and statutes, seeking to regulate all aspects of shipping and ocean commerce, such as insurance, salvage, and contracts for carriage of goods by sea. It is international to the extent that firm general principles exist, but these have no legal force except as they are incorporated by individual countries into their own legal systems; they are often modified in the process. Many derive from decisions of medieval maritime courts. In the United States, maritime law is administered by the federal district courts.

Maritime Provinces *See:* Atlantic Provinces.

Marius, Gaius (157-86 B.C.), Roman general and politician. After successes on the battlefield, he was elected consul 7 times between 107 and 86 B.C.
See also: Rome, Ancient.

Marivaux, Pierre (1688-1763), French playwright and novelist, best known for his witty comedies. Sparkling dialogue is still termed *marivaudage*. Among his works are the comedy *The Game of Love and Chance* (1730) and the novel *The Successful Peasant* (1735-36).

Marjoram, perennial herb of the mint family, native to the Mediterranean region and Asia. It is cultivated in the United States for flavoring foods and for use in toilet soaps. Sweet marjoram is *Marjorana hortensis*. Common marjoram (*Origanum vulgare*) is also called oregano.

Mark Antony *See:* Antony, Marc.

Mark, Saint, or John Mark (fl. 1st century A.D.), Christian evangelist and traditional author of the second Gospel, which derived information from St.Peter in Rome. Mark accompanied Barnabas (his cousin) and Paul on their missionary journeys. His feast day is Apr. 25.
See also: Christianity.

Marketing, refers to all activities concerned with the flow of goods and services from the producer to the consumer. It includes the various physical movements of the product including the pricing, wholesaling, transporting, and retailing of the product. It also involves packaging, design, and advertising. Marketing may be said to include everything that has to do with *how* a product is sold. In earlier times, when economic activities were simpler, people concentrated on the actual manufacture of the product. The business of taking it to a market and selling it was relatively simple. Today, with a huge range of products to choose from (often almost indistinguishable from each other) marketing is an important operation. Most companies employ a team of people, working under a marketing director, to plan the marketing of a product. They have to decide, on the basis of market surveys, just what the consumer wants. Then they design and package the product to match the requirements of the consumer. Marketing decisions involve a whole complex of considerations: what country and climate, for example, the product will be sold in; which social groupings among the population will buy it; how it will be distributed—through supermarkets, department stores, or mail order; and whether, and how, it should be advertised.
Marketing plays a vital role in ensuring prosperity since, it is argued, consumers are given what they want at a convenient location and packaged in the most efficient way possible. On the other hand,however, there is the objection that too much money is spent on marketing and that it is sometimes more concerned with persuading people that they need a certain product, rather than finding out what they want.

Market research, process of gathering and analyzing information for marketing decision making. It dates back to the early 20th century in the United States before spreading to Europe and Japan. Business employs market research to identify customers (markets) for its products, to analyze their needs (through such techniques as polls and surveys), and to suggest strategies to develop interest among those customers for their products.

Markham, Edwin (1852-1940), U.S. poet and lecturer whose poem of social protest, "The Man with the Hoe" (1899), based on a painting by Millet, brought him a fortune and worldwide acclaim.

Markova, Dame Alicia (1910-), leading English ballerina. She was a member of Sergei Diaghilev's Ballets Russes (1925-29) and became a prima ballerina with London's Vic-Wells Ballet in 1932. She founded her own company with Anton Dolin in 1935. This grew into the London Festival

Ballet, which they headed from 1944-52. She also directed the Metropolitan Opera Ballet (1963-69) and taught at the University of Cincinnati (1969-74).

Marlborough, Duke of (John Churchill; 1650-1722), English soldier and politician, one of the country's greatest generals. He helped suppress the Duke of Monmouth's rebellion (1685) for James II, but in 1688 transferred his allegiance to William of Orange, who made him an earl and a member of the Privy Council. His wife, Sarah Churchill, was the closest friend and attendant of Princess (later Queen) Anne; together they had great influence with the queen. After Anne's accession in 1702 Marlborough commanded English, Dutch, and German forces in the war of the Spanish Succession. In 1704 he won a great victory over the French at Blenheim. Further victories followed at Ramillies (1706), Oudenarde (1708), and Malplaquet (1709). His wife fell from favor with the queen in 1711, and Marlborough was dismissed; in 1714, however, he was restored to favor by George I.
See also: United Kingdom.

Marlin, gamefish related to the sailfish and the swordfish, found in warm oceans. The marlin is armed with a long spike extending from its upper jaw. Most marlins weigh 50-400 lb (23-180 kg), although the blue marlin (genus *Makira*) can reach 1,000 lb (454 kg).

Marlowe, Christopher (1564-93), English poet and dramatist, a major influence on William Shakespeare. He developed the use of dramatic blank verse. His best-known plays are *Tamburlaine the Great* (c. 1587); *Dr. Faustus* (c. 1588), in which he developed a new concept of tragedy, that of a heroic character doomed to failure because of his ambition and power; and *Edward II* (c.1593). He also wrote the unfinished long poem *Hero and Leander* (1598) and the lyric "The Pastoral Shepherd to His Love."

Marmara, Sea of, sea between the Asian and European sections of Turkey. It is connected to the Black Sea on the northeast by the Bosporus and to the Aegean Sea on the southwest by the Dardanelles. The sea covers 4,300 sq mi (11,100 sq km) and is a key waterway for the passage of ships between the Mediterranean and the southern ports of the former USSR.

Marmoset, the world's smallest monkey, usually growing to less than 1 ft (30 cm) long. It is a member of the family Callitrichidae. Some marmosets have striking ear tufts. The pygmy marmoset (*Cebuella pygmaea*) is 5.5 to 6.25 in (14-16 cm). Marmosets live in the forests of South America, feeding on insects, leaves, and fruit.

Marmot, large round squirrel (genus *Marmota*) found in much of the Northern Hemisphere. Marmots dig burrows, where they hibernate in winter, and live in colonies. Most live in hill country, although the woodchuck, or groundhog (*M. monox*), prefers open areas. Marmots grow from 1-2 ft (30-61 cm) long.

Marne, Battles of the, two World War I battles fought in the Marne River area of France. In the first (Sept. 1914), the German advance on Paris was halted by an Allied offensive. The second (July 1918) countered the last German offensive.
See also: World War I.

Marne River, chief tributary of the Seine River, France, rising on the Langres Plateau of eastern France and flowing through 310 mi (500 km) of rich farmland before joining the Seine southeast of Paris. Several key battles fought there during World War I saved Paris from being overrun by the German army.

Marquand, J(ohn) P(hillips) (1893-1960), U.S. novelist best known for his detective stories centered on the Japanese agent Mr. Moto and for his gentle satires of New England society, such as *The Late George Apley* (1937), for which he won a Pulitzer Prize, and *Point of No Return* (1949).

Marquesas Islands, 2 clusters of mountainous and volcanic islands in the South Pacific, about 900 mi (1,400 km) northeast of Tahiti. The islands are governed by France. Their total area is about 492 sq mi (1,274 sq km). The largest islands are Hiva Oa and Nuku Hiva. The population is made up mainly of Polynesians. The islands are fertile, producing breadfruit, coffee, vanilla, and copra (dried coconut meat) for export.

Marquette, Jacques (1637-75), French Jesuit missionary and explorer. With Louis Joliet he traced the course of the Mississippi River, discovering that it flowed into the Gulf of Mexico (1673).
See also: Jesuits.

Marrakech, or Marrakesh (pop. 332,700), city of southwestern Morocco, near the Atlas Mtns. Founded in 1062, Marrakech was the capital of the Berber Empire and a center of commerce and culture in the 15th century. It was captured by the French in 1912. Marrakech is a popular tourist attraction for its fine examples of Islamic architecture and its outdoor markets (*souks*). It is also a food-processing and leather manufacturing center.
See also: Morocco.

Marriage, union between man and woman for the purpose of cohabitation and usually also for raising children. The modern trend is towards monogamy, union between one man and one woman only. Many societies still permit polygamy, but it is increasingly rare. Forms of group and communal marriage have been tried from time to time, though with little success or social acceptance.
Marriage is in some senses a contract, often involving property and in some societies a dowry. In U.S. law marriage creates special ownership rights in marital property. It is still also a religious matter in many countries; marriage is a minor sacrament of the Roman Catholic Church.
Most societies limit marriage in certain ways. It is forbidden in most countries between partners who have too close a blood relationship, although the degree permissible varies widely among countries, religions, and U.S. states. In U.S. common law a purported marriage involving bigamy is void; other conditions, such as non-consummation, render marriage void or voidable, generally through the courts. A marriage is also void if not carried out in the prescribed legal form, although in some states common law marriage may arise after long cohabitation without any formality. Most societies have some provision for divorce. Marriages in the U.S. are performed either by a civil authority or by a religious ceremony with civil authorization; the ceremonies of most denominations are so authorized in most states. In general, a marriage

valid in one state is recognized in the others. Some states require banns to be posted.

Marryat, Frederick (1792-1848), English author. An officer in the British Navy who spent 24 years at sea, Marryat's books all had maritime adventure themes. His best-known works are *Frank Mildmay* (1829), *The King's Own* (1830), and *Mr. Midshipman Easy* (1836).

Mars, the fourth planet from the Sun, with a mean solar distance of 141.6 million mi (227.9 million km) and a mean diameter of 4,223 mi (6,796 km). Mars takes about 687 earth-days to orbit the Sun. The planet's temperature ranges from −191° to 81°F (−124° to 27°C), and its tenuous atmosphere consists mainly of carbon dioxide. The distinctive Martian polar caps are composed of frozen carbon dioxide and water ice.
Telescopically, Mars appears as an ocher-red disk marked by extensive dark areas; these latter have in the past been erroneously termed *maria* (seas). Several observers in the past reported sighting networks of straight lines on the Martian surface—the famous canals—but observations with large telescopes and the photographs sent back by the United States' Mariner (1965, 1969, 1971) and Viking (1976) space probes showed these to be an optical illusion. Mars actually has a cratered surface marked with canyons, ancient volcanoes, and jumbled terrains.
No probe has yet found evidence that life ever existed on the planet. Mars has 2 satellites (moons), Phobos and Deimos. In 1996 scientists of NASA, Lockheed Martin, and universities in Montreal, Georgia, and Stanford announced they had found fossil traces on a meteorite from Mars. These traces could be the result of early biological activity on Mars. Although this discovery was not seen as evidence of life on Mars, it led to other meteorites from Mars being studied more closely.
See also: Planet; Solar System.

Mars, in Roman mythology, the god of war. He was originally the god of agriculture, but later was identified with Ares, the Greek god of war. Second in importance only to his father, Jupiter, Mars had several children by Venus and was also regarded as the father of Romulus, legendary founder of Rome. His altar on the Campus Martius was the scene of festivals in Mar. (his month) and Oct.
See also: Mythology.

Marseille (pop. 807,700), second largest city in France, located in the southeastern part of the country. It serves as France's chief seaport and is a major industrial center. The oldest city in France, was settled by the Greeks c.600 B.C. and annexed by Rome in 49 B.C. The city's expansion began with the conquest of Algeria and the opening of the Suez Canal in the 19th century. Marseille's port handles about one third of French maritime trade.

Marsh, flat wetland area characterized by grassy plant growth. Distinguished from swamps where trees grow, marshes often occur in coastal regions where tidal flows add salt water to fresh water, usually at the mouths of rivers (estuarine marshes). Freshwater marshes occur in low-lying inland areas and both types of marshes are home to a wide variety of fish and wildlife.

Marshall, Alfred (1842-1924), English economist, professor of political economy at Cambridge (1885-1908). His *Principles of Economics* (1890) systematized economic thought up to that time and was the standard text for many years. Through his work on cost, and value, and distribution Marshall developed a concept of marginal utility.

Marshall, George Catlett (1880-1959), U.S. general and politician. As chief of staff (1939-45) he influenced Allied strategy in World War II. As secretary of state (1947-49) under President Harry S. Truman, he introduced the European Recovery Program, or Marshall Plan, for which he was awarded the 1953 Nobel Peace Prize. As U.S. secretary of defense (1950-51), he was active in the creation of the North Atlantic Treaty Organization (NATO).
See also: Marshall Plan; North Atlantic Treaty Organization.

Marshall, James Wilson (1810-85), discoverer of gold in California. On Jan. 24, 1848, while building a sawmill for John Sutter on the American River, Marshall found several gold nuggets in the water. Word of the discovery spread quickly and triggered the California Gold Rush of 1849.
See also: Gold Rush.

Marshall, John (1755-1835), fourth chief justice of the United States, known as the "Great Chief Justice." He established the modern status of the Supreme Court. He served in the Revolutionary War, studied law, and was elected to the Virginia legislature in 1782. A staunch Federalist, he supported acceptance of the Constitution. He declined ministerial posts but became one of the U.S. negotiators who resolved the XYZ Affair (1797-98). Elected to Congress in 1799, he was made secretary of state by President John Adams (1800-01). In 1801 he became chief justice. He labored to increase the then-scant power and prestige of the Supreme Court. In *Marbury* v. *Madison* he established the Court's power to review a law and, if necessary, declare it unconstitutional. An opponent of states' rights, he established in *McCulloch* v. *Maryland* and *Gibbons* v. *Ogden* the superiority of federal authority under the Constitution.
See also: Supreme Court of the United States.

Marshall, Thurgood (1908-93), U.S. judge, first black member of the United States' Supreme Court. He served as chief counsel for the National Association for the Advancement of Colored People (1938-61) and U.S. solicitor general (1965-67), before being nominated to the Supreme Court by President Lyndon B. Johnson in 1967. As associate justice, Marshall was known for his liberal positions on issues as capital punishment and free speech.
See also: Supreme Court of the United States.

Marshall Islands, 2 curving chains, each about 650 mi (1,050 km) in length, of altogether 34 coral atolls and islands in the west central Pacific: the eastern *Radak* (Sunrise) chain and the western *Ralik* (Sunset) chain. Formerly Japanese, the islands were self-governing in free association with the United States from 1986-90, when the islands became independent. Their total land area is 70 sq mi (180 sq km). The main atolls are Majuro, Amo, Ailinglaplap, Jaluit, and Kwajalein, which the United States uses as a missile range. After

---

Marshall Islands

Capital:	Dalap Uliga Darrit
Area:	70 sq mi
	(180 sq km)
Population:	50,000
Language:	English
Government:	Republic
Independent:	1990
Head of gov.:	President
Per capita:	U.S. $7,560
Mon. unit:	1 U.S. dollar = 100
	cents

World War II the United States used the Eniwetok and Bikini atolls as atomic testing grounds. The island's population is predominantly Micronesian. Breadfruit is the main crop, and copra (dried coconut meat) is the chief export. The islands are named for a British sea captain, John Marshall, who discovered them in 1788.

Marshall Plan, or European Recovery Program, program designed to help Europe's economic recovery after World War II, named for its originator, U.S. Secretary of State George C. Marshall. From 1948 to 1948 to 1952, material and financial aid amounting to almost $13 billion dollars was sent by the United States to the 17 European countries who formed the Organization for European Economic Cooperation (OEEC). The plan was administered by the Economic Cooperation Administration (ECA). *See also:* World War II.

Marsh, Reginald (1898-1954), U.S. painter. He began as a newspaper illustrator and later turned to the realistic depiction of New York life in paintings such as *"Why Not Use the 'L' ?"* (1930).

Marsh gas *See:* Methane.

Marsh hawk *See:* Northern harrier.

Marsh mallow (*Althaea officinalis*), herb found mainly in Europe, although it is now grown in the United States. The marsh mallow grows from 2 to 4 ft (61 to 120 cm) and has large leaves covered by soft hair.

Marsh marigold *See:* Cowslip.

Marston, John (1576-1634), English playwright best known for his comedy *The Malcontents* (1604). His *Antonio's Revenge* (1600) is one of the first examples of English tragedy.

Marsupial, any of an order (Marsupialia) of pouched mammals found mainly in Australia, Tasmania, and New Guinea. With few exceptions, marsupials do not develop placenta. They give birth to undeveloped young that attach themselves to the mother's teats inside a pouch on her abdomen, where they continue their development. Members of the order include the kangaroo, koala, and wombat.

Martel, Charles *See:* Charles Martel.

Marten, any of several large mammals (genus *Martes*) of the weasel family with valuable fur. The home of the marten is the pine forests of North America, Europe, and Asia. In Europe martens are also called sables. Their prey is mainly squirrels. American species include the American marten and the larger fisher or pekan.

Martha's Vineyard, island off the coast of southeast Massachusetts. About 100 sq mi (260 sq km) in area, it is separated from Cape Cod by Vineyard Sound. Named by Barthelomew Gosnold (1602), it was settled in 1632. A major whaling center in the 18th and 19th centuries, it is now a popular summer resort.

Martí, José Julian (1853-1895), Cuban poet and hero of the independence movement. While in exile in the United States (1881-95) he founded the Cuban Revolutionary Party. His best known poems appear in *Ismaelillo* (1882), *Versos sencilles* (1891), and *Versos libres* (1913). A leader of the 1895 Cuban rebellion against Spanish rule, Martí was killed at the battle of Dos Rios.

Martial (Marcus Valerius Martialis; c.A.D. 40-104), Spanish-born Latin poet. He lived in Rome 64-98 and was favored by emperors Titus and Domitian. Martial wrote 15 books of epigrams famous for their wit and their unusual poetic meter.
See also: Epigram.

Martial law, temporary superimposition of military on domestic civil government, usually in wartime or other national emergency. The army takes over executive and judicial functions, and civil rights such as habeas corpus may be suspended. When an invading army assumes control of a country, it is said to act not under martial law but as a military government.

Martin, any of several birds of the swallow family. The best-known member of the species is the purple martin (*Progne subis*), valued throughout the Southern United States for its consumption of large quantities of mosquitoes and other insect pests. They are native to most of the United States and the lower portions of Canada and often flock together in large numbers, consuming swarms of winged insects in flight.

Martin V (Oddone Colonna; 1368-1431), 15th-century Roman Catholic pope. Elected to the papacy in 1417 at the Council of Constance, his accession ended the Great Schism in the church. Martin worked for reforms within the church structure and hierarchy and arranged agreements (concordats) with the most powerful nations of Europe. He also called several councils aimed at receiving input for the continued unity and betterment of the church.

Martin du Gard, Roger (1881-1958), French novelist known for his objective but somber exploration of human relationships and the large backgrounds in which he sets them. In *Jean Barois* (1913) it is the Dreyfus Affair; in *The Thibaults* (1922-40), an 8-part novel cycle, it is World War I. In 1937 he won the Nobel Prize for literature.

Martineau, Harriet (1802-76), British writer and social reformer. A writer of fiction as well as nonfiction on many topics, she is best known for her works on economics and social reform, particularly her *Illustrations of Political Economy* (1832-34) and *Illustrations of Taxation* (1834), written for the layperson, and *Society in America* (1837), presenting her antislavery views.

Martinique, island in the Windward group in the east Caribbean, an overseas department of France since 1946. A volcanic island discovered by Columbus c.1502, Martinique was colonized by France as a sugar-growing center after 1635. Slave labor was used until 1848, and much of the present population is of African descent. The economy still rests on sugar, as well as rum, fruit, and tourism. The island is rugged and mountainous but very fertile. Its main town is Fort-de-France.

Martin of Tours, Saint (c.316-397), bishop of Tours. Son of a pagan, he served in the Roman army but after a vision of Christ sought a religious life. Bishop of Tours from c.371, he encouraged monasticism and opposed execution of heretics.
See also: Tours.

Martins, Peter (1946-   ), Danish dancer. He danced with the Royal Danish Ballet 1964-67, then joined the New York City Ballet, where he became a leading male dancer in such works by George Balanchine as *Violin Concerto* and *Duo Concertant* (both 1972). In 1983, following Balanchine's death, he became ballet master-in-chief (with Jerome Robbins).
See also: Ballet.

Marvell, Andrew (1621-1678), English metaphysical poet. Assistant to John Milton from 1657, Marvell was also a member of Parliament from 1659. A Puritan, he was known as a wit and satirist, but is best remembered today for his lyric poetry, including such works as "To His Coy Mistress" and "The Garden."

Marx, Karl (1818-83), German philosopher and social and economic theorist, founder of modern socialism. Born in Prussia of Jewish parents, Marx studied philosophy in Bonn and Berlin. When the Cologne newspaper he edited the *Rheinische Zeitung*, was suppressed (1843), he moved with his wife Jenny von Westphalen to Paris, where he met Friedrich Engels in 1844, and later to London, where he spent most of his life in great poverty.
In 1848 Marx and Engels published the *Communist Manifesto*, which established the theoretical basis for a socialist movement based on class struggle and sociological analysis rather than moral appeals to natural rights. Marx and Engels later cofounded (1864) International Workingmen's Association, the first international revolutionary organization. Marx wrote prolifically on questions of philosophy, history, and politics, but his greatest work

was *Capital*, his analysis of the system of capitalism. Only the first volume was published in his lifetime (1867). After his death, Engels completed the second (1885) and third (1894) volumes. Building on his criticism of the theories of Adam Smith and David Ricardo, Marx developed the theory of surplus-value to explain the exploitation of workers under capitalism. He predicted that the working class, or proletariat, would grow in numbers and power and would eventually overthrow capitalism, and establish socialism. The economic and political analysis of capitalism was integrated into a broader theory called historical materialism, which analyzed human history in terms of a sequence of kinds of society based on different forms of ownership of the means of production. Marx's influence has been widespread, and he is universally regarded as one of the major thinkers of the 19th century.
See also: Communism; Marxism.

Marx brothers, U.S. comedy team whose main members were Groucho (Julius; 1890-1977), Harpo (Arthur; 1888-1964), and Chico (Leonard; 1886-1961). Gummo (Milton; 1897-1961) left the team after their vaudeville days, and Zeppo (Herbert; 1901-79) left in 1934. The Marx brothers made about a dozen movies (1933-46). Their anarchic humor made hits of such memorable movies as *Duck Soup* (1933) and *A Night at the Opera* (1935).

Marxism, foundation philosophy of modern communism, originating in the work of Karl Marx and Friedrich Engels. Three of its basic concepts are that productive labor is the fundamental attribute of human nature; that the structure of any society is determined by its economic means of production; and that societies evolve by a series of crises caused by internal contradictions, analyzable by dialectical materialism.
Marx held that 19th-century industrial capitalism, the latest stage of the historical process, had arisen from feudalism by class struggle between the aristocracy and the rising bourgeois capitalist class. Dialectical materialism predicted conflict between these capitalists and the working class, or proletariat, on which the new industrialism depended. The triumphant dictatorship of the proletariat, an idea further developed by Lenin, would give way to a classless, stateless communist society where all would be equal, contributing according to their abilities and receiving according to their needs.
A key concept of Marxist economics is the labor theory of value, that value is created by labor and profit is surplus value creamed off by the capitalist. The fact that the capitalist owns the means of production makes this exploitation possible. It also means that the worker cannot own the product of his labor and thus suffers alienation from part of his own humanity and the social system. Marx believed capitalism would be swept away by the last of a catastrophic series of crises.
Among numerous later Marxist theorists are Karl Kautsky and Rosa Luxemburg. In *The Accumulation of Capital* (1913), Luxemburg argued that capitalism was able to adapt and survive by exploitation of its colonial empires. In the USSR Stalin proclaimed Marxist-Leninism an active philosophy of society in forced evolutionary conflict. In China Mao Zedong adapted Marxism to an agricultural peasant situation. Yugoslavia's Tito gave Marxism a nationalist bias, still more marked in the thinking of Fidel Castro of Cuba. Some western economists, sociologists, and historians have been widely influenced by Marxism.
See also: Marx, Karl.

Mary, in the Bible, the mother of Jesus, also called the Blessed Virgin. The chief events of her life related in the Gospels are her betrothal to Joseph; the annunciation of Jesus's birth; her visit to her cousin Elizabeth, mother of John the Baptist; the birth of Jesus; and her witnessing his crucifixion. In the Roman Catholic Church Mary is accorded a special degree of veneration superior to that given to other saints, and is regarded as mediatrix of all graces and coredemptress. Roman Catholic doctrine holds she was born free from sin, remained always a virgin, and was assumed bodily into heaven.
See also: Bible; Jesus Christ; United Kingdom.

Mary, name of 2 English queens. **Mary I** (1516-58), daughter of Henry VIII and Catherine of Aragon, succeeded Edward VI in 1553. She strove to restore Roman Catholicism in England. Some 300 Protestants were burnt as heretics—a persecution unparalleled in England, which earned her the name "Bloody Mary." Her unpopular alliance with and marriage to Philip II of Spain (1554) led to war with France and the loss of Calais (1558). **Mary II** (1662-94) was the Protestant daughter of James II and the wife (1677) of her cousin William of Orange, the Protestant ruler of the Netherlands. She helped found the College of William and Mary in Virginia in 1693. In the Glorious Revolution of 1688, William's forces attacked England, causing James to flee. Mary II was proclaimed joint sovereign with William in 1689.

Mary, Queen of Scots (1542-87), queen of Scotland (1542-67), daughter of James V and Mary of Guise. Brought up in France, she married (1558) the Dauphin, King Francis II (died 1560). Returning to Scotland (1561), she married (1565) Lord Darnley. In 1566 he murdered her counselor, David Rizzio; later Darnley himself was murdered, supposedly by the Earl of Bothwell, whom Mary married. Public outrage and Presbyterian opposition forced her abdication, and in 1568 she fled to England. Mary, heir presumptive of Elizabeth I and a Roman Catholic, soon became the natural focus of plots against the English throne. Parliament demanded her death; only in 1587, after Anthony Babington's plot, did Elizabeth reluctantly agree. Mary's trial and execution at Fotheringay castle inspired Schiller's tragedy *Maria Stuart*.
See also: Scotland; United Kingdom.

Mary, Virgin *See:* Mary.

Maryknoll Fathers, popular name for the Catholic Foreign Mission Society of America. It was founded in 1911 with headquarters at Maryknoll, N.Y. It has sent missions to Asia, Latin America, and the Pacific islands.

Maryland, state in the mid-Atlantic region of the eastern United States; bordered by Pennsylvania to the north, Delaware and the Atlantic Ocean to the east, Virginia and the District of Columbia to the south, and West Virginia to the south and west.
Land and climate. Chesapeake Bay, a jagged arm of the Atlantic Ocean, almost cuts the state in two from north to south. Maryland's 3,190 mi (5,134 km) of coastline—only 31 mi (49 km) of which are on the Atlantic—include many fine harbors. Maryland can be divided into 3 major regions. The Atlantic Coastal Plain (often called Tidewater Maryland) includes land south

Maryland

Capital:	Annapolis
Statehood:	Apr. 28, 1788 (7th state)
Familiar names:	Old Line State, Free State
Area:	10,577 sq mi (27,394 km); ranks 42nd
Population:	5,094,000 (1997); ranks 19th
Elevation:	Highest—3,360 (1,024 m), Backbone Mountain Lowest—sea level
Motto:	*Fatti Maschii, Parole Femine* (Manly Deeds, Womanly Words)
Flower:	Black-eyed Susan
Bird:	Baltimore oriole
Tree:	White oak
State song:	"Maryland, My Maryland"

and east of the fall line, which runs between Washington, D.C., and Baltimore. The part of the plain east of Chesapeake Bay (called the Eastern Shore) is very flat. The part west of the bay (the Western Shore) is fairly flat, but includes some hills. The central Piedmont-Blue Ridge region is an area of foothills and plateaus. The Appalachian-Allegheny area, which stretches from Hagerstown to the western border, is the state's highest region. Maryland's major rivers all flow into Chesapeake Bay. They include the Potomac, Patapsco, and Susquehanna. All Maryland's lakes are artificial. Forest covers approximately 40% of the state. Maryland has hot summers and mild winters. Principal cities are Baltimore, Silver Spring, and Dundalk.

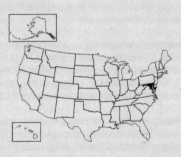

Economy. Maryland's economy is based on service industries. Many federal office buildings and support services are here, due to Maryland's proximity to the U.S. capital. Manufacturing and tourism are the principal industries. Manufactured products include electrical equipment, processed foods, chemicals, printed materials, and transportation equipment. Tourist attractions include horse- and yacht-racing events, shore resorts, and historic Fort McHenry. Maryland's fishing industry is another major source of income. Its production of clams and oysters is one of the nation's highest, and it is known for its crabs and other seafood. About 35% of the state's area is farmland. Broilers (chickens), beef cattle, and milk are the leading livestock products; greenhouse and nursery plants, cotton, soybeans, and rice are the major crops. Mineral products include construction sand and gravel, crushed stone, and coal.

Government. Maryland's present constitution was adopted in 1867. The governor serves a 4-year term. The state legislature, called the General Assembly, consists of 47 senators and 141 delegates; all serve 4-year terms.

In the U.S. Congress, Maryland is represented by 2 senators and 8 representatives.

History. Maryland was home to several Native American tribes before Spanish explorers, the first Europeans, arrived in the 1500s. One of the original 13 colonies, Maryland played an active part in the American Revolution. During the War of 1812, a battle at Baltimore's Fort McHenry inspired Francis Scott Key to write "The Star-Spangled Banner," which later became the U.S. national anthem. Maryland officially supported the Union in the Civil War, but its people were sharply divided. Afterward, its economy grew and became more diverse, booming after World War I, crashing in the Great Depression, and rising again after World War II. Today, Maryland is a center of research and development for the U.S. space program.

Mary Magdalene, in the New Testament, the woman of Magdala from whom Jesus cast out 7 demons (Luke 8:2). She became his devoted follower and may have been present at his death and burial. Mary was the first person to see the risen Jesus.
See also: New Testament.

Masaccio (Tommaso Guidi; 1401-28), Florentine painter of the Renaissance, one of the great innovators of Western art. Possibly a pupil of Masolino, Masaccio produced paintings that inspired such painters as Michelangelo and Raphael. Through austere composition and inspired use of light Masaccio created expressive monumental paintings and frescoes, notably in the Brancacci Chapel of Santa Maria del Carmine in Florence. Other works include the *Trinity* fresco in Santa Maria Novella and the *Virgin with St. Anne* in the Uffizi Palace, both in Florence.
See also: Renaissance.

Masada, mountaintop rock fortress near the southeastern coast of the Dead Sea, Israel. The castle-palace complex, built (37-31 B.C.) largely by Herod the Great, was seized from Roman occupation by Jewish Zealots in A.D. 66. A 2-year seige, 72-73, was needed to recover it, but the Zealots committed suicide rather than surrender. The site has been excavated (1963-65) and restored.

Masai, people of eastern Africa who speak the Masai language of the Sudanic group. The nomadic pastoral Masai of Kenya, the largest Masai tribe, practice polygamy and organize their society on a system of male age sets, graded from junior warrior up to tribal elder. They subsist almost entirely by herding.

Masaryk, name of 2 Czechoslovakian politicians. **Thomas Garrigue Masaryk** (1850-1937), was chief founder and first president of Czechoslovakia (1918-35). Professor of philosophy at the Univ. of Prague from 1882, he was a fervent nationalist. During World War I he lobbied Western statesmen for Czech independence. His son **Jan Garrigue Masaryk** (1886-1948) was foreign minister of the Czech government-in-exile in London in World War II, broadcasting to his German-occupied country. He continued as foreign minister in the restored government (1945). Soon after the Communist coup (1948) he was said to have committed suicide.

Mascagni, Pietro (1863-1945), Italian opera composer of the *verismo* (realist) school, known for the one-act *Cavalleria Rusticana* (Rustic Chivalry,

1890). In 1929 he became musical director of La Scala, Milan. Although he composed 15 operas, among them *L'Amico Fritz* (1891), Mascagni did not repeat his initial success.
See also: Opera.

Masefield, John (1878-1967), English poet, novelist, and playwright. As a youth he served on a windjammer ship, and love of the sea pervades his poems. He won fame with such long narrative poems as *The Everlasting Mercy* (1911), *Dauber* (1913), and *Raynard the Fox* (1919). In 1930 he became poet laureate.

Maser, in technology, acronym for Microwave Amplification by Stimulated Emission of Radiation, a device capable of amplifying or generating radio frequency radiation. Maser amplifiers are used in satellite communication ground stations to amplify the extremely weak signals received from communication satellites.
See also: Laser.

Maseru (pop. 109,400), capital of Lesotho, a landlocked independent state in southern Africa. Standing near Lesotho's northwestern border with the Orange Free State (South Africa), the town is linked by a short railroad with the Bioemfontein-Natal line in South Africa. Maseru has a public library, hospital, and technical training school.
See also: Lesotho.

Maslow, Abraham Harold (1908-70), U.S. psychologist, the major figure in the humanistic school of psychology. Rejecting behaviorism and psychoanalysis, he saw human beings as creative entities striving for self-actualization. His books include *Motivation and Personality* (1954), *Toward a Psychology of Being* (1962), and *The Psychology of Science* (1966).
See also: Psychology.

Mason, Charles *See:* Mason and Dixon's Line.

Mason, George (1725-92), U.S. politician who helped draft the U.S. Constitution, but refused to sign it because of its compromise on slavery and other issues. His Virginia declaration of rights (1776) became the basis for the Bill of Rights. Much of the Virginia Constitution was also his work.

Mason and Dixon's Line, Mason-Dixon Line, traditional dividing line between the northern and southern states of the United States. Surveyed by Charles Mason and Jeremiah Dixon in 1767, the line formed the east-west boundary between Pennsylvania and Maryland and the north-south boundary between Maryland and Delaware. In 1779 the east-west line was extended to form the boundary between Virginia and Pennsylvania.

Mason and Slidell, Confederate diplomats; their seizure while aboard a British vessel nearly touched off a war between the United States and Great Britain during the Civil War. James Murray Mason (1798-1871) served in the U.S. Senate and House of Representatives from Virginia. John Slidell (1793-1871) served in both houses of Congress from Louisiana. On Nov. 8, 1861, they were captured along with the British ship *Trent*, as they sailed

toward Europe to seek diplomatic recognition for the confederacy. They were released on Jan. 2, 1862.
See also: Civil War, U.S.

Masonry, or freemasonry, common name for the practices of the order of Free and Accepted Masons, one of the world's largest and oldest fraternal organizations. Members participate in elaborate, secret rituals and are dedicated to the promotion of brotherhood and morality. Membership, of which there are several grades, is restricted to men; allegiance to some form of religious belief is required. Modern Masonry emerged with the Grand Lodge of England, founded in 1717, although masons trace their ancestry to the craft associations or "lodges" of medieval stone masons. The first U.S. lodge was founded in Philadelphia, Pa. in 1730. There are associated organizations for women, boys, and girls. The worldwide membership is more than 6 million.

Masqat *See:* Muscat.

Masque, or mask, dramatic entertainment popular in the early-17th-century English court. It concentrated on spectacle rather than plot. Members of the aristocracy often took part with the actors, and masks were generally worn (hence the name). Ben Jonson was the most famous masque writer, and Inigo Jones designed many of the lavish sets.

Mass, term for the celebration of Holy Communion in the Roman Catholic Church and in Anglo-Catholic churches. Roman Catholics believe that the bread (host) and the wine become Christ's body and blood, which are offered as a sacrifice to God. The text consists of the "ordinary," spoken or sung at every celebration, and the "proper," sections which change according to the day or occasion—for example, the requiem mass has its own proper. In High Mass, celebrated with priest, deacon, and choir, the text is sung to plainsong with choral responses. Medieval choral settings of the mass were the first great masterpieces of Western music, remaining a major musical form into the 20th century. Low Mass, said by a single priest, is the basic Roman Catholic service. In 1965 the Vatican sanctioned the use of vernacular languages in place of Latin.

Mass, in physics, measure of the linear inertia of a body, i.e., of the extent to which it resists acceleration when a force is applied to it. Alternatively, mass can be thought of as a measure of the amount of matter in a body. This view seems validated when one remembers that bodies of equal inertial mass have identical weights in a given gravitational field. The exact equivalence of inertial mass and gravitational mass is only a theoretical assumption, albeit one strongly supported by experimental evidence. According to Einstein's theory of relativity, the mass of a body is increased if it gains energy, according to the equation $E=mc^2$, where m is the change in mass due to the energy change E, and c is the electromagnetic constant. It is an important property of nature that in an isolated system mass-energy is conserved. The international standard of mass is the international prototype kilogram.
See also: Inertia.

Massachusetts, state in New England, the northeastern region of the United States; bordered by Vermont and New Hampshire to the north, the Atlantic

Massachusetts

Capital:	Boston
Statehood:	Feb. 6, 1788 (6th state)
Familiar name:	Bay State
Area:	8,284 sq mi (21,456 km); ranks 45th
Population:	6,118,000 (1997); ranks 13th
Elevation:	Highest—3,491 ft (1,064 m), Mt. Greylock; Lowest—sea level, along the Atlantic coast
Motto:	Ense Petit Placidam Sub Libertate Quietem (By the Sword We Seek Peace, But Peace Only Under Liberty)
Flower:	Mayflower
Bird:	Chickadee
Tree:	American elm
Song:	"All Hail to Massachusetts"

Ocean to the east and south, Rhode Island and Connecticut to the south, and New York to the west.

Land and climate. Massachusetts can be divided into six land regions. The Coastal Lowlands is a flat or gently sloping plain in the eastern third of the state. Most of the state's people and principal manufacturing centers are here.

The hilly Eastern New England Upland extends west of the Lowlands for 40-60 mi (64-97 km). The land then dips into the broad, fertile Connecticut Valley, which is about 20 mi (32 km) wide. West of there, the land rises into the most rugged regions of the state—the Western New England Upland (including Mt. Greylock, the state's highest point), the Berkshire Valley, and the Taconic Mountains. Although there are more than 4,200 mi of rivers in Massachusetts, the Connecticut River is the state's only major navigable waterway. The

Merrimack River furnished the water power for Massachusetts's early industries. The state has more than 1,000 lakes and ponds. The climate is humid, with sharply defined seasons. Western Massachusetts is colder and snowier than the east. Principal cities are Boston, Worcester, and Springfield.

Economy. The state's economy is based on such service industries as banking, health care, real estate, and retail trade. Principal manufactured goods are machinery (particularly computers), electrical equipment, scientific instruments, printed materials, transportation equipment, chemicals, and food, plastic, and paper products. Tourism, an important part of the economy, thrives in Boston, Cape Cod, and the Berkshires. Agriculture, fishing, and mining, once of prime importance, are now minor branches of the economy.

Government. The Massachusetts constitution, the oldest state constitution still in use, was adopted in 1780. The governor serves a four-year term. The state legislature, called the General Court, consists of 40 senators and 160 representatives; all serve 2-year terms. In the U.S. Congress, Massachusetts is represented by two senators and 10 representatives.

History. Native American peoples were the area's first known settlers, more than 3,000 years ago. The first European explorers may have been Vikings, about A.D. 1000. The Pilgrims, who came from England in 1620, built the first European settlement. English Puritans settled at and around Boston. The Massachusetts Bay Colony was one of the original 13 British colonies. Indian opposition culminated in King Philip's War (1675-76). The Boston Massacre (1770) and the Boston Tea Party (1773) helped spark the American Revolution, whose first battles were at Lexington and Concord (1775). The new state's commerce flourished, especially in the major seaport of Boston. In 1814, one of the first U.S. factories was built at Waltham; Massachusetts soon became the most industrialized state in the nation. Massachusetts supported the Union during the Civil War. Between that war and World War I, an immigration boom swelled the state's population and helped power its industrial rise. The state economy suffered during the 1920s and 1930s, but World War II brought recovery. Massachusetts, known for its historic universities and colleges (including Harvard and MIT), attracts research and development industries that supported it during the economic slump of the late 1980s.

Massachusetts Bay Company, English joint stock company set up by royal charter in 1629 and styled the "Governor and Company of the Massachusetts Bay in New England." The charter gave the company self-government, subject only to the king; it effectively became the constitution of the colony. In 1630 almost 1,000 immigrants landed in Massachusetts, led by John Winthrop, who became the first governor. The franchise was then restricted to Puritan "freemen," and the colony became an independent Calvinistic theocracy; it coined its own money and restricted freedom of worship. As a result, the charter was revoked in 1684 and Massachusetts became a royal colony

Massasoit (1580?-1661), powerful Wampanoag chief who signed a treaty with the Pilgrims under Governor John Carver of Plymouth Colony in 1621. He befriended the Plymouth colony, teaching the settlers how to survive, and kept up friendly relations until his death.
See also: Plymouth Colony.

Massenet, Jules (1842-1912), French composer. Best known for his operas *Manon* (1884), *Werther* (1892), and *Thaïs* (1894), he frequently used spoken (accompanied) dialogue in the place of recitative.

Massey, Vincent (1887-1967), Canadian diplomat. The first Canadian-born governor-general of Canada (1952-59), he became Canada's first minister in Washington (1926). From 1935-46 he was high commissioner in London. Massey also became chairperson of the Royal Commission on National Development in the Arts, Letters and Sciences (1949) and chancellor of the Univ. of Toronto (1947-53). In 1961 he founded Massey College. He also published several books of his speeches, and his autobiography, *What's Past Is Prologue* (1963).

Massine, Léonide (1896-1979), Russian-born U.S. ballet dancer and choreographer. He worked with Diaghilev as principal dancer and choreographer (1914-21, 1925-28), and directed the Ballet Russe de Monte Carlo 1932-42. His works include *Parade* (1917) and *Jeux d' Enfants* (1943).

Massinger, Philip (1583-1640), English dramatist known for satirical comedies. Among his works are *A New Way to Pay Old Debts* (1621), *The City Madam* (1632), and the romantic tragedy *The Duke of Milan* (1621). He often collaborated with others, such as John Fletcher. A moralist, he criticized the frivolity in society.

Mass media *See:* Advertising.

Mass number *See:* Atom.

Masson, André (1896-1987), French painter and graphic artist. Influenced by surrealism, he developed a style of drawing ("automatic drawing") intended to be spontaneous and without a specific subject.

Mass production, production of large numbers of identical objects, usually by use of mechanization. The root of mass production is the assembly line, essentially a conveyer belt that transports the product so that each worker may perform a single function on it (e.g., add a component). The advantages of mass production are cheapness and speed; the disadvantages are lack of job satisfaction for the workers and resultant sociological problems.
See also: Assembly line; Machine tool.

Mass spectroscopy, spectroscopic technique in which electric and magnetic fields are used to deflect moving charged particles according to their mass; employed for chemical analysis, separation, isotope determination, or finding impurities. The apparatus for obtaining a mass spectrum (i.e., a number of "lines" of distinct charge-to-mass ratio obtained from the beam of charged particles) is known as a mass spectrometer or mass spectrograph, depending on whether the lines are detected electrically or on a photographic plate. In essence, it consists of an ion source, a vacuum chamber, a deflecting field, and a collector. By altering the accelerating voltage and deflecting field, particles of a given mass can be focused to pass together through the collecting slit.
See also: Spectrometer.

Masters, Edgar Lee (1869-1950), U.S. poet, novelist, biographer, and playwright whose best-known work is *Spoon River Anthology* (1915), which reveals the life of a small town as seen through the epitaphs of its inhabitants. He also wrote critical biographies of Abraham Lincoln and Mark Twain.

Masters, William H. (1915-   ), and Virginia E. Johnson (1925-   ), U.S. sex researchers whose book *Human Sexual Response* (1966) was the first complete study of the physiology and anatomy of sexual activity.

Masterson, Bat (1853-1921), U.S. pioneer and peace officer. He is best known as assistant to Wyatt Earp, a deputy U.S. marshall in Tombstone, Ariz., 1881. Masterson was a deputy marshall in Dodge City, Kans. (1876), sheriff of Ford county (1878-80), and city marshall of Trinidad, Colo. (1882).

Mastodon, any of a genus (*Mammut*) of the extinct mammals resembling elephants. Different from mammoths and elephants because of their molar teeth, they sometimes had 4 tusks (2 on the lower jaw, 2 on the upper jaw). Forest dwellers, mastodons lived in Africa during the Oligocene epoch.
See also: Mammoth.

Mata Hari (Margaretha Geertruida Zelle; 1866-1917), Dutch-born dancer and spy for Germany in World War I. She belonged to the German secret service in Paris. The mistress of many French officials, she passed on military secrets to the Germans, for which she was tried and executed.
See also: World War I.

Maté, also known as yerba maté or Paraguay tea, evergreen tree of the holly family. Its leaves are dried to make a tea containing caffeine that is widely drunk in South America.

Materialism, in philosophy, any view asserting the primacy of physical matter in explaining the nature of the world. The earliest materialists were the classical atomists, e.g., Democritus and Leucippus. Modern science has revived materialism, argued as a prerequisite for scientific thought, particularly in psychology.
See also: Democritus; Leucippus; Marx, Karl.

Mathematics, field of thought concerned with relationships involving concepts of quantity, space, and symbolism. Over the past several centuries mathematics developed to include *axiomatic-deductive reasoning*. This aspect of mathematics is credited to the classical Greeks and is traced back to Euclid, who formalized it in 300 B.C. with his work *Elements*. Axiomatic-deductive systems are based on elementary ideas assumed self-evident (*axioms*) and formal rules governing the mathematical system. Consequences (*theorems*) can then be deduced systematically and logically from axioms. All mathematical systems have this quality. Familiar examples include algebra, where relationships between known and unknown quantities are represented symbolically; arithmetic, the science of quantity and space concerned with numbers and rules for manipulating them such as addition or multiplication; calculus, dealing with relationships involving rates of change; and geometry, concerned with spatial relationships. Mathematics is pursued to solve practical problems as well as to enhance its logical and often abstract nature. Consequently it is often categorized as *applied* and *pure*. The applied mathematician uses or develops mathematics as a tool, solving problems or relationships in other fields. Physicists and engineers often apply calculus to questions of motion, economists apply concepts of linear algebra to determine cost effective solutions, and statistics and probability are frequently used by psychologists. The scholar of pure mathematics investigates logical relationships of abstract quantities or objects. Questions of the completeness and consistency within given mathematical constructs are addressed in pure mathematics.
Major contributions in the development of western mathematics came from Egypt (3000-1600 B.C.), Babylonia (1700-300 B.C.), Greece (600-200 B.C.), and the Hindu and Arab world (600 B.C.-A.D. 1450). Major achievements before modern times have also occurred in China, Japan, and Incan and Aztec empires.

Mather, family of American colonial ministers. **Richard Mather** (1596-1669) fled England (1635) for Massachusetts seeking religious freedom. A Puritan and pastor of Dorchester, he wrote the *Platform of Church Discipline* (1649), the basic creed of Massachusetts Congregationalism. **Increase Mather** (1639-1723), son of Richard, was president of Harvard College (1685-1701). A renowned Puritan pastor and scholar, he helped negotiate the colony's new charter and intervened against witchcraft persecution. **Cotton Mather** (1663-1728), son of Increase, was a famous preacher and scholar who contributed to the witchcraft hysteria. He helped found Yale Univ.; because of his broad scientific interests he was the first American colonist elected to the Royal Society of London.

Mathewson, Christy (Christopher Mathewson; 1880-1925), U.S. baseball player. Mathewson, a right-handed pitcher for the New York Giants (1900-16) and Cincinnati Reds (1916) is considered one of the best pitchers of all time and is credited with developing the screwball. His achievements include being the first pitcher of the 1900's to win 30 games or more for 3 consecutive seasons (1903-05), 373 career wins, and winning 20 games or more for 12 consecutive seasons (1901-14). Mathewson was among the first group of players inducted into the National Baseball Hall of Fame (1936). A victim of poison gas in World War I, he died of tuberculosis.

Matisse, Henri (1869-1954), French painter, sculptor, and lithographer. He is regarded, with Picasso, as one of the 2 most important artists of the 20th century. He was a leader of the fauves and was noted for his brilliant, expressive use of color in such paintings as *The Green Line* (1905) and *Landscape at Callioure* (1905). Earlier he had explored impressionism, as in his painting *The Dinner Table* (1897). In his last years he created abstract compositions out of handpainted cut paper, a technique he called "drawing with scissors." From 1948 to 1951 he designed and decorated the Dominican chapel at Vence, France.

Matter, material substance existing in space and time. All matter has inertia, measured quantitatively by its mass and weight, exerting its gravitational pull on other such bodies. There are 3 common states of matter: solid, liquid and gas; scientists consider plasma a fourth. Atoms and molecules make up ordinary matter.

Matterhorn, 14,691-ft (4,478-m) high mountain in the Alps on the Swiss-Italian frontier. It was first climbed by Edward Whymper in 1865.

Matthew, Saint, one of the twelve apostles, traditionally the author of the first gospel. His gospel, the fullest of the 4 gospels, was probably written for Jewish Christians. By its many Old Testament quotes it shows Jesus as the promised Messiah. His feast day is Sept. 12.
See also: Apostles.

Mattingly, Don (Donald Arthur Mattingly; 1961-   ), U.S. baseball player. As first baseman for the New York Yankees, American League (AL), he distinguished himself as a batter and fielder. He was named AL Most Valuable Player in 1985, and batted over .300 for 6 consecutive seasons

(1984-89). In 1991 Mattingly became the tenth captain in New York Yankees history.

Maugham, W(illiam) Somerset (1874-1965), British author. A playwright, short story writer, and novelist, his writing frequently was characterized by irony and cynicism. Maugham's novels include the autobiographical *Of Human Bondage* (1915), *The Moon and Sixpence* (1919), and the satirical *Cakes and Ale* (1930).

Maui *See:* Hawaii.

Mauldin, Bill (1921-), U.S. cartoonist. His cartoons of World War II GIs, Willie and Joe, published in the armed forces newspaper *Stars and Stripes*, became the national embodiment of the American infantrymen. He won the Pulitzer Prize for cartooning in 1945 and 1959. *Up Front* (1945) and *Brass Ring* (1971) are 2 of his books of cartoons.
See also: Cartoon.

Mau Mau, terrorist organization in Kenya (chiefly the Kikuyu tribe) whose main aim was to expel the British. Organized as a secret society, the Mau Mau ran a campaign of murder and sabotage (1952-60); after 1956 the British put an end to most of the bloodshed.

Mauna Kea, dormant volcano in Hawaii. At 13,796 ft (4,205 m) high, Mauna Kea ("white mountain") is the world's highest island mountain. At the top of its snow-covered summit are several astronomical observatories and large telescopes.

Mauna Loa, active volcano in the Hawaii Volcanoes National Park. The world's largest volcano, it erupts every 3.5 years. It is 13,680 ft (4,170 m) high. Kilauea volcano is on its southeastern side.

Maundy Thursday, the Thursday before Easter, commemorating Jesus's washing of his disciples' feet and institution of Holy Communion at the Last Supper.
See also: Holy Week.

Maupassant, Guy de *See:* De Maupassant, Guy.

Mauriac, François (1885-1970), French author. A nonconformist Catholic, his novels concern man's vulnerability to sin and evil. Winner of the 1952 Nobel Prize for literature, his works include *The Desert of Love* (1925), *Thérèse Desqueyroux* (1927), and *The Knot of Vipers* (1932).

Maurice of Nassau (1567-1625), Prince of Orange from 1618, Dutch statesman, and military leader. A son of William the Silent, he conducted a successful war against Spanish rule and was an architect of the emerging Dutch republic. He was virtual ruler of the Netherlands, executing his former ally Johan van Oldenbarneveldt in 1619 and establishing the supremacy of the house of Orange.
See also: Netherlands.

Mauritania, Islamic Republic of, former French colony in western Africa. Mauritania is some 398,000 sq mi (1,030,700 sq km) in area and is bordered

Mauritania

Capital:	Nouakchott
Area:	398,000 sq mi
	(1,030,700 sq km)
Population:	2,511,000
Language:	Arabic, French
Government:	Presidential
	republic
Independent:	1960
Head of gov.:	Prime minister
Per capita:	U.S. $460
Mon. unit:	1 Ouguiya =
	5 khoum

by Morocco, Western Sahara and Algeria to the north, Mali and Senegal to the south, Mali to the east, and the Atlantic Ocean to the west.

Land and climate. Mauritania is principally a dry, rocky plateau averaging 500 ft (152 m) above sea level, a southern extension of the Sahara. There is a fertile grain growing district along the Senegal River in the south and cattle raising grasslands in the southeast. The climate is hot throughout the country, but rainfall varies considerably from less than 4 in (10 cm) annually in the north to about 24 in (61 cm) annually toward the south.

People. Some 80% of the population are Berbers or Moors and the remaining 20% are black Africans. About 50% of the people live in towns. The Berbers and Moors live a nomadic life principally in the north and the black Africans live in rural villages in the south. The capital is Nouakchott. The official languages are French and Arabic. Islam is the official religion.

Economy. There are large deposits of iron ore, gypsum, and copper, which account for about 80% of all exports. Farmers in the south raise millet, sorghum, rice, and other cereals and vegetables while nomads raise sheep, goats, cattle, and camels. Recent droughts have dealt a serious blow to livestock.

History. In the 11th century, the Ghanaian Empire, to which most of Mauritania then belonged, was invaded by nomadic Berbers of the Almoravid group. In the 13th century South Mauritania fell to the Mali Empire and Islam was firmly established. The Portuguese probed the coast in the 15th century; the French penetrated the interior in the 19th century. In 1920 Mauritania became the colony of French West Africa. In 1960 it gained full independence and became a Muslim state under President Mokhtar Ould Daddah. The military seized power in 1968. During the 1970s a war against the Polisario Front guerrillas over claims to the Western Sahara brought political and economic instability. Mauritania relinquished its claim to the territory in 1979. In 1984, Lt. Col. Maaouga Ould Sidi Ahmed Taya replaced Lt. Col. Mohamed Khouma Ould Haidalla as head of state. In the 1991 Gulf War, Mauritania supported Iraq. As a result, relations with the U.S., France, and the Gulf states deteriorated and economic support of Mauritania was reduced or even terminated. In 1993 France and the Gulf states continued their economic aid.

Mauritius	
Capital:	Port Louis
Area:	788 sq mi
	(2,040 sq km)
Population:	1,168,000
Language:	English, French
Government:	Republic
Independent:	1968
Head of gov.:	Prime minister
Per capita:	U.S. $3,380
Mon. unit:	1 Mauritian rupee =
	100 cents

Mauritius, island republic 500 mi (805 km) east of Madagascar in the Indian Ocean, comprising the islands of Mauritius, Rodrigues, and associated archipelagos.

Land and climate. The main island, Mauritius, is surrounded by coral reefs. The island is principally a plateau and approximately 788 sq mi (2,040 sq km) in area. The climate is warm and humid with a cyclone season from Dec. to Mar.

People. More than 60% of the population consists of Indians, about 30% are Creole, a mixture of French and black African, and the remainder are principally Europeans, African, and Chinese. Religions reflect the diversity of the people and include the Hindu religion, Christianity, and Islam. The official language is English and the capital is Port Louis.

Economy. Sugar was the single most important export until the 1980s when it was surpassed by textile products. Tea and tobacco are also cash crops and tourism contributes to the economy as well. But with more than 1,000,000 inhabitants, overpopulation and unemployment are persistent problems for Mauritius.

History. Formerly uninhabited, Mauritius was settled by the Portuguese in the early 1500s but soon abandoned. After a period of Dutch occupation in the 17th century, the French settled the island in 1715, founded the sugar industry, and imported slaves from Africa to work the plantations. The British took Mauritius in 1810, during the Napoleonic Wars and when they abolished slavery in the colonies in 1831, the planters resorted to indentured laborers from India. The British first initiated moves toward representative government for the colony in the late 19th century. Mauritius was granted full independence in 1968. Until 1992 Mauritius was a constitutional monarchy in the British Commonwealth, with the British Queen as the head of state. In 1992 the country became a republic with Cassan Uteem as the first elected president.

Maurois, André (Émile Herzog; 1885-1967), 20th-century French author. A soldier in World War I, his earliest works were novels about his war experiences, including *The Silence of Colonel Bramble* (1918) and *Les Discours du Docteur O'Grady* (1921). Maurois is known for his biographies of authors Percy Bysshe Shelley, Lord Byron, George Sand, Victor Hugo, and Alexandre Dumas and politicians George Washington, Benjamin Disraeli, and Chateaubriand. His *Memoirs: 1885-1967* was published posthumously in 1970.

Maurya Empire, Indian imperial dynasty, 325-183 B.C., founded by Chandragupta Maurya. Its capital was near modern Patna. Chandragupta Maurya's grandson Asoka (d. 232) brought almost the whole subcontinent under one rule and made Buddhism the state religion. Under Mauryan art, there was a flowering of the Indian Buddhist culture.
See also: Asoka; Chandragupta, Maurya.

Maury, Matthew Fontaine (1806-73), U.S. naval officer, head of the Depot of Charts and Instruments (1844-61). His study of the bed of the Atlantic Ocean and his *Physical Geography of the Sea* (1855) helped pioneer the science of oceanography.

Maverick, Samuel Augustus (1803-70), Texas politician and cattle rancher. He was a member of the convention that founded the Republic of Texas (1836) and served as a member of the Texas Congress and its first state legislature. Owner of a large cattle ranch, Maverick did not brand his herd, and neighbors called his strays, "mavericks." The word came to mean all unmarked cattle. Today the term applies largely to politicians who have no distinct affiliations or party loyalties.

Maxim, U.S. family of inventors. **Sir Hiram Stevens Maxim** (1840-1916) invented (1854) the automatic, rapid-firing gun (Maxim machine gun) and tested a steam-powered aircraft (it successfully lifted off the ground). **Hudson Maxim** (1853-1927), Sir Hiram's brother, invented an explosive more powerful than dynamite, a smokeless powder, and a torpedo propellant. **Hiram Percy Maxim** (1869-1936), Sir Hiram's son, invented the gun silencer, designed an electric automobile, and helped develop mufflers for automobiles and jet engines.
See also: Explosive; Machine gun.

Maximilian, name of 2 Habsburg Holy Roman emperors. **Maximilian I** (1459-1519) reigned from 1493. He married, first, Mary of Burgundy (1477) and then Bianca, daughter of the Duke of Milan (1494). He arranged other family marriages that brought the Habsburgs much of Burgundy, the Netherlands, Hungary, Bohemia, and Spain. Maximilian I reorganized imperial administration and set up a supreme court of justice. However, he had to recognize Switzerland's independence (1499), and failed to hold Milan. His finances were severely strained by continual warfare in support of his ambitions. **Maximilian II** (1527-76), emperor from 1564, was also king of Bohemia from 1549 and of Hungary from 1563. He was the son and successor of Ferdinand I. A humanist, he adopted a policy of religious toleration. Maximilian II arranged a truce with Turkey, according to which he would pay tribute to the sultan for his part of Hungary.
See also: Holy Roman Empire.

Maximilian (1832-1867), emperor of Mexico from 1864 until his death. An Austrian archduke, he was given the throne by the French emperor Napoleon III, who hoped to extend his empire. Maximilian believed that the Mexicans would welcome him and attempted to rule liberally and benevolently, but found French troops essential against popular support for President Benito Juárez. After the troops withdrew (1866-67), Maximilian was defeated by Juárez's forces and executed.

Maxwell, James Clerk (1831-79), Scottish theoretical physicist. His most important work was in electricity, magnetism, and his kinetic theory of gases. He also studied color vision, elasticity, optics, Saturn's rings, and thermodynamics. *Maxwell's equations*, 4 linked differential equations, extend the work of Michael Faraday and others and completely define the classical theory of the electromagnetic field. Maxwell's most famous work was *Treatise on Electricity and Magnetism* (1873). Its main concepts are considered to be the basis for Albert Einstein's theory of relativity and the quantum theory.
See also: Electromagnetic waves.

Maxwell's rule, law stating that every part of an electric circuit is acted upon by a force tending to move it in such a direction as to enclose the maximum amount of magnetic flux.

May apple, or mayapple (*Podophyllum peltatum*), woodland plant native to eastern North America. Also known as mandrake, it produces white flowers between Apr. and June and edible yellow berries often used in jellies. A member of the barberry family, may apple roots are used to manufacture types of herbal medicines.

Mayas, Middle American Indian confederation of Central America, covering the Yucatán peninsula, East Chiapas state in modern Mexico, most of Guatemala, and the western parts of El Salvador and Honduras. Its civilization was at its height A.D. 300-900. A farming people of the rain forests, the Mayas grew corn, cassava, cotton, beans, and sweet potatoes and kept bees for wax and honey. They had a hierarchy of priest-nobles under a hereditary chief. The Mayans developed an involved hieroglyphic form of writing, still undeciphered, and a knowledge of mathematics, astronomy, and chronology superior to that in contemporaneous Europe. The priests devised 2 calendars: a 365-day civil year and a sacred year of 260 days. Mayan art comprises fine sculpture, both in the round and in relief; painted frescoes and manuscripts; ceramics, and magnificent architecture, including the lofty stone pyramid topped by a temple. By 900 their main centers, such as Palenque, Peidras, and Copán, had been abandoned to the jungle for reasons unknown. A "postclassical" tradition, under Toltec influence, sprang up in new centers, notably Chichén Itzá, but in the early 1500s the entire region came under Spanish rule.

May beetle *See:* June bug.

May Day, spring festival on May 1. Traces of its pagan origins survive in the decorated maypoles and May queens of England. Declared a socialist labor festival by the Second International in 1889, it is celebrated, particularly in communist countries, by parades and demonstrations.

Mayer, Julius Robert von (1814-78), German physician and physicist who contributed (1842) to the formulation of the law of conservation of energy.
See also: Heat; Joule, James Prescott.

Mayflower, ship that carried the Pilgrims to America in 1620. It left Plymouth, England, on Sept. 21 and reached Provincetown, Mass., on Nov. 21. The Pilgrims settled what is now Plymouth, Mass., after signing the Mayflower Compact. The *Mayflower* a 2-decker ship, probably 90 ft (27 m) long and about 180 tons (163 metric tons), has not survived, but an English-built replica, *Mayflower II*, sailed the Atlantic in 1957. It is now at Plymouth, Mass.

Mayflower Compact, agreement signed by 41 of the Pilgrims on Nov. 21, 1620. Having landed outside any civil jurisdiction and fearing that their group might split up, they undertook to form a "civil body politic," governed by majority rule, and to "frame just and equal laws." The compact became the basis of the government of the colony of Plymouth.
See also: Plymouth Colony.

Mayfly, common insect (order Ephemeroptera) of ponds and rivers. The larvae live in the water and emerge to molt as subadults. The subadults immediately molt again into full adults. The adults have 3 fine "tails" (as have the larvae), large transparent forewings, small or no hindwings, and weak legs. The mouthparts are also weak; adult mayflies do not feed during their short life, which may last no longer than an afternoon.

Mayo, U.S. family of surgeons. **William Worrall Mayo** (1819-1911) founded St. Mary's Hospital, Rochester, Minn. (1889), which was to become the famous Mayo Clinic. His sons, **William James Mayo** (1861-1939), and **Charles Horace Mayo** (1865-1939), traveled to many countries to discover new surgical techniques and to attract foreign surgeons to the clinic; in 1915 they set up the Mayo Foundation for Medical Education and Research. Charles's son, **Charles William Mayo** (1898-1968), was also a distinguished surgeon.

Mayo Clinic, one of the world's largest medical centers. It was founded in 1889 at Rochester, Minn., as a voluntary association of physicians. It grew from an emergency hospital set up by Dr. William W. Mayo (1861-1939) to help cyclone victims. The Clinic treats about 175,000 patients a year and is financed by the Mayo Foundation.

Mays, Willie (1931-   ), U.S. baseball player. An outfielder for the New York (later, San Francisco) Giants (1951-72), he hit 660 home runs in his career (third on the all time list) and was named the National League's most valuable player twice (1954, 65). He was inducted into the National Baseball Hall of Fame in 1979.

Ma Yuan (c.1160-1225), Chinese Southern Sung period artist, who created some of China's greatest landscape paintings in ink. A contemporary of the painter Xia Gui (also spelled Hsia Kuei), Ma Yuan was noted for his spare and dramatically asymmetrical compositions. His romantic landsape style influenced the Japanese ink painters Shbun (early 15th century) and Sessh, and the early masters of the Kan school during the Muromachi period (1338-1573).

Mazarin, Jules Cardinal (1602-61), Italian-born French politician and cardinal. Born Giulio Mazarini, he strengthened the French monarchy and by successful diplomacy increased France's influence abroad. After the deaths of Cardinal Richelieu (1642) and Louis XIII (1643), he became the trusted chief minister of the regent, Anne of Austria, and educator of her son, the future Louis XIV. His policy of centralized power and his imposition of taxes provoked the revolts known as the Fronde of the Parlement (1648-53), which he eventually crushed decisively. In foreign policy he gained favorable terms in the treaties that ended the Thirty Years War (1648) and the war with Spain (1659). He was patron of the arts.

Maze *See:* Labyrinth.

Mazepa, Ivan (1640?-1709), Cossack chief who vainly aided Charles XII of Sweden against Peter the Great, hoping to win independence for his native Ukraine. Byron's *Mazeppa* immortalizes a youthful incident in which he is said to have been tied to a wild horse by a jealous Polish nobleman.

Mazzei, Philip (1730-1816), Italian-born U.S. patriot. A physician and wine merchant, Mazzei came to the United States in 1773 and was befriended by Thomas Jefferson. In the years before the American Revolution, he wrote articles calling for independence that Jefferson translated into English. During the war he was sent on an intelligence-gathering mission to Italy. In 1796, while living in France, Mazzei received a letter from Jefferson that was critical of the Federalist government; it caused a political uproar on publication.

Mazzini, Giuseppe (1805-72), Italian patriot and a leading propagandist of the secret society, the Risorgimento, the nationalist involvement that achieved Italian unification. Exiled in 1831, he formed the Young Italy societies, and from France, Switzerland, and England promoted his ideal of a united, democratic Italy. In 1849 he became a leader of the short-lived republic of Rome, but was soon in exile again, continuing his revolutionary propaganda and organizing abortive uprisings. The actual unification of Italy, in which he took little part, fell short of his popular republican ideals.

Mbabane (pop. 38,600), town, administrative capital of Swaziland. Founded as a mining camp in a mountainous region of the former British colony, Mbabane is the center of a prosperous tin mining and agricultural region. Most of the city's residents are Swazi, a Bantu-speaking people of southern Africa, but English is also widely spoken there.

Mboya, Tom (1930-1969), Kenyan political leader. General secretary of the Kenya Federation of Labor (1953-63) and a member of the colonial legislative assembly (1957), he played a key role in securing Kenya's independence. Economics minister from 1964, he was established as a likely successor to Jomo Kenyatta. His assassination (1969) led to rioting and political tension.

McAdam, John Loudon (1756-1836), British engineer and surveyor. He developed a method of paving roads using layers of crushed stone, that revolutionized road building throughout the world. Macadamized roads built in the early 1800s lasted until the 20th century and were the forerunners of many highways still in use today.

McCarran, Patrick Anthony (1876-1954), U.S. Democratic senator from Nevada (1933-54). He sponsored 2 controversial measures, the McCarran-Wood Act (1950), which required the registration of communists, and the McCarran-Walter Act (1952), which tightened controls over aliens and immigrants.

McCarthy, Eugene Joseph (1916-), U.S. Democratic senator from Minnesota (1959-71). A consistent opponent of the Vietnam War, he campaigned for the presidential nomination in 1968 and attracted considerable support. Although he lost the nomination to Hubert Humphrey, his campaign helped to consolidate public opposition to the war.

McCarthy, Joseph Raymond (1908-57), U.S. Republican senator from Wisconsin (1947-57). The "McCarthy era" was born in the early 1950s as a result of his sensational investigations into alleged communist subversion of U.S. life. These investigations were first made (1950) in federal departments, then in the army and among prominent civilians. *McCarthyism* became a word for charges made without proof and accompanied by publicity. After the Army focused national publicity on his activities during the McCarthy hearings (1954), McCarthy was formally censured by fellow senators, and his influence steadily diminished.

McCarthy, Mary (1912-89), U.S. writer, best known for her satirical novel *The Group* (1963), about the lives of a generation of Vassar graduates. Her nonfiction works include *Memories of a Catholic Girlhood* (1957), *Vietnam* (1967), and a body of outstanding literary criticism.

McCarthyism, political movement named after Republican Senator Joseph R. McCarthy of Wisconsin that investigated suspected Communist activities in the United States in the early 1950s. Fearing a Communist takeover of the U.S. government, McCarthy conducted public investigations of suspected officials (and civilians). None of his suspicions were substantiated. He was "condemned" by the Senate in 1954, after having ruined many lives and careers. In contemporary terminology, McCarthyism denotes accusations of disloyalty to the United States or subversive activities based on insufficient evidence.

McCartney, (James) Paul (1942-   ), English singer, guitarist, and songwriter, member of the Beatles (1959-70). Most of the Beatles' songs were sung and written by McCartney and John Lennon. McCartney's contributions were predominantly ballads, including "Yesterday" (1965), "Hey Jude" (1969), and "Let It Be" (1970). McCartney and his wife, Linda Eastman McCartney (1942-1998), subsequently formed and performed with the rock band Wings (1971-81), recording such albums as *Band on the Run* (1973). His more recent solo albums include *Tug of War* (1982), *Off the Ground* (1993), and *Flaming Pie* (1996).
See also: Beatles.

McClellan, George Brinton (1826-85), controversial Union general in the U.S. Civil War. In July 1861 he was given command of the Army of the Potomac, and later that year the supreme command. His hesitation in taking the offensive and his failure to take Richmond led to his dismissal. After

being reinstated, McClellan failed to follow up his success at the Battle of Antietam and was again dismissed in 1862. In 1864 he ran unsuccessfully for the presidency against Abraham Lincoln.
See also: Civil War, U.S.

McClintock, Barbara (1902-92), U.S. geneticist. She won the 1983 Nobel Prize in physiology or medicine for her discovery in the 1940s of the mobility within the chromosome of genetic elements that had been believed to be stationary. McClintock found that certain genetic material is transferred unpredictably from generation to generation, and offered a means of understanding cell differentiation. Her work, considered a great contribution to DNA research, led to greater understanding of some human and animal diseases.
See also: Genetics.

McCloskey, John Cardinal (1810-85), U.S. Roman Catholic prelate. He became archbishop of New York (1864) and was created the first U.S. cardinal (1875). He was responsible for the completion of St. Patrick's Cathedral in New York City.

McClure, Samuel Sidney (1857-1949), editor and publisher who founded (1884) the first U.S. newspaper syndicate. *McClure's Magazine*, of which he was founder (1893) and editor, presented many famous writers to the U.S. public.

McClure, Sir Robert John Le Mesurier(1807-73), English arctic explorer and naval officer. On a search (1850-53) in the Arctic Archipelago for Sir John Franklin, he discovered McClure Strait and became the first to prove the existence of the Northwest Passage.
See also: Northwest Passage.

McCollum, Elmer Verner (1879-1967), U.S. biochemist and professor. While teaching at the Univ. of Wisconsin, he pioneered the study of nutrition and was responsible for assigning letters of the alphabet to the individual vitamins (1915). He also studied the role of other minerals in the diet and the effects of Vitamin D. His published works include *The Newer Knowledge of Nutrition* (1918) and *Foods, Nutrition and Health* (1933).
See also: Biochemistry; Vitamin.

McCormack, John (1884-1945), Irish-American tenor. He began his operatic career in London, first appearing in the U.S. in 1909. He gained his greatest popularity as a concert singer.
See also: Opera.

McCormick, Cyrus Hall (1809-84), U.S. inventor and industrialist. He invented (1831) an early mechanical reaper (patented 1934) that contained innovations used commonly in harvesting machines. The first models appeared under license from 1841 onward.
See also: Reaper.

McCormick, Robert Rutherford (1880-1955), U.S. newspaper editor and publisher who became sole owner of the *Chicago Tribune* after World War

I. Pursuing an extreme right-wing policy, it won the largest circulation of any paper in the Midwest.

McCoy, Elijah (1844?-1929), U.S. engineer and inventor. He developed an efficient system of reducing friction on industrial machinery through the invention of the lubricator cup, which fed a continuous supply of lubricants to the moving parts of machinery, thereby enabling factories to increase their productivity. The popular expression, "the real McCoy" originated when buyers of new machinery insisted that they contain real McCoy lubricators.

McCrae, John (1872-1918), Canadian physician and poet of World War I, famous for his poem "In Flanders Fields," which was written under fire. It was first published in the magazine *Punch* in Dec. 1915.

McCullers, Carson (1917-67), U.S. writer. She is best known for her novels portraying small-town life in the South, and particularly for her lonely, isolated characters, as in *The Heart Is a Lonely Hunter* (1940) and *Member of the Wedding* (1946; adapted by McCullers as a play, 1950). Her *Collected Stories* were published posthumously (1987).

McCulloch v. Maryland, case before the U.S. Supreme Court in 1819, in which Congress was ruled to have implied powers other than those specifically granted by the Constitution. The case involved the Baltimore branch of the Bank of the United States, which refused to pay a tax imposed by Maryland. The court ruled that the tax was unconstitutional because it interfered with Congress, which had the implied power to charter a bank, being responsible for the fiscal operations of the national government.

McEnroe, John (1959-   ), U.S. tennis player. Known for his powerful serve and speed, he won 4 U.S. Open singles titles (1979-81, 1984) and 3 Wimbledon singles titles (1981, 1983-84).

McGillivray, Alexander (1759?-93), Native American leader of the Creek tribe. During the American Revolution he sided with the British and helped protect Creek tribal lands from encroachment by colonial settlers. Between 1785 and 1787 he led the Creeks (backed by the Spanish) in wars against Georgia and Tennessee, and in 1790 he signed a treaty with the United States guaranteeing the Creeks sovereignty over certain lands they held.

McGovern, George Stanley (1922-   ), U.S. senator from South Dakota and the 1972 Democratic presidential candidate. A leading advocate of an end to the Vietnam War, he campaigned for a broad program of social and political reforms. He initially attracted substantial support from liberals, but encountered serious party divisions that hurt his campaign. Richard Nixon won with a record 61% of the popular vote. McGovern unsuccessfully sought his party's nomination again in 1984.

McGraw, John Joseph (1873-1934), U.S. professional baseball player and manager. A star third baseman for the American League's Baltimore Orioles, he became manager of the team in 1901. He then managed the New York Giants (1902-32), who won 10 league championships and 3 World Series.

McGuffey, William Holmes (1800-73), U.S. educator and clergyman. His series of 6 *Eclectic Readers* (1836-57) sold an estimated 122 million copies. Almost universally used in elementary schools in the Midwest and South, they had an immense influence on public education. McGuffey was also president of Ohio Univ. (1839-45).

McKay, Alexander (?-1811), early Canadian explorer and fur trader. He was a member of Alexander Mackenzie's first trans-Canadian expedition that reached the Pacific Coast in 1793. As a member of the North West Company (later Hudson's Bay Company), McKay agreed to help John Jacob Astor build Astoria, Ore. in 1810. A year later he brought his ship into the columbia River to begin work on the settlement but hostile Native Americans boarded it, killing everyone on board.

McKay, Claude (1890-1948), U.S. poet and novelist born in Jamaica. His was the first and most militant voice of the New York Negro movement in the 1920s. His works include poetry, *Harlem Shadows* (1922), and the novel *Home to Harlem* (1927).

McKay, Donald (1810-80), Canadian-born U.S. naval architect, master builder of clipper ships. His *Great Republic* (1853) at 4,555 tons (5,020 metric tons) was the biggest clipper ever built. The use of steam brought a decline in business that forced him to close his Boston shipyards in 1855.

McKean, Thomas (1734-1817), U.S. patriot. He as a signer of the Declaration of Independence and Delaware representative to the Continental Congress (1774-1783). He served as president of the Congress (1781), chief justice of Pennsylvania (1777-99), and governor of Pennsylvania (1799-1808). He also wrote most of the Delaware state constitution.

McKim, Charles Follen (1847-1909), U.S. architect, founder of the firm McKim, Mead, and White (1878) and of the American Academy in Rome. His best-known projects, such as the University Club in New York City (1900), are in a neoclassical style.

McKinley, William (1843-1901), 25th president of the United States. McKinley—last in a long line of presidents who had fought in the Civil War—led the U.S. during its war with Spain, and presided over a nation emerging from a period of isolation to become a world power.

William McKinley

25th U.S. President	
Born:	Niles, Ohio; Jan. 29, 1843
Term:	Mar. 1897-Sept. 1901
Vice presidents:	Garret A. Hobart; Theodore Roosevelt
Political party:	Republican
Spouse:	Ida Saxton McKinley
Children:	2
Died:	Buffalo, N.Y.; Sept. 14, 1901

Early life. McKinley attended Allegheny College at Meadville, Pa., but illness forced him to return home after a few months. He taught school until the Civil War broke out. McKinley, then 18, enlisted in the 23rd Ohio Volunteers. His bravery in the Battle of Antietam earned him a higher commission; by the war's end, he had reached the rank of brevet major. After studying law in Albany, N.Y., he was admitted to the bar in 1867 and set up a practice in Canton, Ohio. In 1871, he married Ida Saxton; they had two children.

Political career. McKinley entered Republican party politics soon after moving to Canton. In 1876, he was elected to the U.S. House of Representatives, where he served, except for one term, until 1891. He sponsored the McKinley Tariff Act of 1890, which set record-high protective duties. The tariff's unpopularity contributed to his reelection defeat in 1890, but he was elected governor of Ohio in 1891 and 1893. In 1896, the Republicans nominated him for the presidency. McKinley was elected after a bitter campaign in which opponent William Jennings Bryan, the famous orator, portrayed McKinley and his running mate, Garret A. Hobart, as supporters of "rule of the rich."

President. In his administration's early years, McKinley had to cope with the nation's economic problems. By 1898, however, the depression that had lasted for five years was ending. As the severe economic and social problems of the 1880s and 1890s subsided, U.S. attention turned outward and foreign-affairs problems took center stage. Spanish outrages during a Cuban insurrection that had begun in 1895 aroused indignation in the U.S. war hysteria grew after the battleship U.S.S. *Maine* was blown up in Havana's harbor on Feb. 15, 1898. McKinley hoped to avoid war, but eventually yielded to public opinion and that of many Congress members and other high officials by asking Congress to authorize U.S. intervention in Cuba. On Apr. 24, two days after Congress authorized a U.S. blockade of Spanish ports, Spain declared war on the U.S.

The Spanish-American War, which lasted only 113 days, brought the U.S. into the arena of international politics and made it an imperial power. During the war, the U.S. annexed Hawaii; the following year, the U.S. demanded equal trade opportunities with China.

The war had brought on a period of booming prosperity, helping McKinley and running mate Theodore Roosevelt, who promised "a full dinner bucket" for four more years, to win the 1900 election.

Assassination. In 1901, McKinley took a national speaking tour to call for freer trade and an end to U.S. isolation. As he greeted a crowd in Buffalo, N.Y., he was shot by anarchist Leon Czolgosz. McKinley died eight days later.

McKissick, Floyd Bixler (1922-), African-American political leader. In the 1960s he was the national chairperson and director of the Congress of Racial Equality (CORE) and one of the leading advocates of Black Power. McKissick and other Black Power proponents urged African-Americans to take control over the destinies of their own communities and to foster a greater sense of pride in their social and cultural heritage.
See also: Black Power.

McKuen, Rod (1933-   ), U.S. poet and songwriter. His poetry collections include *Lonesome Cities* (1968) and *In Someone's Shadow* (1969). He has performed and recorded many of his own songs, and has also written film scores.

McLoughlin, John (1784-1857), Canadian pioneer of the Oregon Territory. Directing (1824-46) the operations of the Hudson's Bay Company in the region of the Columbia River, McLoughlin was credited with achieving peace between Native American tribes and European-American settlers of the Columbia and Willamette river valleys. Often called the "father of Oregon," McLoughlin's efforts contributed to the formation of the Oregon Territory (1848) and the achievement of statehood (1859).
See also: Oregon.

McLuhan, Marshall (1911-80), Canadian professor of humanities and mass communications specialist. He is best known for his influential *Understanding Media* (1964). It contains the famous phrase, "the medium is the message"—that is, the content of communication is determined by its means, with the implication that modern mass communications technology is creating a "global village" and transforming our way of thinking and perceiving.
See also: Communication.

M'Clure, Sir Robert John Le Mesurier *See:* McClure, Sir Robert John Le Mesurier.

McNamara, Robert Strange (1916-), secretary of defense under presidents Kennedy and Johnson (1961-68), who played an important part in the shaping of U.S. defense policy, including Vietnam War policy. Before this he had been president of the Ford Motor Company, and in 1968 he became president of the World Bank, serving until 1981. In his book *In Retrospect. The Tragedy and Lessons of Vietnam* (1995), he admits that America has made mistakes concerning the war in Vietnam.

McPherson, Aimee Semple (1890-1944), U.S. evangelist, famed for her flamboyant preaching. She worked as a missionary in China, then returned to the United States to become an itinerant preacher and faith-healer. She opened the Angelus Temple (1923) and founded the International Church of Foursquare Gospel (1927), both in Los Angeles. She was involved in numerous legal actions, including a sensational one for fraud, of which she was acquitted.

Mead, Margaret (1901-78), U.S. cultural anthropologist known for *Coming of Age in Samoa* (1928), *Growing Up in New Guinea* (1930), *the Mountain Arapesh* (3 vols., 1938-49), and *Male and Female* (1949), among other works. Her autobiography, *Blackberry Winter*, appeared in 1972. She was adjunct professor of anthropology at Columbia Univ. after 1954, and was associated with New York's American Museum of Natural History from 1926 until her death.
See also: Anthropology.

Meade, George Gordon (1815-72), Union general of the U.S. Civil War. He performed with distinction in 1862 at the Seven Days Battles, Bull Run, and Antietam, and afterwards at Fredericksburg and Chancellorville. As commander of the Army of the Potomac, he won the Battle of Gettysburg.

Criticized for not following up his victory, he kept his command under Ulysses S. Grant's direction.
See also: Civil War, U.S.

Meadowlark, common North American field bird of the family Icteridae, with a distinctive black V on its yellow underside. It is a relative of the blackbird and oriole. Also called a meadow starling, the meadowlark eats insects rather than grain and builds its nest on the ground. The eastern meadowlark, known for its whistling song, lives in moister areas than the western meadowlark.

Meany, George (1894-1980), U.S. labor leader, president (1955-79) of the American Federation of Labor and Congress of Industrial Organizations (AFL-CIO). He was president of the New York State Federation of Labor (1934) and secretary-treasurer (1939) and president (1952) of the AFL.
See also: Labor movement.

Measles, common infectious disease usually seen in children and caused by a virus. It involves a characteristic sequence of fever, headache, and malaise, followed by conjunctivitis and rhinitis, and the development of a typical rash, with blotchy erythema (redness) affecting the skin of the face, trunk, and limbs. Complications can include pneumonia and encephalitis. Vaccination confers temporary immunity; one attack confers lifelong immunity.

Measuring worm, also known as inchworm or looper, hairless caterpillar, moth larvae found on every continent. Measuring worms move by extending their front end and holding on with their legs, then bringing up the rest of the body in a loop so that the rear end practically meets the front end. They move in this way because they have only 2 or 3 (rather than the usual 5) pairs of leglike structures on the back part of their bodies. Many measuring worms are difficult to detect when not moving, as they often resemble twigs and rest in twiglike positions.

Meat packing, industry that involves the butchering and processing of meat-producing animals for human consumption. Meat packing companies purchase large herds of cattle, sheep, and hogs from ranchers and farmers or from terminal markets. In the packing plants, the animals are slaughtered and cut up into their edible sections (dressed). The meat is treated to preserve freshness, frozen to keep it from being spoiled by bacteria, and shipped to consumer markets.

Mecca (Arabic: *Makka*; pop. 550,000), is the chief city of the Hejaz region of Saudi Arabia. It is the birthplace of the prophet Muhammad, the founder of Islam, and the most holy city of Islam. Only Muslims may enter the city. The courtyard of the great Haram mosque encloses the sacred shrine, the Kaaba, which Muslims face when they pray; nearby is the holy Zem-Zem well. Pilgrimage to Mecca, "haji," is a duty of all Muslims able to perform it; each year over a million pilgrims arrive. The economy of Mecca depends on the pilgrims.
See also: Islam; Saudi Arabia.

Mechanical engineering *See:* Engineering.

Mechanics, branch of applied mathematics that deals with the effects of forces on solids, liquids, and gases at rest or in motion. Dynamics studies the way in which forces produce motion; statics addresses the forces acting on a motionless body; kinematics deals with relationships among distance, time, velocity, and acceleration. Solid mechanics examines the motions of rigid bodies and deformable solid bodies and the causative forces. Continuum mechanics addresses deformable bodies, such as gases, liquids, and deformable solids.
See also: Aerodynamics; Hydraulics.

Mecklenburg, German state, renamed Mecklenburg-Western Pomerania upon Germany's reunification (1990). Primarily a farming region along Germany's Baltic coastal plain, Mecklenburg was ruled by powerful German princes and kings throughout the Middle Ages. It was divided many times into separate states, following wars during the 17th through the 19th centuries, and powerful landowners (Junkers) controlled vast estates from the mid-18th century through the end of World War II. Captured by the Communist army in 1945, Mecklenburg was an East German state until 1952, when it was divided into 3 districts.
See also: Germany.

Medal *See:* Decorations, medals, and orders.

Medawar, Sir Peter Brian (1915-87), Brazilian-born British zoologist who shared with Sir Macfarlane Burnet the 1960 Nobel Prize for physiology or medicine for their work on immunological tolerance. Inspired by Burnet's ideas, Medawar showed that if fetal mice were injected with cells from eventual donors, skin grafts made onto them later from those donors would "take," thus showing the possibility of acquired tolerance and hence, ultimately, organ transplants.
See also: Zoology.

Medea, in Greek mythology, sorceress and princess of Colchis. Through her magical powers she helped Jason obtain the Golden Fleece in Colchis where she was the daughter of King Aites. Returning with Jason to the Greek city of Iolkos where he claimed the throne, Medea conspired to kill King Pelias who had seized the throne from Jason's father. When Jason tried to divorce her, Medea had his bride-to-be killed and after plotting to kill the oldest son of the king of Athens, she was banished.
See also: Mythology.

Medellín (pop. 1,595,000), city in west-central Colombia. Medellín is the capital of Antioquia department and the hub of a rich mining and agricultural region. It was founded in 1675 near several gold mines and later became a textile, manufacturing, and coffee-processing center. Medellín also houses 3 universities and is a major educational center.

Medfly *See:* Mediterranean fruit fly.

Media, homeland of a nomadic people, the Medes, it was located in what is now northern Iran. Its history has been traced back to 836 B.C., when the Assyrians, under King Shalmaneser III, invaded Media in the first of many invasions. The Medes reached their peak under Cyaxares, who reigned from 625 to 585 B.C. His son, Astyages, the last Median king, was defeated by Cyrus the Great of Persia about 550 B.C. Media became a part of the Persian Empire.

Media, the plural form of "medium." The term is used to apply to communication systems, such as books, newspapers, radio, and television.
See also: Newspaper; Radio; Television.

Medicaid, U.S. government-financed system of medical aid to low-income people under 65. It was introduced in 1965 along with the Medicare legislation. The federal government pays from 50% to about 80% of the costs for anyone eligible, as determined by each state separately. To participate, a state must meet the standards of the federal government.

Medical Association, American *See:* American Medical Association.

Medicare, U.S. government-financed system of medical and hospital insurance for people aged 65 and over. It was set up in 1965 by legislation supported by President Lyndon B. Johnson. It was opposed by the American Medical Association, which objected on principle to possible government intervention, although the cost of private treatment had risen beyond the means of most older people. In 1972 Medicare was extended to cover disabled Social Security beneficiaries and persons of any age suffering from chronic kidney disease.

Medici, Italian family of bankers, princes, and patrons of the arts who controlled Florence almost continually from the 1420s to 1737 and provided cardinals, popes (Leo X, Clement VII, and Leo XI), and 2 queens of France. The foundations of the family's power were laid by **Giovanni di Bicci de'Medici** (1360-1429), who achieved wealth through banking and commerce. His elder son, **Cosimo de'Medici** (1389-1464), was effectively ruler of Florence from 1434 and was voted "Father of the Country" after his death. He founded the great Laurentian Library and patronized artists including Donatello and Lorenzo Ghiberti. His grandson **Lorenzo** (1449-92), called "the Magnificent," was Italy's most brilliant Renaissance prince. Himself a fine poet, he patronized Sandro Botticelli, Domenico Ghirlandaio, the young Michelangelo, and many other artists. Lorenzo helped make Florence a powerful and beautiful Italian state, and took over the state government. His son **Pietro** (1471-1503) was expelled from Florence (1494) by a popular rising led by Girolamo Savonarola. The family was restored in 1512; Pietro's son **Lorenzo** (1492-1519) ruled from 1513 under the guidance of his uncle **Giovanni** (1475-1521), who was Pope Leo X and a bountiful patron of the arts in Rome. The ruthless **Cosimo I** (1519-74) doubled Florentine territory and power and was made grand duke of Tuscany in 1569. **Catherine de Médicis** (1519-89) was the wife of Henry II and mother of 3 French kings. She virtually ruled France from 1559. **Marie de Médicis** (1573-1642), the wife of Henry IV, reigned after his death (1610) until her son, Louis XIII, became king. The later Medicis were less distinguished; the line died out with Gian Gastone (1671-1737).
See also: Catherine de' Medici; Clement VII; Leo.

Medicine, the art and science of treating disease. Within the last 150 years medicine has become dominated by scientific principles. Prior to this, healing was mainly a matter of tradition and magic. The Greeks introduced anatomy and physiology and provided the Hippocratic oath, in use today. In the 17th century, William Harvey researched blood circulation and the heart; in the 18th century, Edward Jenner introduced vaccination; in the 19th century, Louis Pasteur proposed the germ theory and anesthesia made advances in surgery possible. Medicine in the 20th century uses new diagnostic techniques (x-rays, CAT scans, MRIs), organ transplants, a better understanding of nutrition and immunity, and new drugs, especially antibiotics.

Medicine, patent *See:* Patent medicine.

Medieval period *See:* Middle Ages.

Medill, Joseph (1823-99), Canadian-born U.S. editor and publisher of the *Chicago Tribune*, and a builder of the Republican Party. A strong emancipationist and supporter of Abraham Lincoln, he served at the Illinois Constitutional Convention of 1869 and as mayor of Chicago (1872-74).

Medina (pop. 350,000), holy Muslim city and place of pilgrimage in Hejaz, Saudi Arabia, 210 mi (338 km) north of Mecca. The prophet Muhammad came to Medina after his *hegira* (flight) from Mecca (A.D. 622), and the chief mosque contains his tomb. A walled city, Medina stands in a fertile oasis noted for its dates, grains, and vegetables.
See also: Muslims; Saudi Arabia.

Medina, Harold Raymond (1888-1990), U.S. jurist. A Columbia University law professor from 1915 to 1947. Medina was appointed a federal judge in 1947. Two years later he presided over the trial of 11 American Communist party leaders convicted of advocating the overthrow of the U.S. government by force. He stepped down from the bench in 1958.

Mediterranean fruit fly, or Medfly (*Ceratitis capitata*), pest of fruit in Africa, Australia, and the United States, attacking, in particular, peaches, apricots, and citrus fruits. The larvae destroy the fruits, and whole harvests may be lost. The maggots are capable of prodigious leaps of about 4 in (10 cm) high and over distances of 8 in (20 cm).

Mediterranean Sea, intercontinental sea between Europe, Asia, and Africa (over 965,000 sq mi—2,500,000 sq km). It opens into the Atlantic Ocean in the west through the Strait of Gibraltar, and into the Black Sea through the Dardanelles and Bosporus. The Suez Canal provides the Mediterranean Sea's link with the Red Sea and on to the Indian Ocean. Peninsular Italy, Sicily, Malta, and Pantelleria and Tunisia's Cape Bon mark the dividing narrows between the eastern and western basins. The many islands of the western basin include Sicily, Sardinia, Elba, Corsica and the Balearics. Crete, Cyprus, Rhodes, and the numerous Aegean islands are included in the eastern basin. Geologically the Mediterranean Sea is a relic of a sea that separated Eurasia from Africa about 200 million years ago, and was partially uplifted to form the Alps, South Europe, and the Atlas Mountains. The name (Latin, "middle [of the] land"), reflects the sea's central position and importance in the ancient world. Limited access from the Atlantic Ocean and confined entries to both the Black and Red seas have given the Mediterranean Sea great strategic importance throughout history.

Medusa, in Greek mythology one of three equally hideous-looking sisters (Gorgons). She and her sisters, Stheno and Euryale, had snakes growing from their heads in place of hair and fangs for teeth. Anyone looking directly at them turned to stone but Perseus slew Medusa by looking at a reflection of her as he cut off her head. Later he gave the head to Athena.
See also: Mythology.

Medusa *See:* Jellyfish.

Meeker, Ezra (1830-1928), U.S. author and explorer of the Oregon Trail. In 1852, Meeker and his family made an ox-cart journey on the Oregon Trail from Iowa to Portland, Ore. He made the return trip some years later in 1906 and once again by automobile in 1915. His books are *Ox-Team Days on the Oregon Trail* (1922) and *Kate Mulhal* (1926). Meeker was the founder of the Oregon Trail Association.
See also: Oregon Trail.

Meerkat, or suricate (*Suricata suricatta*), small, insect-eating mammal of the family Herpestidae, native to dry regions of southern Africa. The meerkat's slim body and long tail measure about 20 in (51 cm) long, and it weighs about 2 lb (900 gm). It has silvery brown fur with dark markings. Its sturdy hind legs allow it to stand upright to search for predatory birds. Meerkats live in burrows in colonies of up to 30 animals. The name "meerkat" is also sometimes applied to various mongooses.

Mehta, Zubin (1936-), Indian-born U.S. conductor who studied at the Vienna Academy of Music and later became musical director of the Montreal Symphony (1961-67), Los Angeles Philharmonic (1962-78), and New York Philharmonic (1978-91).

Meighen, Arthur (1874-1960), 2-term Canadian prime minister. Elected to the Canadian House of Commons in 1908, Meighen, a Conservative, held 3 Cabinet posts under Prime Minister Sir Robert Borden. Following Borden's retirement in 1920, Meighen took office on July 10. On Dec. 29, 1921, he was replaced by William Lyon Mackenzie King. He won a second term as prime minister in 1926, serving from June 29 to Sept. 25 and was replaced by King again.

Meiji (1852-1912), emperor of Japan (1867-1912); his given name was Mutsuhito. The long isolation of Japan under the shoguns ended in 1868 with the restoration of imperial power. Meiji guided the transformation of Japan from a feudal empire into a modern industrial nation with a central admini-stration. The court was moved from Kyoto to Tokyo.

Mein Kampf (German, "My Struggle"), Adolf Hitler's book detailing his life and beliefs, published in 2 volumes (1925, 1927; English trans., 1933, 1939). The book, which advocates Germany's conquest of the world and

expresses Hitler's views on the superiority of the German "master race" and the inferiority and evil of Jews, became the Nazi manifesto.
See also: Hitler, Adolf; Nazism.

Meir, Golda (1898-1978), Israeli leader, prime minister of Israel (1969-74). Born Golda Mabovitch in Kiev, USSR, she was raised in the United States and emigrated to Palestine in 1921. She was a prominent figure in the establishment of the State of Israel (1948). Elected to the Knesset (parliament) in 1949, Meir became foreign minister in 1956; in 1966 she was elected general secretary of the dominant Mapai party, later the Israel Labor Party (1968). In 1969 she succeeded Levi Eshkol as premier and formed a broad coalition government. During her time in office the Israelis fought off a 1973 Syrian-Egyptian surprise attack (the Yom Kippur War). In 1974 she resigned because of criticism of her lack of preparedness for that war.
See also: Israel.

Meitner, Lise (1878-1968), Austrian physicist who worked with Otto Hahn to discover protactinium (1917). Following the experiments of German physical chemists Hahn and Fritz Strassmann in bombarding uranium with neutrons, Meitner and her nephew, Otto Robert Frish (1904-), correctly interpreted the results as showing nuclear fission and predicted the chain reaction. This work contributed to the development of the atomic bomb and other uses of nuclear energy.
See also: Nuclear energy; Physics.

Mekong River, one of the chief rivers of the southeastern region of Asia, rising in the Tibetan highlands. It flows 2,600 mi (4,180 km) southward through the Yunnan province of China and Laos, along the Thailand border, and through Cambodia to its wide fertile delta in southern Vietnam, on the South China Sea. The lower 340 mi (547 km) can accommodate medium-sized vessels. Phnom-Penh is an important port. The Mekong River's lower valley produces much of the world's rice.

Melaka (pop. 88,100), Malaysian port city. Located on the strategic Strait of Malacca, Melaka (formerly Malacca) is the capital of the state of the same name. In the 15th century, it was one of the most important ports in Southeast Asia and was captured by Portugal (1511), the Netherlands (1641), and Great Britain (1795). Melaka remained in British hands until Malaysia was granted independence (1957) as the Federation of Malaya.
See also: Malaysia.

Melanchthon, Philipp (1497-1560), German scholar and humanist, second to Luther in initiating and leading the Protestant Reformation in Germany. His *Loci communes rerum theologicarum* (1521), a systematic statement of Lutheran beliefs, was the first great Protestant work on religious doctrine; and his *Augsburg Confession* (1530) was one of the principal statements of faith in the Lutheran Church.
See also: Reformation.

Melanesia *See:* Pacific Islands.

Melanin *See:* Skin.

Melbourne (pop. 3,080,900), second-largest city in Australia and capital of Victoria, on the Yarra River. Founded by settlers in 1835 and named (1837) in honor of the British prime minister Lord Melbourne, the city is now one of the nation's chief ports; it ranks with Sydney as a major industrial center. Manufactures include textiles, leather goods, ships, automobiles, and aircraft; oil refineries also have been built. Melbourne was the seat of the Australian federal government (1901-27).
See also: Australia.

Mellon, Andrew William (1855-1937), U.S. financier, industrialist, U.S. treasury secretary (1921-31), and U.S. ambassador to Britain (1931-32). After taking control of his father's banking firm and founding other banks, he increased his holdings in such companies as oil, coal, locomotives, hydroelectricity, bridge construction, insurance, and steel. He served under 3 presidents, and reduced the national debt by some $9 billion. A multimillionaire himself, he founded the Mellon Institute of Industrial Research. His vast art collection formed the basis (1937) of the National Gallery of Art in Washington, D.C.

Mellon Foundation, Andrew W., philanthropic organization that grants funds to educational, scientific, public affairs and cultural institutions. Named after Andrew W. Mellon, former secretary of the treasury (1921-32), the foundation was started by Mellon's daughter and son in 1969. It is one of the 10 wealthiest foundations in the United States.

Melodrama, originally a term used to refer to a passage in opera spoken over an orchestral accompaniment but more usually used to describe the sentimental drama of the 19th century in which characters were either good or bad. Melodramas were often based on romantic novels or bloodthirsty crimes. Thrills and narrow escapes played an important part in the plot.

Melon, fruit of *Cucumis melo*, a plant of the gourd family that grows wild in Africa and Asia. It is now widely cultivated in the United States, where the climate is hot and dry. The 2 main kinds of melon are the *watermelon* and the *muskmelon*, which includes *honeydews*, *casabas*, and *Persian melons*. The *cantaloupe* spoils rapidly, whereas the others will last for months, becoming softer as they ripen. The *tsamma melon*, a watermelon, supplies vital water to the Bush people of the Kalahari Desert. The round melons can grow to 1 ft (30 cm) across and vary in color.

Melos *See:* Mílos.

Meltdown *See:* Nuclear reactor.

Melville, Herman (1819-91), U.S. writer. His reputation rests mainly on the masterpiece Moby-Dick (1851), and the short novel Billy Budd, Foretopman, published posthumously (1924). Melville's whaling and other voyages provided material for several of his earlier, popular books. Typee (1846), his first, was based on his adventures and capture by cannibals after jumping ship in the Marquesas islands. Moby-Dick, a deeply symbolic work, combines allegory with adventure. Too profound and complex for its audience, this great novel was not successful; subsequent books did not recapture

Melville's former popularity. Only in the 1930s did his talent receive full recognition.

Melville Island, Canadian island in the Arctic Ocean. Covering an area of 16,369 sq mi (42,396 sq km), Melville Island is one of the Parry Islands, discovered in 1819 by the British explorer Sir William Parry. The straits and seas surrounding the island are frozen most of the year; herds of musk-oxen inhabit the island, which is without human habitation. Melville Island is administered by the District of Franklin, Northwest Territories.

Memel *See:* Klaipeda.

Memling, Hans (1430-94), Flemish painter famous for his portraits and religious works, including the paneled *Shrine of St. Ursula* (1489). The German-born Memling (or Memlinc) worked in Bruges, Belgium, and was probably a pupil of Rogier van der Weyden.

Memorial Day, or Decoration Day, U.S. holiday honoring the dead of all wars, observed on the last Mon. in May. Memorial Day originated in the South after the Civil War when the graves of both Confederate and Union soldiers were decorated.

Memphis, capital of the Old Kingdom of ancient Egypt until c.2200 B.C. Probably founded (c.3100 B.C.) by Menes, the first king of a united Upper and Lower Egypt, the city stood on the West bank of the Nile, about 15 mi (24 km) south of modern Cairo. Excavations have revealed the temple of Ptah, god of the city, and the 2 massive statues of Ramses II; cemeteries and pyramids also remain.

Memphis (pop. 610,300), largest city and chief river port of Tennessee, seat of Shelby County, on the high east banks bluffs of the Mississippi River below the mouth of the Wolf River. It was founded in 1819 and incorporated in 1826. Memphis is a leading market for cotton, hardwood lumber and livestock, as well as meat packing center and a transportation hub. Its manufactures include cottonseed products, textiles, farm machinery, paper, and drugs. It has foundries and rice mills. The city, noted for its fine churches, also has many educational institutions, including the medical divisions of the University of Tennessee. Memphis is the site of Beale Street, made famous by the composer W.C. Handy, and of Elvis Presley's estate, Graceland, a popular tourist attraction.
See also: Tennessee.

Menander (342-c.291 B.C.), leading Greek writer of New comedy. Of over 100 plays, only *Dyscolos* (The Grouch) survives complete; adaptations of his other plays, by the Roman playwrights Plautus and Terence, influenced 17th-century comedy. His plots are based on love affairs, and he is noted for his elegant style and debt characterization.

Mencius (Mengke; 370-290 B.C.), Chinese philosopher. A follower of Confucius, he was influential in the development of Confucianism. He held that humanity is naturally good and that the principles of true moral conduct are inborn. He was a champion of the ordinary people and exhorted rulers to treat their subjects well.
See also: Confucianism.

Mencken, H(enry) L(ouis) (1880-1956), U.S. journalist and author, caustic critic of U.S. society and literature. He wrote for the *Baltimore Sun* and founded and edited the *American Mercury* (1924). His collected essays appeared in *Prejudices* (6 vols., 1919-27). Among other works, he also wrote an authoritative study, *The American Language* (1919).

Mendel, Gregor Johann (1822-84), Austrian botanist and Augustinian monk who laid the foundations of the science of genetics. His results with experiments on dwarf pea plants provided a mechanism justifying Charles Darwin's theory of evolution by natural selection; however, contemporary lack of interest and his unsuccessful experiments with the hawkweeds discouraged him from carrying this work further. Only in 1900, when scientists found his published results, was the importance of his work realized.
See also: Genetics; Heredity.

Mendeleev, Dmitri Ivanovich (1834-1907), Russian chemist who formulated (1869) the Periodic Law, stating that the properties of elements vary periodically with increasing atomic weight. This work enabled him to draw up the Periodic Table.
See also: Chemistry; Periodic table.

Mendelevium, chemical element, symbol Md; for physical constants see Periodic Table. An artificial radioactive element, mendelevium was discovered by Albert Ghiorso and his co-workers in 1955. Einsteinium-253 was bombarded with helium ions in the 60-inch cyclotron in Berkeley. Mendelevium-256, having a half-life of 76 minutes, was produced. That is the longest-lived isotope of the element known. It is a metallic element and a member of the actinide series. Fourteen radioactive isotopes of mendelevium have been produced.

Mendel's laws *See:* Genetics; Mendel, Gregor Johann.

Mendelssohn, Felix (1809-47), German Romantic composer. He wrote his concert overture to *A Midsummer Night's Dream* at age 17. Other works include his *Hebrides Overture* (also known as "Fingal's Cave," 1830-32), *Scotch* (1842) and *Italian* (1833) symphonies, a violin concerto, chamber music, and the oratorio *Elijah*. He was also a celebrated conductor, notably of the Leipzig Gewandhaus orchestra, and he revived interest in the music of Johann Sebastian Bach.

Mendelssohn, Moses (1729-1786), German-Jewish philosopher and scholar, a leading figure of the Enlightenment in Prussia, and a promoter of Jewish assimilation into German culture. He wrote *Phädon* (1767) and *Jerusalem* (1783).
See also: Age of Reason; Philosophy.

Mengele, Josef (1911-79?), Nazi war criminal. A doctor who conducted often inhuman medical experiments on inmates of Auschwitz, a Nazi concentration camp. Mengele is believed responsible for 400,000 deaths there. Captured by the Allies at the end of World War II, he was inadvertently released and fled to South America. Charged with war crimes by West

Germany (1959), Mengele eluded capture for 20 years before dying in Brazil. Remains believed to be his were unearthed in a Brazilian cemetery in 1985. *See also:* Auschwitz; Nazism.

Menhaden, marine fish (*Brevoortia tyrannus*) of the herring family. Inhabiting the Atlantic coastal waters from Nova Scotia to Brazil, menhaden measure 12-18 in (30-46 cm) and weigh up to 1 lb (0.5 kg). They are edible but are most often processed for their oil or as livestock feed and fertilizer.

Meningitis (cerebrospinal meningitis), inflammation of the menninges caused by bacteria or viruses. Bacterial meningitis is of abrupt onset, with headache, vomiting, fever, neck stiffness, and sensitivity to light. Early and appropriate antibiotic treatment is essential as permanent damage may occur, especially in children. Viral meningitis is a milder illness with similar signs; only symptomatic measures are required. Tuberculous meningitis is an insidious chronic type that responds slowly to antituberculous drugs. Some fungi, unusual bacteria and syphilis may also cause varieties of meningitis. Diagnosis is made through an examination of the cerebrospinal fluid via a spinal tap.

Menninger, U.S. family of psychiatrists. **Charles Frederick Menninger** (1862-1955), along with his sons **Karl Augustus** (1893-1990) and **William Claire** (1899-1966) established the clinic (1920) and foundation (1941) that bears their name in Topeka, Kans. Karl and William served as officials for the Menninger Foundation which specializes in research, treatment of mentally ill patients, and the training of psychiatric professionals. Published works include Karl's *The Human Mind* (1930), *Man Against Himself* (1938), and *The Crime of Punishment* (1968) and Williams's *Psychiatry in a Troubled World* (1948).
See also: Psychiatry.

Mennonites, Protestant sect originating among the Anabaptists of Zurich, Switzerland. They became particularly influential in the Netherlands, and are named for the Dutch reformer Menno Simons. They base their faith solely on the Bible, believe in separation of Church and State, pacifism, and baptism only for adults who renounce sin. They are known for the strict simplicity of their life and worship. The Amish Church is a well-known, conservative division of the Mennonites in the United States.
See also: Anabaptism.

Menominee, Native American tribe of the Algonquian linguistic group. For more than 5,000 years they lived in upper Michigan and Wisconsin, along the western shore of Green Bay, gathering wild rice (*Menominee* means *wild rice people*). In 1854 they were settled on a reservation on the Wolf and Oconto rivers in Wisconsin, now a county, where their descendants still live and work in the lumber business. In 1953, through the policy of termination, the U.S. government abolished the Menominee reservation, but reestablished it in 1975.

Menotti, Gian Carlo (1911-), Italian-born U.S. composer of operas and founder (1958) of the Festival of Two Worlds at Spoleto, Italy. His works include *The Medium* (1946) and the television opera *Amahl and the Night*

Visitors (1951). *The Consul* (1950) and *The Saint of Bleecker Street* (1954) won Pulitzer prizes for music.

Mensheviks, name for the position of the minority group in the Russian Social Democratic Workers' Party-opposition to the Bolsheviks, the majority group led by Vladimir Ilyich Lenin. Unlike Lenin, the Menshevik theoretician Georgi Plekhanov favored mass membership and believed a spell of bourgeois rule must precede communism. Led by L. Martov (Yuly Osiporich Tsederbaum), the Mensheviks emerged in 1903, backed Aleksandr Feodorovich Kerensky's short-lived government (1917), and opposed the Bolshevik seizure of power. By 1921 they had been eliminated.
See also: Bolsheviks; Russian Revolution.

Menstruation, in women of reproductive age, specifically the monthly loss of blood (period), representing shedding of womb endometrium; in general, the whole monthly cycle of hormonal, structural, and functional changes, punctuated by menstrual blood loss. After each period, the endometrium (womb-lining) starts to proliferate and thicken under the influence of gonadotrophins (follicle-stimulating hormone) and estrogens. In midcycle an egg is released from an ovarian follicle (ovulation). The endometrium is prepared for implantation of a fertilized egg. If the egg is not fertilized, pregnancy does not ensue; then blood-vessel changes that occur lead to the shedding of the endometrium and some blood, sometimes with pain or colic. The cycle then restarts. Cyclic patterns are established at puberty (menarche) and end in middle life (age 45-60) at the menopause, the "change of life." Disorders of menstruation include heavy, irregular, or missed periods; bleeding between periods or after the menopause; and excessively painful periods. These disorders are studied in gynecology.
See also: Reproduction.

Mental age *See:* Intelligence quotient.

Mental illness, any of several diseases of the mind manifesting itself as disordered thoughts or feelings, or behavior which is apparently irrational or which deviates from socially and culturally accepted norms. The modern concept of mental illness rests on 3 foundations. The oldest of these consists of norms of feeling, development, and behavior defined by society and prevailing in a culture at a particular time. One example of an important area bearing on an individual's mental health that is strongly defined by custom and belief is sexuality. Our definition of mental illness also proceeds from rationalism, the idea that a healthy mind is predominantly a logical mind. And we rely upon science, particularly neurophysiology and neurochemistry, for research into the organic causes of mental illness. Though it is widely accepted that many, if not most, mental illnesses are caused or can be treated organically, there are many mental disorders that have no known organic cause but whose symptoms may be masked or alleviated by drugs. Organic disorders include delirium, which may be accompanied by illusions or hallucinations, and dementia, characterized by lapses of one or more of the mental faculties. Delirium can be caused by alcoholism or certain illnesses; dementia often accompanies aging. Schizophrenia, a severe form of psychosis, has recently been associated with chemical imbalances in the brain and there are indications it may be hereditary. Affective disorders, including mania, depression, and manic-depression, are profound disturbances of mood which can be managed to some degree with antidepressants or tranquilizers.

Other forms of mental illness include a variety of anxieties such as obsessive-compulsive behavior or phobias (agoraphobia, or fear of public places, and claustrophobia, or fear of closed places, are examples). There are also dissociative disorders in which a person may suffer a change or loss of identity. These can manifest as one of several kinds of amnesia or as multiple personality disorder, in which a person has more than 1 personality with now one, then the other, being dominant. The underlying causes of these conditions are as yet unknown.

There are also certain kinds of mental illness unique to a particular age group. Children, for example, may be hyperactive or they may be afflicted with autism, a disorder in which the child appears remote, expressionless, and unresponsive. Alzheimer's, a disease of the brain cells that leads to impairment of the mental faculties, attacks people in their 40s and older.

The principal health professionals concerned with diagnosing and treating the mentally ill are psychiatrists and psychologists. Psychiatrists are medical doctors; psychologists are usually Ph.D.s in psychology. Treatment for the mentally ill may include drug therapy, various forms of psychotherapy, or periods of institutionalization. In many cases, a combination of therapies is used. For some patients, psychoanalysis is found useful, while others respond best to behavior modification. In extreme cases, electroshock treatments and even psychosurgery may be necessary, though both are highly controversial forms of treatment which now raise fundamental moral, ethical, and legal questions.

For the most part, society's treatment of the mentally ill has not been a bright page in human history. Mental disorders have been seen as curses and the work of malevolent spirits and the mentally ill, as often as not, were shunned, tormented, or persecuted. Among the Greeks, Hippocrates made a major advance in the 5th century B.C. by offering a rational explanation for mental illness as being due to imbalances in certain bodily fluids. But it would be another 2,000 years before humane and rational treatment of the mentally ill became the accepted standard. It was in the 1700s that Philippe Pinel, a French doctor, and the British merchant William Tuke, introduced modern reforms into mental institutions. Their innovations were taken up by Benjamin Rush in America, and reform of the country's mental institutions was hastened by the writings of Dorothea Dix. Reform was also advanced by the work of Clifford W. Beers, a former mental patient, whose book, *A Mind That Found Itself*, helped improve public understanding of the problems of the mentally ill. In 1909, he founded the National Committee for Mental Hygiene, which later became the National Association for Mental Health.

Simultaneously with institutional reform came medical advances and new forms of treatment and therapy. Toward the end of the 19th century, Emil Kraepelin and Eugen Bleuler classified most mental disorders. Early in the 20th century, Sigmund Freud introduced his psychoanalytic method and his ideas on the structure and development of the mind. Research into various forms of psychotherapy, the development of behaviorist theories, research into the physiology and chemistry of the brain and the nervous system, and the development of psychotropic drugs, have all had a significant effect upon the care and treatment of the mentally ill. But they are still, in many ways, feared, ignored, or discriminated against, and problems of care, treatment, and integration of the mentally ill into society are as urgent as the need for continued medical research.

Mental retardation, low intellectual capacity, arising not from mental illness but from impairment of the normal development of the brain and nervous system. Causes include genetic defect (as in Down's syndrome); infection of the embryo or fetus (hydrocephalus or inherited metabolic defects), injury at birth, including cerebral hemorrhage and fetal anoxia (lack of oxygen), and disease in infancy (for example, encephalitis). Retardation is initially recognized by slowness to develop normal patterns of social and learning behavior; it is confirmed through intelligence measurements. Although mental retardation cannot be cured, it is most important that affected children receive adequate social contact and education, for their development is generally retarded, not arrested. Special schooling may help them achieve a degree of learning and social competence. Proper prenatal, perinatal, and postnatal care may help prevent some cases of mental retardation.

Menuhin, Yehudi (1916-), U.S. violinist and conductor. He made his concert debut in San Francisco at age 7, played for Allied forces in World War II, and later performed to raise cash for war victims. He has revived forgotten masterpieces, promoted interest in Eastern music, and toured internationally with the Menuhin Festival Orchestra. In 1963 he opened the Yehudi Menuhin School of Music for musically gifted children in Suffolk, England.

Mephistopheles, in medieval legend, the devil to whom Faust sold his soul. He is primarily a literary creation and appears in the famous plays by Christopher Marlowe and Johann Goethe.
See also: Devil.

Mercantilism, economic system prevailing in 16th- to 18th-century western Europe that reflected the increased importance of the merchant. Mercantilism was based on the concepts that a country's wealth was founded on its supply of gold and silver, and that in a world of limited resources one nation could prosper only at the expense of another. Mercantilists favored tariffs in order to secure a favorable international trade balance and thereby maintain reserves of previous metals. Their protectionism was succeeded by the free trade arguments of the French physiocrats and later the policy of laissez faire. Today, mercantilism sometimes refers to policies that protect domestic businesses from foreign competition.
See also: Colonialism.

Mercator, Gerardus (Gerhard Kremer; 1512-94), geographer and cartographer best known for his world map. With this map Mercator introduced a new map projection, or method of transferring features of the earth's surface onto a flat sheet of paper. On a map using the so-called Mercator projection, the lines of latitude, which are equidistant on a globe, are drawn with increasing separation as their distance from the equator increases. While this exaggerates the sizes of areas as they move away from the equator, it preserves their shapes. Mercator's method is still in use today by navigators.
See also: Geography.

Merchandising *See:* Marketing.

Merchant marine, commercial shipping operations of a maritime nation and the personnel who operate the ships. Privately-owned cargo ships make up the largest percentage of most nations' fleets, but state-owned vessels are operated in some countries, particularly those of the Communist bloc. Gross tonnage, the total cargo capacity of all ships of a nation's registry, is the figure used to measure a merchant marine's size.

Merchant Marine Academy *See:* United States Merchant Marine Academy.

Mercury (element), chemical element, symbol Hg; for physical constants see Periodic Table. Mercury was known to the ancient Chinese and Hindus. It is a silvery-white, heavy, liquid metal. Compared with other metals, it is a poor conductor of heat and a fair conductor of electricity. Mercury is the only common metal that is liquid at ordinary temperatures. It easily forms alloys with many other metals. Both the element and most of its compounds are poisonous. Mercury and its compounds are used in electrolytic cells, dentistry, thermometers, barometers, diffusion pumps, electrical switches, mercury-vapor lamps, paint, batteries, explosive detonators, and in medicine.

Mercury (mythology), in Roman mythology, god of commerce and wealth; associated with Hermes in Greek mythology. Known as the messenger of the gods, he delivered his messages with great speed because he wore winged sandals. Mercury was the son of Jupiter, and Maia, a goddess. He was depicted as both crafty and deceptive.

Mercury (planet), in astronomy, planet closest to the sun, with a mean solar distance of 36 million mi (57.9 million km). Its eccentric elliptical orbit brings it within 28.5 million mi (46 million km) of the sun at perihelion (point nearest to the sun) and takes it 43.5 million mi (70 million km) from the sun at aphelion (point farthest from the sun). Its diameter is 3,031 mi (4,878 km), and its mass about 0.054 that of the earth. Mercury revolves around the sun in just under 88 days—faster than any other planet—and rotates on its axis in about 59 days. Albert Einstein's successful prediction that Mercury's orbit would advance by 43 in (109 cm) per century is usually regarded as a confirmation of the general theory of relativity. Night surface temperature on this dry and airless planet is believed to be about –315ÉF (–É193C), midday equatorial temperature over 648ÉF (342ÉC). No plant life is believed to exist. Mercury also has no known satellites. The U.S. Mariner space probe revealed (1974-75) that Mercury has a moonlike, heavily cratered surface and a slight magnetic field.
See also: Planet; Solar System.

Mercury program *See:* Space exploration.

Meredith, George (1828-1909), English novelist and poet. His novels include the tragicomic *The Ordeal of Richard Feverel* (1859), *The Egoist* (1879), and *Diana of the Crossways* (1885). The sonnet sequence *Modern Love* (1862) grew out of the breakdown of his marriage. His writing offers piercing character and social analyses.

Merganser, fish-eating duck of the family Anatidae, found in many parts of the world. It is also called the sawbill because of its long serrated bill. Both sexes have a large head crest—the male dark, and the female brown. Mergansers nest in tree holes. They include the American, red-breasted, and hooded mergansers, all of which can be found in North America.

Mergenthaler, Ottmar (1854-99), German-American inventor of the Linotype machine, an automatic typesetting device. Patented in 1884 and produced in 1886, the Linotype made the printing process more efficient and cost-effective, thus producing widespread changes in publishing. *See also:* Linotype.

Mérida (pop. 557,300), founded in 1542, now the largest city on the Yucatan Peninsula in Mexico. Mérida is surrounded by farmland and is located near the the ancient Mayan sites of Chichén Itzá and Uxmal. The city contains a magnificent cathedral and examples of early Spanish architecture.

Mérimée, Prosper (1803-70), French author, historian, archeologist, and linguist. He is best known for his novelettes (long short stories such as "Mateo Falcone" (1829), "Colomba" (1840), and the romance "Carmen" (1845), which was the source of Georges Bizet's opera. Mérimée also wrote essays and translations in the 1850s intended to interest the French in Russia and its literature.

Merit badge *See:* Boy Scouts.

Merlin *See:* Round Table.

Merovingian, dynasty of Frankish kings (A.D. 428-751) who governed Gaul. They were named for the 5th-century king Merovech; his grandson Clovis I first united much of France. The kingdom was later partitioned, but enlarged and reunited (A.D. 613) under Clotaire II. The Merovingians governed through the remnants of the old Roman administration and established Catholic Christianity. After Dagobert I in the 7th century, the kings became known as *rois-fainéants* (do-nothings), and power passed to the mayors of the palace, nominally high officials. The last of these, Pepin the Short, deposed the last Merovingian, Childeric III, and founded the Carolingian dynasty. *See also:* Carolingian; Gaul.

Merrill, Robert (1919-), internationally acclaimed New York-born baritone opera singer. Known for his powerful voice and technical proficiency, he has performed extensively worldwide, notably with the Metropolitan Opera and on Broadway. Among his famous roles are Renato in Verdi's *Un Ballo in Maschera*, Amonasro in *Aïda*, and Escomillo in Bizet's *Carmen*. He wrote an autobiograhy, *Once More from the Beginning* (1965), and a novel, *The Divas* (1978).

Merrimack *See:* Monitor and Merrimack.

Merrimack River, stream of New England, flows 110 mi (177 km) from the White Mountains of New Hampshire through northeastern Massachusetts to the Atlantic Ocean. The river and its 6 waterfalls provided water power for the first U.S. textile factories; it now is harnessed to produce hydroelectricity. *Merrimack* means "swift water."

Mersey, River, major trade waterway rising in the Pennine Hills of northwest England and entering the Irish Sea. About 70 mi (110 km) long, the river has underwater tunnels for railroads and automotive traffic. Its many docks and basins, serving the cities of Liverpool and Birkenhead, have contributed to the development of Birkenhead as an important market for cattle. A canal connects the river to the city of Manchester.

Merton, Robert King (1910-   ), U.S. sociologist. His seminal work on the sociology of science produced *Science, Technology and Society in Seventeenth Century England* (1938), expressing the view that English Puritanism helped lead to the modern scientific age. He wrote an analysis of the function of deviant behavior in society (*Social Theory and Social Structure*, 1949), and was instrumental in developing quantitative (statistical) research methods in sociology.
See also: Sociology.

Merton, Thomas (1915-68), U.S. religious writer of poetry, meditative works and an autobiography, *The Seven Storey Mountain* (1948). A convert to Roman Catholicism, he became a Trappist monk (1941) and was later ordained a priest. The French-born Merton also wrote *The Waters of Siloe* (1949) and *The Sign of Jonas* (1953) about the Trappist life.

Merv, ruined city in the Turkmen Soviet Socialist Republic, situated near the modern city of Mary. Since ancient times an oasis in the desert, Merv was once a prosperous city and center of Islamic learning. Destroyed by the Mongols in 1221, it was rebuilt in the 15th century and occupied by the Russians in 1884. Farming is its main occupation.
See also: Turkmenistan.

Mesa (Spanish, "table"), used in the western and southwestern United States for a steep-sided, flat-topped hill or isolated tableland, such as Mesa Encantada (Enchanted Mesa) in New Mexico and Mesa Verde (Green Mesa) in Colorado. Often red or yellow, mesas were long ago part of much larger plateaus of softer rock that were gradually worn down. The mesas escaped erosion because they were capped by hard rock layers protecting the softer strata below.

Mesabi Range, hills in northeastern Minnesota, northwest of Lake Superior from Babbitt to Grand Rapids; highest point is 2,000 ft (610 m). The range is famous for its iron ore deposits, which lie near the surface and have been mined since the 1890s. *Mesabi* means "hidden giant."

Mescaline, nonaddictive hallucinogen derived from the Mexican peyote cactus (*Lophophora williamsii*). Because peyote is bitter-tasting and causes a burning sensation and itching of mucous membranes, the "buttons" are brewed with tea or chewed while drinking beverages. Pure mescaline is more potent than peyote powder, which may be mixed with gelatine or injected intravenously in decoctions. About 10 minutes to 3 hours after taking

mescaline, and lasting about 12 hours, one experiences nausea, dizziness, sweating, headache, palpitations, heat or chilliness, and cramps in chest, neck, or abdomen. Effects include multicolored visions; hypersensitivity to sound; disturbed senses of touch, taste, smell, space, and time; and a distorted concept of one's own body. Euphoria and glee are followed by anxiety (sometimes depression and hostility), loss of concentration and control over speech and action, and possibly general but temporary schizophrenic psychosis. U.S. law prohibits the use of mescaline except by members of the Native American Church.
See also: Drug; Drug abuse.

Meshed (pop. 1,120,000), capital city of Khorsn province, northeastern Iran. Meshed, center of the northern wool trade, is also a religious center, visited by over 100,000 pilgrims annually. It contains the tombs of the caliph Hrn ar-Rashd (A.D. 809) and his son-in-law, religious leader Alar-Rid.
See also: Iran.

Mesmer, Franz, or **Friedrich Anton** (1734-1815), Austrian physician who theorized (1775) that a person may transmit universal forces to others through "animal magnetism." Controversy over his unusual techniques and theories, involving the beneficial effects of a magnet upon an occult force within the subject, forced Mesmer to flee Austria (1778) for Paris. Interest in mesmerism led the British surgeon James Braid, the French neurologist Jean Charcot, and the Viennese psychologist Sigmund Freud to develop the ancient practice of hypnotism for the study of psychology.
See also: Hypnosis.

Mesolithic Period *See:* Stone Age.

Meson, subatomic particle of a family called hadrons, which act via a strong nuclear force that holds together an atomic nucleus. Mesons are unstable particles that decay; they carry a positive, negative, or neutral electric charge. They consist of a quark and an antiquark. Mesons include pions (or pi-mesons), upsilon particles, k-mesons (or kaons), and psi particles (or J particles). British physicist Cecil Powell discovered the meson (1947) in cosmic radiation.
See also: Hadron; Quark.

Mesopotamia (Greek, "between the rivers"), ancient region between the Tigris and Euphrates rivers in southwestern Asia. Called "the cradle of civilizations" Mesopotamia mainly lies in Iraq, between the Armenian and Kurdish Mountains in the north and the Persian Gulf in the south. The north is mainly grassy, rolling plateau; the south is a sandy plain leading to marshes. Since ancient times the rivers have been used to irrigate the area; however, the ancient systems degenerated under Mongol invasion and Ottoman rule and were not replaced until the 20th century. Neolithic farming peoples settled Mesopotamia by 6000 B.C. By 3000 B.C. the Sumerians, who created the first system of writing (cuneiform), had developed a civilization of independent city-states in the south. From c.3000-625 B.C. Mesopotamia was dominated successively by Sumer, Akkad, the Sumerian dynasty of Ur, the empires of Babylonia and Assyria, and Chaldea. In 539 B.C. the Persian Empire absorbed Mesopotamia; in 331 B.C. it was conquered by Alexander the Great. It subsequently came under Roman, Byzantine, and Arab rule. The Abbasid caliphs made Baghdad their capital in 762, but prosperity collapsed with the Mongol invasion of 1289. After Ottoman rule (1638-1918), Mesopotamia was largely incorporated into Iraq. Today it is generally barren, but contains rich oil fields.

Mesosphere, layer of the atmosphere immediately above the stratosphere, marked by a temperature maximum (about 10°C/ 50°F) between altitudes of about 30 mi-50 mi (58-80 km).
See also: Atmosphere.

Mesozoic Era *See:* Dinosaur; Reptile.

Mesquite, or screw bean, tough shrub or tree (genus *Prosopis*) that grows in the stony deserts of the southwestern United States and similar regions. The roots may penetrate as much as 70 ft (21 m) into the ground. It bears spines and small olive-colored leaflets. A member of the pea family, mesquite has seeds that develop into edible pods that can be used to make bread and a fermented beverage. The pods, wood, and gum from the stem have commercial value as food, fuel, and lumber.

Messenia, region in the southern peninsula of Greece and seat of the ancient Mycenaean civilization. Under Spartan domination for hundreds of years, the Messenians were finally freed in the 4th century B.C. by Theben leader Epaminondas. Messenia is noted for its Frankish and Turkish castles, and for its rich farmland.
See also: Mycenae.

Messiaen, Olivier (1908-92), French composer, organist, teacher, and theorist. Much of his music, such as *The Ascension* (1935), was influenced by Roman Catholic mysticism. Others are based on Oriental music, such as the *Turangalila* symphony (1949), or on birdsong, such as the *Catalog of Birds* (1959). He influenced many modern composers, among them Pierre Boulez of France and Karlheinz Stockhausen of Germany.

Messiah (Hebrew, "anointed one"), according to Israelite prophets, especially Isaiah, the ruler whom God would send to restore Israel and begin a glorious age of peace and righteousness. He would be a descendant of King David. Christians recognize Jesus of Nazareth as the Messiah (or Christ); his role as "suffering servant" was alien to Jewish hopes of a political deliverer. The concept of a forthcoming divine redeemer is common to many religions.
See also: Religion.

Messier, Charles (1730-1817), French astronomer and compiler of an extensive catalog of celestial sources of light that are not stars. Among these are galaxies, nebulae, and star clusters. In attempting to distinguish between nebulae and comets, he discovered 21 comets and predicted the return of Halley's Comet in 1758-59.
See also: Astronomy.

Messina (pop. 232,900), city on Sicily's northeast coast, on the Strait of Messina. First mentioned in history as an ancient Sicilian colony (c.730 B.C.)

it was occupied by the Greeks in the 700s B.C. and became a flourishing Greek colony. Throughout history it has been fought over and survived many rulers. Earthquakes in 1783 and 1908 almost destroyed Messina, which also sustained great damage during World War II. A gateway to Sicily, its principal exports are fruits, wine, olive oil, chemicals, pharmaceuticals, and medicinal products.
See also: Sicily.

Metabolism, sum total of all chemical reactions that occur in a living organism. It can be subdivided into *anabolism*, which describes reactions that build up more complex substances from smaller ones, and *catabolism*, which describes reactions that break down complex substances into simpler ones. Anabolic reactions require energy, while catabolic reactions liberate energy.
Metabolic reactions are set off by enzymes in a highly integrated and finely controlled manner so that there is no overproduction or underutilization of the energy required to maintain life. All this energy is ultimately derived from sunlight by the photosynthesis in plants, and most organisms use the products of photosynthesis either directly or indirectly.

Metal, element that has high specific gravity; high opacity and reflectivity to light (giving a characteristic luster when polished); ability to be hammered into thin sheets and drawn into wires (i.e., is malleable and ductile); and is a good conductor of heat and electricity, its electrical conductivity decreasing with temperature. Roughly 75% of the chemical elements are metals, but not all of them possess all the typical metallic properties. Most are found as ores and in the pure state are crystalline solids (mercury, liquid at room temperature, being a notable exception), their atoms readily losing electrons to become positive ions. Alloys are easily formed because of the nonspecific nondirectional nature of the metallic bond.

Metallurgy, the science and technology of extracting metals from ores, the methods of refining, purifying, and preparing them for use, and the study of the structure and physical properties of metals and alloys. A few unreactive metals such as silver and gold are found native (uncombined), but most metals occur naturally as minerals (i.e., in chemical combination with nonmetallic elements). *Hydrometallurgy* uses chemical reactions in aqueous solutions to extract metal from ore. *Electrometallurgy* uses electricity for firing a furnace or electrolytically reducing a metallic compound to a metal. *Pyrometallurgy* covers roasting, smelting, and other high temperature chemical reactions.

Metamorphic rock, one of the 3 main classes of rocks of the earth's crust—the class that has undergone change owing to heat, pressure, or chemical action. In plate tectonic theory the collision of lithospheric plates leads to widespread *regional metamorphism*. Igneous intrusion leads to changes in the rocks close to the borders or contacts of the cooling magma, and these changes, largely due to the application of heat, constitute *contact (thermal) metamorphism*. Common metamorphic rock types include marble, quartzite, slate, schist, and gneiss. Some occurrences of granite are also thought to be of metamorphic origin.
See also: Rock.

Metamorphosis, in zoology, changes undergone from larvae to a mature adult stage. The term, meaning "transformation," is generally used only for insects and amphibians, although other animals also have distinct larval and adult stages. Metamorphosis of insects may be *complete*, occurring in abrupt steps, or *incomplete*, a gradual process. Butterflies and moths have complete metamorphosis, changing from caterpillar to adult via one intermediate stage, the pupa. Grasshoppers and cockroaches mature gradually in a series of molts (the young are called *nymphs*) until they develop into adults. Metamorphosis of amphibians is generally from a water-dwelling, gill-breathing larva, such as a tadpole, into a less aquatic air-breathing adult, such as a frog.
See also: Zoology.

Metaphysical poets, early 17th-century English lyric poets whose style relied on the metaphysical conceit, an elaborate metaphorical image. Most famous among them is John Donne; others include Andrew Marvell, George Herbert, Richard Crashaw, Henry Vaughan, and Thomas Carew. The Metaphysical poets (a term first used by Samuel Johnson in 1744) extended the range of lyric poetry by writing about death, decay, immortality, and faith. They declined in popularity after about 1660, but their complex intellectual content and rich exploration of feeling was a major influence on 20th-century poetry.

Metaphysics, branch of philosophy that addresses the fundamentals of existence or reality, such as the existence and nature of God, immortality of the soul, meaning of evil, the problem of freedom and determinism, and relationship of mind and body. Metaphysical systems have included Aristotelian scholasticism and the 17th-century rationalistic systems of Descartes, Spinoza, and Leibniz. Metaphysical thinking was criticized in the 18th century by Immanuel Kant, who claimed that traditional metaphysics, while raising morally necessary questions, sought to go beyond the limits of human knowledge. In the 20th century, the concerns of metaphysics were rejected as being meaningless by the logical positivists.
See also: Philosophy.

Metaxas, Ionannis (1871-1941), Greek general and from 1936 ultraroyalist premier and dictator of Greece. He made important social and economic reforms. He tried to maintain Greek neutrality in World War II, but after successfully resisting the Italian invasion in 1940 joined the Allied powers.
See also: Greece.

Metazoan, in zoology, multicellular animal, member of the group Metazoa, distinguished from single-celled protozoans. With increase in the number of cells comes differentiation of function of cells, tissues, and organs. Many zoologists divide the Metazoa group into sponges (Parazoa) and all other multicelled animals (Eumetazoa).

Metchnikoff, Élie (1845-1916), Russian biologist who shared with Paul Ehrlich the 1908 Nobel Prize for physiology or medicine for his discovery of phagocytes (in humans, called leukocytes) and their role in defending the body from, for example, bacteria.
See also: Biology.

Meteor, small speck of material from space, about the size of a grain of sand. Meteors become visible as they burn up in the earth's atmosphere. Friction with the air causes them to glow and vaporize, resembling a swift streak of light (*shooting star* or *falling star*). When the earth crosses the orbit of a comet, whole swarms of meteors, called *meteor showers*, can be seen burning up in the atmosphere. A *meteorite* is a meteor that reaches the earth's surface before completely burning up in the atmosphere. An estimated 1,000 tons of meteoric material lands on the earth each day

Meteorology, study of the atmosphere and its phenomena, weather, and climate. Based on atmospheric physics, meteorology is mainly applied in weather forecasting and control. The rain gauge and wind vane were known in ancient times. The other basic instruments—anemometer, barometer, hygrometer, and thermometer—were invented by 1790; however, simultaneous observations over a wide area were impracticable until the development of the telegraph. Since World War I, observations of the upper atmosphere have been made using airplanes, balloons, and radiosonde, and since World War II, using radar, rockets, and artificial satellites. Observed phenomena include clouds, precipitation and humidity, wind and air pressure, air temperature, storms, cyclones, air masses, and fronts.
See also: Atmosphere.

Meter, basic unit of length in the metric system. One meter is equal to 39.37 in. and to 1.1 yd.
See also: Metric system.

Methadone, synthetic narcotic used extensively to treat heroin addicts. Methadone causes less severe and dangerous withdrawal symptoms than other narcotic drugs, although it is also addictive. It is also used as an analgesic, particularly in terminally ill patients, and sometimes in very small doses as a cough suppressant.

Methamphetamine, generic name of a powerful drug that is a derivate of and similar to amphetamine. Also known as "speed," methamphetamine enables a user to work and talk for long periods. Legally obtainable only with a doctor's prescription, methamphetamine can be hazardous if misused. Withdrawal symptoms may occur when use is stopped.
See also: Amphetamine.

Methane (CH_4), colorless, odorless gas; the simplest alkane. It is produced by decomposing organic matter in sewage and in marshes (hence the name *marsh gas*), and is the "firedamp" of coal mines. Nontoxic but highly flammable, methane when mixed with air, oxygen, or chlorine is explosive. It is the chief constituent of natural gas, occurs in coal gas and water gas, and is produced in petroleum refining. Methane is used as a fuel, for making carbon-black, and for chemical synthesis.

Methanol (CH_3OH), also called methyl alcohol or wood alcohol, type of alcohol with many industrial uses. Methanol is clear, colorless, flammable, and poisonous. Ways of lowering its manufacturing costs and enlarging its use as an alternate fuel are being sought.

Methodists, doctrine and polity of Protestant churches that originated in the 18th-century evangelical revival led by John and Charles Wesley. The name Methodist was first used in 1729 for members of the "Holy Club" of Oxford University, led by the Wesleys, who lived "by rule and method." Influenced by the Moravian Church, Methodism began as an evangelical movement in 1738 when the Wesleys and George Whitefield began preaching. Banned from most Anglican pulpits, they preached in the open air and drew vast crowds. After Wesley's death in 1791, Methodist societies formally separated from the Church of England and became the Wesleyan Methodist Church. The American Methodist movement was established after 1771 by Francis Asbury and Thomas Coke. Methodist polity in Britain is in effect Presbyterian; in the United States it is Episcopal. Methodism traditionally stresses conversion, holiness, and social welfare.
See also: Protestantism; Wesley.

Methuselah, oldest person in the Bible. According to the Bible (Gen. 5.25-27) he lived to the age of 969. He was the grandfather of Noah. The term "old as Methuselah" is a popular expression denoting an old person.
See also: Bible.

Methyl alcohol *See:* Methanol.

Methylbenzene *See:* Toluene.

Metre *See:* Meter; Metric system.

Metric system, decimal system of measurement, first adopted in France during the Revolution (1790s), called the Système International d'Unités, or SI. This simple system is used to measure length and distance, surface, volume and capacity, weight and mass, time, and temperature. The modern version of the metric system currently in use worldwide includes 7 base units: meter (length or distance), kilogram (mass), second (time), ampère (electricity),degrees (temperature, Celsius or Kelvin), candela (light), and mole (chemical substance).

Metropolitan Museum of Art, largest and most comprehensive art museum in the United States, founded in 1870 in New York City. Its collections include art, pottery, jewelry, and sculpture from ancient Egypt, Greece, Rome, Babylonia, and Assyria; Eastern paintings, sculptures, and artifacts; American art, sculpture, and period rooms; African art; and modern art, photography, and industrial design. The Uris Center hosts educational activities. Medieval art is housed in the Cloisters, located in Fort Tryon Park. It features parts of European medieval buildings, outdoor gardens, and medieval art, such as tapestries, ivories, and stained glass.

Metternich (Clemens Wenzel Nepomuk Lothar von Metternich; 1773-1859), Austrian diplomat. After a diplomatic career in Saxony, Prussia, and France he became Austrian foreign minister (1809-48). He gradually dissociated Austria from France and organized an alliance of Austria, Russia, and Prussia against Napoleon. However, at the Congress of Vienna (1814-15) he reestablished a system of power whereby Russia and Prussia were balanced by the combined power of Austria, France, and England. Appointed state

chancellor in 1821, his authority declined after 1826, and he was overthrown in 1848. The period 1815-48 is often called the Age of Metternich.
See also: Austria; Vienna, Congress of.

Metz (pop. 123,900), city in northeastern France on the Moselle River, a center for iron and coal mining. Of pre-Roman origin, it became a bishopric and capital of the Frankish kingdom of Austrasia. France annexed it in 1552, and Germany held it from 1871 to 1918.
See also: France.

Meuse River, rises in the Langres Plateau, France, and flows north for about 580 mi (933 km) across Belgium and the Netherlands, where it is named *Maas*, into the North Sea. It is an important thoroughfare and line of defense for France and Belgium.

Mexicali (pop. 602,400), city in Mexico founded in 1903. Mexicali is the capital and second largest city of the Mexican state of Baja California Norte. The name is a combination of the words "Mexico" and "California." Mexicali is a popular tourist attraction that offers beautiful architecture, handicrafts, and exciting sporting events like rodeos and bullfights.
See also: Mexico.

Mexican Americans *See:* Hispanic Americans.

Mexican hairless, dog that derives its name because it has no coat of hair. It typically weighs about 12 lb (5 kg) and is pinkish in color. The dog was brought to the New World from China.

Mexican turnip *See:* Jicama.

Mexican War (1846-48), conflict between Mexico and the United States that resulted in the defeat of Mexico and America's acquisition of territory that became California, Nevada, Utah, most of New Mexico and Arizona, and parts of Colorado and Wyoming. The war took place against a background of expansionist sentiment (Manifest Destiny) in the United States, which held that it was destined to become a continental power and the dominant nation of the Western Hemisphere.
Causes of the war. In 1835, when the region comprising Texas, then under control of Mexico, revolted and declared its independence, Mexico warned the United States that it would break off diplomatic relations if Texas were admitted to the union. President James K. Polk, elected in 1844, favored expansionism and backed the annexation of Texas. When Texas was accepted into the union in 1845, Mexico broke relations. The matter could have been negotiated peacefully except that other issues, notably the boundary dispute between Texas and Mexico, stymied agreement. Mexico put the boundary at the Nueces River while Texas claimed it was the Rio Grande farther to the south. In addition, American citizens claimed damages from the Mexican government for losses sustained in Mexico's war of independence from Spain, which ended in 1821. Also, U.S. expansionists had designs on the vast California territory, then under Mexican rule but which had experienced an influx of English-speaking people. Polk sent John Slidell to offer Mexico a solution whereby the United States would pay Mexico $25

million and assume all American claims against it if Mexico, in turn, would accept the Rio Grande boundary and agree to sell the New Mexico and California regions to the United States. When Mexico declined to deal on these terms, Polk resorted to force.

Outbreak of the war. In April 1846, General Zachary Taylor was ordered to advance his 3,000 troops from the Neuces to the Rio Grande. Mexico saw this as an invasion, and a slight engagement of forces occurred—excuse enough for Polk, on May 13th, to get a declaration of war on Mexico. Even before that reached Taylor, he had won the battles of Palo Alto and Resaca de la Palma, forcing the Mexicans across the Rio Grande.

Course of the war. U.S. strategy involved a 3-pronged attack on Mexico: an invasion of New Mexico and California, a naval blockade of both the Gulf of Mexico and California, and a major thrust from the north. The first 2 objectives were quickly attained. General Stephen W. Kearny, with about 1,700 troops, took New Mexico in August 1846, then moved on to California where, in January 1847, forces under Kearny and Commodore Robert F. Stockton won the Battle of San Gabriel, completing the conquest of California. Taylor took Monterrey in September 1846, but Mexico still refused to negotiate. Polk sent General Winfield Scott to land an army at Veracruz on Mexico's east coast, and to menace Mexico City. Many of Taylor's best troops were transferred to the Veracruz campaign, leaving him vulnerable when challenged by a large Mexican force led by General Antonio López de Santa Ana. In February 1847, Taylor only narrowly won the hard-fought battle of Buena Vista. Scott took Veracruz in March and drove toward Mexico City. In April, his troops defeated Santa Ana at the mountain stronghold of Cerro Gordo; and in August, near Mexico City, after hard fighting they defeated Mexican forces at the battles of Contereras and Churubusco. A 2-week armistice ensued, but when negotiations broke down, fighting resumed. Moving on Mexico City, Scott took the strong points of Casa Mata and Molino del Rey and stormed the fortress of Chapultepec. On September 14, 1847, U.S. troops entered Mexico City, ending the war.

Outcome of the war. By the Treaty of Guadalupe Hidalgo (February 1848), Mexico ceded to the United States two-fifths of Mexican territory (nearly all of present-day Arizona, California, Colorado, Nevada, New Mexico, and Utah)—more than 500,000 sq mi. The United States agreed to pay Mexico $15 million and to assume all outstanding claims of American citizens against Mexico. The war deeply divided the American people, not least because some feared an extension of slavery into the new territories. The Compromise of 1850 made California a free state but allowed the people of the other territories to decide whether they should be slave or free states. Bitter disputes followed, 12 years later contributing to the chain of events that led to the American Civil War.

Mexico, the United Mexican States, a federal republic occupying the southernmost portion of the North American continent. Mexico is bounded by the United States to the north, Guatemala and Belize to the south, the Caribbean Sea and the Gulf of Mexico on the east, and the Pacific Ocean on the west. *Land and climate.* Mexico is nearly 1,200 mi/1,930 km long with an area of 761,530 sq mi/1,972,544 sq km. Two mountain ranges run most of the length of the country from northwest to southeast, the Sierra Madre Occidental along the Pacific coast and the Sierra Madre Oriental along the Atlantic coast. Between the two ranges lies the great central plateau rising 3,000 to 4,000

Mexico

Capital:	Mexico City
Area:	761,530 sq mi (1,972,544 sq km)
Population:	98,553,000
Language:	Spanish
Government:	Federal presidential republic
Independent:	1821
Head of gov.:	President
Per capita:	U.S. $3,320
Mon. unit:	1 Peso = 100 centavos

ft/914 to 1219 m in the north to 8,000 ft/2,438 m in the south. Mexico City, the capital, is situated near the southern end of the plateau at an elevation of about 7,400 ft/2,256 m.

Mexico is a land of dramatic contrasts. Its mountain ranges include the extinct volcanoes Popocatépetl (17,888 ft/5,452 m), Ixtacihuatl (17,343 ft/5,286 m), and Orizaba (18,406 ft/5,610 m). Its high plateau gives way to semi-tropical coastal regions. To the northwest lies Baja California, mountainous desert, and to the southeast the low limestone plateau of the Yucatan which includes tropical forests in the south. As a result, Mexico's climate varies considerably from the mountains to the desert, from the temperate plateau to the tropical lowlands. In all, less than 15% of the land surface is cultivable and most of it is on the central plateau.

People. The majority of Mexicans are mestizos, a mixture of native Americans and Spanish, but nearly one-tenth of the population remains pure native American and many of Mexico's native Americans speak only their native languages. About 10% of the population is of pure Spanish descent. Spanish is the official language and the people are overwhelmingly Roman Catholic.

Economy. Despite considerable industrialization since World War II, agriculture remains the major employer in the Mexican economy with more than 25% of the work force. The chief subsistence crops are corn and beans. The main commercial crops are wheat, corn, beans, cotton, coffee, sugarcane, sisal, and citrus fruits. The country also has valuable forests and fisheries which contribute to its economy. Mexico is rich in minerals and exports silver, zinc, lead, manganese, and sulfur. Abundant reserves of iron ore and uranium await development. Huge petroleum reserves, perhaps the second largest in the world, were discovered in the mid 1970s. Major industries include iron and steel, textiles, chemicals, electric goods, ceramics, paper, footwear, and processed foods. Mexico is plagued by inflation, government debt, and, more recently, a severe drop in world oil prices. Its economic problems are compounded by unemployment and illiteracy.

History. Prehistoric remains indicate that Mexico was inhabited as early as 10,000 B.C. Between A.D. 300 and 800, four classical native American civilizations developed in Mexico including the Maya of the Yucatán Peninsula. By the 15th century the Aztecs established the last Indian civilization in Mexico with its capital at Tenochtitlán, the site of present day Mexico

City. It was this empire, under Montezuma, which was conquered by the Spanish under Hernán Cortés in 1521 thereby ushering the Spanish dominion. The Spanish consolidated their rule, exploiting the labor and mineral wealth of the colony they named New Spain. The colony was governed by a line of 62 viceroys appointed by the Spanish throne until independence in 1821. At the same time, the Roman Catholic church pursued a thorough policy of converting the Indians to Christianity and acquired considerable power. In September 1810, Father Miguel Hidalgo raised a rebellion against Spain which was subsequently crushed. another priest, José María Morelos, took up the struggle in 1813, but he too was defeated. Finally, backed by conservative elements seeking independence from a more liberal Spain, the country achieved independence in 1821 under Augustín de Iturbide. Emperor Augustín I was deposed in 1823 by Antonio Lopes de Santa Anna who dominated the turbulent politics of the new federal republic until 1855. During that period, Mexico waged a costly war with the U.S., the Mexican-American War (1846-48), which led to the loss of Texas and Mexico's considerable northwest territories in the U.S.

In 1855 Benito Pablo Juarez overthrew Santa Anna and introduced a more liberal constitution. Civil war between liberals and conservatives followed. In the ensuing turmoil, the French invaded and Napoleon III installed Maximilian of Austria as emperor in 1864. He was overthrown and executed in 1867. From 1876 to 1911 Mexico was governed by Gen. Porfirio Díaz, who brought a measure of stability and economic growth to the country. But his oligarchic regime generated deep and widespread resentment. Pancho Villa, Emiliano Zapata, and Francisco Madero raised rebellions which led to the downfall of Díaz in 1911. In 1917 Venustiano Carranza established control and promulgated a new liberal constitution. President Alvaro Obregon (1920-24) began a program of land redistribution and education and carried on a struggle with the Roman Catholic church which was not settled until 1929 when the church was granted autonomy in religious matters only. In 1929 Plutarco Elías Calles established the Institutional Revolutionary Party (PRI) which has effectively governed Mexico ever since. President Lázaro Cárdenas continued educational reform and nationalized some industries. Since World War II, Mexico has been politically relatively moderate and stable, concentrating primarily on economic development. Despite progress, significant signs of strain and resistance were apparent under the presidencies of Luis Echeverria and his successor José Lopez Portillo. Mexico's economy suffered in the 1970s, due in part to the worldwide oil glut. Miguel de la Madrid Hurtado was elected president in 1982, promising new programs to deal with Mexico's grave economic problems, such as the crushing foreign debt and high unemployment. De la Madrid's programs failed, and Carlos Salinas de Gortari succeeded him in 1988. Under De Gortari's leadership, Mexico's economy has enjoyed a substantial revival, helped by new foreign investment and the turning over of government-run industries to the private sector. Although the rule of the PRI is challenged since the 1980s, PRI candidate Ernesto Zedillo Ponce de Leon was elected president in 1994. At the 1997 elections, the PRI lost its absolute majority for the first time.

Mexico City (pop. 8,236,900), capital and largest city of Mexico. Located at an altitude of about 7,500 ft (2,300 m) and at the southern end of Mexico's central plateau, it is surrounded by the mountain ranges of Ixtacihuatl and

Popocatepétl. The climate is cool and dry, but the city has often been damaged by local floods. Mexico City is on the site of the old Aztec capital of Tenochtitlán, founded in 1325. Cortés captured the city in 1521, and for the next 300 years it was the seat of the viceroyalty of New Spain; consequently it possesses some of the finest Spanish colonial architecture. The city was hit by a severe earthquake in 1985 and suffers greatly from air pollution. *See also:* Mexico.

Meyer, Julius Lothar (1830-1895), German scientist who developed the periodic chart of the elements which organizes the elements according to atomic weight and property. He also demonstrated the relationship between atomic weights and the properties of elements.
See also: Chemistry; Periodic table.

Meyerbeer, Giacomo (1791-1864), German composer. His romantic and spectacular operas, with librettos by A.E. Scribe, set the vogue for French opera. Most famous are his *Robert le Diable* (1831), *Les Huguenots* (1836), and *L'Africaine* (1865). Meyerbeer's music influenced that of Richard Wagner.

Miami (city) (pop. 367,000), city in southeast Florida, at the mouth of the Miami River on Biscayne Bay. Its near-tropical climate, fine hotels, beaches, and recreational facilities make it a world-famous resort center. Miami was chartered in 1896, when Henry Flagler brought the railroad to Biscayne Bay. Now an agricultural processing and shipping center, Miami is also a center for aircraft and ship rebuilding and textiles.

Miami (tribe), member of Algonquian-speaking Native American group, of the Great Lakes region. The Miami tribe hunted buffalo and grew crops. In the 18th century enemies drove them to northwest Ohio, where they numbered not more than 1,750. The Miamis were allies of the French during the French and Indian Wars and aided the British during the American Revolution. In 1867 most of the Miami tribe was moved to an Oklahoma reservation.

Mica, group of minerals that split into thin, flat sheets of aluminum, silicon, and oxygen. Varieties of mica include muscovite, biotite, phlogopite, and lepidolite. Mica can be found in glistening rocks such as igneous and metamorphic. In its sheet, scrap, or ground form, it has a wide variety of industrial uses. Most scrap mica is produced in the United States.

Micah, Book of, sixth of the Old Testament Minor Prophets. These prophets were oracles of the Judean prophet Micah, who flourished in the late 8th century B.C. (Chapters 4 through 7 are believed to have been written later.) Ethical in tenor, the book prophesies judgment for sin and redemption by the Messiah.
See also: Old Testament.

Michaelmas daisy *See:* Aster.

Michel, Hartmut (1948-), German biochemist, head of biophysics division (Frankfurt am Main) of the Max Planck Institute for Biochemistry (1987-). Michel, Johann Deisenhofer, and Robert Huber shared the 1988 Nobel Prize

for chemistry for their study of the structure of protein molecules involved in photosynthesis. Michel crystallized the proteins in 1982, enabling Deisenhofer and Huber to analyze them.
See also: Biochemistry; Photosynthesis.

Michelangelo (Michelangelo Buonarroti; 1475-1564), Italian sculptor, painter, architect, and poet. As a child he was apprenticed to the Florentine painter Ghirlandaio; in adolescence he was a protégé of Lorenzo de Medici. He went to Rome in 1496, where his marble *Pietà* in Saint Peter's (1498-99) established him as the foremost living sculptor. In Florence Michelangelo sculpted the magnificent *David* (1501-04). In 1505 he returned to Rome to work on a sepulchral monument tomb for Pope Julius II. There he painted the ceiling of the Sistine Chapel (1508-12), one of the most influential works in the history of art. After living in Florence (1515-34) and building the Medici Chapel and Laurentian Library for the Medici family and assisting as engineer in the defense of Florence, Michelangelo moved permanently to Rome. He painted the *Last Judgment* in the Sistine Chapel (1536-41) and was chief architect of Saint Peter's Basilica (1546-64). His architectural designs were influential throughout Italy and in France and England.
See also: Renaissance.

Michener, James Albert (1907-97), U.S. author. His Pulitzer Prize-winning *Tales of the South Pacific* (1947), based on his U.S. Navy experiences in World War II, inspired the famous musical *South Pacific* (1949) by Rodgers and Hammerstein. He also wrote such ambitious, historically based novels as *Hawaii* (1959), *The Source* (1965), *Centennial* (1974), *Chesapeake* (1978), *Poland* (1983), *Texas* (1985), and *Caribbean* (1989).

Michigan, state in the Great Lakes region of midwestern United States; it consists of two separate land masses, the Upper Peninsula and the Lower Peninsula. The Upper Peninsula is bordered by Lake Superior to the north, St. Marys River (dividing it from Canada) to the east, the Straits of Mackinac and Lake Michigan to the south, and Wisconsin to the south and west. The Lower Peninsula is bordered by the Straits of Mackinac to the north; Lake Huron, Canada, and Lake Erie to the east; Ohio and Indiana to the south; and Lake Michigan to the west.
Land and climate. Michigan's two main land regions are the Superior Upland and the Great Lakes Plains. The Superior Upland region, in the Upper Peninsula's western half, is a rugged, forested area possessing some of the nation's richest iron and copper deposits. The Upper Peninsula's eastern half and the entire Lower Peninsula has thin soil; the northern Lower Peninsula is a rolling and hilly plateau; the southern Lower Peninsula has the best farmland. High bluffs and sand dunes border parts of Lake Michigan. Bordered by four of the five Great Lakes, Michigan has the longest coastline of any inland state: 3,288 mi (5,292 km). It has thousands of lakes and ponds. Most of Michigan's rivers and streams flow into the Great Lakes. Some 500 islands lie off Michigan's shores. Michigan's climate is moist, with cold winters and summers that are cool in the north, warm in the south. Principal cities are Detroit, Grand Rapids, Warren, and Flint.
Economy. Michigan's economy is based on service industries, the most important being wholesale and retail trade. Michigan is one of the foremost manufacturing states, producing transportation equipment, machinery, food

Michigan

Capital:	Lansing
Statehood:	Jan. 26, 1837 (26th state)
Familiar name:	Wolverine State
Area:	58,527 sq mi (151,586 sq km); ranks 23rd
Population:	9,774,000 (1997); ranks 8th
Elevation:	Highest—1,980 ft (604 m), Mt. Curwood; Lowest—572 ft (174 m) at Lake Erie
Motto:	*Si Quaeris Peninsulam Amoenam, Circumspice* (If You Seek a Pleasant Peninsula, Look Around You)
Flower:	Apple blossom
Bird:	Robin
Tree:	White pine
Song:	"Michigan, My Michigan" (unofficial)

products, chemicals, and metal, rubber, and plastic goods. It leads the nation in the manufacture of automobiles; Detroit is called the "Automobile Capital of the World" and "Motor City." The most valuable mineral is petroleum, followed by iron ore, natural gas, salt, limestone, and copper. Michigan is a leading producer of iodine, gypsum, peat, and sand and gravel. The chief livestock product is milk, followed by cattle, hogs, and eggs. The chief crops are corn, wheat, soybeans, dry beans, oats, hay, sugar beets, and fruits. Tourism is a major contributor to the economy.

Government. Michigan's present constitution was adopted in 1964. The governor serves a 4-year term. The state's legislature consists of 38 senators serving 4-year terms and 110 representatives serving 2-year terms. In the U.S. Congress, Michigan is represented by 2 senators and 18 representatives.

History. Native Americans, including the Chippewa, Menominee, and Miami, were Michigan's first settlers. French explorers—the first Europeans—arrived about 1620. France ceded the area to Britain in 1763, after the French and Indian Wars. After the American Revolution, it became part of the United States' Northwest Territory; it became a state in 1837. The Civil War (in which Michigan supported the Union), was followed by rapid expansion. Lumber production was the main industry until the early 1900s, when the automobile industry was established in Detroit. Michigan's economy boomed through World War I, slumped during the Depression of the 1930s, then recovered with World War II. It suffered again during the nationwide recessions of the 1970s and 1980s, when Michigan's unemployment rate led the nation.

Michigan, Lake, third largest of the Great Lakes, in North America. It is the largest freshwater lake wholly within the United States, with an area of

22,178 sq mi (57,441 sq km). Important ports on the lake include Milwaukee, Wis., Chicago, Ill., and Gary, Ind. In the north, Lake Michigan empties into Lake Huron by the Straits of Mackinac. It is part of the navigable Great Lakes-Saint Lawrence Seaway; a series of connections link it to the Mississippi River and the Gulf of Mexico.
See also: Great Lakes.

Micmac, Canadian Native Americans of New France (Nova Scotia, New Brunswick, Prince Edward Island, and coastal Quebec), of the Algonquian language group. They lived by hunting and fishing, using canoes for transportation. They traded with the French explorer Jacques Cartier, who arrived in 1534, and strove unsuccessfully with the French to ward away the British. They numbered about 3,000 in the 17th and 18th centuries. They came under Canadian government in 1867. The Micmacs survive today as a tribal group engaged in guiding and farming.

Microbe, see: Microbiology.

Microbiology (formerly called bacteriology), study of microorganisms, including bacteria, viruses, fungi, protozoans, yeasts, and algae. Microbiology includes anatomy, physiology, genetics, taxonomy, and ecology, along with branches of medicine, veterinary sciences, and plant pathology, since many microorganisms are disease causing by nature. Microbiologists also play an important role in the food industry, particularly in baking and brewing. In the pharmaceutical industry, they supervise the production of antibiotics.
See also: Bacteriology.

Microcomputer, complete small computer system, consisting of hardware and software, whose main processing parts are made of semiconductor integrated circuits. The various applications include video games, traffic control systems, scientific instruments, credit card verification and cash machines, blood analyzers, pinball machines, microwave ovens, flow meters, sewing machines, pollution monitors, and control units for hundreds of other devices.
See also: Computer.

Microelectronics, branch of technology and electronics that deals with the production of miniature electronic devices that use minimal electric power. Approaches include forming integrated circuits, thin-film techniques, and solid logic modules.

Microfiche *See:* Microfilm.

Microfilm, photographic film used for recording and storing graphic information in a reduced size. Microfilm comes in rolls, often called microform, and rectangular sheets called microfiche. It is used extensively in government offices, libraries, banks, and businesses.

Micronesia (Federated States of), Island state of 670 islands and atols in the western Pacific Ocean. Formerly part of the UN Trust Territory of the Pacific Islands, Micronesia became independent in 1990. Despite its independence,

Micronesia

Capital:	Pohnpei
Area:	270 sq mi
	(700 sq km)
Population:	130,000
Language:	English
Government:	Federal republic
Independent:	1990
Head of gov.:	President
Per capita:	U.S. $3035
Mon. unit:	1 U.S. dollar = 100
	cents

foreign policy and defense are administered by the US government. The US use a number of islands as a military base.

Microorganism *See:* Microbiology.

Microphone, instrument (invented c.1880) for transmitting or intensifying sounds, by means of electricity that converts sound waves into electrical waves. It is used in radio and television broadcasting and the film and recording industries. Types of microphones include carbon, crystal and ceramic, moving coil, ribbon, and capacitor.

Microprocessor, integrated circuit that performs the functions of a large computer on a tiny "chip" of silicon. Unlike a computer, which can be programmed to solve many different problems, a microprocessor is designed for a specific task. Microprocessors are called very large-scale integrated circuits because they may contain more than 100,000 transistors. First produced in 1971, microprocessors today can perform about 66 million functions per second. Microprocessors are used in a variety of "smart" devices, including appliances used at home, businesses, and industrial plants. *See also:* Computer; Integrated circuit.

Microscope, instrument for producing enlarged images of small objects. In the compound microscope a magnified, inverted image of an object resting on the "stage" (a platform) is produced by the objective lens, or lens system. This image is viewed through the eyepiece (or ocular) lens, which acts as a simple microscope, giving a greatly magnified image. Generally the object is viewed by transmitted light, illumination being controlled by mirror, diaphragm, and "substage condenser" lenses. Near-transparent objects are often stained to make them visible; phase-contrast microscopy, in which a "phase plate" produces a diffraction effect, is an alternative to staining. Objects too small to be seen directly can be made visible in dark-field illumination, in which an opaque disk prevents direct illumination; the object is viewed in the light diffracted from the remaining oblique illumination. Although theoretically the magnifying power of the optical microscope is unlimited, magnifications greater than about 2,000 offer no improvement in

resolving power for light of visible wavelengths. The shorter wavelength of ultraviolet light allows better resolution and hence higher useful magnification. For yet finer resolution, physicists use electron beams and electromagnetic focusing. The field-ion microscope, which offers the greatest magnifications is quite dissimilar from the optical microscope. The compound microscope was invented in the early 17th century.
See also: Leeuwenhoek, Anton van.

Microwave, electromagnetic wave in the superhigh frequency radio spectrum (890 to 300,000 megacycles per sec). Microwaves are electromagnetic radiations of wavelength between .03937 in (1 mm) and 1 ft (30 cm). Microwaves first received attention through the use of radar in World War II (1939-45); today they are used in radar, telecommunications, and spectroscopy and for cooking (microwave ovens).
See also: Radio; Television; Ultrahigh frequency waves.

Midas, in Greek mythology, king of Phrygia who was given the power by the god Dionysus to turn whatever he touched into gold. At first a cause for celebration, this power soon became a curse when even Midas' food turned to gold. With the aid of Dionysus, Midas was able to reverse his powers by bathing himself in the Pactolus River.
See also: Mythology.

Middle Ages (A.D. 400-1500), also known as the medieval period, era in western European history between the fall of the Roman Empire and the beginnings of modern European civilization. By the year 400 A.D., Germanic tribes, called barbarians by the Romans, began to invade the territories of Rome. By this time, the Roman Empire had lost much of its power and could not prevent the invasions. Tribes such as the Visigoths, Angles, Jutes, Saxons, Franks, and Ostrogoths divided the huge Roman Empire into different kingdoms. Because of the primitive legal and economic structures of these tribes, much of the Roman legacy in law, trade, and education was destroyed or lost for centuries. It is for this reason that the term "Dark Ages" is sometimes incorrectly applied to this era. The laws that once provided safety and security to Roman citizens gave way to tribal allegiances and superstitions. The great network of roads built by Rome to maintain trade and communication were destroyed by the barbarians. In the absence of a trade economy, money was no longer necessary. Farming became the economic mainstay of Europe. By the 9th century, most of western Europe was organized into large estates called manors. The manors were owned by a handful of wealthy landowners, but the actual work was accomplished by peasants. The increased power of the manor diminished the need for towns and the need for a merchant class. Consequently, the Middle Ages is characterized by a diminishment in urban life and the loss of culture. Education and cultural institutions were almost totally destroyed during this period. Knowledge of Greece and Rome was lost, the Latin language was unknown to most, and the disciplines of literature, painting, and architecture were forgotten. The sole civilizing force during the Middle Ages was the Christian Church, which saved western Europe from intellectual and cultural oblivion. By the 11th and 12th centuries some powerful lords had succeeded in establishing stable governments that provided peace and security. This, in turn, stimulated thought and economic activities—merchants and towns reappeared, trade routes were established, technological advances occurred, and people ventured far beyond the borders of the manor. This era also experienced remarkable artistic and intellectual achievements such as the cathedral of Notre Dame, the writings of St. Thomas Aquinas, the introduction of the works of Aristotle, and the establishment of universities. Between the 14th and 16th centuries, the Middle Ages slowly yielded to a more modern Europe characterized by the advances of the Renaissance.

Middle East, region, mostly in southwestern Asia but extending into southeastern Europe and northeastern Africa. Today the term usually includes Bahrain, Cyprus, Egypt, Iran, Iraq, Israel, Jordan, Kuwait, Lebanon, Libya, Saudi Arabia and the other countries of the Arabian peninsula, and Sudan. Politically, other countries of predominantly Islamic culture, such as Algeria, Morocco, and Tunisia, are sometimes included. The site of early civilization (including that of Sumer and Egypt, 3500-3100 B.C.), the Middle East was also the birthplace of Judaism, Christianity, and Islam. It has been the seat of many great empires, including the Ottoman Empire, which began in the 14th century and survived until 1923. The Tigris-Euphrates and the Nile are the Middle East's 2 major river systems; agriculture has been its most important economic activity. Today, the Middle East has assumed geopolitical importance as the world's primary oil-producing region; it is also the focus of international tensions and strife.

Middleton, Arthur (1742-87), South Carolina planter and one of the signers of the Declaration of Independence. At the center of the struggle for American independence, he served as a delegate to the Continental Congress (1776, 1777) and to the Congress of the Confederation (1781). In 1780, he was captured by the British at the siege of Charleston but was released as a result of a prisoner exchange.

Middleton, Thomas (1580-1627), English dramatist. He wrote lively, naturalistic comedies, the Lord Mayor of London's pageants and various masques, and 2 tragedies concerning human corruption: *The Changeling* (1621) and *Women Beware Women* (1657). *A Game at Chesse* (1624) was his satire on political marriages with Spain, suppressed under James I.

Midge, large group (about 2,000 species) of tiny flies belonging to the Chironomidae family. Although related to biting midges and resembling mosquitos, midges do not bite. They often appear in swarms around streams and ponds. Their larvae, found in water, mud, tree bark, or manure, provide food for certain varieties of insects and fish.

Midget, human dwarf having normal body proportions, mental capacity, and sexual development. This type of dwarfism is caused by a deficiency of pituitary growth hormone.
See also: Dwarf.

Midway Island, group of islands (2 sq mi/5.2 sq km) northwest of Honolulu. Annexed by the United States in 1867 and used as a naval base, the island was the site of the Battle of Midway, the first important U.S. naval victory of World War II.
See also: World War II.

Mies van der Rohe, Ludwig (1886-1969), German-born U.S. architect, famous for functional but elegant buildings in the International Style, constructed of brick, steel, and glass. His work includes the Illinois Institute of Technology campus (1939) in Chicago, and the Seagram Building (1958, with Philip Johnson) in New York. Although he had no formal training, he was a director of the Bauhaus school and one of the leading architects.
See also: Architecture; Bauhaus.

Mifflin, Thomas (1744-1800), American soldier and political leader. A member of the First Continental Congress (1774-76, 1782-84) during the Revolutionary War he rose to the rank of quartermaster general (1775-77). He was later a delegate to the Constitutional Convention (1787) and the first governor of Pennsylvania (1790-99).

Mignonette, decorative garden plant belonging to the Resedaceae family. Found in North America and Europe, it has bushy leaves and tall spikes on which appear small, fragrant, yellowish-white or flowers with reddish pollen sacs.

Mikan, George (1924-   ), U.S. basketball player. Known for his strength and accurate hook shot, he was named the Associated Press' Player of the Half Century. Standing at 6-ft 10-in (208-cm), Mikan became the first center known for scoring (11,764 career points). He played in the National Basketball Association (NBA) for the Minneapolis Lakers (1946-55), and led them to 5 championships (1949, 50, 52-54). In 1967, he was named commissioner of the newly founded American Basketball Association. Mikan was inducted into the Basketball Hall of Fame in 1960.

Mikulic, Branko (1928-), premier of Yugoslavia (1986-88). He joined the League of Communists in 1943 and was a member of the Central Committee Presidium (1984-86). Mikulic was appointed as premier, but he and his entire cabinet resigned Dec. 30, 1988 over disputes with the Yugoslav parliament regarding economic planning.

Milan (pop. 1,358,600), city in northern Italy, capital of Lombardy. An important European trade and transportation hub, it is Italy's major industrial and commercial center, producing automobiles, airplanes, textiles, chemicals, electrical equipment, machinery, and books. Founded by the Celts c.400 B.C., Milan was a major late Roman city; it was the principal city state of Lombardy under the Visconti (1277-1447) and Sforza families. Spanish from 1535, Milan fell to Austria in 1714 and became a center of the 19th-century Risorgimento. Artistic treasures include the Milan Cathedral, Leonardo da Vinci's *Last Supper*, the Brera palace and art gallery, and La Scala opera house.

Milan Decree, order issued by Napoleon I of France in December, 1807. Hoping to bring about a complete economic blockade of Britain, the decree stated that even neutral ships were subject to capture. Although its effect was felt by the neutral nations—including the United States—the decree could not be enforced due to the superior naval strength of the British.
See also: Continental System; Napoleon I.

Mildew, general name for superficial growth of many types of fungi often found on plants and material derived from plants. Powdery mildews, numbering about 50, are caused by fungi belonging to the Ascomycetes order Erysiphales; the powdery effect is due to the masses of spores. Downy mildews are caused by Phycomycetes. Both types of disease can be controlled by the use of fungicides.

Miles, Nelson Appleton (1839-1925), U.S. soldier, army commander in chief (1895-1903). A Union general in the Civil War, in the Indian Wars he campaigned against the Sioux and also accepted the surrenders of Chiefs Joseph (1877) and Geronimo (1886). He also commanded in Cuba and Puerto Rico (1898).

Milhaud, Darius (1892-1974), French composer, one of the Parisian group called Les Six, noted for his polytonality (the simultaneous use of different keys). His vast output includes the jazz-influenced ballet *Creation of the World* (1923), *Saudades do Brasil* (1921), and various operas, among them *Christophe Colombe* (1930).

Military Academy, U.S. *See:* United States Military Academy.

Military service, compulsory *See:* Draft, military.

Milk, liquid secreted by the mammary glands of female mammals. It contains water, protein, fat, sugar, vitamins A, C, and D, and some B vitamins, as well as inorganic salts and minerals (calcium and phosphorus). In any species, milk serves as a complete food for the young of that species until weaning. Milk for human use is commercially produced by cows and water buffalo (especially in India); goat's milk is also commonly used in some areas, particularly the Middle East. An extremely perishable liquid, milk must be cooled to a temperature of not more than 10°C (50°F) within two hours of milking and maintained at that temperature until delivery.

Milk snake, small kingsnake (*Lampropeltis triangulum*), found in North America, from the northeastern United States to Mexico. About 4 ft (1.2 m) long, milk snakes are bright red, black, and yellow when young and gray and brown when adult.

Milkweed, any of various perennial plants (genus *Asclepias*) that secrete latex. They are common in fields and waste areas of North America. Milkweed is poisonous in large quantities especially for children.

Milky Way, spiral galaxy with a radius of about 50,000 light-years, containing some 100 billion stars. The Milky Way is shaped like a flat disk about 10,000 light-years thick in most places, about 30,000 light-years at the center. It is a modest-sized galaxy. Our solar system is in one of its spiral arms, just over 30,000 light-years from the galactic center. The galaxy rotates about a roughly spherical nucleus, the sun circling the galactic center once every 230 million years or so. The Milky Way is surrounded by a spheroidal halo some 165,000 light-years in diameter composed of gas, dust, occasional stars, and globular clusters. The name of the galaxy is derived from its appearance as

a hazy, milklike band of stars in the night sky. Irregular dark patches are caused by intervening clouds of gas dust.
See also: Galaxy; Solar System.

Mill, name of British literary family famed for their work in history, philosophy, economics, and psychology. **James Mill** (1773-1836) gained recognition with his book *A History of British India* but whose great contribution came through his work as the disciple of Jeremy Bentham, the father of utilitarianism. Mill was instrumental in explaining the fundamental tenets of the utilitarian doctrine. He also wrote a work on psychology, *Analysis of the Phenomena of the Human Mind* (1829); the first textbook of English economics, *Elements of Political Economy* (1821); and a work on moral philosophy, *Fragment on Mackintosh* (1835). His other accomplishments include being a Presbyterian minister, journalist, and head of the East India Company (1830-36). **John Stuart Mill** (1806-73), son of James Mill, is considered one of the most important thinkers of the 19th century. Mill was the head of the utilitarian movement and worked actively to promote the rights of workers and women. His most important work, *System of Logic* (1834), is a seminal work. Other works include *Principles of Political Economy* (1848), the famous *On Liberty* (1859), *The Subjection of Women* (1869), and *Autobiography* (1873). Mill was a brilliant child, who by the age of 14, mastered Latin, classical literature, history, mathematics, economics, and philosophy. He followed in his father's footsteps and became head of the East India Company but then went on to become a member of Parliament in 1865. **Harriet Taylor Mill** (1807-58), wife of John Stuart Mill, was instrumental in the thinking and writing of her husband's works. Her only work of actual authorship is her essay "Enfranchisement of Women" which appeared in one of her husband's works.
See also: Economics; Philosophy; Psychology.

Millais, Sir John Everett (1829-96), English painter, a founder of the Pre-Raphaelite "brotherhood" (1848). The realism of his *Christ in the Carpenter's Shop* (1850) caused a scandal. Later works such as *The Blind Girl* (1856) and *Bubbles* (1886) were more sentimental.

Millay, Edna St. Vincent (1892-1950), U.S. poet. Her reputation was established with *A Few Figs from Thistles* (1920). *The Harp Weaver* (1922) won a Pulitzer Prize. Other works include *Wine from These Grapes* (1934) and the verse drama *Aria da Capo* (1920).

Miller, Arthur (1915-), U.S. playwright. He has explored individual and social morality in plays like *Death of a Salesman* (1949; Pulitzer Prize); *The Crucible* (1953), about the witch trials in Salem, Mass.; *A View from the Bridge* (1955; Pulitzer Prize); the partly autobiographical *After the Fall* (1964); and the screenplay *The Misfits* (1961), written for his second wife, Marilyn Monroe. His autobiography, *Time Bends*, was published in 1987.

Miller, Glenn (1904-44), U.S. trombonist and bandleader of the big band "swing" era of the late 1930s and early 1940s. His blend of instrumental colors, the "Glenn Miller sound," had great success. Among his most popular recordings were *In the Mood*, *Moonlight Serenade*, and *Chattanooga Choo-Choo*. He died in a plane crash in Europe during World War II.

Miller, Henry (1891-1980), U.S. writer, noted for his candid treatment of sex and his espousal of the "natural man." *Tropic of Cancer* (1934) and *Tropic of Capricorn* (1939) were banned as obscene in the United States until 1961. Other books include the trilogy *The Rosy Crucifixion* (1949-60). He was a major influence on the Beat Generation of writers.

Miller, Lewis *See:* Chautauqua Movement.

Millerites *See:* Adventists.

Millet, common name for several varieties of cereal that grow on poor soil and ripen rapidly in hot sun. These characteristics have made it a popular crop in hot, dry countries, particularly in Africa and Asia. The grains can be stored for a long time and are richer in protein than rice, though the yield is small. Fermented millet grain is used to make beer in some countries, e.g. South Africa. In western countries millet is generally grown as cattle feed and for cage-birds. The tall elephant grass of Africa is a millet.

Millet, Jean François (1814-75), French painter. His peasant subjects, for example *The Gleaners* (1857) and *The Angelus* (1859), are naturalistic, though romanticized in style.
See also: Barbizon school.

Milligan, ex parte *See:* Ex Parte Milligan.

Millikan, Robert Andrews (1868-1953), U.S. physicist. He was awarded the 1923 Nobel Prize for physics for determining the electron's charge and for his work on the photoelectric effect. He also studied and named cosmic rays.
See also: Photoelectric effect.

Milliliter, in the metric system, unit of capacity equal to one-thousandth (.001) of a liter.
See also: Metric system.

Millimeter *See:* Metric system.

Millimicrosecond *See:* Metric system.

Millipede, segmented arthropod having two pairs of legs on each body segment (unlike centipedes, which have only one pair of legs per segment). Millipedes live in damp soil, rotting vegetation, or under stones. They eat mainly decaying vegetation. Some roll into a ball when molested, while others squirt a spray of poison that can burn the skin. Some tropical millipedes grow to several inches in length, and a few are brightly colored. One species, living among the sequoias of California, is luminous.

Mills, C(harles) Wright (1916-62), U.S. sociologist and critic of U.S. capitalism and militarism whose work was influential with radical social scientists of the 1970s. His books include *White Collar* (1951), *The Power Elite* (1956), and *The Sociological Imagination* (1959), which argues that sociologists should not be passive observers but agents of social change.
See also: Sociology.

Mills, Robert (1781-1855), U.S. architect and engineer. Official architect of public buildings in Washington, D.C. (1836-51), he aimed at an American neoclassical style. He designed the Washington Monument, the Treasury, and the Old Post Office building.
See also: Washington Monument.

Milne, A(lan) A(lexander) (1882-1956), English writer and dramatist. His fame rests on stories and poems he wrote for his son Christopher Robin: *Winnie-the-Pooh* (1926), *The House at Pooh Corner* (1928), *When We Were Very Young* (1924), and *Now We Are Six* (1927).

Milo *See:* Sorghum.

Mílos, or Milo, one of the Greek Cyclades islands in the Aegean Sea. The seat of ancient Athenian civilization, it is known as the place where the celebrated statue of Venus de Milo was discovered in 1820. Tourism is important to the economy of the island. Other industries include olive and tobacco production.
See also: Greece.

Miltiades (c.540?-488? B.C.), Athenian general who defeated the invading Persians at the battle of Marathon (490 B.C.). Earlier, he had served the Persian king Darius I against the Scythians.
See also: Greece, Ancient; Marathon.

Milton, John (1608-74), English poet. His blank-verse epic *Paradise Lost* (1667), detailing Lucifer's revolt against God and the fall of Adam and Eve in the Garden of Eden, is one of the masterpieces of English literature. His major early works are the ode "On the Morning of Christ's Nativity" (1629), "L'Allegro" (1630), "Il Penseroso" (c. 1631), *Comus* (c. 1632), and "Lycidas" (1638). A supporter of the anti-monarchists during the English Civil War, he wrote many political pamphlets and a defense of freedom of the press, *Areopagitica* (1644). He retired after the Restoration (1660), and though totally blind, dictated his final great works: *Paradise Lost, Paradise Regained* (1671), and *Samson Agonistes* (1671).

Milwaukee (pop. 617,000), largest city in Wisconsin, seat of Milwaukee County, in the southeast region of the state. An industrial center and leading Great Lakes port (on Lake Michigan), Milwaukee was incorporated in 1848. Notable landmarks include the Greek Orthodox Annunciation Church, designed by Frank Lloyd Wright; the War Memorial Center, housing the Milwaukee Art Center, designed by Eero Saarinen; the Performing Arts Center (1969); and the Civic Center downtown. The city has many spacious parks. Its educational institutions include the University of Wisconsin at Milwaukee, Marquette University, and 16 other universities and colleges.
See also: Wisconsin.

Mimosa, any of several tropical American plants (genus *Mimosa*) of the pulse family, with pink flowers and small leaves. One variety is called the sensitive plant (*M. pudica*), because its leaves fold together when touched, though after a few minutes they return to the normal position.

Mindszenty, József (1892-1975), Hungarian Roman Catholic cardinal who was sentenced (1949) to life imprisonment for his opposition to communism. Released in the uprising of 1956, he took refuge in the U.S. legation in Budapest. He refused to leave until the charges against him were rescinded. In 1971, after an agreement between the Vatican and the Hungarian government, Mindszenty left for Rome.

Mineral, in biology, inorganic element vital to human health. Minerals are usually obtained from food. The essential ones are calcium, chlorine, cobalt, copper fluorine, iodine, iron, magnesium, manganese, phosphorus, potassium, sodium, sulphur, and zinc. Other minerals, known as trace elements, are present in the body in minute quantities and are presumed to be necessary for health: aluminum, boron, bromine, chromium, molybdenum nickel, silicon, and silver.

Mineral, in geology, naturally occurring inorganic substance with a particular chemical composition and definite physical properties. The rocks of the earth's crust are composed of minerals, which are generally classified in order of increasing complexity: elements, sulfides, oxides, halides, carbonates, nitrates, sulfates, phosphates, and silicates

Minerva, in Roman mythology, daughter of Jupiter. She was modeled on the Greek goddess Athena. Worshiped for her skill in handicrafts as well as for her artistic and intellectual gifts, Minerva came to symbolize military prowess and was often depicted wearing a helmet and suit of armor. *See also:* Mythology.

Mineworkers of America, United (UMW), U.S. labor union for workers in coal mines and coal industries. The UMW is an industrial union, with membership based on an industry rather than on job skills. Founded in 1890, it was a member of the American Federation of Labor (AFL) until 1936 (rejoining briefly 1946-47). Under the leadership of John L. Lewis, union president 1919-60, it then became a moving force in the formation of the Congress of Industrial Organizations (CIO; 1935). It resigned from the CIO in 1942 and is an unaffiliated union. *See also:* Unions, labor.

Ming dynasty, imperial family that ruled China from 1368-1644. Following years of Mongolian rule, this period was characterized by a return to civil service and an emphasis on scholarship, the arts, and architecture. Achievements included the building of the imperial palace in Beijing's Forbidden City and the creation of exquisite porcelain vases. *See also:* China.

Miniature schnauzer, dog breed developed in Germany in the 19th century. Standing at 12 to 14 inches (30 to 36 centimeters) and possessing a variety of colorations, it is characterized by wiry hair that bristles out in its spiky eyebrows and beard. It is considered to be intelligent, energetic, affectionate, and a good watchdog and mouser.

Minimalism, art movement initiated in the 1960s that stressed pure color and geometry. In both painting and sculpture—generally executed with great precision—it rejected emotionalism, striving for an "exclusive, negative, absolute, and timeless" quality. Minimalism comprises, among styles and techniques, color-field painting, hard-edge painting, pop art, the shaped canvas, serial imagery, and primary structures.

Mining, extraction of minerals and ores from the earth. There are various types of mines. The open pit mine is used when the desired minerals lie near the surface. It usually consists of a series of terraces that are worked back in parallel so that the mineral is always within reach of the excavating machines. In strip mining a surface layer is peeled off to reach a usually thin mineral seam (often coal). When minerals lie far below the surface, various deep mining techniques must be used. Access to the mineral-bearing strata is obtained through a vertical shaft or sloping incline dug from the surface or through a horizontal adit driven into the side of a mountain. Underground mines require ventilation and lighting, facilities for pumping out any ground-water or toxic gases, and some means (railroad or conveyor) for carrying the ore and waste to the surface. Several serious occupational diseases (e.g., pneumoconiosis, or "black lung") are associated with mining and extractive metallurgy, particularly where high dust levels and toxic substances are involved.

Mink, semiaquatic carnivore (genus *Mustela*) of the weasel family, extensively farmed for its fur. There are two species: *M. lutreola*, of European distribution, and *M. vision*, originating in North America but now widely distributed throughout Europe. Feeding on small fish, eggs, young birds, and small mammals, minks are avid hunters, often killing more than they can eat.

Minneapolis (pop. 362,700), largest city of Minnesota and seat of Hennepin County, on the upper Mississippi River, contiguous to its twin city, St. Paul. Minneapolis is a manufacturing, trading, and financial center noted for its many large flour mills and grain elevators. Its products include farm machinery, electronic equipment, linseed oil, paint, precision instruments, and furniture. Site of the University of Minnesota, the city also has an institute of art, a symphony orchestra, and a repertory theater.
See also: Minnesota.

Minnehaha, in Henry Wadsworth Longfellow's poem *The Song of Hiawatha* (1855), a young Native American woman. She became the wife of Hiawatha.

Minnesinger, minstrel-poet of medieval Germany. Minnesingers composed and sang songs of courtly love (*minne*). Heirs to the Provençal troubadours, they flourished from c.1150 to c.1350.

Minnesota, state in the Great Lakes region of the midwestern United States; bordered by Canada to the north, Lake Superior and Wisconsin to the east, Iowa to the south, and South Dakota and North Dakota to the west.
Land and climate. Minnesota's 4 main land regions are the Superior Upland, the Young Drift Plains, the Dissected Till Plains, and the Driftless Area. The Superior Upland, in northeastern Minnesota, includes some of the most rugged and isolated parts of the state. The gently rolling Young Drift Plains cover most of the rest of the state. This region has the state's most important

Minnesota

Capital:	St. Paul
Statehood:	May 11, 1858 (32nd state)
Familiar name:	Gopher State
Area:	84,402 sq mi (218,601 sq km);
Population:	4,686,000 (1997); ranks 20th
Elevation:	Highest—2,301 ft (701 m), Eagle Mountain;
	Lowest—602 ft (83 m), along Lake Superior
Motto:	L'Etoile du Nord (The Star of the North)
Flower:	Pink and white lady's-slipper
Bird:	Common loon
Tree:	Norway pine
Song:	"Hail! Minnesota"

farmlands. In the Dissected Till Plains, at the state's southwestern corner, the soil is a thick mixture of sand, gravel, and clay. Parts of this region are good farmland. The Driftless Area in the southeastern corner is nearly flat in the east, but with deep valleys cut by swift streams in the west. Minnesota has as many as 22,000 lakes; more than 15,000 of them are 10 acres or larger. The nation's greatest river, the Mississippi, has its source in Minnesota. Other major rivers include the Red River of the North, the Rainy River, and the St. Louis River. Minnesota has long, cold winters and warm-to-very-hot summers. Principal cities are Minneapolis, St. Paul, and Duluth.

Economy. Minnesota's principal industries are agri-business, forest products, mining, manufacturing, and tourism. The chief manufactured products are nonelectrical machinery, food products, fabricated metal products, chemicals, paper and paper goods, and adhesive tapes and industrial adhesives. Livestock and dairy products account for about more than half of the state's farm income; chief crops are corn, soybeans, hay, and wheat. Chief mineral products are iron ore, taconite, granite, limestone, and clay.

Government. Minnesota's constitution was adopted in 1858. The governor serves a 4-year term. The state's Legislature consists of 67 senators serving 4-year terms and 134 representatives serving 2-year terms. In the U.S. Congress, Minnesota is represented by 2 senators and 8 representatives.

History. Sioux were living in the region when the first whites arrived in the late 1600s; Chippewa came soon after. French fur traders and missionaries settled the area. At various times, parts of Minnesota were held by France, Spain, and Britain. Some of Minnesota became part of the U.S. after the American Revolution, the rest with the Louisiana Purchase. In 1851, the Sioux were forced to sign treaties that opened most of Minnesota to white settlement, which boomed. Minnesota, which became a state in 1858, supported the Union during the Civil War. In 1862, the Sioux rose in a bloody uprising that the U.S. Army and state militia eventually quashed. After the Civil and Indian Wars, industries developed rapidly and immigration increased. World War I raised demand for Minnesota's iron and steel, but the Depression of the 1930s devastated the state's economy. World War II brought recovery. Since then, industry's importance has grown, while farming's has declined. During the 1970s and 1980s, a major concern was finding ways to develop Minnesota's rich resources without damaging its environment, especially the lakes and rivers, wooded parks, and ski areas that draw millions of vacationers a year.

Minnow, common name for many small freshwater fishes found throughout the world except for South America and Australia. The original minnow is a 3-in (7.6-cm) European fish, but the name has also been extended to its relatives, which include carp, cutlips, shiners, roach, and tench. Minnows feed on insects and crustaceans and are important in the food chain, since larger fish feed on them. The largest American minnow is the squawfish, or Pacific pike, which may grow to several feet. Minnows have long pharyngeal teeth around their gills. They lay their eggs in gravel or in special nests.

Minoan civilization, Bronze Age culture that flourished on the island of Crete during the 3rd and 2nd millenniums B.C. The first great Aegean civilization—with cities, palaces, a highly developed art and architecture, writing, extensive trade, and complex religious beliefs—Minoan culture reached its high point c.2200-1500 B.C. The city of Cnossus on the north coast of Crete was its center, from which the Minoan fleet carried goods to Egypt, Syria, Phoenicia, Asia Minor, Sicily, and Greece. By c.1000 B.C. Minoan civilization had declined, and its remains were incorporated by Greece. The word "Minoan" comes from the legendary King Minos, who was said to have ruled in Cnossus.
See also: Crete; Greece, Ancient.

Minorca, or Menorca, one of the Balearic Islands off the eastern coast of Spain. The second largest of the islands, it was seized several times by France and by England, who eventually ceded it to Spain in 1802. Minorca is known for its farm crops, light manufacturing, lobster fishing, and beaches. Tourism is also important.

Minor leagues *See:* Baseball.

Minos, in Greek mythology, wealthy king of Crete who commanded the artisan Daedalus to construct a labyrinthine prison for a beast called the Minotaur, to whom the young people of Athens were regularly sacrificed. One of these, Theseus, succeeded in killing the Minotaur and running away with Minos' daughter Ariadne. Minos was married to Pasiphaë; his other children included Androgeous, Glaucus, and Phaedra.
See also: Mythology.

Minot, George (1885-1950), U.S. physician who developed a cure for the once-fatal blood disease called pernicious anemia. He found that feeding patients a diet consisting largely of raw liver normalized their red blood count. He was awarded the Nobel Prize for medicine (1934, with G.H.

Whipple and W.P. Murphy). Minot wrote numerous articles on blood disorders and dietary deficiency.
See also: Anemia.

Minsk (pop. 1,613,000), capital city of the Byelorussia, located on the Svisloch River. After suffering extensive damage during World War II, the city was revitalized by the creation of factories and new housing. Among the goods produced in Minsk are trucks, machine parts, tools, and radios. The city is also noted for its academic and cultural institutions.
See also: Byelorussia.

Minstrel, wandering professional entertainers who flourished in medieval Europe. Known variously as *troubadours* or *jongleurs* in France, *bards* in Ireland, *skalds* in Scandinavia, and *minnesingers* in Germany, they were generally singers but also used storytelling and mime. Because they wandered from town to town, they spread local news and helped to preserve oral traditions. They began to die out in the 15th century, largely due to the appearance of the printing press.

Minstrel show, form of entertainment popular in the United States from about 1840 to 1900. White performers blackened their faces in imitation of African Americans and alternated jokes with African American songs, many of which thus became well-known American folk songs. Minstrel shows reinforced negative stereotypes of blacks that lasted for decades after the shows had ceased to exist.

Mint, in botany, family of square-stemmed plants with white, blue, purple, or red flowers in the form of a lipped tube. Many are aromatic. Familiar examples are lavender, sage, oswego tea, marjoram, and thyme. The true mints (genus *Mentha*) include spearmint (*M. spicata*) and peppermint (*M. piperita*).

Minto, Earl of (1845-1914), British governor general of Canada (1898-1904) and viceroy of India (1905-10). As governor general, he was criticized by French-speaking Canadians for sending Canadian troops to South Africa during the Boer War. As viceroy, he angered Indian nationalists by instituting reforms that resulted in the intensification of divisions between Hindus and Muslims.

Minuit, Peter (c.1580-1638), Dutch colonial administrator in North America. He was the first director-general of New Netherland for the Dutch West India Company and is remembered for buying Manhattan island from the Native Americans (1626) for about $24 worth of trinkets. He founded New Amsterdam (now New York City) and later (1638) established New Sweden on the Delaware River.

Minuteman, member of a volunteer militia during the American Revolutionary War, ready to take up arms "at a minute's notice." Massachusetts minutemen fought at the battles of Lexington and Concord (1775). Maryland, New Hampshire, and Connecticut also had such militias.
See also: Revolutionary War in America.

Miocene, last epoch but one of the Tertiary period, which lasted from 25 to 10 million years ago.

Mira, variable star about 270 light-years away from the earth. The German astronomer Fabricius first observed the brightening and dimming of the star in 1596; later, variations in diameter and temperature were also noted. The diameter of Mira can be imagined as equal to that of the sun and all nearby planets, extending to a point somewhere beyond Mars. It is visible to the naked eye for about half the year; otherwise it can be seen through a telescope.
See also: Star.

Mirabeau, Comte de (1749-91), French revolutionary leader. A powerful orator, he became an early leader of the moderate wing of revolutionary forces, representing the third estate (the commoners) in the States-General (the French parliament). He worked secretly to establish a constitutional monarchy but was mistrusted by both revolutionaries and royalists. He was elected president of the National Assembly in 1791 but died a few months later.
See also: French Revolution; Jacobins.

Miracle play *See:* Mystery play.

Mirage, optical illusion in the atmosphere in which the refraction of light passing through air layers of different densities causes non-existent images to be seen. Distant objects may appear to be reflected in water, as light rays traveling initially toward the ground have been bent upward by layers of hot air close to the surface. In some mirages objects seem to float in the air. This commonly occurs over cold surfaces such as ice or a cold sea, where warmer air overlies cooler air and bends light rays downward.

Miramichi River, Canadian waterway located in New Brunswick. About 135 mi (48 km) long, the river has its mouth near Newcastle and empties into the Gulf of St. Lawrence. It is an important source of salmon and provides passage for large ships.

Miranda, Francisco de (1750-1816), Venezuelan patriot who fought for the forces of freedom on 3 continents. While an officer in the army of Spain he served in the American Revolution, receiving the British surrender at Pensacola, Fla. He later joined the French revolutionary forces, fighting in several major battles. When in 1810 patriots in Venezuela formed a provisional government, he returned home, where he and Simón Bolivar proclaimed the first South American republic, in Caracas on July 5, 1811. Captured by royalists, he died in prison in Spain.
See also: Venezuela.

Miranda v. Arizona, U.S. Supreme Court case (1966) establishing the rights of criminal suspects in police custody. In its 5-4 ruling the Court specified that prior to any sort of questioning suspects must be informed of their rights to remain silent and to have a lawyer present. Miranda had been questioned by police in Arizona and had confessed to a crime without having been told of these rights. The Court ruled that the confession was therefore inadmissible evidence.

Miró, Joan (1893-1983), Spanish painter. A pioneer of surrealism, Miró produced freely drawn works characterized by bright colors and clusters of abstract symbolic forms. His work includes murals and large ceramic decorations for UNESCO in Paris.

Misdemeanor, crime that is not as serious as a felony. In general, offenses punishable only by a fine or short imprisonment in county jails are misdemeanors. These may include traffic violations, assault and battery, and theft of small amounts of money. Convictions that carry punishment by imprisonment in state penitentiaries are felonies.
See also: Crime.

Mishima, Yukio (Kimitake Hiraoka; 1925-70), Japanese author. His writing is obsessed with the conflict between traditional and post-World War II Japan. He formed a private army devoted to ancient martial arts and committed hara-kiri. His work includes the novels *The Temple of the Golden Pavilion* (1956), *Sun and Steel* (1970), *Sea of Fertility* (4 vols., 1970), and *Patriotism* (1966), on ritual suicide, and modern Kabuki and Noh plays.

Missile, guided *See:* Guided missile.

Missionary, individual sent to a foreign territory or country to educate others in particular religious tradition. While their goal is religious conversion, missionaries also work to provide agricultural information, social services, and literacy skills. The Christian church, with the greatest number of missionaries, sponsors activities in Asia, Latin America, Africa, and the Pacific islands.

Mississippi, state in the Deep South region of the United States; bordered by Tennessee to the north, Alabama to the east, the Gulf of Mexico to the south, Louisiana to the south and west, and Arkansas to the west.
Land and climate. Mississippi has 2 main land regions. The Mississippi Alluvial Plain, often called "the Delta," lies on the state's western edge along the Mississippi River. Its rich lowlands, built up by river deposits, support good cotton and soybean crops. Small, slow-moving streams called bayous connect this region's lakes and rivers. The rest of the state lies in the East Gulf Coastal Plain, which consists of low, rolling hills with some prairie and lowland. Pine forests cover much of this region's southern portion; the northeast is a fertile agricultural area. Forests, which originally covered nearly the entire state, now cover more than half of it. Mississippi's complex river system drains into the Gulf of Mexico—directly, or via the Mississippi River. Other large rivers include the Yazoo, Tallahatchie, Tombigbee, Pearl, and Pascagula. A system of *levees* (dikes) helps to control the lower Mississippi River during flood season. All of the state's larger lakes are man-made reservoirs. Mississippi has a warm, humid climate, with long, hot summers and short, mild winters. Principal cities are Jackson, Biloxi, and Meridian.
Economy. Mississippi's principal industries are manufacturing, food processing, seafood, government, and wholesale and retail trade. Cotton, though no longer "king," remains the most important crop. Other important agricultural products include soybeans, catfish, and rice. Timber, petroleum, and natural gas are the main natural resources.

Mississippi

Capital:	Jackson
Statehood:	Dec. 10, 1817 (20th state)
Familiar name:	Magnolia State
Area:	47,689 sq mi (123,515 sq km);
Population:	2,731,000 (1997); ranks 31st
Elevation:	Highest—806 ft (246 m), Woodall Mountain;
	Lowest—sea level, along the Gulf of Mexico coast
Motto:	Virtute et Armis (By Valor and Arms)
Flower:	Magnolia.
Bird:	Mockingbird
Tree:	Magnolia
Song:	"Go Mississipi"

Government. Mississippi's present constitution was adopted in 1980. The governor serves a 4-year term. The state's legislature consists of 52 senators and 122 representatives; all serve 4-year terms. In the U.S. Congress, Mississippi is represented by 2 senators and 5 representatives.

History. Chickasaw, Natchez, and Choctaw were living in Mississippi when the first white settlers arrived. The first European to visit the area was de Soto, a Spanish explorer, in 1540. In 1683, the French explorer La Salle claimed the entire Mississippi Valley for France. In 1763, after the French and Indian Wars, France ceded the region to Britain. After a series of border changes and

land conflicts, Mississippi became the Union's 20th state in 1817. Indians had controlled most of the area throughout its territorial days, but whites had full control by 1840. By 1860, black slaves outnumbered the white population and Mississippi had become the Union's top cotton-producing state. The second state to secede from the Union, Mississippi was a leading member of the Confederacy during the Civil War. The state's economy was ruined by the war; Reconstruction and the postwar military government did nothing to restore it. Depression-era programs helped improve Mississippi's agriculture and industry somewhat; modest industrial growth continued during the 1940s and 1950s. During the 1960s, Mississippi was the scene of some of the worst violence in the civil-rights movement. Race relations improved during the 1970s and 1980s—as did the state's economy. But many farm workers are jobless, and many educated young people leave the state to seek employment elsewhere.

Mississippian *See:* Mound Builders.

Mississippi River, chief river of the North American continent and the longest river in the United States, flowing about 2,350 mi (3,780 km) south from Lake Itasca in northwestern Minnesota to its enormous delta at the Gulf of Mexico, below New Orleans. Called the "father of waters" by Native Americans, the Mississippi drains an area of about 1.25 million sq mi (3,237,500 sq km). With the Missouri and Ohio rivers (its chief tributaries), it forms the world's third longest river system, after the Nile and the Amazon. It receives more than 250 tributaries in all. The Mississippi is noted for sudden changes of course, its length varying by 40-50 mi (64-80 km) per year. The river's average discharge is 1.64 million cu ft (46,412 cu m) per sec, but in high water season this soars to some 2.3 million cu ft (65,090 cu m) per sec. Flooding is a serious problem, but dikes and levees contain its periodic massive overflows. The river is a major transportation artery of the United States and was of fundamental importance in the development of the North American continent.

Missoula (pop. 33,388), large city in western Montana known for its wood products. A regional headquarters for the U.S. Forest Service, it has a training center for *smoke jumpers*—firefighters who descend into remote forest areas by parachute. Founded in the 1860s as a trading post, its growth was triggered by the creation of the Northern Pacific Railway.

Missouri, state in central United States, considered part of the Midwest; bordered by Iowa to the north; the Mississippi River and Illinois, Kentucky, and Tennessee to the east; Arkansas to the south, and Oklahoma, Kansas, and Nebraska to the west.
Land and climate. Missouri's 4 land regions reflect a unique blending of North, South, East, and West. The state's southeastern corner is part of the rich Mississippi Alluvial Plain. The flattest, lowest, and most fertile part of the state, it recalls the Deep South. The forested Ozark Plateau, in central and southern Missouri, is the state's largest land region. This area of poor, stony soil but great scenic beauty resembles the hill country of eastern Tennessee and Kentucky. The Osage Plains region in western Missouri is a relatively flat prairie area much like the Great Plains. The upper third of the state is part of the fertile Dissected Till Plains region, which is part of the Midwest's Corn Belt. The nation's 2 largest rivers, the Mississippi and the Missouri, enrich the state's soil and make it an important waterway, railroad, and highway hub. Missouri's climate is humid, and the weather is extremely changeable. Summers are long and winters are brisk. Principal cities are St. Louis, Kansas City, and Springfield.
Economy. Missouri's main industries are agriculture, manufacturing, aerospace, and tourism. Soybeans, corn, wheat, and cotton are the main crops. Missouri is a leading beef-cattle state; other important livestock products are dairy cattle, hogs and pigs, sheep, eggs, turkeys, and chickens. Chief manufactured products are transportation equipment, food products, chemicals and related products, and electrical machinery and equipment. The most important mineral resources are lead, crushed stone, limestone, sand and gravel, coal, zinc, and silver.
Government. Missouri's present constitution was adopted in 1945. The governor serves a 4-year term. The state legislature, called the General Assembly, consists of 34 senators serving four-year terms and 163 representatives serving two-year terms. In the U.S. Congress, Missouri is represented by two senators and nine representatives.
History. Native Americans known as Mound Builders lived in Missouri long before the first whites, French explorers Marquette and Joliet, arrived in

Missourri

Capital:	Jefferson City
Statehood:	Aug. 10, 1821 (24th state)
Familiar name:	Show Me State
Area:	69,697 sq mi (180,516 sq km); ranks 19th
Population:	5,402,000 (1997); ranks 16th
Elevation:	Highest—1,772 ft (540 m), Taum Sauk Mountain; Lowest—230 ft (70 m) along the St. Francis River near Cardwell
Motto:	Salus Populi Suprema Lex Esto (The Welfare of the People Shall be the Supreme Law)
Flower:	Hawthorne
Bird:	Bluebird
Tree:	Flowering dogwood
Song:	"Missouri Waltz"

1673. France claimed the entire Mississippi Valley after La Salle's voyage down the river in 1682. The U.S. acquired the area in the 1803 Louisiana Purchase. In 1812, Congress created the Missouri Territory. By 1815, fighting between Indians and settlers ended in treaties that followed further white settlement. Most new settlers were slave owners from the South, which caused problems when Missouri requested statehood. After three years of controversy, the Missouri Compromise of 1820 allowed Missouri to enter the Union as a slave state in 1821. Missouri became known as the "Gateway to the West" as thousands of settlers left from Independence to travel west on the Santa Fe and Oregon Trails and St. Joseph became the starting point of the Pony Express. During the Civil War, Missouri was bitterly divided; heavy fighting took place there. Postwar recovery was slow. Since about 1830, manufacturing, rather than agriculture, has been the state's chief source of income. World War II brought new industries. Missouri battled urban problems during the 1970s and a farm crisis and financial problems in the 1980s.

Missouri Compromise, package of measures adopted by the U.S. Congress in 1820-21, to resolve issues relating to the extension of slavery. At the time of Missouri's first petition to become a state (1819), there were 11 free and 11 slave states in the Union. Missouri's addition would have changed the balance of power in the U.S. Senate and reopened the bitterly contested issue of whether slavery should be permitted to spread in the United States. Action on Missouri's petition was delayed until Maine requested admission as a free state, and both were admitted. The compromise also barred slavery from

being extended to the rest of the territory of the Louisiana Purchase north of 36°30' latitude. The compromise was repealed in 1854 by the Kansas-Nebraska Act.
See also: Kansas-Nebraska Act; Slavery.

Missouri River, second-longest river in the United States (about 2,500 mi/4,023 km) and chief tributary of the Mississippi, with which it forms the world's third-largest river system. Rising in southeastern Montana in the Rocky Mountains, the Missouri river flows north and then east through Montana; it then crosses North Dakota, and continues generally southeast until emptying into the Mississippi north of St. Louis. Its main tributaries include the Cheyenne, Kansas, Osage, Platte, Yellowstone, James, and Milk rivers. The Missouri was explored by Joliet and Marquette in 1673 and by the Lewis and Clark expedition in 1804-05. Like the Mississippi, it is subject to serious flooding, which is under control since three decades.

Mistletoe, any of many species of evergreen parasitic plants of the family Loranthaceae with small, inconspicuous flowers. In Europe the common mistletoe (*Viscum album*) grows on apples, poplar, willow, linden, and hawthorns, while common U.S. mistletoes (*Phoradendron flavescens*, for example) occur on most deciduous trees and some conifers. Mistletoes derive some of their nutrients from the host plants, but they also produce some by photosynthesis. Their seeds are spread by fruit-eating birds.

Mistral, Frédéric (1830-1914), French poet. He won the 1904 Nobel Prize for literature and for his work as leader of a movement to restore the former glories of the Provençal language and culture. Among his works are the epic poems *Mirèio* (1859), *Calendau* (1867), *Nerto* (1884), and *Lou Pouémo dúo Rose* (1897).

Mistral, Gabriela (Lucila Godoy Alcayaga; 1889-1957), Chilean poet, educator, and diplomat awarded the Nobel Prize for literature in 1945. Her simple, lyrical poems express sympathy with nature and mankind. Her works include *Desolation* (1922) and *Tenderness* (1924).

Mitanni, kingdom that flourished in northern Mesopotamia (now southeastern Turkey) from about 1500 B.C. A warfaring people renowned for their skills with horses and chariots, the early Mitannians fought the Egyptians for control of Syria, but the threat of a common enemy—the Hittites—caused these empires to form an alliance. Ultimately, the kingdom of Mitanni was captured in 1350 B.C. and became part of the Assyrian Empire.

Mitchell, Billy (1879-1936), U.S. army officer and aviator. After leading U.S. air services in World War I, he became an outspoken champion of a strong air force independent of army or naval control. Court-martialed for insubordination (1925) and suspended from duty for five years, he resigned from the army in 1926.

Mitchell, John Newton (1913-88), U.S. attorney general (1969-72) and convicted Watergate felon. A former law partner of Richard M. Nixon, he served as Nixon's campaign manager in 1968. In 1972, as director of the Committee to Reelect the President, he was involved in the burglary of the

Democratic Party headquarters, resulting in his 1977 conviction and prison sentence. He was paroled in 1979 after serving 19 months.
See also: Watergate.

Mitchell, Margaret (1900-49), U.S. writer. Her best-selling and only novel *Gone With the Wind* (1936) won the 1937 Pulitzer Prize and was made into a successful film (1939).

Mitchell, Maria (1818-89), U.S. astronomer who discovered a comet in 1847. She was the first woman to be elected to the American Academy of Arts and Sciences (1848) and was professor of astronomy at Vassar College (1865-88).
See also: Astronomy.

Mitchell, Wesley Clair (1874-1948), U.S. economist and educator. He helped organize the National Bureau of Economic Research (1920), and was its research director (1920-45). He served on many government boards and was a leading authority on business cycles.
See also: Economics.

Mite, tiny arachnid, a relative of the spider with a rounded body and four pairs of legs. Mites feed by sucking the juices of plants and animals. Some are pests and may carry diseases, e.g. scrub typhus. Others cause itching and scabs when they get under the skin. Chiggers are the larvae of one form of mite.

Mithra, ancient Indo-Iranian sun-god, one of the ethical lords, or gods, of Zoroastrianism. He was the chief Persian deity during the 5th century B.C., and his cult spread over most of Asia Minor reaching Rome, according to Plutarch, in 68 B.C.. Mithraism was especially popular among the Roman legions. Roman Mithraism, which competed with early Christianity for converts, thought that the forces of good and evil waged a struggle in the world. It made ethical demands on its followers and offered them the hope of immortality. It declined after A.D. 200 and was officially suppressed in the 4th century.
See also: Zoroastrianism.

Mithridates VI (132 B.C.-63 B.C.), king of ancient Pontus, on the Black Sea, who fought three wars against the Roman state. In the first (88-84 B.C.), he overran Asia Minor but was subsequently forced to make peace. He won the second war (83-81 B.C.) but lost the third (74-63 B.C.). Pompey drove him into exile in the Crimea, where he had himself killed by a mercenary.
See also: Pontus.

Mitterrand, François Maurice (1916-96), French politician, president of the republic from 1981-95. A cabinet minister in 11 governments during the Fourth Republic (1946-58), he opposed De Gaulle's establishment of the Fifth Republic in 1958. A socialist and candidate of the non-Communist left, he first ran for the presidency in 1965, but was defeated by De Gaulle. He became head of the Socialist Party in 1971 and ran unsuccessfully for the presidency a second time in 1974, losing to Valéry Giscard d'Estaing. He finally won in 1981. His party also won a majority in the National Assembly

and initiated a program of mild nationalization and social reform. In the late 1980s his government became increasingly moderate.
See also: France.

Mix, Tom (1880-1940), U.S. film actor and director whose popular westerns featured spectacular photography and daring horseriding. He starred in the silent films *Desert Love* (1920) and *Riders of the Purple Sage* (1925) and in numerous films of the 1930s.

Moabite stone, ancient, black-basalt stone containing writing in Hebrew-Phoenician characters. Probably inscribed about 865 B.C., the stone stands 3 ft, 8 in (112 cm) high and 2 ft, 3 in (68 cm) wide. Its inscription narrates the deeds of Mesha, king of the Moabites, in his wars against Israel and against the Edomites.

Mobile (pop. 476,923), city in southwestern Alabama, on Mobile Bay, and connected by a deepwater channel to the Gulf of Mexico. Alabama's only seaport, Mobile exports cotton, iron, steel products, and lumber. The city was settled by the French in 1702, and from 1711 to 1720 was the capital of French Louisiana. It was taken successively by the English and the Spanish and became part of the U.S. in 1813.

Möbius, August Ferdinand (1790-1868), German mathematician and astronomer who developed the field of topology, which derived from his work in geometry. Topology studies the qualities of a geometric form that do not change when subject to twisting, bending, and stretching.
See also: Topology.

Mobutu Sese Seko (1930-97), president of the Republic of Zaïre (formerly the Belgian Congo) from 1966-97. He took power in a coup and in 1967 established a dictatorial regime with himself as president. In 1997 he was ousted by Laurent Kabila and went into exile.

Moccasin flower *See:* Lady's-slipper.

Moccasin snake *See:* Water moccasin.

Mockingbird, any of several species of birds of the family Mimidae native to the Americas, with long tails, short rounded wings and well-developed legs. They feed on insects and fruit. The name is derived from their ability to mimic the calls of other birds.

Mock orange, or syringa, small garden bush belonging to the saxifrage family and known for its clusters of tiny, light-colored, often-fragrant flowers. Various hybrids are grown in the United States and Mexico.

Model Parliament, English parliament set up in 1295 by King Edward I. The Model Parliament's wide representation (clergy, earls, barons, two knights from each county, and two burgesses from each borough) was symbolic of Parliament's developing representational role, although the principles of membership were by no means strictly observed through much of the 14th century.
See also: Parliament.

Modigliani, Amedeo (1884-1920), Italian painter and sculptor best known for his nudes and portraits, works characterized by elegant elongated forms. He was influenced by African sculpture and by Constantin Brancusi.

Modoc, Native Americans who occupied parts of what is now California and Oregon. They are closely related to the Klamath, with whom they agreed in 1864 to move to an Ore. reservation. In 1870 a Modoc group, led by Chief Kintpuash (Captain Jack), fled back to northern California. The group was attacked by a U.S. army unit, bringing about the Modoc War (1872-73). Some of the Modoc subsequently returned to Oregon; others were sent to Oklahoma.

Moffat Tunnel, U.S. railroad tunnel, one of the longest, running for over 6 mi (9.7 km) through James Peak, Colo. The tunnel shortens the rail distance from Denver to Salt Lake City by 176 mi (283 km).

Mogadishu, or Mogadiscio (pop. 1,000,000), capital and major port city of the Somali Democratic Republic, located on the Indian Ocean. Long under Arab rule, it was made the colonial capital of Italian Somaliland in 1905. When Somalia gained its independence in 1960, Mogadishu remained as its capital. Both Arabic and Italian influences are evident in the city, which was heavily damaged during the civil war in the early 1990s.

Mogul Empire, Muslim empire in northern India (1526-1857), founded by Babur, who invaded India from Afghanistan. His son Humayun was defeated by the Afghan Sher Shah Sur, but Mogul power was restored by Akbar (1556-1605), who established centralized government throughout Afghanistan and northern and central India. The Mogul "golden age" was in the reign of Shah Jehan (1628-58). During this time, the Taj Mahal, the Pearl Mosque of Agra, and many of Delhi's finest buildings were erected. In the 1700s, the rising power of the Hindu Mahratetas weakened the empire. In 1857 the British deposed the last Mogul emperor, Bahadur Shah II.
See also: Akbar.

Mohammad *See:* Muhammad.

Mohammad Reza Pahlavi (1919-80), shah of Iran (1941-79). The British forced his pro-German father, Reza Pahlavi, to abdicate in 1941. Mohammad Reza Pahlavi left the country briefly during the rule of the left-wing Nationalist Muhammad Mossadegh (1953), but returned with CIA-backing to consolidate his power. He instituted certain western social reforms, but exercised a dictatorship bolstered by a pervasive secret police, the Savak. An Islamic revolution forced him into exile in 1979. He died in exile in Egypt.

Mohawk River, chief tributary of the Hudson River. Formed in Oneida county, central New York State, the Mohawk flows south and east for about 145 mi (233 km) joining the Hudson at Cohoes. The Mohawk Valley, a historic route from the Hudson to the Great Lakes, saw fierce fighting during the French and Indian Wars and the Revolutionary War.

Mohawks, Native American tribe, of what is now New York State, one of the five tribes of the Iroquois League, which had a highly developed culture that flourished through the 17th and 18th century.

Mohegan, North American Indian tribe of the Eastern Woodlands. Mohegans formed a branch of the Mahican group, which occupied southwestern Connecticut in the 17th and 18th centuries. In the 1600s, the Mohegan chief, Uncas, and the settlers formed an alliance against hostile native groups. In the 1700s, however, many Mohegans were driven from the land, had died of disease, or were converted to Christianity. A few remaining descendants still live on a Connecticut reservation. Both Mohegans and Mahicans are sometimes called Mohicans, after the fictional tribe in James Fenimore Cooper's *The Last of the Mohicans*.
See also: Mahican.

Mohican *See:* Mahican; Mohegan.

Moholy-Nagy, László (1895-1946), Hungarian painter, designer, and member of the German Constructivist school. He was professor at the Bauhaus, 1923-28. He founded the Institute of Design at the Illinois Institute of Technology in Chicago in 1939 and was an important influence on U.S. industrial design.

Mohorovicic discontinuity, or Moho, seismic boundary of the earth originally regarded as separating the crust and mantle, evidenced by rapid increase in the velocity of seismic waves.

Moisture *See:* Humidity; Weather.

Mojave Desert, barren area of mountains and desert valley in southeastern California. It includes Death Valley in the north and the Joshua Tree National Monument in the south.

Molar *See:* Teeth.

Mold, general name for a number of filamentous fungi that produce powdery or fluffy growths on fabrics, foods, and decaying plant or animal remains. Best known is the blue bread mold caused by penicillium, from which the antibiotic penicillin was first discovered.
See also: Fungi.

Moldova, Republic in Eastern Europe, between Romania in the south and the Ukraine in the north. The capital is Chisinau.
Land and climate. Moldova lies between the Prut River and the Dnestr River. Almost everywhere in Moldova, the soil consists of fertile black soil. The climate is continental, in the south it is slightly more moderate. In the deciduous forests wolves can still be found.
People. Moldavians constitute 65% of the population; Ukranians and Russians are important minorities. The official language is Moldavian. The most important churches are the Romanian-orthodox Church and the Russian-orthodox Church.
Economy. Agriculture is important to the country's economy. After the disintegration of the Soviet Union, the viniculture and the defense industry broke down. After 1994 the economy improved.

Moldova

Capital:	Kishinev
Area:	13,010 sq mi
	(33,700 sq km)
Population:	4,457,000
Language:	Moldavian
Government:	Federal republic
Independent:	1991
Head of gov.:	Prime minister
Per capita:	U.S. $920
Mon. unit:	1 Leu = 100 bani

History. Moldavia was a region in eastern Romania, divided by the Prut River form the Moldavian Soviet Socialist Republic (MSSR), part of the Soviet Union. Modavia belonged to Romania from 1918 to 1940, when a portion of ist was annexed by the Soviets as the MSSR, with Kishinev as its capital. After the collapse of communism in the USSR in 1991, the MSSR became an independent republic, named Moldova.
See also: Romania; Union of Soviet Socialist Republics.

Mole, any of various small burrowing insect-eating mammals of the family Talpidae native to the Northern Hemisphere. Moles have spade-shaped front feet and long, mobile muzzles. Their eyes are small and often covered with fur, and they have no external ears, though their sense of hearing is acute.

Mole, in chemistry, a quantity of particles equal to Avogadro's number, or 6.02252×10^{23}. One mole of a given compound is that number of molecules of the compound. The gram-atomic weight of an element is the weight, in grams, of a mole of that element. The gram-molecular weight of a compound is the weight in grams of a mole of molecules of that compound.
See also: Chemistry.

Mole, in dermatology, pigmented spot or nevus in the skin, consisting of a localized group of special cells containing melanin. Dramatic change in a mole, such as an increase in size, change of color, or bleeding, may indicate that the mole has developed in to a cancerous tumor called a melanoma, which can spread to other parts of the body.

Molecular biology, study of the structure and function of the molecules that make up living organisms. This includes the study of proteins, enzymes, carbohydrates, fats, and nucleic acids, and their interactions in the life processes.
See also: Biology.

Molecular weight, sum of the atomic weights of all the atoms in a molecule, expressed in atomic mass units.

Molecule, smallest particle of a chemical compound that retains all the chemical properties of that compound. Molecules are made up of atoms joined to one another by chemical bonds. The composition of a molecule is represented by its molecular formula. Molecules range in size from two atoms to macromolecules (chiefly proteins and polymers), which may be composed of 10,000 or more atoms.

Molière (1622-73), French playwright of high comedy and farce, also known for his skills as an actor and director. He was born Jean Baptiste Poquelin. Granted patronage by Louis XIV and given his own theater, Molière wrote satiric plays with controversial themes that often offended religious groups. Among these were *The School for Wives* (1662), *The Imposter* (1664), and *The Misanthrope* ('1666).

Mollusk, any of many soft-bodied invertebrate animals (phyllum Mollusca), typically having a shell into which the body can withdraw. Mollusks constitute the second largest phylum of invertebrates. They include slugs and snails, limpets, winkles, clams, mussels, and oysters, as well as octopuses and squids. Mollusks have adapted to niches in the sea, in fresh water, and on land. Major groups of mollusks include bivalves, cephalopods, chitons, and gastropods.

Molly Maguires, secret society of Irish-Americans in the Pennsylvania coal-mining area, 1862-75. The name was borrowed from an Irish anti-landlord organization. Their purpose was to help miners in resisting oppressive conditions and intimidation by mine owners, but they frequently resorted to violence against private police hired by owners. In 1875 the organization was broken by Pinkerton agents who infiltrated the group. Twenty members were executed by hanging.

Molnár, Ferenc (1878-1952), Hungarian author and playwright. His play *Liliom* (1909) was adapted as the musical *Carousel* (1945). He also wrote novels and short stories. He lived in the United States from 1940.

Moloch, or Molech, Canaanite god of fire, to whom children were sacrificed, identified in the Old Testament as a god of the Ammonites. His worship, introduced by King Ahaz, was condemned by the prophets, and his sanctuary at Tophet near Jerusalem later became known as Gehenna.

Molokai *See:* Hawaii.

Molotov, Vyacheslav Mikhailovich (1890-1986), Soviet diplomat and politician. Born Vyacheslav Mikhailovich Skriabin he became a Bolshevik in 1906. After the Russian Revolution of 1917 he quickly rose to power in the ruling Communist Party. He was Soviet Premier (1930-41) under Joseph Stalin. As foreign minister (1939-49 and 1953-56) he negotiated the 1939 nonaggression pact with Germany and played an important role in the USSR's wartime and postwar relations with the West. Expelled from the party central committee in 1957 for opposing Nikita Khrushchev, he held only minor posts. In 1964 he was expelled from the party itself, but he was reinstated in 1984.
See also: Union of Soviet Socialist Republics.

Monaco

Capital:	Monaco
Area:	0.7 sq mi
	(1.9 sq km)
Population:	32,000
Language:	French
Government:	Parliamentary
	monarchy
Independent:	1489
Head of gov.:	Prime minister
Per capita:	U.S. $9,386
Mon. unit:	1 French franc = 100
	centimes

Molting, shedding of the skin, fur, or feathers by an animal. It may be a seasonal occurrence, as a periodic renewal of fur or plumage in mammals and birds, or it may be associated with growth, as in insects or crustaceans. In birds and mammals the molt is primarily to renew worn fur or feathers so that pelage or plumage is kept in good condition for waterproofing, insulation, or flight. It also may serve to shed breeding plumage or to change between summer and winter coats. In invertebrates the rigid external skeleton must be shed and replaced to allow growth within. In larval insects the final molts are involved in the metamorphosis to adult form.

Moltke, Helmuth Karl Bernhard von (1801-91), Prussian and, later, German chief of staff (1858-88). A strategist of genius, he won victories against Denmark (1864), Austria (1866), and France (1870), greatly furthering German unification.

Molybdenum, chemical element, symbol Mo; for physical constants see Periodic Table. Molybdenum was discovered by Karl Scheele in 1778. It occurs in nature in the minerals wulfenite and powellite and is obtained principally from molybdenite, a sulfide. Molybdenum is a silvery-white, hard, ductile, unreactive, metal. It is a valuable alloying agent for steels and for nickel-based, heat-resistant, and corrosion-resistant alloys. Molybdenum and its compounds are used in nuclear energy applications, missile and aircraft parts, ultra-high-strength steels, high-temperature lubricants, and as catalysts.

Mombasa (pop. 425,600), large port city in Kenya, on the Indian Ocean, an international center of shipping and industry. It contains an airport, state buildings, an oil refinery, and tourist facilities. Its major industries include cement, food processing, and glass. First settled by the Persians and Arabs in the 8th century, Kenya was later ruled variously by Portugal, Oman, and Great Britain until it was declared independent in 1963.

Monaco, independent principality on the Mediterranean near the French-Italian border, about 370 acres (150 hectares) in area. It is a tourist center, with a yachting harbor and a world-famous casino. The reigning constitu-

tional monarch, Prince Rainier III, succeeded to the throne in 1949 and married the U.S. film actress Grace Kelly in 1956. In 1962, after a crisis with France over Monaco's tax-free status, Rainier proclaimed a new constitution, guaranteeing fundamental rights, giving the vote to women, and abolishing the death penalty. The government consists of three councilors, headed by a minister of state who must be French. There is an 18-member National Council, elected for five-year terms by universal suffrage, which shares legislative powers with the Prince. In 1993 the country joined the United Nations.
1997 commemorated the fact that in 1297 the Genoese Grimaldi became Monaco's sovereign.

Mona Lisa *See:* Da Vinci, Leonardo.

Monarchy, form of government in which sovereignty is vested in one person, usually for life. The office may be elective but is usually hereditary. A monarch who has unlimited power is an *absolute monarch*; one whose power is limited by custom or constitution is a *constitutional monarch*. In modern parliamentary democracies a monarch is usually a nonparty political figure and a symbol of national unity

Monasticism, religious way of life, usually communal and celibate, generally involving withdrawal from worldly concerns. People who join a monastic order are secluded from society; men (called monks) live in *monasteries* and women (called nuns) in *convents*. Monasticism exists in various religions, including Buddhism, Islam, and Christianity (also Greek Orthodox church). In Christianity, monasticism is mostly a phenomenon of Catholicism. Monastic orders include Franciscans, Carmelites, and Dominicans.

Monazite, yellow to brown mineral containing phosphates of the rare earth elements cerium, lanthanum, and neodymium. It also contains yttrium and thorium. Found mainly in India, Brazil, and Australia, monazite is the prime source of thorium, a nuclear fuel. The rare earths, important for the manufacture of glass are also extracted from monazite

Monck, Viscount (1819-94), Irish-born governor general of British North America (1861-67) and first governor general of the Dominion of Canada (1867-68). Monck's support of confederation helped to bring about the establishment of the dominion.

Moncton (pop. 55,500), city in New Brunswick and the center of distribution and transportation for the Maritime Provinces of Canada. It provides railway, ferry, and highway access to Prince Edward Island and Nova Scotia, as well as regular air flights to the Canada mainland and the U.S. Industries include metal products, wood, and textiles.
See also: New Brunswick.

Mondale, Walter (1928-), 41st U.S. vice president (1977-81), under Jimmy Carter. His early career was furthered by Hubert Humphrey. As a Democratic senator from Minnesota (1964-77) he was known as a liberal and populist reformer. Carter and Mondale ran again in 1980 but lost to Ronald Reagan and George Bush. Mondale was the Democratic nominee for president in

1984. His running mate, Geraldine Ferraro, was the first woman to be chosen for the vice presidency by a major U.S. party. Mondale and Ferraro lost to Reagan and Bush. In 1993, Mondale became ambassador to Japan.

Mondrian, Piet (1872-1944), Dutch painter and theorist, a founder of the Stijl movement. At first a symbolist, he was later influenced by cubism and evolved a distinctive abstract style relating primary colors, black, white, and gray in gridlike arrangements.

Monera, group of primitive one-celled organisms that have no nucleus. Scientists place monera in the Monera kingdom or in the plant or protist kingdom. Bacteria and blue-green algae comprise the group's single division. Monera, found throughout the world, live in soil (parasitic species live in organisms) and are able to survive the extreme temperatures of hot springs and frozen tundra.

Monet, Claude (1840-1926), French painter, leading exponent of impressionism, a term coined after his picture Impression, Sunrise (1872). He painted his landscapes outside, in natural light, applying paint in a multitude of variously colored strokes and swatches, thus conveying the appearance of a subject in a particular light, in a particular season, and at a particular time of day. His last pictures of water lilies are virtually abstract patterns of color.

Monetarism, theoretical position in economics, chiefly associated with the work of Milton Friedman of the University of Chicago. This contemporary theory is based on the 19th-century "quantity-of-money" theory, which directly related changes in price levels to changes in the amount of money in circulation. Monetarism, which stands generally in opposition to Keynesianism, advocates curing inflation and depression not by fiscal measures but rather by control of the nation's money supply—for instance, by varying the interest rate charged by the Federal Reserve System and expanding or limiting the sale of treasury bills.
See also: Economics.

Money, in an economic system, anything accepted as a medium of exchange, measure of value, or means of payment. In primitive societies, barter, or direct physical exchange, was commonly used. The precise origin of money is unknown. It evolved gradually out of the needs of commerce and trade. Many objects have at one time or another been used as money: shells, nuts, wampum, beads, and stones. Gradually, metal was adopted because of its easy handling, durability, divisibility, and—especially with gold or silver—for its own value. The oldest coinage dates back to 700 B.C., when coins of gold and silver alloys were made in Lydia (Asia Minor). Paper money was known in China as early as the 7th century A.D., but it did not develop in Europe until the 17th century. The stability and value of paper currency is usually guaranteed by governments or banks (those invested with legal authority to issue currency) with some bullion holdings.
The monetary system of the United States during most of the 19th century was based on bimetallism, which meant that both gold and silver were legal money. With the passing of the Gold Standard Act of 1900, the dollar was

Mongolia	
Capital:	Ulaanbaatar (Ulan Bator)
Area:	604,800 sq mi (1,566,500 sq km)
Population:	2,579,000
Language:	Mongolian
Government:	Republic
Independent:	1921
Head of gov.:	Prime minister
Per capita:	U.S. $310
Mon. unit:	1 Tögrög = 100 möngö

defined only in terms of gold. The Gold Reserve Act of 1934 reduced this dependence on gold, and in 1971 the nation went off the gold standard altogether. The nation's money supply is controlled by the Federal Reserve System, a central banking system created in 1913. Most currency in circulation today consists of Federal Reserve notes.

Mongol Empire, empire founded in the early 13th century by Genghis Khan (1167?-1227). Superb horseriders and archers, the Mongols of Central Asia were united into a well-disciplined, highly mobile army that conquered northern China by 1215 and then swept west through the Middle East and southern Russia, establishing a vast empire with its capital at Karakorum, in Mongolia. After Genghis Khan's death, the Mongol invasions were continued under his son Ogotai. During 1237-40 the Mongol general Batu Khan, a grandson of Genghis Khan, crossed the Volga, crushed the Bulgars and Kumans, and invaded Poland and Hungary. Baghdad, seat of the Abbasid caliphate, was sacked in 1258. The Mongol troops had a reputation for great ferocity, in particular when attacking and destroying cities.
By about 1260 the Empire was organized into four Khanates, centered in Persia, southern Russia, Turkestan, and China. Kublai Khan's rule in China (1260-94) saw the foundation of the Yüan Dynasty. The Mongol tradition of conquest was revived by Tamerlane in the 14th century and by Babur (founder of the Mogul Empire) in the 16th century.
See also: Genghis Khan; Kublai Khan.

Mongolia, area in east central Asia divided into Outer Mongolia, or the Mongolian People's Republic, and Inner Mongolia, or the Inner Mongolia Autonomous Region of China. Mongolia as a whole is bordered by Russia to the north and by China to the south, east, and west.
Land and climate. The land is largely a steppe plateau with an average elevation of 3,000 ft/914 m. The Hentiyn, Sayan, and other mountain ranges hem the area to the north and northeast and the Altai Mountains mark the end of the plateau to the southwest. Much of the southeast is part of the Gobi Desert which straddles a large part of Outer and Inner Mongolia. The climate is harsh with great extremes of heat and cold. The capital is Ulan Bator.
People. Although both Inner and Outer Mongolia were communist, many

Mongolians continued to practice Tibetan Buddhism (Lamaism). Mongolian is the official language.

Economy. The economy is based upon livestock farming, the principal livelihood of a traditionally nomadic people. There is also some agriculture. Coal, iron ore, gold, and other minerals are mined. Industry is limited to felts, furniture, and other consumer goods. The chief exports are livestock, wool, hides, meat, and ores.

History. Formerly the heartland of the Mongol Empire founded by Genghis Khan in the 13th century, Mongolia became a province of China in 1691. Mongolia declared its independence in 1911, but was reoccupied by China in 1919. With support from the Soviet Union, Outer Mongolia declared its independence again in 1921. In 1924 it became the Mongolian People's Republic, the world's second communist state although China did not recognize Mongolia's independence until 1946. In 1990 the country became a multiparty democracy, and Punsalmaagiyn Ochirbat was elected president. In 1997 he was succeeded by Bagbandy.

Mongolism *See:* Down's syndrome.

Mongoose, small carnivorous mammal with a reputation for killing snakes and stealing eggs. There are about 48 species occupying a variety of habitats around the Mediterranean, in Africa, and in southern Asia. Most are diurnal, feeding on lizards, snakes, eggs, and other small mammals. Mongooses generally resemble weasels.

Monitor, any of a family of mostly tropical lizards of the Eastern Hemisphere that includes the world's largest, the 10-ft (3-m) Komodo dragon, of Indonesia.

Monitor and Merrimack, pioneer ironclad warships that fought the world's first battle between iron-armored vessels, at Hampton Roads, Va., on Mar. 9, 1862, during the U.S. Civil War. The *Merrimack* was a scuttled Union steam frigate, salvaged by the Confederates and renamed the *Virginia*. The Union's *Monitor* was equipped with a revolving gun turret. Neither vessel was victorious in the engagement.

Monk, Thelonious (1917-82), U.S. composer, pianist, bandleader, and one of the innovators of modern jazz in the 1940s. His compositions "Round Midnight," "52nd Street Theme," "Epistrophy," and "Straight No Chaser" are jazz standards.

Monkey, any of several primates, suborder Anthropoidea. There are two superfamilies of monkeys, New World and Old World. Though there is little uniformity in the group, monkeys have flattened faces, the Old and New World families being distinguished by nose shape. Monkeys are normally restricted to tropical or subtropical areas of the world. Old World forms include langurs, colubuses, macaques, guenons, mangabeys, and baboons. Monkeys of the New World include sakis, uakaris, howlers, douroucoulis, squirrel monkeys, and capuchins.

Monkey bread *See:* Baobab.

Monkey flower, name of large group of herbs and shrubs (genus *Mimulus*) in the figwort family. Found mostly on the western coast of North America in wet areas, these plants grow to a height of 6 to 36 in (15 to 91 cm). The spots on their petals give the impression of a monkey.

Monmouth, Duke of (1649-85), illegitimate son of King Charles II of England. When he did not inherit his father's throne, he invaded England (1685) with his own army and demanded that his father's successor, James II, relinquish the crown to him. Monmouth's army lost the battle that ensued. He was captured and executed.

Monnet, Jean (1888-1979), French economist and politician, known as the architect of a united Western Europe. His Monnet Plan (1947) helped France's economic recovery after World War II. He served as first president of the European Coal and Steel Community (ECSC), and helped organize the Common Market (European Community).
See also: European Community.

Monongahela River, river formed in West Virginia by the junction of the West Fork and Tygart rivers in Marion County. It flows 128 mi (206 km) northeast into Pennsylvania, joining the Allegheny at Pittsburgh to form the Ohio River.

Mononucleosis, also called infectious mononucleosis or glandular fever, infectious disease commonly affecting adolescents and young adults. Symptoms include severe sore throat, headache, fever, and enlargement of the lymph nodes and spleen. It is believed to be caused by a herpes virus. Severe cases may require steroids, and convalescence may be lengthy.
See also: Herpes; Epstein-Barr (EB) virus.

Monopoly, economic term describing significant control or ownership of a product or service (and thereby its price) because of command of the product's supply, legal privilege, or concerted action. There are different kinds of monopoly. Patents and copyrights are legal monopolies granted by a government to individuals or companies. A nationalized industry or service, such as the U.S. Postal Service, has a monopoly. A franchise granted by government to a public company to run a public utility (such as an electrical company) creates a monopoly.
Trading and industrial monopolies have the power to decide upon supply and price of goods. Sometimes labor unions act as monopolies in the supply of workers' services. In the case of national monopolies it is considered that they can provide mass-produced goods or services at a lower price, or more efficiently, than could be provided in a competitive situation; in practice this is not always true. Business or manufacturing monopolies may often discourage competitors from entering the field of competition. There is legislation designed to control monopolies that conspire to restrain price or trade.

Monotheism, belief in one God, contrasted with polytheism, pantheism, or atheism. Classical monotheism is held by Judaism, Christianity, and Islam; some other religions, such as early Zoroastrianism and later Greek religion, are monotheistic to a lesser degree. In the theories of Sir Edward B. Tylor, religions have evolved from animism through polytheism and henotheism (the worship of one god, ignoring others in practice) to monotheism. There

is, however, evidence for residual monotheism (the "High God") in primitive religions.
See also: Religion.

Monroe, James (1758-1831), fifth president of the United States. Monroe held office during the "Era of Good Feeling," a period marked by the absence of party conflict and by exceptional national growth.

Early years. Monroe entered the College of William and Mary at age 16, but left after 2 years to fight in the American Revolution. In 1780 he began to study law under the direction of Thomas Jefferson, then governor of Virginia.

Public service. Monroe was elected to the Virginia Assembly in 1782, and he later served in the Congress of the Confederation and attended the Annapolis Convention. In 1790 the Virginia legislature chose him to fill a vacancy in the U.S. Senate.

Monroe was U.S. minister to France from 1794 to 1796, under President George Washington. He served as governor of Virginia from 1799 to 1802. In 1803, as President Jefferson's special envoy to France, he helped negotiate the Louisiana Purchase, which doubled the size of the United States.

Monroe's diplomatic service continued with a stint as U.S. minister to Great Britain (1804-7). In 1811, he was once again elected governor of Virginia. Later that year, however, President James Madison appointed Monroe secretary of state, a position he held until 1817.

In 1816 Monroe, a Democratic-Republican, ran for president and defeated his Federalist opponent easily. Four years later, with the Federalist party virtually dead, Monroe was reelected with only a single electoral vote cast against him.

President. Monroe believed that Congress rather than the president should have a leading role in legislative issues. But he did take a strong stand on certain matters, such as the debate over whether Missouri should be admitted to the Union as a slave or a free state. Monroe left Congress to try to resolve the issue, but he made it clear that he would veto any bill that admitted Missouri but prohibited slavery in the state.

It was in foreign affairs that Monroe's administration had the greatest impact. With the help of Secretary of State John Quincy Adams, Monroe reached an agreement with Spain that acquired Florida for the United States and recognized a U.S. border with Mexico all the way to the Pacific Ocean. Monroe also reached agreements with Great Britain banning military installations on the Great Lakes and establishing the border between the United States and Canada as far west as the Rocky Mountains. Monroe was sympathetic to the newly independent states of Latin America and urged that they be recogni-

---

James Monroe

5th U.S. president

Born:	Westmoreland, County, Va.; Apr. 28, 1758.
Term of office:	March 1817-March 1825.
Vice president:	Daniel D. Tompkins.
Party:	Democratic-Republican.
Children:	3.
Died:	New York, N.Y.; July 4, 1831

zed. Again with Adams's help, he formulated the famous Monroe Doctrine, which stated U.S. opposition to further interference by European countries in the affairs of the Americas. The Monroe Doctrine became an important foundation for later U.S. foreign policy decisions.

Retirement. Monroe left office at the height of his prestige. He retired to his Virginia estate, but in his last years financial difficulties caused him to move to New York City, where he lived with one of his daughters. He died there on July 4, 1831.

Monroe, Marilyn (Norma Jean Baker; 1926-62), U.S. movie star who became world famous as a sex symbol. A comic actress of considerable talent, she acted in such films as *Gentlemen Prefer Blondes* (1953), *The Seven-Year Itch* (1955), *Bus Stop* (1956), and *Some Like It Ho*t (1959).

Monroe Doctrine, declaration of U.S. policy toward the newly independent states of Latin America, issued by President James Monroe on Dec. 2, 1823. It stated that the United States would not tolerate any European interference with the former colonies of the Americas, which were "henceforth not to be considered as subjects for further colonization by any European powers." President Theodore Roosevelt's corollary to the doctrine (1904) asserted that the United States had the right to intervene to prevent any interference in the affairs of the hemisphere by outside governments and to ensure that acceptable governments were maintained there. This became known as the "big stick" policy and was invoked often by Presidents Taft and Wilson to justify armed U.S. intervention in the Caribbean.

Monrovia (pop. 425,000), capital city of Liberia, in West Africa, on Bushrod Island. Situated on the Atlantic coast at the mouth of the Saint Paul River, it is the administrative, commercial, cultural, and educational center of Liberia. Monrovia's modern harbor is the main source of its revenue. Monrovia, named for the U.S. president James Monroe, was founded in 1822 by the American Colonization Society as a place where freed U.S. slaves could live.
See also: Liberia.

Monsoon, wind system in which the prevailing wind direction reverses in the course of the seasons, occurring where large temperature (hence pressure) differences arise between oceans and large land masses. Best known is that of Southeast Asia. In summer, moist winds, with associated hurricanes, blow from the Indian Ocean into the low-pressure region of northwestern India caused by intense heating of the land. In winter, cold, dry winds sweep south from the high-pressure region of southern Siberia.

Montagnais, tribe of people that dwelled in Canada's Labrador Peninsula. Because the climate was too cold to grow adequate crops, the Montagnais ("Mountaineers") traveled the land in bands of 50-100 people to hunt and fish for their food. Their diet included moose, seals, fish, and small game. In the 1600s, the Montagnais became active in fur trading with the French. By the 1700s, the population of large animals had declined severely, leading to starvation among the Montagnais. Today, approximately 7,000 Montagnais remain, living in Quebec and Labrador.

Montaigne, Michel Eyquem de (1533-92), French writer, generally regarded as the originator of the personal essay. The first two books of his
Essays (1580), written in an informal style, display insatiable intellectual
curiosity tempered by skepticism. A third book of essays, which appeared in
1588, includes his last reflections. The essays deal with a range of subjects,
most revolving around the nature of human life and the requirements of
knowledge and happiness.

Montale, Eugenio (1896-1981), Italian poet and literary critic. Recipient of
the 1975 Nobel Prize for literature, his books of poetry include *Cuttlefish
Bones* (1925), *The Occasions* (1939), *Satura* (1971), and *Notebook of Four
Years* (1977). In his writings, Montale expressed the complexity of modern
life and the difficulty of achieving happiness. Montale also wrote short
stories and essays, and translated English writings by Emily Dickinson, T.S.
Eliot, and William Shakespeare into Italian.

Montana, state in the northwestern United States in the Rocky Mountain
region; bordered by Canada to the north, North Dakota and South Dakota to
the east, Wyoming to the south, and Idaho to the south and west.
Land and climate. Montana's two main land regions are separated by the
Continental Divide, which marks the division between streams flowing west
toward the Pacific and those flowing east toward the Atlantic. The Great
Plains, in the eastern three-fifths of the state, are part of the huge Interior
Plain of North America. They consist of high flat or gently rolling land: the
northern section has numerous lakes. The Rocky Mountains, in the state's
western two-fifths, is very high, rugged land with many snow-capped or
heavily forested peaks. Montana has many rivers, the two principal ones
being the Missouri and the Yellowstone. Grassland covers about half of
Montana's area; forests cover another fourth. Many wild animals—including
deer, pronghorn antelope, bear, moose, mountain goats and sheep, wolves,
coyotes, and elk—live in the state. Montana's varied elevations make for
great differences in climate. West of the Continental Divide, summers are
cooler and winter's warmer than east of the divide. Principal cities are
Billings, Great Falls, and Butte.
Economy. Montana's main industries are manufacturing, agriculture, mining, and tourism. Chief manufactured goods are lumber and wood products,
petroleum products, primary metals and minerals, farm machinery and
processed foods. Chief crops are wheat, barley, sugar beets, hay, and oats;
chief livestock products are cattle, hogs, sheep, and wool. Petroleum and coal
are the top mineral products, followed by gold, silver, copper, and lead. The
manufacture of lumber and wood products is Montana's leading industry,
even though trees in the national parks cannot be logged. (The U.S. government owns about 30% of Montana's land.) National parks and forests,
fishing, hiking, skiing, and dude ranches are popular with tourists.
Government. Montana's present constitution was adopted in 1973. The
governor serves a four-year term. The state's legislature consists of 50
senators serving four-year terms and 100 representatives serving two-year
terms. In the U.S. Congress, Montana is represented by two senators and one
representative.
History. The area was home to many Native American tribes before the
arrival of whites. French trappers probably entered the area in the 1700s, but
the Lewis and Clark expedition of 1803-06 was the first recorded visit by

Montana

Capital:	Helena
Statehood:	Nov. 8, 1889 (41st state)
Familiar name:	Treasure State
Area:	147,046 sq mi (380,848 sq km); ranks 4th
Population:	879,000 (1997); ranks 44th
Elevation:	Highest—12,799 ft (3,901 m), Granite Peak;
	Lowest—1,800 ft (549 m) along the Kootenai River
	in Lincoln County
Motto:	Oro y Plata (Gold and silver)
Flower:	Bitterroot
Bird:	Western meadowlark
Tree:	Ponderosa pine
Song:	"Montana"

whites. For decades after, fur trappers and traders were the only whites in the region. The discovery of gold at Gold Creek in 1852 swelled the white population—as well as lawlessness.

To better control the area, Congress created the Montana Territory in 1864. Conflicts between whites and Indians peaked in the 1870s; "Custer's Last Stand" was fought at Montana's Little Bighorn River in 1876. Montana became a state in 1889. During the early 1900s, Montana developed its natural resources. Its economy suffered during the Great Depression of the 1930s, then boomed after World War II. The petroleum industry and tourism expanded in the mid-1900s. During the 1980s, thousands of jobs were lost in Montana's farming, mining, and lumber industries. Today, Montana is working to develop its natural resources, new businesses, and tourism.

Montcalm, Marquis de (1712-59), French general, military commander in Canada from 1756 during the French and Indian Wars. He captured Fort Ontario (1756) and Fort William Henry (1757) and repulsed the British at Ticonderoga (1758). He was defeated and killed on the Plains of Abraham (Sept. 13, 1759), while unsuccessfully defending Quebec against the British General James Wolfe, who was also killed.
See also: Quebec, Battle of.

Monte Carlo (pop. 13,100), town in Monaco, on the Mediterranean coast. An international resort with a gambling casino, a yacht harbor, and an annual automobile rally, it is the home (and tax haven) of many international firms.
See also: Monaco.

Monte Cristo, small Italian island. Located in the Tyrrhenian Sea between Italy and Corsica, this mountainous island has an area of 6 sq mi (16 sq km) and rises to 2,116 ft (645 m) above sea level. Ruins of a 13th-century Benedictine monastery abandoned in 1553 after pirates destroyed it still stand there. Alexandre Dumas made the island famous in his novel *The Count of Monte Cristo* (1844).
See also: Italy.

Montenegro, smallest of the two constituent republics of the Federal Republic of Yugoslavia. Its capital is Podgorica. Its former capital, Cetinje, was absorbed into Serbia after World War I. The area is mountainous with heavy forests. Mining, agriculture, and the raising of livestock are its chief occupations.

Monterey (pop. 27,558), city in northern California on the Pacific coast, situated about 120 mi (193 km) south of San Francisco. Until 1850, Monterey was the capital of California, under Spanish, Mexican, and U.S. rule. The 18th-century Spanish Presidio, formerly the capitol, is now the home of the U.S. Army Language School. The city, with its surrounding area, including Carmel, is a popular tourist resort and artists' colony.

Montesquieu (Charles de Secondat; 1689-1755), French political philosopher. He inherited the title Baron de la Brède et de Montesquieu. His theory that governmental powers should be separated into legislative, executive, and judicial bodies to safeguard personal liberty was developed in his most important work, *The Spirit of Laws* (1748). His ideas influenced the framers of the U.S. Constitution. Montesquieu's *Persian Letters* (1721), which satirized contemporary French sociopolitical institutions, won him early fame.

Montessori, Maria (1870-1952), Italian psychiatrist and educator. The first woman to gain a medical degree in Italy (1894), she developed a system of preschool teaching, the Montessori Method, which is designed to encourage individual initiative. Children of three to six are given a wide range of materials and equipment that enables them to learn by themselves or with minimal adult intervention. There are more than 600 schools in the United States using this method.
See also: Psychiatry.

Monteverdi, Claudio (1567-1643), Italian composer. His innovative operas were the predecessors of modern opera, in which aria, recitative, and orchestral accompaniment enhances dramatic characterization. *Orfeo* (1607) is considered the first modern opera. His other compositions include many madrigals, *Vespers* (1610), much other sacred music, and the operas *The Return of Ulysses to His Country* (1641) and *The Coronation of Poppaea* (1642).
See also: Opera.

Montevideo (pop. 1,247,900), capital and largest city of Uruguay, located in the south on the Rio de la Plata. It is the country's industrial, cultural, and transportation center, as well as a seaport and popular resort. Founded in 1724, it became the capital in 1828.

Montezuma, or Moctezuma, name of two Aztec rulers of Mexico before the Spanish conquest. Montezuma I (1390-1469) was a successful military leader who ruled from 1440. His descendant, Montezuma II (1466?-1520), was the last Aztec emperor (c.1502-20). When the Spanish conquistadors arrived, Montezuma failed to resist them because he believed Cortés to be the god Quetzalcoatl. When Montezuma was taken hostage, the Aztecs rebelled against the Spanish, and Montezuma was killed in the struggle. *See also:* Aztecs.

Montfort, Simon de (1208?-65), Anglo-French leader who mounted a revolt against King Henry III. The Baron's War, led by de Montfort, followed Henry's annulment (1261) of the Provisions of Oxford which he had been forced to sign in 1258. The war was ended with the capture of the king (1264). The parliament of 1265, summoned by Montfort and including representatives from every shire, town, and borough, was a landmark in English history. In subsequent fighting Montfort was killed at the Battle of Evesham.

Montgolfier, Joseph Michel(1740-1810) and **Jacques Étienne** (1745-99), French brothers noted for their invention of the first manned aircraft, the first practical hot-air balloon, which they flew in 1783. Later that same year Jacques Montgolfier assisted Jacques Charles in the launching of the first gas (hydrogen) balloon. *See also:* Balloon.

Montgomery (pop. 194,000), capital of Alabama. Lying in the cotton-belt, it is a major Southern agricultural market center. Its other industries include manufacturing of furniture, glass, machinery, paper, and textiles. Named after Brigadier General Richard Montgomery, a Revolutionary War hero, Montgomery played a key role in the Civil War, and is often referred to as the "Cradle of the Confederacy." In 1861, the Confederate States of America were established there, Montgomery was made the first Confederate capital, and Jefferson Davis was inaugurated as president of the Confederacy in its capital. More recently, Montgomery was a focus in the Civil Rights Movement. Dr. Martin Luther King, Jr. led demonstrations there to promote equal treatment for all people. In 1956, Montgomery was one of the first Southern cities to ban racial segregation on buses.

Montgomery, Bernard Law (1887-1976), British field marshal who defeated the Germans by Gen. Rommel at El Alamein (1942), thus driving the Germans out of northern Africa. Montgomery later commanded the British forces in the invasion of Normandy (1944). After the war he served as supreme commander of NATO (1951-58). *See also:* North Atlantic Treaty Organization.

Monticello, 640-acre (260-hectare) estate planned by Thomas Jefferson in Virginia, just outside Charlottesville. Construction of the neoclassical mansion atop a small mountain began in 1770; Jefferson moved in before it was completed and lived there for 56 years. His tomb is nearby. The house was declared a national shrine in 1926 and is open to the public.

Montpelier (pop. 8,241), capital of Vermont. Located on the Winooski and North Branch rivers in central Vermont, many of its citizens are employed by the state government and insurance offices in the area. Products manufactured in Montpelier include lumber, granite, plastics, and stone-finishing and sawmill equipment. It is a tourist center.

Montreal (officially Montréal; pop. 3,127,200), city in southern Quebec, Canada, located on the island of Montréal at the confluence of the St. Lawrence and Ottawa rivers. A major inland port on the St. Lawrence Seaway, Montreal is Canada's largest city. It is named for 764-ft (233-m) Mount Royal, which rises in the city's center. A French mission was built on the site in 1642, which soon become an important fur-trading center. Ceded to Britain in 1763, the city has retained much of its French character. In the 19th century Montreal grew into an important transportation and industrial center, aided by its many natural resources and an abundance of hydroelectric power. It is the site of McGill University and the University of Montréal.

Mont Saint Michel, rocky isle off the northwestern French coast. A tourist attraction, it contains a small town and a Benedictine abbey founded in 708. The abbey's church is renowned for its Gothic architecture.

Montserrat, Leeward Island in the West Indies, situated southeast of Puerto Rico. It was discovered and named in 1493 by Christopher Columbus, and colonized by the British in 1632; they took possession of it in 1783. Montserrat contains 3 mountain groups within an area of 38 sq mi (98 sq km). A British dependency, Montserrat has been self-governing since 1960. Plymouth is its capital. Its chief crops include cotton, limes, and vegetables. In 1997 the Soufrière Hills volcano erupted after having been dormant for four centuries. As a result, the largest part of the island became uninhabitable.

Moody, Helen Wills *See:* Wills, Helen Newington.

Moon, natural satellite of the earth. The moon is 2,160 mi (3,476 km) in diameter, or about one-fourth the size of the earth, and has a smaller mass than the earth. It would take 82 moons to tip the scales against the earth. The moon is about 239,000 mi (384,623 km) from earth.
The moon takes just under a calendar month, or 27.322 days, to orbit the earth. In fact, the word "month" is derived from the word "moon." As it orbits the earth, it also rotates on its axis. The result is that the moon always presents the same side toward the earth.
In the course of its orbit, the moon is seen to go through phases. It reflects sunlight and its phases are the result of the progressive increase and decrease of the portions of its surface reflecting sunlight as it orbits the earth. The new moon occurs when the moon's reflecting surface is turned away from the sun and is completely in shadow. The full moon occurs when the whole of the moon's reflecting surface is illuminated by the sun.
With the naked eye, the moon appears to be divided unevenly into bright and dark areas. Through a telescope astronomers are able to identify the bright regions as upland areas and the dark regions as lowlands, plains, or depressions. The plains are called "maria," from the Latin for "seas," because they were once thought to be expanses of water. It is not certain whether there are bodies of water on the moon, although in 1972 Apollo 17 did discover possible traces of water. Neither is there a lunar atmosphere. Without an

insulating atmosphere the daytime temperature of the lunar surface reaches 200°F (93°C), and at night it falls to –250°F (–157°C).

The "seas" of the moon are lowland areas that appear to have been flooded with volcanic lava. Scientists reason that the lava has obliterated many craters. But for more than a century, scientists argued about the origin of the moon's many craters. One theory was that the moon's features were the result of explosive impacts by giant meteors. Opponents of that view argued that some form of volcanic action had built up the craters. Closeup photographs by orbiting space probes have provided evidence of both processes. On July 20, 1969, the United States succeeded in landing the first man on the moon. In March of 1998, measurements made by the space probe Lunar Prospector indicated that ice caps might be present on the moon.
See also: Solar System.

Moonflower, flowering climbing plant (*Ipomaea bona-nox* or *Calonyction aculeatum*) in the morning glory family. The vine can grow to a height of 10 ft (3 m). It bears large, heart-shaped leaves and large, white, funnel-shaped flowers that bloom at night. The flowers have a delicate fragrance and can grow to be from 3 to 6 in (8 to 15 cm) across.

Moore, Clement Clarke (1779-1863), U.S. educator and poet. He wrote the popular Christmas poem "A Visit from St. Nicholas," which begins "'Twas the night before Christmas" (1823), and for 29 years was a professor of Oriental and Greek literature at New York City's General Theological Seminary.

Moore, Douglas Stuart (1893-1969), U.S. composer and teacher. Most of his major works deal with American themes and people. In 1951 he won the Pulitzer Prize for music for *Giants in the Earth*, an opera about the difficulties faced by Norwegian farmers in the Dakotas in the 1800s. His other operas include *The Devil and Daniel Webster* (1939), set in New England, and *The Ballad of Baby Doe* (1956), set in Colorado. He also wrote orchestral pieces, such as *Pageant of P.T. Barnum* (1924) and *Moby Dick* (1928). He taught music at Columbia University. His book *From Madrigal to Modern Music* (1942), is a study of musical styles.

Moore, George Augustus (1852-1933), Irish writer. Influenced by the realism and naturalism of Honoré de Balzac and Émile Zola, he stirred English literary society with his realistic novels *Esther Waters* (1894) and *Héloise and Abélard* (1921). He contributed greatly to the Irish renaissance revival and to the success of the Abbey Theatre.

Moore, Henry (1898-1986), English sculptor. His inspiration came from natural forms, such as stones, roots, and bones, and was often expressed in curving abstract shapes perforated with large holes. His work, with repeated themes, such as mother and child, is monumental. It includes *Family Group* (1949) and *Reclining Figure* (1965).

Moore, Marianne (1887-1972), U.S. poet, winner of the 1952 Pulitzer Prize for her *Collected Poems*. She edited *Dial* magazine (1925-29) and translated La Fontaine's *Fables* (1954).

Moor hen *See:* Gallinule.

Moorish art *See:* Islamic art.

Moors, North African nomadic people who adopted Islam and became ethnically fused with the Arabs during the expansion of Islam in the 7th century. The Moors went on to conquer much of Spain and Portugal in the early 8th century, crossing into France, where they were stopped by the army of Charles Martel in 732. Their rule in Spain, centered in the cities of Córdoba and Granada, saw an unparalled development of philosophy, the sciences, and architecture. The Moors lost much of their land in Spain by the late 13th century. They were finally driven from the Iberian peninsula (along with the Jews) by Christian forces under King Ferdinand and Queen Isabella in 1492.

Moose, large, long-legged mammal (genus *Alces*) of the deer family, native to cold climates. The species *A. alces*, found in Europe, is called an elk. The males have large, palmate antlers, as wide as 7 ft (2 m) across. Often living near water, the moose feeds on aquatic plants and bushes and mature trees.

Moose Jaw (pop. 35,100), city in Canada, located in southern Saskatchewan, at the point where Thunder Creek and Moose Jaw River meet. Situated on a major railway line, Moose Jaw is an agricultural and livestock processing and distribution center. Available facilities include grain storage, flour milling, stockyards, dairies, slaughterhouses, and meatpacking. Moose Jaw also has several oil refineries. Manufactured products include chemicals, clothing, and lumber.
See also: Saskatchewan.

Moose River, in northeastern Ontario, Canada. The Moose River begins at the confluence of the Mattagami and Missinaibi rivers and flows 75 mi (121 km) into Hudson Bay. Moose River and the streams and rivers that empty into it drain almost the entire northeastern Ontario area.

Mora, Juan Rafael (1814-1860), president of Costa Rica (1849-59). His accomplishments included creating a public school system, building public buildings, establishing the first Costa Rican national bank, and promoting the coffee industry. Considered a hero for his defense of Central America in 1956 and 1957 against William Walker of the United States, he was nevertheless ousted by rebels in 1859 and executed during a revolution in 1860.
See also: Costa Rica.

Morality play, form of drama popular at the end of the Middle Ages, from about the 14th to the 16th century. It was intended to instruct its audience on the eternal struggle between good and evil for human souls. The characters were personifications of virtues and vices. The most noted English example is *Everyman* (from the late 15th century), which is still sometimes performed. Morality plays grew out of earlier religious pageants and were an important step in the secularization of drama.

Moral Majority, strictly, the U.S. religious-political organization headed by the Rev. Jerry Falwell; loosely, the entire religious constituency of the New Right. In this second sense the Moral Majority is the same as the New Christian (or Religious) Right. Led chiefly by TV evangelists, it represents fundamentalist Christian beliefs and proved a potent force in the 1980 presidential and congressional campaigns, especially in the Sun Belt and West.

Moravia, eastern region of the Czech Republic, bounded on the west by the Bohemian highlands and on the east by the Carpathian Mountains. Historically the homeland of the Moravian Empire, from 1029 Moravia was a province of Bohemia. In 1526 it passed under Hapsburg rule, and was part of Austria-Hungary until 1918. Moravia is a fertile and now highly industrialized region. Brno, the largest city, is noted for textile manufacturing. *See also:* Czech Republic.

Moravian Church, Protestant church, also known as the *Unitas Fratrum* (Unity of Brethren), formed in 1457 by Bohemian followers of Jan Hus. They believed in simple worship and strict Christian living, with the Bible as their rule of faith. They broke with Rome in 1467. During the Thirty Years' War (1618-48), they were persecuted almost to extinction, but they revived in Silesia and in 1732 began the missionary work for which they are still known. The first American settlements were in Pennsylvania (1740) and North Carolina (1753). The Moravian church has about 50,000 members in the United States and has been very influential in shaping modern Protestantism. *See also:* Hus, Jan; Protestantism.

Moray *See:* Eel.

More, Saint Thomas (1478-1535), English statesman, writer, and saint who was executed for his refusal to take the oath of supremacy recognizing Henry VIII as head of the English church. A man of brilliance, subtlety, and wit, he was much favored by the king. When Cardinal Wolsey fell in 1529, More was made lord chancellor. Probably because of Henry's determination to divorce Catherine of Aragon in defiance of the pope, More resigned only 3 years later. Considered dangerously influential even in silence and retirement, More was condemned for high treason. His best-known work is *Utopia*, a description of an ideal society based on reason. Long recognized as a martyr by the Catholic church, More was canonized in 1935. *See also:* Utopia.

Morgagni, Giovanni Battista (1682-1771), anatomist, the first person to make the study of diseases a science. An anatomy professor at the University of Padua, Morgagni believed that the key to diagnosing and treating diseases lay in knowledge of the body and how it functions. He studied hundreds of corpses to find the causes of their deaths. His findings are recorded in *On the Seats and Causes of Diseases* (1761). *See also:* Anatomy; Pathology.

Morgan, U.S. banking family famous for its immense financial power and its philanthropic activities. The banking house of J.S. Morgan & Co. was founded by Junius Spencer Morgan (1813-90) and developed into a vast financial and industrial empire (J.P. Morgan & Co.) under his son, John Pierpont Morgan (1837-1913). Many of J. P. Morgan's commercial activities aroused controversy, and in 1904 his Northern Securities Company was dissolved as a violation of the Sherman Antitrust Act. Notable philanthropic legacies include part of his art collection to the Metropolitan Museum of Art, as well as the Pierpont Morgan Library, which was endowed by his son. John Pierpont Morgan, Jr. (1867-1943) was U.S. agent for the Allies during World War I, when he raised huge funds and organized contracts for military supplies. Most of the large postwar international loans were floated by the house of Morgan.

Morgan, John Hunt (1825-64), Confederate general in the U.S. Civil War, famous for his skilled and daring raids behind Union lines. His great raid (1863) through Kentucky, Indiana, and Ohio ended in his capture, but he escaped to resume fighting until killed at Greenville, Tenn.
See also: Civil War, U.S.

Morgan, Sir Henry (1635-88), English adventurer and leader of the West Indies buccaneers. The destruction of Panama City (1671), his most daring exploit, took place after the signing of a treaty between England and Spain. Recalled under arrest, he was subsequently pardoned, knighted (1673), and made lieutenant governor of Jamaica (1680-82).

Morgan, Thomas Hunt (1866-1945), U.S. biologist who, through his experiments with the fruit fly *Drosophila*, established the relation between genes and chromosomes and thus the mechanism of heredity. For his work he received the 1933 Nobel Prize for physiology or medicine. His books include *The Physical Basis of Heredity* (1919), *Evolution and Genetics* (1925), and *Embryology and Genetics* (1934).
See also: Genetics; Heredity.

Morgan's Raiders *See:* Morgan, John Hunt.

Morgenthau, Henry, Jr. (1891-1967), U.S. secretary of the treasury (1934-45). During World War II he raised billions of dollars through the sale of government bonds. In 1945 he helped establish the World Bank and the International Monetary Fund, organizations to help countries develop self-sufficiency and economic prosperity.

Mörike, Eduard (1804-75), German lyric poet. His poetry, first collected in the volume *Gedichte* (1838), is small in quantity but varied in theme and technique. He also wrote a novel *Maler Nolten* (1832) and some short stories.

Morison, Samuel Eliot (1887-1976), U.S. historian and Harvard professor who wrote the official 15-volume history of the U.S. Navy during World War II. He won Pulitzer Prizes for his *Admiral of the Ocean Sea* (1942), a life of Christopher Columbus, and *John Paul Jones* (1959).

Morisot, Berthe (1841-95), French impressionist painter. Her paintings, which often included family members, were noted for the originality of their design and their exquisite color. Morisot was a prominent figure in the Parisian art world, and was good friends with Degas, Renoir, and Eduard Manet, whose brother she married.

Morley, Thomas (1557?-1603?), English composer noted for his madrigals. A pupil of William Byrd and organist of St. Paul's Cathedral, he also wrote

A Plaine and Easie Introduction to Practicall Musicke (1597), an invaluable source of information on Elizabethan musical practice.

Mormon cricket, insect (*Anabrus simplex*) belonging to the family of grasshoppers and katydids. Found in the Great Plains and Western United States, Mormon crickets grow to a length of approximately 2 in (5 cm) and can be black, green, or brown. Although they have small wings, they cannot fly. In 1848 Mormons in Utah almost lost all their crops to a swarm of these insects. Miraculously, a flock of seagulls appeared in time and ate the crickets. Farmers today use poisons and baits to destroy them.

Mormons, members of The Church of Jesus Christ of Latter-Day Saints, founded in 1830 by Joseph Smith. Mormons accept Smith as having miraculously found and translated a divinely inspired record of the early history and religion of America, the *Book of Mormon*. With Smith's own writings and the Bible, this forms the Mormon scriptures. The Mormons' attempts to settle in Ohio and Missouri met with recurrent persecution, culminating in the murder of Smith in 1844. In 1847 Brigham Young led the Mormons west to Salt Lake City (still the location of their chief temple). In 1850 Congress granted them the Territory of Utah, with Young as governor. Hostility to the flourishing agricultural community that developed focused on the Mormon sanction of polygamy and came to a climax with the "Utah War" (1857-58). In 1890 the Mormons abolished polygamy, and Utah was admitted to the Union in 1896. The Mormons have a president and counselors; their membership is about 3 million.
See also: Utah; Young, Brigham.

Morning-glory, common name for herbs, shrubs, and small trees of the family *Convolvulaceae*. Predominantly climbing plants, morning-glories are found in warm climates. Their fast-growing vines bear colorful, funnel-shaped flowers (some of which only open in the morning) and can grow to heights of 10-20 ft (3-6 m). The sweet potato, bindweed, moonflower, and garden morning glory are some plants belonging to this family.

Morning star *See:* Evening star.

Morocco, kingdom in northwest Africa bordered by the Mediterranean Sea on the north, the Atlantic Ocean to the west, Algeria and Western Sahara.
Land and climate. Morocco occupies an area of c.177,117 sq mi (458,730 sq km). In the north and east of the coastal plain, the ridges of the Rif Mountains form an arc from Ceuta to Melilla, 2 ports under Spanish suzerainty. South of the Rif, the Atlas Mountains extend southwestward across central Morocco. And southeast of the Atlas Mountains is the Sahara Desert and the as yet undefined section of the border with Algeria. The climate of the fertile coastal plain is Mediterranean, with hot dry summers and mild winters. The climate of the interior plains and mountainous regions is harsh. Morocco's capital is Rabat, and its cities include Casablanca, Marrakesh, and Fez.
People. Moroccans are mostly of Arab descent, but about one-third of the people are Berbers, and there are Jewish, French, Spanish and Tuareg communities. Less than one-third of the people live in the cities and towns. The official language is Arabic.

Morocco

Capital:	Rabat
Area:	177,117 sq mi
	(458,730 sq km)
Population:	29,114,000
Language:	Arabic
Government:	Parliamentary
	monarchy
Independent:	1956
Head of gov.:	Prime minister
Per capita:	U.S. $1,110
Mon. unit:	1 Moroccan dirham
	100 centimes

Economy. Morocco's economy rests primarily on mining and agriculture. Farming accounts for about 10% of the gross domestic product and wheat, barley, corn, beans, dates, citrus, and other fruits are grown. Coal, manganese, iron ore, lead, cobalt, zinc, silver, and some are produced, but the principal source of export revenue is phosphate. Morocco leads the world in production of this important mineral. Tourism and handicrafts also contribute to the economy.

History. Once ruled by Carthage and then Rome, Morocco was later invaded by the Vandals (429 A.D.). The Arabs conquered in 683 A.D. and Moroccan Berbers helped them in their subsequent conquest of Spain. In the 11th century, Morocco was part of the great Almoravid empire. A haven for pirates in the 18th century, Morocco was coveted by France, Spain, and Germany, and they struggled for dominance throughout the 19th century. In the Algeciras Conference of 1906, the great powers pledged Moroccan independence but ceded special rights to France, enabling that country to establish a protectorate in 1912, part of which was ceded to Spain. The Moroccans resisted and effective French and Spanish control was not complete until 1930. Resistance continued after World War II and Morocco was granted its independence in 1956, though Ceuta, Melilla, and a few small islands remain under Spanish control. King Muhammed V governed from 1957 to 1961 and was succeeded by his son Hassan II. He reigned as absolute monarch, but his rule was constantly threatened by attempted coups and assassinations. In 1970, a new constitution was adopted and, in 1972, amended to further limit Hassan's powers. Morocco, though not one of the hard-line Arab states, supported Syria in the 1973 Arab-Israeli War. Since the discovery of oil in the Middle Atlas Mountains, Hassan has pressed Morocco's claims to the western Sahara. The Polisario Front has resisted those claims, and with Algerian aid and backing has waged a guerrilla war against the king's forces. Attempts to find a political solution to the dispute have failed so far. In 1998 a referendum will be held regarding the Western Sahara.

Morpheus, in Greek mythology, one of the many offspring of Hypnos (Somnus), god of sleep. Morpheus and 2 brothers are gods of dreams; while he is responsible for the appearance of humans in dreams, his brothers

Phobetor (Ikelos) and Phantasus produce forms of animals and inanimate objects.
See also: Mythology.

Morphine, addictive opium derivative used as a narcotic painkiller. It suppresses anxiety and produces euphoria. Morphine also weakens mental and physical powers and reduces sex and hunger urges. It depresses respiration and the cough reflex, induces sleep, and may cause vomiting and constipation. Medically it is valuable in the treatment of heart failure and as a premedication for anesthetics.
See also: Drug; Drug abuse.

Morris, Gouverneur (1752-1816), U.S. politician responsible for planning the U.S. decimal coinage system. He was a member of the New York provincial congress (1775-77). At the Constitutional Convention of 1787 he argued for a strong, property-based federal government and was responsible for much of the wording of the U.S. Constitution. He was minister to France (1792-94) and later played a leading part in promoting the Erie Canal.

Morris, Lewis (1726-98), U.S. patriot and signer of the Declaration of Independence. A member of the Continental Congress, he helped supervise the storing and distribution of military supplies during the Revolutionary War and also served as a major general of New York State's militia. From 1777 to 1790 he was a member of the New York state legislature.

Morris, Robert (1734-1806), U.S. financier who funded the American Revolution and signed the Declaration of Independence. As superintendent of finance (1781-84) he saved the nation from bankruptcy by raising money (chiefly from the French) to establish the Bank of North America.

Morris, William (1834-96), English artist, poet, and designer. One of the Pre-Raphaelites, he sought to counteract the effects of industrialization by a return to the aesthetic standards and craftsmanship of the Middle Ages. In 1861 he set up Morris and Co. to design and make wallpaper, furniture, carpets, and stained glass. Influenced by John Ruskin, he formed the Socialist League (1884). His founding of the Kelmscott Press (1890) had a primary impact on typographical and book design.

Morrison, Toni (Chloe Anthony Wofford; 1931-), U.S. novelist. She is known for imaginative, poetic, emotional portrayals of individuals in relation to society and the African American experience in such novels as Song of Solomon (1977), Tar Baby (1981), the best-seller Beloved (1987, Pulitzer Prize), and Paradise (1998).

Morse, Samuel Finley Breese (1791-1872), U.S. inventor of an electric telegraph and portrait painter. Morse spent 12 years developing the range and capabilities of his system; he was granted a U.S. patent for his telegraph in 1840. His famous message—"What hath God wrought!"—was the first sent on his Washington-Baltimore line on May 24, 1844. For this he used Morse code, which he devised in 1838.
See also: Telegraph.

Morse code, telegraphic signal system devised (1838) by Samuel Morse for use in transmitting messages. Letters, numbers, and punctuation are represented by combinations of dots (brief taps of the transmitting key) and dashes (3 times the length of dots).

Morton, John (1724-77), U.S. patriot and signer of the Declaration of Independence. In 1765 he was a Pennsylvania delegate to the Stamp Act Congress, representatives from 9 colonies who protested British taxation of American colonists. From 1774 to 1777 he served in the Continental Congress, representatives from the 13 colonies who founded the U.S.

Morton, William Thomas Green (1819-68), U.S. dentist who pioneered the use of diethyl ether as an anesthetic (1844-46). In later years he engaged in bitter litigation over his refusal to recognize Crawford W. Long's prior use of ether as an anesthetic.
See also: Anesthesia; Ether.

Mosby, John Singleton (1833-1916), Confederate U.S. Civil War hero who led Mosby's Partisan Rangers, a cavalry troop known for its daring raids behind enemy lines in Maryland and Union-occupied Virginia. After the war he became a Republican and entered government service.

Moscow (Russian: *Moskva*; pop. 8,801,000), capital of the Russian Federation and capital of the former USSR, on both banks of the Moskva River. It is Russia's largest city, and its political, cultural, commercial, industrial, and communications center. Some leading industries are chemicals, textiles, wood products, and a wide range of heavy machinery, including aircraft and automobiles. Moscow became the capital of all Russia under Ivan IV in the 16th century. Superseded by St. Petersburg (now Leningrad) in 1713, it regained its former status in 1918, following the Russian Revolution. At the city's heart is the Kremlin, location of government headquarters and a palace housing architectural relics of tsarist Russia. Red Square, the site of parades and celebrations, along with the Lenin Mausoleum and St. Basil's Cathedral, is nearby. Among outstanding cultural and educational institutions are the Bolshoi Theater, the Moscow Art Theater, the Maly Theater, Moscow University, the Academy of Sciences, the Tchaikovsky Conservatory, and the Lenin State Library.

Moscow Art Theater, influential Russian repertory theater famed for its ensemble acting and its introduction of new techniques in stage realism. Founded in 1897 by Konstantin Stanislavski and Vladimir Nemirovich-Danchenko, it introduced plays by Chekhov, Dostoyevsky, Gorky, and Tolstoy.
See also: Stanislavski, Konstantin.

Moselle, or **Mosel River**, tributary of the Rhine River, about 339 mi (545 km) long, arising in northeastern France; it flows into Germany, where it empties into the Rhine at Koblenz. Along its French banks lie power stations and iron and steel plants. In the German Moseltal, the renowned Moselle wines are produced.

Moses (c.13th century B.C.), Hebrew lawgiver and prophet who led the Israelites out of Egypt. According to the Bible, the infant Moses was found

and raised by the pharaoh's daughter. After killing an Egyptian, he fled to the desert. Speaking from a burning bush, God ordered Moses to return and demand the Israelites' freedom under threat of ten plagues. At last, Moses led them out of Egypt (the "exodus"); the Red Sea miraculously parted to let them cross to safety. On Mt. Sinai Moses received the Ten Commandments. After years of ruling the wandering Israelites in the wilderness, Moses died within sight of the promised land. Traditionally he was the author of the first five books of the Bible, the Torah.
See also: Bible.

Moses, Edwin Corley (1955-), U.S. track and field athlete in hurdling events. He won the 1976 and 1984 Olympic gold medals for the 400-m (438-yd) hurdle, and held the world record in that event from 1983. In 1990 he became eligible to represent the United States in international bobsled competitions.

Moses, Grandma (Anna Mary Robertson Moses; 1860-1961), U.S. artist of the primitive style. Self-taught, she began painting at age 76 and won wide popularity with her lively, unpretentious pictures of rural life in upstate New York.

Moses, Phoebe Ann *See:* Oakley, Annie.

Mosque, Muslim place of worship. The name derives from the Arabic *masjid*, meaning "a place for prostration" (in prayer). Mosques are typically built with one or more *minarets* (towers); a courtyard with fountains or wells for ceremonial washing; an area where the faithful assemble for prayers led by the *imam* (priest); a *mihrab* (niche) indicating the *qiblah* (direction) of Mecca; a *mimbar* (pulpit) and sometimes, facing it, a *maqsurah* (enclosed area for important persons). Some mosques include a *madrasah* (religious school).
See also: Islam.

Mosquitia *See:* Mosquito Coast.

Mosquito, any of 35 genera of small insects belonging to the fly order Diptera of the family *Culicidae*. Mosquitoes have long legs and 2 wings capable of beating about 1,000 times a second. Males survive on plant juices; females feed on the blood of mammals. They are able to pierce skin with needlelike parts in their proboscises. Certain species transmit diseases such as malaria, yellow fever, and encephalitis.

Mosquito Coast, coastal landstrip in Nicaragua and Honduras, along the Caribbean Sea. It begins at the San Juan River on the eastern coast of Nicaragua and continues to the Aguan River on the northeastern coast of Honduras, it is about 40 mi (65 km) wide and 200 mi (320 km) long and is named after the indigenous Mosquito tribe.

Mosquito hawk *See:* Nighthawk.

Moss, primitive plants related to the liverworts. The mosses and liverworts together make up the phylum bryophyta. Of the 2 groups, the mosses are the more advanced because they have a vertical stem with simple leaves and roots. From the tip of the leafcovered stem springs a tall stalk bearing a capsule containing the spores. Mosses display alternation of generations, with both sexual and asexual stages in their life cycles. Mosses are dependent on water for their life and reproduction. They are found in damp woods, crevices, bogs, and a few live underwater in ponds. They play an important part in preventing erosion and in the formation of soil. The peat mosses, are of considerable economic importance. They are extremely absorbent, taking up over 100 times their weight of water, and have been used in surgical dressings. Their rotted remains collect in bogs to form peat, which is used in many parts of the world as fuel and in garden cultivation.

Mössbauer, Rudolf Ludwig (1929-), German physicist. In 1961 he shared the Nobel Prize for physics for his discovery (1957) of the Mössbauer effect, a method of producing gamma rays. Among other applications, Mössbauer's work led to the verification of Albert Einstein's theory of relativity. Mössbauer taught physics briefly at the California Institute of Technology (1961) before returning to Munich to teach at its Technical University.
See also: Gamma rays.

Mossbunker *See:* Menhaden.

Moth, insect that, together with the butterfly, makes up the order *Lepidoptera*. Most moths have intricately patterned, dull-colored wings to camouflage them. When a moth larva, or caterpillar, hatches out from its egg, it eats the leaf, plant, or fabric on which it was laid. Caterpillars cause extensive damage to trees, crops, and clothes. As caterpillars grow, they shed their skin. In the final stage of growth, when it is known as a pupa, the caterpillar changes into an adult moth. Most moths sleep during the day and come out at night. They are drawn by the radiation around bright lights. There are about 120,000 known species of moths, ranging from minute wingless forms to giants several inches across.

Mother Carey's chicken *See:* Petrel.

Mother Goose, fictitious character who wrote many collections of fairy tales and nursery rhymes. The name seems to have been first associated with Charles Perrault's French *Tales of Mother Goose* (1697). Others say the American *Mother Goose Melodies* (1719) was the origin.

Mother Jones *See:* Jones, Mary Harris.

Mother of Canada *See:* Saint Lawrence River.

Mother Teresa *See:* Teresa, Mother.

Motherwell, Robert (1915-91), U.S. painter and theoretician, a leading exponent of abstract expressionism. His work is characterized by restrained colors and large, indefinite shapes. His best-known series is *Elegies to the Spanish Republic* (1975).

Motion, perpetual *See:* Perpetual motion machine.

Motion pictures, the art of interpreting reality and presenting entertainment or information by projecting a series of connected photographs in rapid succession onto a screen. The illusion of motion pictures rests upon the eye's tendency to retain an image for a fraction of a second after that image has been withdrawn. If a series of pictures is prepared showing, in gradual progression, the different phases of an action and the pictures are then viewed in rapid succession, the eye tends to connect the pictures, resulting in the illusion of a moving image. In fact, a movie is a series of still photographs printed on a long strip of celluloid. The strip is run through a projector which, by means of a shutter, shows each picture, or frame, for a split second. Modern movies run at a speed of 24 frames per second; silent films ran at 16 frames a second. Thomas A. Edison and his assistant, W.K.L. Dickson, made the first significant step toward the development of a motion picture camera by exploiting this principle. Dickson, using the new celluloid film developed by another American inventor, George Eastman, contrived a method of moving the film through the camera using sprocket wheels. By 1894, Edison had perfected the Kinetoscope, in which a viewer could see minute-long scenes from vaudeville acts and boxing matches. European inventors, adapting the Kinetoscope, devised a means of projecting pictures onto a screen for public showings, and projectors were developed almost simultaneously by Robert Paul in London and the Lumière brothers in Paris. Nickelodeons were replaced by movie theaters, and soon moving pictures were shown in many of the world's major cities.

Following the work of early pioneers, like the French magician Georges Méliès and the U.S. director Edwin S. Porter, D. W. Griffith brought the art of movie-making to its first maturity. In films such as *The Birth of a Nation* (1915) and *Intolerance* (1916), he refined the elements of film language to create a highly effective narrative technique and style. He made conscious use of selective editing, closeups, and carefully considered camera positioning and movement. At about the same time, Mack Sennett produced superb silent comedies starring comedians like Charlie Chaplin, Buster Keaton, and Harold Lloyd. The studio star system developed.

Relying upon an ever more sophisticated technology and the cooperation of large groups of skilled and semiskilled professionals, the new art form also became a new industry. Until 1912, the U.S. movie industry was dominated by the Motion Picture Patents Company. But as movies attracted rapidly growing audiences, production companies learned they could ensure profits through distributing movies to chains of theaters they had bought or built. Theater owners, for their part, banded together and formed their own studios. Until World War I, the movies were international, but after the war the United States dominated the industry. By 1920, the combination of the star system, distribution monopolies at home, and large markets abroad made Hollywood the world's film capital and the center of a multimillion-dollar industry. Its great stars included Clara Bow, Lon Chaney, Charlie Chaplin, Greta Garbo, Lillian Gish, Tom Mix, Gloria Swanson, and Rudolph Valentino. Westerns and slapstick comedies were the most popular movies.

Europe did less movie-making in this era, but its work was influential. German directors like F. W. Murnau and G. W. Pabst introduced original and highly expressive techniques into film-making, which were studied and adapted by Hollywood. And in Russia, after the revolution, Sergei M. Eisenstein perfected his montage technique in *Battleship Potemkin* (1925).

In the meantime, technicians were advancing the new art form. An American, Lee De Forest, devised a method for recording sound onto the margin of the film alongside the frames. The innovation was demonstrated in 1923, but it was not until 1927, with the release of *The Jazz Singer* featuring two songs sung by Al Jolson, that "talkies" revolutionized the movies. Overnight, silent films were abandoned. Studios embraced talking pictures and, a few years later, the technological breakthrough of color films. Joining the ever-popular dramas, costume epics, and screwball or romantic comedies, the new genres of musical and gangster films dominated the movies in the 1930s and 1940s. Joining Garbo and a few other silent stars who made the transition, a new generation arose, among them Fred Astaire, Humphrey Bogart, James Cagney, Claudette Colbert, Bette Davis, Marlene Dietrich, Judy Garland, Cary Grant, Katharine Hepburn, Edward G. Robinson, and Spencer Tracy; the innovative new directors included George Cukor, Howard Hawks, Alfred Hitchcock, Preston Sturges, William Wyler, and actor Orson Welles.

The end of World War II and the advent of television brought a period of ferment to the movie industry. Hollywood studios turned to making TV films and shooting their movies throughout the United States and abroad. The studio system's virtual monopoly on the international film scene gave way to foreign influences. The Italians and French broke new ground under directors like Michelangelo Antonioni, Federico Fellini, Roberto Rossellini, Luchino Visconti, Jean-Luc Godard, and François Truffaut, as did the Japanese with Akira Kurosawa and Yasujiro Ozu. Meanwhile, technology continued to redefine the industry and its markets, most recently with the production of videocassettes for home viewing and the construction of multitheater complexes. The result is an industry and art form that continue to be as dynamic as they were in their formative years.

Motmot, indigenous forest-bird family of South America. Motmots are beautiful birds with feathers of blue, black, green, and orange. Motmots possess an unusual tail configuration caused by the loss of feathers which creates paddlelike shapes at the end of the tail.

Motor *See:* Electric motor; Engine; Rocket.

Motor car *See:* Automobile.

Motorcycle, motorized bicycle developed in 1885 by Gottlieb Daimler. The engine of a motorcycle may be either 2-stroke or 4-stroke and is usually air cooled. Chain drive is almost universal. In lightweight machines ignition is often achieved by means of a magneto inside the flywheel. Motorcycles were first widely used by dispatch riders in World War I. Between the wars the motorcycle industry was dominated by simple, heavy British designs. After World War II Italy developed the motor scooter, designed for convenience and economy, with 150cc 2-stroke engines. In the 1960s the Japanese introduced a series of highly sophisticated, lightweight machines that are now used all over the world.

Mott, Lucretia Coffin (1793-1880), U.S. reformer, pioneer of women's rights. She founded the Philadelphia Female Anti-Slavery Society (1833) and with Elizabeth Cady Stanton organized the first women's rights convention at Seneca Falls, N.Y., in 1848.
See also: Stanton, Elizabeth Cady.

Moultrie, William (1730-1805), patriot general during the Revolutionary War. In 1776 he defeated the British fleet at Charleston harbor in South Carolina, defending a fort that was later named in his honor. In 1779 he drove British troops from Beaufort. He was captured in 1780 when Charleston surrendered to the British, and was freed 2 years later in a prisoner exchange. After the end of the war he served 2 terms as governor of South Carolina (1785-87, 1792-94).
See also: Revolutionary War in America.

Mound bird, any of 12 species of birds in the megapode family. Found from Australia westward to the Nicobar Islands, this bird is also known as mound builder or incubator bird because of the mound in which it incubates its eggs. The male uses his large feet to heap plant matter into a mound, which may take up to 11 months to build; the female lays her eggs in it, and then covers them with more matter. As the materials in the mound decay, they release heat. That and the heat of the sun keep the mound warm, and the eggs hatch in 6-7 weeks. Mound birds use the same mound year after year, adding to it each time. A mound can become as large as 14 ft (4 m) high and 70 ft (21 m) across.

Mound Builders, in archeology, early native North Americans who built large mounds, primarily in valleys of the Mississippi and Ohio rivers and the Great Lakes region. The chief mound building peoples were the Adena, the Hopewell and the Mississippian. Mound Builders were active from approximately 5000 B.C. to 600 B.C. Their mounds served as burial places, fortresses, or as platforms for temples or official residences. The pottery, jewelry, weavings, and stone carvings found buried in the mounds show that their builders were skilled craftspeople, and confirm that they were ancestors of Native Americans. Built entirely by human labor, thousands of mounds remain, ranging in size from 1 to 100 acres (0.4 to 40 hectares). Their shapes vary from geometric patterns to those resembling animals.

Mount Aetna *See:* Mount Etna.

Mountain, land mass elevated substantially above its surroundings. Most mountains occur in ranges, chains, or zones. The earth's crust is made up of various moving fragments; hence, land masses are in constant motion. Thus the Andes have formed where the Nazca oceanic plate is being forced under the South American continental plate, and the Himalayas have arisen at the meeting of 2 continental plates.
Mountains are classified as volcanic, block, or folded. Volcanic mountains occur when lava and other debris build up a dome around the vent of a volcano. Block mountains occur where land has been uplifted between earthquake faults. Folded mountains occur through deformations of the earth's crust; when vast quantities of sediments accumulate, their weight causes deformation. Erosion eventually reduces all mountains to plains.

Mountain ash, name for various trees and shrubs of genus *Sorbus*, rose family, native particularly to high elevations in the Northern Hemisphere. The leaves are compound, with leaflets opposite each other on the leaf stem. The white clustered flowers develop into clusters of orange or red berrylike fruit. The mountain ash provides food for wildlife, shade, and wood for implements. The American mountain ash (*S. americana*) grows in eastern Canada and the United States.

Mountain beaver, or sewellel (*Aplodontia rufa*), nocturnal, burrowing rodent of western North America. Perhaps the oldest rodent species on earth still in existence, the mountain beaver has lived in North America at least 60 million years. Unrelated to the beaver, it looks like a vole, with a stout body about 1 ft (30 cm) long, short legs, and very short tail. Colonies of mountain beavers live in burrow systems dug in stream banks.

Mountaineering, climbing of hills, cliffs, or mountains for exploration or sport. There are two types of climbing: *free climbing*, in which the climber ascends by using protrusions and cracks in the rocks as holds; and *artificial climbing*, where ladders and slings are used as aids in climbing difficult places having no natural holds. Mountaineers usually climb in a team, roped together for safety. Depending on circumstances, they will use climbing boots, ropes, pitons (steel pegs), small hammers, carabiners (rings to hold rope), and insulating clothing; in addition, for snow climbing, sunglasses, crampons (spikes attached to boots), and ice axes; and on large mountains, concentrated food, signaling devices, medical supplies, camping and cooking equipment, and oxygen masks. Two of the most famous and challenging objectives for mountaineers have been Mount Blanc in the Alps, first scaled in 1786, and Mount Everest in the Himalayas, first conquered in 1953 by Sir Edmund Hillary and his Sherpa guide Tenzing Norkay.

Mountain goat *See:* Chamois; Ibex; Rocky Mountain goat.

Mountain laurel (*Kalmia latifolia*), evergreen shrub or tree in the heath family. Native to eastern North America, it grows on mountains. A shrub can reach a height of 5 to 10 ft (1.5 to 3 m); a tree can grow to be 33 ft (10 m) tall. Mountain laurels have pink or white clustered flowers and dark, long, oval leaves with pointed ends.

Mountain lion, also known as catamount, cougar, panther, or puma, member of the cat family that inhabited the United States and Canada prior to settlement. The mountain lion can be found in Mexico, Central America, and South America. It has a tawny-colored coat and stands about 5 ft (1.5 m) long. The mountain lion is a hunter that feeds on elk and deer.

Mountain men, pioneer fur trappers and traders in the Rocky Mountains in the 1820s and 1830s. Early mountain men included John Colter, who stayed in the area after the Lewis and Clark expedition of 1804-6, Thomas Fitzpatrick, Jedediah Smith, and W.S. Williams. Many mountain men, including James Bridger, took part in William Ashley's expedition up the Missouri River in 1822. The mountain men were the first to begin opening up the Rockies and make the area's potential known. They were quickly followed by the big fur companies, such as the Rocky Mountain Fur Company and the American Fur Company.

Mountain nestor *See:* Kea.

Mountain sheep *See:* Bighorn.

Mountbatten, Louis (Francis Albert Victor Nicholas, 1st Earl Mountbatten of Burma; 1900-79), English admiral and politician. In World War II he was supreme allied commander in Southeast Asia and liberated Burma from the Japanese. After the war he was the last British viceroy of India (1947), and led the negotiations for India's and Pakistan's independence. He later served as first sea lord, admiral of the fleet, and chief of the defense staff (1959-65). He was killed by Irish Republican Army terrorists.

Mounted Police *See:* Royal Canadian Mounted Police.

Mount Elbrus, highest mountain peak in Europe. Located in the Caucasus Mountains in southwestern former USSR, it is 18,481 ft (5,633 m) high and covers an area of 55 sq mi (140 sq km). Covered by approximately 22 glaciers, it is a major tourist and mountain climbing center.

Mount Etna, active volcano on the eastern coast of Sicily. Its height is about 11,000 ft (3,352 m) and its base is approximately 100 mi (160 km) in circumference. It has erupted over 250 times since its first recorded eruption in 700 B.C., some of which have been extremely destructive to nearby inhabitants.

Mount Everest, highest mountain on earth. Located in the Himalayas, in Tibet and Nepal, it rises to a height of about 29,000 ft (8,839 m). Reaching its top has been the goal of many climbing expeditions. The first to succeed were Sir Edmund Hillary and Tenzing Norkay in 1953. Several other expeditions have since been successful. According to the Sherpa tribes of the area, Mt. Everest is the abode of the Abominable Snowman, or Yeti.
See also: Hillary, Sir Edmund Percival.

Mount Fuji, highest mountain in Japan. Situated on Honshu, an island west of Tokyo, it is 12,388 (3,776 m) high. Its slopes create almost a perfect cone. The Japanese revere Mount Fuji as a sacred place; thousands climb to its top yearly. Fuji contains an inactive volcano.

Mount Kilimanjaro *See:* Kilimanjaro.

Mount McKinley, highest mountain in North America, part of Denali National Park. Located in south-central Alaska near the center of the Alaska Range, it has 2 peaks: South Peak, rising 20,320 ft (6,194 m), and North Peak, 19,470 ft (5,934 m). *Denali*, meaning "High One," is the Native American name for the mountain; McKinley was the name given in honor of William McKinley, U.S. president (1897-1901). In the early 1900s, several attempts were made to reach the mountain's summit. The first successful ascent was made in 1913, by Hudson Stuck, Harry P. Karstens, and 2 companions.

Mount Olympus, highest mountain in Greece. It rises 9,570 ft (2,917 m) at the east end of a 25-mi (50-km) range along the Thessaly-Macedonia border. The summit is snowcapped most of the year. The ancient Greeks believed Olympus to be the home of Zeus and most other gods.

Mount Palomar Observatory *See:* Palomar Observatory.

Mount Parnassus *See:* Parnassus.

Mount Rainier, highest mountain in Washington State; also known as Tacoma, its Native American name. Located in Mt. Rainier National Park, it is part of the Cascade Range. The mountain, a dormant volcano, is 14,410 ft (4,392 m) high.

Mount Royal *See:* Montreal.

Mount Rushmore National Memorial, memorial, carved into the northeast side of Mt. Rushmore, of the heads of U.S. Presidents George Washington, Thomas Jefferson, Theodore Roosevelt, and Abraham Lincoln. Located in the Black Hills of South Dakota, it was designed by the sculptor Gutzon Borglum. He and his son supervised execution of the project, which took 6.5 years of actual work to complete, and used dynamite and drills to sculpt the granite. The heads, each about 60 ft (18 m) high, are the largest sculptures in the world and can be easily seen from many miles away.

Mount Saint Helens, active volcano in the Cascade Range of the southwest region of Washington. Long considered dormant, the volcano became seismically active in Mar. 1980 and erupted for the first time in 120 years on May 18, 1980. Preceded by two magnitude-5 earthquakes, the eruption was the first in the 48 coterminous states since Mt. Lassen erupted in 1915. More than 60 people were killed; there were widespread floods and mudslides. Surrounding forests were scorched or devastated, and much of Washington, Oregon, Idaho, and Montana was blanketed with volcanic ash.

Mount Shasta, inactive volcano in northern California. Located in the southern part of the Cascade Range, it is 14,162 ft (4,317 m) high. The sides of its peak are covered with glaciers.

Mount Sinai *See:* Sinai.

Mount Vernon, restored Georgian home of George Washington (1747-99) on the Potomac River in Virginia, south of Washington, D.C. The tomb of Washington and his wife, Martha, is nearby.
See also: Washington, George.

Mount Vesuvius, only active volcano on mainland Europe, in southern Italy near Naples. Its height (about 4,000 ft/6,440 km) varies with each eruption. Capped by a plume of smoke, it is a famous landmark. Its lower slopes are extremely fertile. In A.D. 79 it destroyed the cities of Pompeii and Herculaneum. Recent eruptions occurred in 1906, 1929, and 1944.
See also: Pompeii.

Mount Washington, mountain with the highest peak in northeastern United States. Part of the Presidential Range of the White Mountains, it has two peaks. The higher peak is 6,288 ft (1,917 m) above sea level and is located in northern New Hampshire. The other peak 2,624 ft (799 m) high, is in southwestern Massachusetts.

Mount Whitney, highest mountain in the United States excluding Alaska. Its peak is 14,495 ft (4,418 m) high. Located in Sequoia National Park in central California, it is part of the Sierra Nevada Range.

Mount Wilson Observatory, astronomical observatory located on Mount Wilson 5,710 ft (1,740 m) above sea level, near Los Angeles, California. The observatory's many powerful telescopes, including both solar and reflecting telescopes, have facilitated the work of such astronomers as Edwin P. Hubble, who discovered the expansion of the universe. Founded in 1904 by the astronomer George Hale to study the solar surface, it was operated by the Carnegie Institute and the California Institute of Technology until 1989, when administrative control was assumed by the Mount Wilson Institute. *See also:* Astronomy.

Mourning dove (*Zenaida macroura*), bird belonging to the pigeon and dove family. Native to North America, it measures about 12 in (30 cm) long and has a long, tapered tail. It is predominantly grayish brown, with pink and violet marks on its neck and a white border on its tail. Its name is derived from the seemingly mournful calling sound it makes. In the winter, mourning doves migrate south to warmer climates.

Mouse, term applied loosely to many small rodents. The house mouse (*Mus musculus*), found worldwide, is gray-brown with large ears, a pointed nose, and a naked tail. It is about 6 in (15 cm) long and weighs under 1 oz (28 grams). The house mouse eats almost everything, nesting in paper. The field mouse is an important herbivore, and in turn important as prey for many birds and mammals.

Mousorgski, Modest *See:* Mussorgsky, Modest.

Mouth, opening through which humans and animals take food. This cavity contains the jawbone, the teeth and gums, the palate, and the tongue. Food passes through the mouth into the digestive tract. The mouth's tongue is also essential for speaking.

Movie *See:* Motion pictures.

Moynihan, Daniel Patrick (1927-), U.S. senator from New York since 1977. A politician with roots in academia, Moynihan distinguished himself as an authority on urban problems, serving as head of Harvard University's and Massachusetts Institute of Technology's Joint Center of Urban Studies (1966-69) and as professor at Harvard (1971-76). He was also a consultant to President Richard Nixon (1969-70), U.S. ambassador to India (1973-75), and ambassador to the United Nations (1975-76).

Mozambique, country in southeast Africa, bordered on the north by Tanzania, on the northwest by Malawi and Zambia, on the west by Zimbabwe and South Africa, on the southwest by South Africa and Swaziland, and on the east by the Indian Ocean. The capital is Maputo.
Land and climate. Mozambique has an area of 303,075 sq mi (784,964 sq km), mostly fertile low-lying plateau and coastal plain. Of the country's many rivers emptying into the Indian Ocean, the most important, and a source

Mozambique

Capital:	Maputo
Area:	303,075 sq mi
	(784,964 sq km)
Population:	18,641,000
Language:	Portuguese
Government:	Republic
Independent:	1975
Head of Gov.:	Prime Minister
Per capita:	U.S. $80
Mon. unit:	1 Metical = 100
	centavos

of hydroelectric power, is the Zambezi, some 820 mi (1,320 km) of which flows in . The highest peak is Monte Binga (7,992 ft/2,436 m). The climate is predominantly humid; the interior uplands are cooler.

People. The Mozambique people are overwhelmingly Bantu-speaking black Africans. Almost half practice native religions but there are sizable numbers of Muslims and Christians as well. Portuguese is the official language.

Economy. Mozambique 's economy depends principally on agriculture, forestry, and fishing. Principal exports are cashews, seafood, and cotton. Mineral wealth remains underdeveloped and a limited industry engages in food processing and cement and fertilizer manufacturing.

History. The Portuguese explorer Vasco da Gama visited the Mozambique coast in 1498, and the first Portuguese settlement was established in 1505. During the next 2 centuries, colonists exploited the native populace for cheap plantation labor and carried on a lucrative slave trade. From the mid- to late-19th century, Portugal expanded its control and private businesses, like the Mozambique Company, were allowed to rule and exploit large areas. After World War II, Mozambique's territory was increased by the addition of land formerly part of German East Africa. Confronted, as in Angola, with active guerrilla movements for independence, dominated by the Mozambique Liberation Front (FRELIMO), the Portuguese maintained strict control over the native population. After a military coup in Portugal, a decade of warfare in Mozambique ended in 1974 with an agreement for joint Portuguese-Frelimo rule. On June 25, 1975, Mozambique became the 45th African state to achieve full independence. The establishment of a black African, Marxist regime was followed by nationalization and the flight of most Europeans from the country. Mozambique's fledgling government supported Zimbabwe nationalists during the war in Rhodesia, and, despite ideological differences, maintains strong economic ties with South Africa. In 1990 Mozambique adopted a new constitution, and the Front for the Liberation of Mozambique (Frelimo) and the Mozambique National Resistance (Renamo) agreed to a limited ceasefire after 15 years of fighting.

Mozart, Wolfgang Amadeus (1756-91), Austrian composer whose brief career produced some of the world's greatest music. A child prodigy of the harpsichord, violin, and organ at the age of 4, he was concertmaster to the archbishop of Salzburg (1771-81). In 1781 he moved to Vienna, where he became Court Composer to Joseph II in 1787. He became a close friend of Haydn and set Lorenzo Da Ponte's opera librettos *The Marriage of Figaro* (1786) and *Don Giovanni* (1787) to music. In 1788 he wrote 3 of his greatest symphonies (numbers 39 to 41). Mozart composed over 600 works, including 50 symphonies, over 20 operas, nearly 30 piano concertos, 27 string quartets, and about 40 violin sonatas. In all these genres his work shows great expressive beauty and technical mastery.

MS *See:* Multiple sclerosis.

Mswati III (Prince Makhosetive; 1968-), king of Swaziland since 1986, son of King Sobhuza II, whom he succeeded to become the world's youngest head of state. He named himself for 19th-century king Mswati (Mswazi), who unified the nation of the Ngwane (who subsequently became known as the Swazi). Mswati III reconstituted the government, dissolving the 12-member supreme council, appointing a new prime minister, and placing his brothers in key cabinet positions.
See also: Swaziland.

Mubarak, Hosni (1928-), president of Egypt since 1981. A graduate of Egypt's military academy, he was trained as a bomber pilot and rose in rank to air force chief of staff (1969) and air force commander (1972). He launched the surprise air attack in the 1973 war with Israel. Chosen by President Anwar Sadat to be Egypt's vice president in 1975, Mubarak became president, by public referendum, after Sadat was assassinated. In 1995, an attempt on his life was made.

Muckraker, term coined in 1906 by President Theodore Roosevelt to journalists specializing in sensational exposés of corrupt businesses and political procedures. The muckrakers included Lincoln Steffens, who wrote about political corruption, Ida Tarbell, who exposed the exploitative practices of an enormous oil company, and Upton Sinclair, who uncovered deplorable conditions in the Chicago meat-packing industry.
See also: Sinclair, Upton; Steffens, Lincoln.

Mucoviscidosis *See:* Cystic fibrosis.

Mud hen *See:* Coot.

Mudpuppy, or water dog (*Necturus maculosus*), salamander growing up to 2 ft (0.6 m) that lives in many North American rivers and streams. It retains its gills even when adult. Mud puppies get their name because they are reputed to emit barking sounds; however, they possess no voice organs of any kind

Mugabe, Robert Gabriel (1924-), president (1987-) and prime minister (1980-) of Zimbabwe. A Marxist, he and Joshua Nkomo shared leadership of a guerrilla movement against the white leaders of Rhodesia. When Rhodesia achieved legal independence (as Zimbabwe) and black majority rule in 1980. Mugabe became prime minister in a government of national unity. In 1982. however, he expelled Nkomo from his cabinet.
See also: Zimbabwe.

Mughal Empire *See:* Mogul Empire.

Mugwump, term for independent voter or political fence straddler. It was particularly used to describe Republicans who voted for Democrat Grover Cleveland for U.S. president in 1884.

Muhammad (570?-632), prophet founder of Islam. Born in Mecca into the ruling Qureish tribe, Muhammad spent his early years as a merchant. At the age of 40 he had a vision of the archangel Gabriel bidding him go forth and preach. His teachings are recorded in the Koran, which Muslims believe is the word of God. Muhammad proclaimed himself the messenger of the one true god, Allah. At first he made few converts, among them his wife (Khadija), his daughter (Fatima), and her husband (Ali). The Meccan rulers persecuted Muhammad's followers. In 622, he escaped to Yathrib, a nearby city, thereafter called Medinat al-Rasul (City of the Prophet), or Medina, for short. The Muslim calendar dates years from this event, known as the Hegira (departure). In Medina, Muhammad formed an Islamic community based on religious faith rather than tribal or family loyalties. He rapidly won converts and his influence grew. In 630, after several years of warfare with Mecca and his victories in the battles of Badr (624) and Uhud (625), he captured Mecca with little bloodshed, making it both the political and religious capital of Islam. By the time of his death, Muhammad had unified the entire Arabian peninsula and the worldwide expansion of Islam had begun. Within a century, the Islamic empire extended from the Iberian peninsula in the west to the borders of India in the east.
See also: Islam.

Muhammad II (1430?-81), sultan and ruler of the Ottoman Empire (Turkey). He founded the Ottoman Empire when he captured Constantinople (1453), which he made his capital. He also conquered other territories in southeast Europe and around the Black Sea. As a ruler, he restructured his government and had government officials trained. He also founded colleges and set up charities, in the interest of his people's welfare.
See also: Ottoman Empire.

Muhammad, Elijah (Elijah Poole; 1897-1975), U.S. Black Muslim leader. In 1931 he met Wali "Prophet" Farad, founder of the first Temple of Islam in Detroit, Mich. Elijah became a prominent disciple, and on Farad's disappearance (1934) he became leader of the movement.
See also: Black Muslims.

Muhammad Ali *See:* Ali, Muhammad.

Muhammadan art *See:* Islamic art.

Muhammad Reza Pahlavi *See:* Mohammad Reza Pahlavi.

Muir, John (1838-1914), Scottish-born U.S. naturalist and writer, an advocate of forest conservation. He described his walking journeys in the northwestern part of the United States and Alaska in many influential articles and books. Yosemite and Sequoia national parks and Muir Woods National Monument in California were established as a result of his efforts.
See also: Sierra Club.

Mukden *See:* Shenyang.

Mulberry, medium-sized deciduous or evergreen tree (family Moraceae) that carries edible fruits, such as berries, figs, and breadfruit. The red mulberry grows in the eastern states and the Mexican mulberry in the southwest. The black mulberry is grown in Asia for its fruit. The leaves of the white mulberry of the Far East form the food of the silkworm.

Mule, infertile offspring of a male donkey and a mare (female horse). Mules have the shape and size of a horse and the long ears and small hooves of a donkey. They are favored for their endurance and surefootedness as draft or pack animals.

Mule deer, medium-sized deer (*Odocoileus hemionus*), of the western United States, closely related to the Virginia, or white-tailed, deer. The two are distinguished by the shape of the antlers and by the Virginia deer's habit of carrying its white tail up when running. Both live in open country and have increased as forests have been cut down. They are the main prey of deer hunters, and in many places their numbers have to be regulated to prevent crop damage.

Mullein, large herbal plants (genus *Verbascum*) of the figwort family. Found in northern regions with mild climates, there are 300 species. The common mullein, which grows to a height of 2 to 7 ft (0.6 to 2 m), has a single stem with large, thick, velvety leaves on the bottom and yellow flowers that grow in clusters, in the form of a spike at the top of the plant. When touched, the mullein's leaves and stem inflame the skin. Its leaves were once used to create a medicinal tea.

Muller, Hermann Joseph (1890-1967), U.S. geneticist awarded the 1946 Nobel Prize for physiology or medicine for his work showing that X-rays greatly accelerate mutation processes.
See also: Genetics.

Müller, Karl Alexander (1797-1840), German philologist and archeologist. He wrote extensively on the ancient Macedonians, Etruscans, and Greeks. His books include *Handbuch der Archaeologie der Kunst* (Handbook on the Archaeology of Art, 1830) and *A History of the Literature of Ancient Greece* (1840).
See also: Archeology.

Müller, Paul Hermann (1899-1965), Swiss chemist. His discovery of DDT (dichlorodiphenyltrichloroethane) as an insecticide won him the 1948 Nobel Prize for medicine or physiology. The subsequent use of DDT led to increased food production in the world and to a decrease in diseases spread by insects. However, its widespread, long-term use eventually led to a buildup of DDT in the environment that threatened animal life and disrupted ecological food chains. As a result, several countries, including the United States, have banned its use.
See also: DDT.

Mullet, any of several species of fish of either the mullet or goatfish families. Fish in the mullet family (also known as gray mullets) have large scales and silvery, stocky bodies that can reach a length of 1 to 3 ft (30 to 90 cm). Their mouths are small and their teeth weak. Living on a mainly vegetarian diet, they inhabit shallow coastal waters in tropical and temperate regions throughout the world. They are fished commercially for their tasty flavor. The common or striped mullet (*Mugil cephalus*) is the best-known species of this family. Mullets in the goatfish family also live in warm waters.

Mulliken, Robert Sanderson (1896-1986), U.S. chemist and physicist awarded the 1966 Nobel Prize for chemistry for his work on the nature of chemical bonding and hence on the electronic structure of molecules.
See also: Chemistry; Molecule.

Mulroney, Brian (1939-), prime minister of Canada (1984-93). He was elected leader of the Progressive Conservative Party in 1983. The Conservatives won a parliamentary majority in the 1984 elections by a landslide victory. Mulroney's reelection (1988) assured passage of the U.S.-Canada Free Trade Agreement.

Multiple sclerosis, degenerative disease of the brain and spinal cord in which myelin sheath around nerve fibers is destroyed. Its cause is unknown, although slow viruses, abnormal allergy to viruses, and abnormalities of fats are suspected. It particularly affects young adults. Episodic symptoms are blurring of vision, double vision, vertigo, paralysis, muscular weakness, and bladder disturbance. Symptoms can disappear and recur over a remission of many years. Steroids, certain dietary foods, and drugs acting on muscles and bladder spasticity can help. The course of the disease is extremely variable, some subjects having only a few mild attacks, others progressing rapidly to permanent disability and dependency.

Mumford, Lewis (1895-1990), U.S. social critic and historian concerned with the relationship between people and environment, especially in urban planning. His books include *The Culture of Cities* (1938), *The Condition of Man* (1944), and *The City in History* (1961).

Mummy, corpse preserved, particularly by embalming. The earliest known Egyptian attempts to preserve bodies were c.2600 B.C., It is believed that the body was being prepared for a reunion with the soul. Natural mummification was seen in bodies buried in Danish peat bogs from 300 B.C. to A.D.300.

Mumps, common viral infection causing swelling of the parotid salivary gland. It can also cause problems in swallowing and fever. Usually occurs in children ages 5 through 15 but can occur in adults. For adults, the condition is more severe and can cause swelling of the testes and sterility. It is highly contagious.

Munch, Edvard (1863-1944), Norwegian painter and printmaker. His work foreshadowed expressionism and was influential in the development of modern art. His powerful, often anguished pictures, for example, *The Shriek* (1893), *The Kiss* (1895), and *Anxiety* (1896) show his obsession with the themes of love, death, and loneliness.

Munich, or München (pop. 1,236,500), capital of Bavaria, southwestern Germany, on the Isar River about 30 mi (48 km) north of the Alps. A cultural center with a cathedral and palace, it is also heavily industrialized (beer, textiles, publishing), and is Germany's third-largest city. Founded in 1158 by Duke Henry the Lion, it was ruled (1255-1918) by the Wittelsbach family (dukes and kings of Bavaria). Munich was the birthplace and headquarters of Nazism and the site of the Munich Agreement in 1938.
See also: Germany.

Munich Agreement, pact signed Sept. 30, 1938, prior to World War II, forcing Czechoslovakia to surrender its Sudetenland to Nazi Germany. The Sudetenland in western Czechoslovakia contained much of the nation's industry and about 700,000 Czechs. The agreement, which allowed an immediate German takeover, was signed by Hitler, Neville Chamberlain (Britain), Edouard Daladier (France), and Benito Mussolini (Italy). Neither the Czechs nor their Soviet allies were consulted. In Mar. 1939 Hitler occupied the rest of Czechoslovakia.
See also: World War II.

Municipal government *See:* City government.

Munro, Hector Hugh (1870-1916), British writer who wrote under the pen name Saki, known for his inventive, satirical, and often fantastic short stories. Among his published works are stories collected in *Reginald* (1904) and *Beasts and Super-Beasts* (1914) and a novel, *The Unbearable Bassington* (1912).

Munsee, Native American group consisting of the Wolf clan of the Delaware tribe. They originally lived around the northern Delaware River and the Hudson River (now southwestern New York State), but were driven to other areas by European settlers in the 18th century, notably to the Susquehanna River (Pennsylvania), the midwestern and southwestern United States, and Ontario, Canada.

Muppets, puppet family created by the master puppeteer Jim Henson in 1955. Henson was strongly influenced by the diversity of the European puppet theater. The first network television appearance of the Muppets occurred on "The Steve Allen Show" in 1956. The Muppets continued to grow in popularity through the early 1960s but it was their appearance on the Children's Television Workshop production of "Sesame Street" that brought them global recognition. The likes of Kermit the Frog, Big Bird, Bert and Ernie, Oscar the Grouch, and Cookie Monster, among many others, provided entertainment and education. In 1976, a new group of Muppets characters that included Kermit began starring in "The Muppet Show," which received a total of 3 Emmy awards during its 5-year run and became the most popular TV show in the world. Another Henson creation, "Fraggle Rock," recently became the first U.S. television series to be broadcast in the USSR. Other Henson creations are the "Muppet Babies" cartoon show, winner of 7 Emmy awards, *The Great Muppet Caper*, *The Dark Crystal*, *The Muppets Take Manhattan*, and "The Storyteller." Henson's philanthropic work included the creation of the Henson Foundation and a close affiliation with the United Nations which issued a Kermit the Frog stamp in 1991. He also supported environmental causes. On May 16, 1990, Jim Henson died of a sudden illness.

Murasaki, Shikibu, or Lady Murasaki (978-1026?), pseudonym of Japanese court figure and author of *The Tale of Genji*, one of the first great works of fiction written in Japanese.

Murat, Joachim (1767-1815), French marshal under Napoleon Bonaparte and king of Naples (1808-15). Murat gained his reputation as a brilliant cavalry leader in the Italian and Egyptian campaigns (1796-99), and contributed to French successes in the Napoleonic Wars. He married Napoleon's sister, Caroline. As king of Naples he fostered the beginnings of Italian nationalism. Although he joined the Allies in 1814, he supported Napoleon during the Hundred Days and was executed after an attempt to recapture Naples.
See also: Napoleon I.

Murdoch, Iris (1919-), Irish-born British novelist. Her novels, such as *A Fairly Honourable Defeat* (1970) , *The Sea, the Sea* (1978), *Nuns and Soldiers* (1980), *The Good Apprentice* (1986), *The Book and the Brotherhood* (1988), and *Jackson's Dilemma* (1995), display wit and a gift for analyzing human relations.

Muriatic acid *See:* Hydrochloric acid.

Murillo, Bartolomé Estéban (1617-82), baroque painter, Spain's most famous in his time, known as the Raphael of Seville. He produced religious narrative scenes expressing deep piety and gentleness, works of realism, and fine portraits. Among his many paintings are the *Vision of St. Anthony* (1656), *The Ragged Boy* (c.1670), and the *Two Trinities* (known as the *Holy Family*) (1678).
See also: Baroque.

Murmansk (pop. 472,000), city in northwestern Russia, lying on the Kola Gulf of the Barents Sea, within the Arctic Circle. An important ice-free port since 1916, it served as an Allied supply base during World War II. It is a shipping and fishing center, with lumber and shipbuilding industries, and is connected by rail with Leningrad.
See also: Union of Soviet Socialist Republics.

Murphy, Audie (1924-71), U.S. soldier and actor. The many medals he received for his gallantry in action during World War II (1939-45) made him the most highly decorated hero of the war. Born in rural Texas, he joined the army in 1942 and served in combat for the war's duration, rising from private to lieutenant. He was decorated several times for his bravery and received the highest military award, the Medal of Honor, for single-handedly holding off 6 German tanks and about 250 German soldiers. His popularity as a war hero led him to embark upon an acting career. *The Red Badge of Courage* (1951) and *To Hell and Back* (1955) were two of his most successful films. He died in a plane crash.
See also: World War II.

Murray, Philip (1886-1952), Scottish-born U.S. labor leader. He was president of the Congress of Industrial Organizations (CIO) from 1940; prominent

leader of the United Mine Workers, 1912-42, and organizer and head of the United Steelworkers from 1942. In 1949-50 he helped rid the CIO of communist unions.
See also: Labor movement.

Murray River, Australia's chief river, an important source of irrigation and hydroelectricity. Rising in the mountains of New South Wales, it flows for 1,609 mi (2,589 km), passing through Hume reservoir and Lake Victoria and on to Encounter Bay and the Indian Ocean.

Murre, seabirds (genus *Uria*) in the auk family. They inhabit cliffs on the coasts of the North Atlantic and North Pacific oceans. Murres, approximately 16 in (41 cm) long, are brownish black, with white breasts. In their breeding season, they nest in large numbers, the female in each pair laying one egg on the bare rock.

Murrow, Edward R(oscoe) (1908-65), U.S. newscaster. He was head of Columbia Broadcasting System's European bureau during World War II; from 1947 to 1960 he produced many acclaimed radio and TV programs, including an exposé of Senator Joseph McCarthy (1954). He also directed the U.S. Information Agency (1961-63).

Muscat, or Maskat (pop. 30,000), capital of Oman. A major port and commercial center, it lies on the Gulf of Oman in southeast Arabia. The city has existed since ancient times. Two Portuguese forts testify to Portugal's occupation of Muscat (1508-1648). In 1741 it became Oman's capital. Muscat and its modern suburbs are known as the Capital Area.
See also: Oman.

Muscle, contractile tissue that produces movement in the body. We consciously control striated muscle at will through the central nervous system, such as when we walk or run. We cannot, however, control the smooth muscle lining most organs, such as organs in the digestive system.

Muscular dystrophy, group of inherited diseases in which muscle fibers are abnormal and become wasted. Duchenne dystrophy occurs only in boys, beginning with swelling of calf muscles before age 3. Death often occurs by age 30. A similar disease, Becker dystrophy, can affect females. There are many variants, largely due to structural or biochemical abnormalities in muscle fibers. A waddling gait and exaggerated curvature of the lower spine are typical. If pneumonia and respiratory failure or heart muscle are affected, early death may result.

Muses, in Greek mythology, 9 patron goddesses of the arts, worshiped especially near Mt. Helicon. Daughters of Zeus and the titan Mnemosyne (Memory), they were attendants to Apollo, god of poetry. The chief muse was Calliope (epic poetry); the others were Clio (history), Euterpe (lyric poetry), Thalia (comedy, pastoral poetry), Melpomene (tragedy), Terpsichore (choral dancing), Erato (love poetry), Polyhymnia (sacred song), and Urania (astronomy).
See also: Mythology.

Museum of Modern Art, one of the world's pre-eminent museums of modern art, New York City. Founded in 1929, it is privately supported and has a collection of more than 100,000 objects, including paintings, sculptures, drawings, architecture and design, decorative arts, crafts, industrial design, prints, and illustrated books. Its holdings of film and photography are especially notable. The museum also has programs of loan exhibitions and publications.

Museveni, Yoweri Kaguta (1944-), president of Uganda since 1986. His Front for National Salvation helped overthrow dictator Idi Amin (1979). After a prolonged struggle he overthrew President Milton Obote by force (1985); when his National Resistance Army seized the capital of Kampala, ousting the ruling military council, Museveni was installed as president. Museveni maintains good relations with Europe and the West and has helped stabilize the country, but has been accused of human rights violations.

Mushroom, popular name given to an umbrella-shaped gill fungi. Edible mushrooms have 5% protein and are mostly water. Poisonous, or inedible, mushrooms are called toadstools. The common field mushroom (*Agaricus campestris*) is the wild species most frequently eaten; *bisporus* is the cultivated mushroom. Some mushrooms are parasites of wood, plantation trees, and garden plants.

Musial, Stan(ley) (1920-   ), U.S. baseball player. An outfielder and first baseman for the St. Louis Cardinals (1941-63), he is acclaimed as one of baseball's great hitters. "Stan the Man" was named the National League's most valuable player 3 times (1943, 46, 48), had a lifetime batting average of .331, hit 475 career home runs, and held the National League record for career hits (3,630) until 1981, when it was topped by Pete Rose. He was inducted into the National Baseball Hall of Fame in 1969.

Music, sound organized and arranged as a means of expression and for sensual and intellectual pleasure. Of the major arts, music may be the most ancient, because the urge to sing and dance in response to feelings of anger, joy, or sorrow springs from the body itself. Music may also be described as sound shaped by time. Its 2 most important elements are rhythm and melody, rhythm being organized in terms of intervals of time and beats to the bar, and melody in terms of notes whose pitch is determined by frequency, or the number of sound vibrations per second. These basic characteristics of music can be considered universal, but musical expressions and traditions are quite distinct and diverse. Oriental music, for instance, does not rely upon harmony, a late but significant development in Western music. And although any music can be arranged according to scale and notated, the development of musical notation was gradual and is a relatively recent phenomenon.
Western music evidently originated in the Middle East, was developed by the Greeks, and, in the form of Byzantine ecclesiastical music, was embraced by the early church. Such music was originally limited to plainsong, a form of chant unadorned by any kind of harmony or accompaniment sung by church or monastery choirs. During the 9th and 10th centuries, choirs began to be divided into sections, each with a different melody line. This gave rise to polyphonic music, the so-called *ars antiqua*, which reached its height in the motet in the 13th century. Following this was the *ars nova*, the new art,

a style of musical composition that departed from the excessive formalism and complexity of the *ars antiqua* and achieved its finest expression in the madrigal of the 14th and 15th centuries. This period also saw the rise and spread of the first comprehensive system of musical notation.

Though the church dominated ancient and medieval music, alongside the ecclesiastical was a lively secular tradition closely related to sung poetry and represented in the works of minstrels, troubadours, and minnesingers. As in the other arts, the secular would become independent and eventually supplant the ecclesiastical, beginning with the Renaissance.

From c.1400 to 1600, great changes in music occurred. It turned to nonecclesiastical themes. New instruments were developed, played by groups of musicians—the nuclei for the modern orchestra. In the work of Claudio Monteverdi, early opera developed. Other composers of the period were Josquin Desprez and Orlando di Lasso in Flanders, Andrea and Giovanni Gabrieli in Venice, and Thomas Morley and John Dowland in England.

The Baroque period was born with Pierluigida Palestrina (c.1526) and culminated in the works of Johann Sebastian Bach (d.1750). The era saw major improvements in instruments, particularly the violin and cello, inspiring composers like Antonio Vivaldi and Arcangelo Corelli. François Couperin and Domenico Scarlatti exploited the newer keyboard instruments. A new harmonic structure of scales and keys familiar today was finally established, and the music of the period achieved a formal complexity, balance, and richness, above all in the work of Bach, which to many remains the highest achievement of Western music.

The late 18th century saw a new age in music, the classical period, pioneered and perfected in the work of Franz Josef Haydn and Wolfgang Amadeus Mozart. The period was marked by the growth and completion of several musical forms—the sonata, symphony, concerto, *opera buffa*—and by works that, as the result of greater mastery and skill with instruments, were musically richer and contained, particularly in Mozart's, an expressiveness that opened new possibilities for music.

Ludwig van Beethoven seized that opportunity and, in the spirit of the times, revolutionized the concept and the practice of the art of music. In his work and influence, Beethoven, in effect, gave a charter of liberties to individual expression that inspired the Romantic movement and, by extension, modern music as well. Franz Schubert, Robert Schumann, Frédéric Chopin, Franz Liszt, Felix Mendelssohn, and Hector Berlioz, Anton Bruckner, Gustav Mahler, and Jan Sibelius completed the Romantic period in music, each with a signal style and distinct sensibility, and each the heir of Beethoven.

As *ars antiqua* gave rise to the rebellion and innovations of *ars nova*, so the classical and Romantic traditions, particularly in the wake of World War I, gave rise to 20th-century modernism in music. It is heard in the neoclassicism of Paul Hindemith and Igor Stravinsky and the more radical atonalism of Arnold Schönberg, which offered an entirely new set of rules for music and gave rise, in turn, to serial and 12-tone music. Influenced by music of non-Western cultures as well as the innovations of jazz and modern technology, often disturbing and unsettling in the way it deliberately explores the untried and the unconventional, serious modern music defies the kind of clear-cut and comfortable categories that make traditional music seem more comprehensible and familiar.

Musil, Robert (1880-1942), Austrian writer. He is known for *The Man Without Qualities* (3 vols., 1930-42), an encyclopedic novel about the ills of prewar Austria. Posthumous collections include *Tonka and Other Stories* (1965) and *Three Short Stories* (1970).

Musk deer (*Moschus moshiferus*), a deer of the family Cervidae. The musk deer stands about 20-24 in (50.8-60.9 cm) at the shoulder, slightly higher at the rump. It has a coarse, gray-brown coat. The male has long upper canine teeth resembling tusks, no antlers, and a musk gland on its abdomen. The deer marks its territory with the musk; people use musk to scent perfumes and soaps. Unlike most deer, musk deer are solitary. They live in the mountains of Asia.

Muskellunge (*Esox masquinongy*), the largest fish of the pike family. Most muskellunges are 2 1/2-4 ft (6.4-10.2 cm) in length and 5-36 lb (2.3-16 kg) in weight. Its slender body may be brown, gray, green, or silver with dark bars or spots on the side. A distinctive feature of the muskellunge is the absence of scales on its lower head. The muskellunge is solitary and carnivorous. It is found in southern Canada and northern United States. A strong fighter, the muskellunge is sought for sport and food.

Musket, shoulder firearm developed in Spain in the 16th century and used into the 19th century. A musket could be 5.5-7 ft (1.7-2.1 m) long and weigh 20-40 lb (9-18.1 kg). It was loaded from the muzzle with a single ball, or a ball plus small lead shot, and fired by igniting a powder charge. Unlike the rifle, the musket had a smooth bore; this made it an inaccurate weapon against targets beyond 100 yd (91 m). The matchlock, the earliest musket, was succeeded by the flintlock, caplock, and wheel lock.

Musk hog *See:* Peccary.

Muskmelon, edible fruit of certain plants (*Cucumis melo*) belonging to the gourd family. Cantaloupes, Persian melons, casabas, and honeydew melons are subspecies of muskmelon. The plants are annual, grow along the ground, and produce hairy, heart-shaped leaves and 5-lobed yellow flowers. The fruit varies: the skin may be smooth, ridged, or latticed, and the flesh white, pale green, or orange. Muskmelons grow best in a hot, dry climate. They are believed to have originated in western Asia.

Musk ox (*Ovibos moschatus*, shaggy-furred, hoofed animal of Arctic America, related to sheep and goats. With a pronounced hump over the shoulders and a musky odor, these highly aggressive animals live in herds of up to 100. When threatened, adults circle the calves, with horns facing outward.

Muskrat, or musquash, aquatic rodent of North America, *Ondrata ziethica*, up to 2 ft (6 m) long. It lives in fresh water or salt marshes, feeding mainly on water plants. The feet are broad; the hindfeet webbed; and the fur is thick and waterproof.

Muslims, practitioners of the religion of Islam as preached by the prophet Muhammad in the 600s. Muslim is an Arabic word meaning one who submits to God. Muslims form the majority of the population of the Middle East,

North Africa, Bangladesh, Indonesia, Malaysia, and Pakistan. The Koran, believed to be the revelations of God (Allah) to Muhammad, is the book to which Muslims are devoted. A dispute, dating back to the first centuries of the Muslim era, caused a fundamental division of Muslims into the Sunni and Shi'te sects.
See also: Islam.

Mussel, two-shelled mollusk that lives in masses on most rocky shores and is exposed at low tide. It feeds on minute particles sifted from the sea and is anchored to the rock by the byssus, a series of strong, silky threads.

Musset, (Louis-Charles) Alfred de (1810-57), French romantic poet and playwright. After an affair with George Sand, he wrote *Les Nuits* (1835-37), some of the finest love poetry in French, and the autobiographical novel *Confession of a Child of the Century* (1836). His witty plays, including *Lorenzaccio* (1834), are often produced today.

Mussolini, Benito (1883-1945), founder of Fascism, dictator of Italy (1924-43). Editor of the Socialist party paper (1912-14), Mussolini split with the Socialists when he advocated Italy's entry in World War I. In 1919 he formed a Fascist group in Milan; in 1921 he was elected to parliament and founded the National Fascist party. In 1922 he led the Fascist march on Rome and was made premier. His dictatorship ended parliamentry government in 1928. As *Duce* leader he signed the Lateran Treaty, creating Vatican City, in 1929. He conquered Ethiopia (1935-36) and annexed Albania in 1939. Joining Hitler in 1940, he declared war on the Allies but suffered great military failures in North Africa and Greece. Mussolini was imprisoned by the king (1943), only to be made a puppet ruler in northern Italy by the Germans. He was shot by partisans after the German defeat.
See also: Fascism; World War II; Italy.

Mussorgsky, Modest (1839-81), Russian composer, one of the first to develop a style around characteristically Russian idioms. His *Boris Gudonov* (1874) is one of the finest Russian operas. Other major works include *Night on Bald Mountain* (1860-66), the piano suite *Pictures at an Exhibition* (1874), later orchestrated by Maurice Ravel; and the song cycle *Songs and Dances of Death* (1875-77).

Mustafa Kemal Pasha *See:* Atatürk, Kemal.

Mustard, any of several herbs (genus *Brassica*) of the Cruciferae family. The Cruciferae include food plants (e.g., many cabbage varieties, watercress, turnip, radish, and horseradish) and such condiment plants as the white mustard (*B. alba*) and black mustard (*B. nigra*), native to the Mediterranean region. They are cultivated for their seeds, which are ground and used as a condiment, or used as medicine.

Mustard gas *See:* Chemical and biological warfare.

Mutsuhito (1852-1912), emperor of Japan (1867-1912); his regal title was *Meiji* ("enlightened rule"). The long isolation of Japan under the shoguns ended in 1867 with the restoration of imperial power. Mutsuhito guided the

Myanmar (formerly Burma)

Capital:	Yangon (Rangoon)
Area:	261,228 sq mi
	(676,577 sq km)
Population:	47,305,000
Language:	Burmese
Government:	Republic
Independent:	1948
Head of gov.:	Chairman of the State
	Peace and Develop-
	ment Council
Per capita:	$765
Mon. unit:	1 Myanmar kyat = 100
	pyas

transformation of Japan from a feudal empire into a modern nation. He established industries, promoted education, gave farmers titles to their land, and modernized the armed forces. Japan's defeat of China (1895) and Russia (1905) and its alliance with England (1902) helped to establish the nation as a great power.

Mutual fund, investment company that pools its shareholders' funds and invests them in a broad range of stocks and shares. A shareholder receives dividends for his or her shares in the fund, rather than for individual company shares. Mutual funds are popular amongsmall investors because of the low risk involved (due to the variety of stocks invested in by the mutual fund) and the expert management provided.

Myanmar, country in Southeast Asia, formerly called Burma, bordered by India, Bangladesh, and the Bay of Bengal on the west, by China on the north and northeast, by Laos and Thailand on the east, and by the Andaman Sea on the south. The capital is Yangon, formerly called Rangoon.
Climate. Myanmar's climate is typical of the tropical monsoon regions of southeast Asia and India. The rainy season lasts from June to October, and rainfall averages 200 in (508 cm) annually.
People. The people are predominantly (about 70%) Burmans, but there are minorities of Karens, Shans, Chins, Kachins, Indians, Chinese, and Bangladeshis. More than 85% are adherents of Theravada Buddhism. Although more than 100 different languages are spoken, the official language is Burmese.
Economy. The majority of Myanmar's work force is engaged in agriculture and forestry. The forests are sources of teak and rubber. There are also rich mineral deposits of oil, silver, tungsten, tin, zinc, and lead. Myanmar is famous for its rubies, sapphires, and rich deposits of jade, but agriculture remains the mainstay of the country's economy.
History. Myanmar was settled in the 9th century by peoples who established a kingdom that reached its height under the Buddhist King Anawrahta in the 11th century. The kingdom and its capital fell to Kublai Khan in 1287, and the area was not reunited until the 16th century. After a series of wars

(1826-85), Britain annexed Burma to its Indian empire. It was granted separate dominion status in 1937. The Japanese occupied the country during World War II, and it was not until after the war, with the foundation of the Union of Burma in 1948, that the country became independent. The first prime minister, U Nu, was overthrown by Gen. Ne Win in 1958. In 1960 U Nu returned to power but was again overthrown by Ne Win in 1962. In 1973 a new constitution made Burma a one-party socialist republic. In 1981 Ne Win resigned the presidency but retained control of the Burma Socialist Program Party. Pro-democracy demonstrations were crushed by the military late in 1988. In elections for a National Assembly in May 1990 the National League for Democracy won 80% of the vote, but the military arrested the League's leaders and the country remained under military rule. The economy deteriorated in the late 1990s. Opposition leader Aung San Suu Kyi continued her fight for the restoration of democracy. The country joined the ASEAN.

Myasthenia gravis, disease of the junctions between the peripheral nerves and the muscles, probably due to abnormal immunity and characterized by muscle fatigue. It commonly affects eye muscles, leading to drooping lids and double vision, but it may involve limb muscles. Weakness of the muscles of respiration, swallowing, and coughing may lead to respiratory failure and aspiration or bacterial pneumonia. Speech is nasal, regurgitation into the nose may occur, and the face is weak, lending a characteristic snarl to the mouth. It is associated with disorders of thymus and thyroid glands. Treatment is with cholinesterase inhibitors; steroids and thymus removal may control the causative immune mechanism.

Mycenae, city of Bronze Age Greece. It was founded c. 2000 B.C. by an Indo-European Greek-speaking people on the southern peninsula. Mycenaean culture benefitted from contact with the Minoans on Crete. By 1600 B.C. Mycenae had risen to cultural, political, and commercial prominence in the Mediterranean world. Between 1400 and 1200 B.C. it was at its height. In 1100 B.C. Mycenae was invaded by the Dorians. Mycenae remained unknown to the modern world until Heinrich Schliemann began excavations at the site and discovered 5 royal tombs (1876).
See also: Greece, Ancient.

My Lai, hamlet in South Vietnam where nearly 350 Vietnamese civilians were massacred by U.S. soldiers in 1968. Subsequent revelations led to army and congressional investigations. Lt. William Calley, in immediate command during the incident, was convicted of killing 22 persons and imprisoned for 3 years. Two generals were censured for failing to conduct an adequate investigation.
See also: Vietnam War.

Myna, several birds of the starling family, native to Indian and Asian forests but dispersed to the Pacific tropics. These noisy birds adapt well to living near people and livestock. The hill or talking myna (*Gracula religiosa*) is kept as a pet and can be trained to mimic the human voice. About 12-15 in (30-38 cm), this glossy black bird has yellow feet, wattles, and beak.

Myocarditis, inflammation of the heart muscle (myocardium). It may be due to a variety of diseases, certain chemicals or drugs, or injury—for instance, electric shock or excessive X-ray treatment.

Myoelectricity *See:* Artificial limb.

Myopia, commonly called nearsightedness, inability to clearly see objects at a distance. The image is focused in front of the retina rather than on it, due to an overly strong refractive power of the eye or an eyeball that is too long. Eyeglasses with concave lenses compensate for myopia.

Myrdal, Gunnar (1898-1987), Swedish economist who wrote a classic work on race relations, *An American Dilemma* (1944), an influential study of Third World economic development, *Asian Drama* (1968), and *Challenge of World Poverty* (1970). He won the 1974 Nobel Prize for economics.

Myrtle, common name for the Myrtaceae family of trees and shrubs. Myrtles are native to temperate Asia and tropical America and Australia. They include the clove, eucalyptus, guava, and pimento. Myrtles are valued for their aromatic oils, timber, spices, and fruit. The common or classical myrtle (*Myrtus communis*) grows in the Mediterranean region. The ancient Greeks associated the glossy evergreen with Aphrodite and awarded Olympic athletes wreaths of myrtle.

Mysteries, secret religious cults of ancient Greece and Rome; their rites were revealed only to initiated persons. The mysteries involved purification rites, dance, drama, and the display of sacred objects such as an ear of corn. The Orphic mysteries were also important.

Mystery play, medieval religious drama based on biblical themes, chiefly those concerning the Nativity, the Passion, and the Resurrection. The form is closely related to that of the miracle play, which is generally based on nonbiblical material, for example, the saints' lives. The distinction between the 2 forms is not clear-cut, and some authorities refer to both as miracle plays. Mystery plays, which are liturgical in origin, can be ambitious in scale, treating the whole of spiritual history from the Creation to Judgment Day in vast cycles. Examples are the English York and Wakefield cycles, the French cycle *Miracle of Notre Dame*, and the Oberammergau Passion of Bavaria.

Mysticism, experience of a transcendental union in this life with God, the divine, through meditation and other disciplines. Cleansing away of physical desires, purification of will, and enlightenment of mind are the stages along the path to unification. Mystics suggest either that God is indwelling and can be reached by delving within, or dwells outside the soul and is reached by the soul's rise in successive stages. Mysticism, which has broad association in English to include the occult and magic, is found in Greek Neoplatonism, Christianity, Judaism, Hinduism, Buddhism, Islam, and Taoism.

Mythology, stories or explanations of the origin and meaning of the world and the universe and their relation to a particular culture or civilization. Mythological stories differ from folk tales and legends in that they tend to be integrated in the religious doctrine of a particular culture and are considered sacred and factual. Mythological stories also contain supernatural and divine elements. Folk tales and legends, on the other hand, are more light-hearted, entertaining, and fictive. Though mythological stories are characteristic of the pre-scientific world many aspects and beliefs of the modern world perpetuate the mythic tradition. The most well-known myths in western civilization are those of ancient Greece. The historic sources for our knowledge of this mythology are the *Theogeny* by Hesiod and the *Illiad* and the *Odyssey* by Homer. All three works date from the 8th century B.C. Other significant mythologic systems are Teutonic, or Norse, mythology of Scandinavia and Germany. The sources for this mythology are the *Eddas* (1200s B.C.).The source for the Hindu mythology of Asia and India are the *Vedas* (1200 to 600 B.C.) The basis of Irish Celtic mythology are three cycles of stories—the mythological cycle, the Ulster cycle, and the Fenian cycle. Other significant mythological systems are those of Africa, Native America, and the Pacific Islands.

Many theories have been developed by scholars about how and why myths began. Some of the more significant theories are those of Euhemerus, the Greek scholar (3rd century B.C.) who believed that myths are based on historical fact; Friedrich Max Muller, a German scholar (late 1800s) who held that mythic heroes were representations of nature; Sir Edward Burnett Tylor, an English anthropologist (1800s) who stated that myths were an attempt to explain the unexplainable events in dreams; Bronislaw Malinowski, a British anthropologist (early 1900s), who held a more psychologic perspective; and Sir James George Frazer, a Scottish anthropologist (early 1900s), who concluded that myths reflect the cyclical nature of life—birth, growth, decay, and rebirth. Frazer is the author of *The Golden Bough*, one of the most famous works in the study of mythology. Among modern psychologists, the work of Sigmund Freud and Carl Jung are significant in their interpretation of myths. In more recent times, the work of Joseph Campbell in the area of comparative mythology has also made a contribution to human knowledge.

N

N, 14th letter of the English alphabet, corresponds with the 14th Semitic letter *nun*, denoting a fish. After it was adopted by the Greeks from the Phoenicians, *nun* became *nu*. Its present form is that used by the Romans. When written with a tilde (common in Spanish words), *n* is pronounced as if it were followed by a *y* (*cañon* = canyon). As an abbreviation, *n* represents noun, neuter, name, and north. In mathematics it may stand for any number. It is the chemical symbol of nitrogen.

NAACP *See:* National Association for the Advancement of Colored People.

Nabokov, Vladimir (1899-1977), Russian-born U.S. novelist and critic. Born in St. Petersburg, he came to the United States in 1940 and taught at Cornell (1948-59). Noted for his originality and satiric wit, he published poetry, essays, short stories, and novels in Russian and in English. His first novel in English was *The Real Life of Sebastian Knight* (1938); he became famous after the U.S. publication of *Lolita* (1958), the story of a middle-aged man's passion for a young girl. Other works include *Pnin* (1957), *Pale Fire* (1962), *Ada* (1969), and an English translation of *Eugene Onegin* (1964).

Nadelman, Elie (1882-1946), Polish-born U.S. sculptor. He interpreted the human form through the eyes of 18th-century folk artists and doll makers, but was also influenced by "classic" sculptors such as Auguste Rodin. Among his more amusing sculptures is *Man in the Open Air* (c.1915).

Nader, Ralph (1934-   ), U.S. consumer crusader and lawyer. The controversy over his book *Unsafe at Any Speed* (1965), a criticism of safety standards in the auto industry, gained him support to investigate other areas of public interest, including chemical food additives, X-ray leakage, and government agencies. His work has resulted in Congressional hearings and remedial legislation.

Nadir, in astronomy, point on the celestial sphere directly opposite the zenith, that is, directly below an observer.
See also: Zenith.

Nadir Shah (1688-1747), shah of Iran (1736-47), often called the Napoleon of Iran. He created an Iranian empire reaching from the Indus River to the Caucasus Mountains by ruthless military conquest, including the capture of the Delhi (and its famous Koh-i-noor diamond and peacock throne).

Nagana *See:* Tsetse fly.

Nagasaki (pop. 439,100), city on western Kyushu Island, Japan, capital of Nagasaki prefecture. A major port on the China Sea, it has been a foreign trading center since 1571. In World War II about 75,000 residents were killed or wounded and much of the city was destroyed when the United States dropped the second atomic bomb (Aug. 9, 1945). Today shipbuilding is the city's major industry.

Nagoya (pop. 2,095,400), capital of Aichi prefecture, Japan, on the island of Honshu. It is a major port and a manufacturing center for textiles, steel, and ceramics. In 1610, the feudal lord Ieyasu Tokugawa built a magnificent castle at Nagoya.

Nagy, Imre (1895?-1958), Hungarian communist leader and premier (1953-55). His criticism of Soviet influence led to his removal from office, but during the Oct. 1956 revolution he became premier again briefly. After Soviet troops crushed the uprising, Nagy was tried and executed in secret.

Nahum, Book of, seventh of the Old Testament Minor Prophets, the oracles of the prophet Nahum. It foretells the fall of Nineveh (612 B.C.).
See also: Bible.

Naiad *See:* Nymph.